In Darkest Alaska

In Darkest Alaska

Travel and Empire Along the Inside Passage

ROBERT CAMPBELL

PENN

University of Pennsylvania Press

Philadelphia

Nature and Culture in America
Marguerite S. Shaffer, Series Editor

Volumes in the series explore the intersections between the construction of cultural meaning and perception and the history of human interaction with the natural world. The series is meant to highlight the complex relationship between nature and culture and provide a distinct position for interdisciplinary scholarship that brings together environmental and cultural history.

Printed in the United States of America on acid-free paper

10   9   8   7   6   5   4   3   2   1

Published by
University of Pennsylvania Press
Philadelphia, Pennsylvania 19104–4112

Library of Congress Cataloging-in-Publication Data

Campbell, Robert B.
   In darkest Alaska : travels and empire along the Inside Passage / Robert
B. Campbell.
      p.   cm. (Nature and culture in America)
   Includes bibliographical references (p.   ) and index.
   ISBN-13: 978-0-8122-4021-4 (hardcover : alk. paper)
   ISBN-10: 0-8122-4021-9 (hardcover : alk. paper)
      1. Tourism—Alaska—19th century.   2. Tourism—Inside Passage—19th
century.   3. Alaska—Description and travel.   4. Inside Passage—Description and
travel.   5. Alaska—History—1867–1959.   6. Alaska—in literature.   I. Title.
   F908 .C36   2007
   917.9802 22   2007023274

Frontispiece: "Muir Glacier from Elevation of 1800 Feet." Photograph by Frank La Roche (*Photographs of Alaska*, Seattle, c. 1892). Courtesy Yale Collection of Western Americana, Beinecke Rare Book and Manuscript Library.

For my father

Contents

Prologue

Voyage to Brobdingnag

> *To the North, the crystal of non-knowledge,*
> *A landscape to be invented.*
>
> —*Octavio Paz*

Alaska was an idea in the minds of Europeans long before they had touched its shores. It was a fantasy before it had a name. (Ages of indigenous names were as yet unknown.) Previous to its becoming an American territory, the north was a space to dream over. And at *this* beginning there was a map.

In 1648 the Russian Cossack Semyon Dezhnev sailed east from the mouth of the Kolyma River in the Asian Arctic through a strait later named after the Danish navigator Vitus Bering, returning with vague rumors of land to the east. Thousands of years earlier other explorers had traipsed across an exposed land bridge—Beringea—leading to the settlement of the new world. The more recent Russian visitors were not aware of these ancient journeys. But Chukchi natives knew well these waters, the land mass, and the people across the strait. Native reports of a continent to the east fueled dreams of the wealth in furs that might be had there. Other ventures followed. The Russians planned "to investigate the islands in the sea and the Great Land," as their native informants had called it, or *bolshaya zemlya*—big land, as another Russian navigator suggested. On the map it remained simply "*Incognita.*"[1]

Not until 1741 did the combined naval squadron of Bering, sailing for Russia, and Aleksei Chirikov make separate landfalls and confirm the rumors. Bering's voyage ended with his death on a remote island beach off the coast of Kamchatka, but the survivors eventually surfaced with nearly a thousand valuable sea otter pelts. Chirikov returned safely, except for the loss, possibly at the hands of local Tlingit, of several crew members who disappeared after landing near present-day Sitka. This

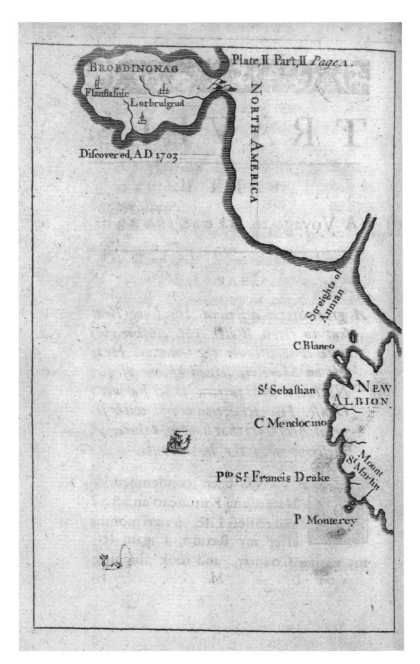

Figure 1. Jonathan Swift's fanciful depiction of Alaska and the northwest coast from *Travels into Several Remote Nations of the World* (1726), now better known as *Gulliver's Travels*. (Courtesy The Bancroft Library, University of California, Berkeley)

first contact between the southeast Alaskan Tlingit and the Russians suggested an inauspicious beginning to what followed.

In the 1720s speculation about the northern extent of the continent had made its way onto European maps and by a more circuitous route into the imagination of a contemporary writer. Early mythmakers were writing about Alaska—and locating it on maps—before they were quite sure it existed.[2] Perhaps the storied strangeness of the fog-begirt lands, the pack ice, and the Arctic mirages helped spur such conjectural mapmaking.

So one should credit the satirist Jonathan Swift with the first travel account regarding this remote—to Europeans at least—northern region. Gulliver urged in his 1726 travelogue that, "They ought to correct their maps and charts, by joining this vast tract of land to the northwest parts of America, wherein I shall be ready to lend them my assistance."[3] To add authenticity to Gulliver's supposed discoveries, Swift enlisted the help of his London coffeehouse colleague, the cartographer Herman Moll, then known for his "New and Correct Map of the Whole World" (1719). Daniel Defoe had relied on Moll's map work to provide a gloss of cartographic verity for *Robinson Crusoe.* Together Moll and Swift conjured an image of this northern terra incognita, complete with the "Straights of Annian"—the fabled Northwest Passage—and a date of discovery, "A.D. 1703." The pursuit of a passage became something of an obsession, as explorers from every European empire sought out the possibility of an easier sea route to the Orient. The mythic and abstract quality of this quest hid its plainly material aspect, the presumed riches that would accrue to its discoverer. It had become a commonplace to adorn those uncharted spaces on a map with imaginary geographies and fanciful creatures. As Swift observed of another region, "So geographers in Afric maps / With savage pictures fill their gaps / and o'er uninhabitable downs / Place elephants instead of towns."[4] Gulliver's ship, blown off course by a North Pacific gale, makes landfall, where he confirms his own suspicion that "our geographers of Europe are in great error, by supposing that nothing but sea [lies] between Japan and California." "For it was ever my opinion that there must be a balance of earth to counterpoise the great continent of Tartary [Asia]." Gulliver's story offers an appropriate, if slightly odd, beginning for the history of Alaskan travel that follows.

In *Gulliver's Travels,* the Anglo-Irishman Swift conjured the future-Alaska as a land of giants. He called these oversized humans Brobdingnags. Beyond the fringe of the known world, the Brobdingnags inhabited a gigantic landscape—mountains thirty miles high, monstrous plants and animals, a territory thousands of miles in breadth. The immensity of this region originated for Swift from impressions that had little connection with geographical information. The as-yet unmapped region allowed for such fantasies. In fact, the writer used the travel-writing genre to satirize the social, political, and scientific pretensions of eighteenth-century Britain. The political meanings of Swift's work have largely been lost, and what remains is a fairy tale, a daydream in miniatures and monstrosities.[5] But it is both the political context of Swift's satire and the imaginative fantasy of Gulliver's discoveries that suggest a beginning for this book.

At the end of Swift's fictional travel narrative, Gulliver comments darkly on "the method of planting Colonies." "A crew of pirates are driven by a storm, they know not whither," he relates.

At length a boy discovers land from the topmast; they go on shore to rob and plunder; they see a harmless people, are entertained with kindness; they give the country a new name; they take formal possession of it for their king; they set up a rotten plank or a stone for a memorial; they murder two or three dozen of the natives, bring away a couple more by force for a sample, return home, and get their pardon. Here commences a new dominion, acquired with a title by divine right. Ships are sent with the first opposition; the natives driven out or destroyed; their princes tortured to discover their gold; a free license given to all acts of humanity and lust; the earth reeking with the blood of its inhabitants; and this execrable crew of butchers employed in so pious an expedition is a modern colony sent to convert and civilize an idolatrous and barbarous people.[6]

Nearly two centuries before the apex of late nineteenth-century imperialism, Swift had laid bare the heart of the colonial drama. The satirist never minced his words when confronting the moral dilemmas of his age. English colonization long predated its New World voyages whether fictive or real. And Swift used Gulliver's fiction to offer his own withering critique of colonialism in Ireland. The memory of Oliver Cromwell's Celtic horrors commingled with the brutal record of England's New World settlement in Swift's mind. His prescient condemnation of the effects of empire, and in particular his precocious sympathy for those destroyed in order to build a colony, prologue the unfolding history of imperial adventures. Born of the Irish experience, "the earth reeking with the blood of its inhabitants," Swift authored the ironic fallacy that the "modern" idea "to convert and civilize an idolatrous and barbarous people" betrayed the colonizers' own barbarities. Out of eighteenth-century London, a world city and the pivot of international trade, Swift staged the dilemmas of empire and its dis-locations. With *Gulliver's Travels,* Swift invoked travel and the then-popular genre of the travelogue as a means to explore—and parody—the spatial reorganizations and uneven developments attendant to the spread of the "boundless market." Swift located the gigantic in the grotesque abstraction of a far-flung exchange economy.[7]

Travelers to Alaska at the end of the nineteenth century had similar difficulty in avoiding the hyperbolic when describing the scenes before them. How strange that Swift's literary depiction of bigness landed in this far northern region? An accident, surely, that searching for a name for the new territory, nineteenth-century Americans decided on "Alaska," an approximation of an Aleut word meaning "The Great Land." Though no secret association linked Gulliver's Brobdingnag to its later formulation, Alaska, once Europeans and then Americans visited the north, the sense of limitless space suggested by Swift was hardly diminished. Immensity seemed a quality of the actual geography. Like Swift's fiction, their reality was imaginative work, full of fanciful distortion.[8] "I see miles and miles of mountain and table-land," a traveler wrote of the Alaska vistas in the late nineteenth century, "covered with snow the depth of which can not be appreciated with the naked eye; there they stand like the palace abodes of some giant race."[9] Indeed, the region reinforced the visitor's sense of scale, as the "abode of some giant race," a Brobdingnag land. In the 1870s another latter-day Gulliver noted a coastal glacier that "resembles a gigantic road torn up by the wheels of some Titan race."[10] And another writer, traveling up the coast in the 1880s, registered what appeared as the gargantuan proportions of Alaska. "I seem to have been adrift in a new creation, such as is sometimes outlined in our dreamland. I am lost in the height of the mountains, the depth of the sea, and the immensity of space. Every thing is on so enlarged a scale that there is no familiar standard of comparative measurement. . . . But this archipelago of mountains and landlocked seas, objects individually so magnificent in themselves as to startle the senses are multiplied and reduplicated until they paralyze one's comprehension!"[11] As Swift had recognized, travel narratives served a vital function in the formation of imperial attitudes, but Gulliver's tale had taken on a life of its own, apart from Swift's meaning.

If, in the minds of late nineteenth-century Americans, the western frontier had closed, then an alternative was found in the North, their last frontier.[12] Following the American purchase of Alaska in 1867, the region appeared to many observers as distant and as unfathomable as Gulliver's tales. And the uncomprehending branded the acquisition with epithets—"Seward's Folly," after the Secretary of State William Seward, who had negotiated the purchase from Russia for $7 million, but also "Icebergia," "Polaria," "Seward's Icebox," and "Walrussia." Boosters soon turned these misrepresentations on their head, promoting instead attractive lures to capital investments in furs, fish, gold, and lumber, but also scenic resources marketed to tourists. Following the first organized steamer excursions in early 1880s, the several-week ventures from west coast ports up the Inside Passage coastal waterway, as far north as Sitka and Glacier Bay, attracted thousands of well-to-do tourists. More than five thousand tourists steamed north along the passage in 1890 alone.[13] Inveterate scribblers, these excursionists wrote and published hundreds of accounts of their travels. Alaska's bigness was reborn.

I use this accident, the connection of scale between Gulliver's Brobdingnag to the Great Land, to make a point. The visiting strangers never merely gazed upon a world transparently evident. If the environment produced statements, then it only did so through a myriad of cultural filters. Their observations projected a host of political, economic, and social meanings embedded in nineteenth-century bourgeois culture, itself a product of empire.[14] The travelers' descriptions of Alaska were fashioned within a wider cultural context through which specific ideologies echoed.

This culture invented a past for itself, tracing a racial legacy back to the forest-dwelling Teutons and the westward-advancing Anglo-Saxons. The north was not "won by weaklings . . . but by men with the heart of Vikings," pronounced the northern versifier Robert Service.[15] Theodore Roosevelt insisted that the winners of the West had more than just heart. They had heredity on their side. The "English-speaking people," according to Roosevelt, held a special destiny in their "blood"; they alone could win "over the world's waste spaces."[16] Bourgeois travelers, wielding words as acts, proved equal to these race warriors.

Other scales of meaning filled these northern spaces. The rocks and beaches, lagoons and precipices had names and stories: frog humans, land otter men, the halibut people, the trickster raven, the puffin's daughter, all animated a land and sea crowded with spirits where the human and the natural converged. Tlingit history, if we may claim it as such, filled the spaces that appeared so empty to the newcomers. These other histories were invisible to the white visitors. The Americans celebrated the bigness of the new acquisition's physical presence, but, unlike Swift, they diminished the natives into insignificance. These so-called "children of nature"—the indigenes—held no gargantuan qualities for the arriving strangers. Instead, they were doomed to "evaporate like snow in the summer sun," as one visitor predicted.

"It must be borne in mind," one guide book celebrated, "how vast a country Alaska is,—as large . . . as the original thirteen states . . . from California it is as far to the western extremity of Alaska as it is to New York; so that the central city of the United States is not Omaha, or St. Paul, but San Francisco!"[17] Each retelling of Alaska's spatial enormity reconstituted again and again the power of the nation's imperial ambitions. Its geographical center had shifted westward. Their words served as claims to possession. "Our New Alaska" helped to fix the newly bought territory within the nation's Pacific ambitions. Alaska, as Secretary of State Seward had predicted, was to be "the drawbridge to Asia." Soon the Philippines, Hawaii, and the markets of the Far East would be theirs.

In the shifting architecture of American cultural identity, Alaska has remained a constant, the attic of the American imagination, a place where heirlooms were stored, precious memories to some, to others nightmares, a place broader and bigger than its actual borders. If elsewhere in the "Great West" the epics chronicled rugged individual struggles in the progressive conquest of the natives and nature, then in Alaska this dreamscape remained alive and fresh for discovery.

Introduction

In Darkest Alaska charts the experiences of travelers and tourists along the southeastern Alaskan coast and interior from the 1867 purchase through the Klondike gold rush. Focusing on the largely ignored late nineteenth-century Alaskan travel literature, this work places several decades of tourist activity at the center of late nineteenth-century northern expansion. The narrative follows travelers along the Inside Passage, the nearly thousand-mile sea lane that weaves a snakelike path up the coast from Puget Sound to Icy Strait. Protected from the fetch of the North Pacific, ships navigated through the islands and fjords, exposed to the open sea only in a few places. Native people along this temperate rain coast had long paddled tremendous cedar canoes along this passage. Under sail the passage proved more hazardous. Not until the advent of reliable steam-powered vessels in the mid-nineteenth century did Europeans, Americans, and Canadians travel regularly and reliably along the full length of the Inside Passage.

A flood of reportage—travelogues, guidebooks, articles, photographs albums, lantern-slide shows—entertained metropolitan audiences with images taken from this northern passage. In this vast literature one finds a remarkably comprehensive preview of the exploitative vision usually associated with the collective fantasies conjured by the Klondike gold rush of the late 1890s. On their northern transits these touring women and men found a ledger-book of nature stocked with aesthetic treasures, tribal artifacts, geological riches, and untold experiential thrills. Boosters may have advertised Alaska as the "Last West," but this work discovers less a settlers' homestead dream than a colder Congo, part of an expanded American empire. These travelers transformed the far north into a model of modern imperial acquisition. With their dreams charted, narrated, illustrated, and published, the tourists blazed the path for later gold seekers. They made Alaska legible for those who followed.

Following these journeys northward, each chapter focuses on stopping points along the Inside Passage—Fort Wrangell, Juneau, Glacier Bay, Sitka. Each stopover highlights different forms of imperial appropriation—sex, curios, minerals, cosmologies, authentic indigenes, and the landscape itself. Here the Inside Passage refers as much to the interior mindscapes of the passengers as it does to the perceived grandeurs of the seascape. While this study highlights the specifically regional experiences of these fin-de-siecle aesthetic Argonauts, it seeks to represent the wider culture of late nineteenth-century bourgeois society.

My aim here is to analyze the forms of tourism practiced in Alaska, and to use this study of travel and tourism as a lens through which to explore the driving forces of capitalism and imperialism—in both an American and a global context. By examining the Alaskan experience, this work reveals the depth of the connections between the experience of tourism and the imperialist agenda; the extent to which the experience of tourism was informed by the racial, class, and gender ideas of the period; and how closely the business of travel fused late nineteenth-century notions of race and empire with capitalist expansion.

In the context of Alaskan history, this book asserts that travel and tourism served as a necessary "prequel" to the story of the Klondike gold rush, more often highlighted by historians of the region. Traditional periodizations of northern history that focus on the Klondike rush as "opening" the north miss the beginnings of Alaskan development. The thirty years of travel preceding the gold rush fixed Alaska's possibilities in the national imaginary. Elite travel and cultural production helped to make American Alaska into a place of colonial conquest and the natural resource extraction it entailed.

Promoters, boosters, and travelers represented Alaska within a wider world of imperial imaginings. They were a motley group, mostly unknown characters—a disenchanted London clerk, a gay ex-sailor, a former society reporter, a Tlingit trader, a neurasthenic minister—but others were well known, such as wilderness advocate John Muir, archetypical imperialist Rudyard Kipling, painter Albert Bierstadt, and photographers Edward Curtis and Eadweard Muybridge.

Spectators all, these Alaskan travelers and writers operated as the secret agents of conquest, acting without being seen to act, because they lived according to a discipline of seeing that made them unwitting functionaries of their class, race, and nation. Though these travelers exerted control upon this new world with less apparent intensity than the miners, trappers, fishers, timber cutters, and other laborers, these passersby put that world at greater risk precisely because, as the critic Elaine Scarry observes, "their own immunity from risk made them inattentive to the forms of alteration they brought about."[1] Alaskan tourists worked invisibly.

Not only were their written words effective at incorporating Alaska into the nation, but the tourists' fleeting physical presence there exerted its own powerful force upon the indigenous north. Their words attracted an international audience that came to understand the north through sightseeing eyes. And their visits, filled as they were with the quest for authentic experiences and souvenirs, extended the ideal of the universal market into the domestic spaces of non-Western communities. For those who followed the tourists—the gold seekers, the miners, and settlers—trooped north certain of one thing, that Alaska was theirs for the taking. The tourists' passages transformed the north. Alaska was a scenic bonanza before it was a mining bonanza. And while the gold has run out, the scenery as yet remains.

Several questions guide this book. First, what was the American relationship to the wider world of nineteenth-century imperialism? And, how might a close examination of this far corner of North America help us to better see and understand such a relationship? Second, How do we come by the ways in which we see nature? That is, how did late nineteenth-century Alaskan travelers interpret the nature they viewed along their passages? And how have American ideas about nature, and more specifically wilderness, been shaped by this Alaskan history? Ideas about nature reflected the social and political worlds of these travelers. It almost goes without saying that the "Last Frontier" state continues to serve as a central fixture in the nation's wilderness imaginary. If empire and wilderness merge in this history, then how have these ideas taken shape together? That is, how did this empire of nature emerge as an historical idea that exerted great power over the native north? And how did the identification of this region as wilderness serve imperial ends? Answers to these questions require that we recognize the ideological character of our own culture's most deeply held myths. Northern nature, far from being merely natural, was, instead, constitutive of a new political order. The title refers to these questions.

"Every frontier has two sides," historian William Macleod wrote unselfconsciously in the 1920s, "Too readily do we forget when we dwell of an evening over the mystery of Rene Maran's *Batouala*, or Joseph Conrad's *Heart of Darkness*, and other stories of the black mystery-continent of Africa, that North America was for long a Dark Continent. And for a longer time, the heart of this continent was dark. The far-flung agents of frontier enterprise in early Virginia felt this, as did the early explorers in the dense woodlands of the Ohio region, for a time the Potomac, and for a longer time the Ohio, were Congos."[2] Alaska too fit within this myth of the Dark (North American) Continent. And while the supposed American frontier had passed out of this darkness in the sweep of westering settlement, Alaska remained a frontier in the national imagination at the turn of the century. "The Soul of Alaska," one observer stressed, was "an integral portion of the 'White Man's Burden' assumed by the

United States when it adopted these children of the Glacier and Fiord."[3] Assuming the "White Man's Burden," as the imperial versifier Rudyard Kipling trumpeted, dominion over the north required little modification to the ideologies of the frontier.

If a too easy comparison between the "barbarous tropics" and the "frigid zone" appears extravagant, then the degree to which contemporary writers drew frequent comparisons between these regions is not exaggerated. The rhetoric of the "Dark Continent" offered a language that might connect the era's supposed civilizing projects where ever they asserted themselves. Mary Hallock Foote betrayed this common metaphor when on joining her engineer husband's attempts to irrigate along the Boise River she exclaimed, "Darkest Idaho! Thousands of acres of desert empty of history."[4] The central position of Africa in the experience of colonialism and empire provided a common grammar. As a counterpart to Africa, Darkest Alaska fit easily in American imaginings of a wider imperial geography. "In Darkest Alaska" headlined a turn-of-the-century article describing the adventures of a survey team, "as much isolated from civilization as was Explorer Stanley in the interior of 'darkest Africa' . . . surrounded for thousands of miles of dreary stretches of uninhabited country."[5] With the closure of the so-called western frontier in 1890, the nation found room for its expansionist imagination in Alaska. In the minds of travelers Alaska held a figurative power akin to other "dark places."

"America's traditional view," as historian William Appleman Williams argued, understood itself as "anti-imperialist throughout its history," save for "a brief and rapidly dispelled aberration at the turn of the century."[6] The nation's history has been understood as "antithetical to the historical experience of imperialism."[7] Celebrated as a final frontier, the obscurantist ideologies of pioneering and rugged individualist struggles against "wild nature," old staples of Alaskan history writing, have hidden this *lebensraum* of the American imagination. Indeed, as Williams insisted, "one of the central themes of American historiography" has been that "there is no American Empire."[8] The challenge to this perception is longstanding. But, Alaskan history has long escaped the critical attentions of historical revisionists. Even the so-called New Western history has generally ignored the role of the north in American empire.[9] In many respects, the New Western history, having raised the question of imperialism, has largely turned away from theories of "process" toward more parochial considerations of "place." Far from being a remote and ignored corner of American national development, Alaska's history serves as an indicator of a far flung culture of imperialism linking Americans to their European imperial counterparts.

Naval bombardment of indigenous villages, summary arrest of native resisters, and administrative reorganization of native communities exacted a powerful imperial control over the native north. But sovereignty over Alaska was seldom grounded on violence alone. Colonization was very much an intellectual and cultural enterprise alongside its more dramatic military, political, and economic conquests. "In place of the old local and national seclusion and self-sufficiency," Karl Marx wrote, "we have intercourse in every direction, universal interdependence of nations. And as in material, so also in intellectual production. The intellectual creations of individual nations become common property. National one-sidedness and narrow-mindedness become more and more impossible, and from the numerous national and local literatures, there arises a world literature."[10] Marx enunciated early on the critical role of language, image, and cultural phenomena to the production of political and economic orders.

Empire in the north was not simply the establishment of a formal American presence. Late nineteenth-century sightseers, transient visitors all, helped to extend the new political order as certainly as did any of the sailors, soldiers, missionaries, or prospectors. These travelers were all the more effective because they were not an official institution of the state apparatus. The type of power they exercised moved invisibly without the imprimatur of state activity, even as they effected critical functions of imperial expansion. Tourists, albeit unwittingly, carried on a distinctly political project. They commanded an imperial "common property," a sort of power over territory and a capacity to mobilize its human and natural resources toward political, economic, and military ends. This well-connected elite acted as a true ruling class, a class which recognized the state as the tool of their shared ideals. The tourists' presences and their written passages exercised a variety of state power while appearing to have no political effect whatsoever.[11]

Their written passages provide a wealth of historical evidence. The texts of this bourgeois cultural world reveal a host of American anxieties at the fin de siècle, that vague sense of decline and decay, but also the spirit of possibility and progress that we may glimpse perhaps most clearly at the edges of the continental empire—"Alaska! The Last West, the great domain of the North," as a travel promotion announced.[12] Focusing on the enormous body of ignored travel literature, both public and private texts, this study takes seriously the reality of what was imagined, and the role such discursive forces had in northern expansion.[13] The flood of travel writing helped to fix a particular vision of the north in the national imaginations of Americans. And these elite travelers were particularly well placed to represent the new northern acquisition to the nation. At the same time that this literature helped shape evolving images and ideas of the new North, the act of travel also proved a constitutive feature of modern American identity, a feature that extended beyond the narrow, leisured upper class. In this way, their travel activities fit within a long tradition of incorporating new land into the national body and national culture. "Tourism," as John Sears observes, "played a powerful force in America's invention of itself as a culture." "It was inevitable when they set out to establish a national culture in the 1820s and 1830s," he argues, "that they would turn to the landscape of America as the basis of that culture." At that early date America was still a country in search of an identity.[14] By the end of the century, Americans had distanced themselves from Europe by establishing a "common national geography" whereby certain places came to characterize America itself as nature's nation distinct from Europe's claim as the historical backdrop of civilization.[15]

Pleasuring summer travelers in Alaska struggled with the meanings of their leisure. Not willing to simply relax, they configured their excursions as edifying ventures. Their play had to constitute some productive form. Nineteenth-century travelers merged the practices of the naturalist and nascent ethnographer with the activities of amateur tourists.[16] Justifying their leisured presence, late nineteenth-century sightseers mimicked their predecessors, relying on the discourse of travel. In their own minds, they were scientific travelers, assembling observed facts— topographical, biological, ethnographical, geological, and political information. Their panoramic sightseeing, tied as it was to the scientific conventions of naturalists, collected information on landforms, flora and fauna, and institutions. No matter that such information had already been gathered. These bourgeois adventurers formed a second or third wave of incorporation, another arm of empire.

While these travelers consistently interpreted what they saw through the blinkers of a metropolitan worldview, this view was given force in their travel experiences. And this view was certainly conditioned by the expansionist geographies elsewhere in the late nineteenth century. As the following chapters will show, Alaska formed one part of a wider web of imperial fashioning that touched many aspects of a developing American culture. Raymond Williams's concept of "structures of feeling" or an alternative he proposed, "structures of experience" is useful here.[17] Williams described "a social experience which is still in *process*, often indeed not yet recognized as social but taken to be private, idiosyncratic, and even isolating, but which in analysis . . . has its emergent, connecting, and dominant characteristics, indeed its specific hierarchies."[18] Few of the travelers and writers considered herein would have recognized the formalized concepts or ideologies that this study attributes to them. Their written passages did, however, contain the power of a dominant worldview hidden as commonsense. Their views of the landscapes of their travels elided the actual social relations of the region. "A working country," according to Raymond Williams, "is hardly ever a landscape. The very idea of landscape implies separation and observation."[19] The tourists' spectacular separation reproduced nature as a landscape to which they felt entitled. The more natural the scenery appeared, the more effectively it naturalized power.[20] Of course one would spend a considerable amount of money to travel north to see the sights. Of course American enterprise would supplant the weak Russian colonies. Of course northern natives would wither and die in their contest with the presumptively superior race. These assumptions of the traveler's everyday consciousness, that assumed possession of the north and presumed superiority over its indigenes, must be interrogated. Their ideas about nature reflected their social world and helped to assemble the new political order.

"All the famous scenic points in Southern Alaska, which have made the Alaska tour famous, will be seen," a tourist brochure advertised, "including Fort Wrangel, Juneau, the Douglas Island gold mines, Lynn Canal, Sitka, and the great Muir Glacier on Glacier Bay . . . everywhere the tourist will have unsurpassed opportunities for scanning the wonderful scenery of our northernmost possessions, and for studying the quaint and primitive native life. The entire route from Puget sound to the farthest northern point reached is lined with scenes of awe inspiring character."[21] For the several decades that are the focus of this study, this itinerary never changed. Each passage stopped at the advertised locations with the tourists well prepared to take in what they had already been told to expect.

It is fashionable, as has been often noted, to see the imperial experience of travel as artificial and simulated, leaving authors "serving the very simulations they expose." In seeking to describe the power of imperial discourse one may end up reproducing its subject positions. But, such hazards admitted, this is not a history of the native north. The Tlingit and other First Nations people are present throughout the succeeding narrative as workers, as residents, and as makers of their own history. But, this study does not seek to give voice to the indigenous people of the Inside Passage. What follows is an examination of a vanguard of bourgeois travelers who exerted a particular kind of power. It is not focused on how their past knowledge or experience was flawed, but, rather, how such knowledge and experience took shape—a kind of critical "ethnohistory" of bourgeois travel.

Dispensing with a traditional chronology, this book moves between a number of interrelated themes and subjects. American national identity imagined itself in a geographically conceived world. These travelers discovered on the Inside Passage an experience that pulled together all experience. Their journeys linked a loose assemblage of contemporary ideas and sensibilities. Questions concerning adventure, empire, health, aesthetics, sexuality, primitivism, industry, and geology, to name some of the central concerns of the succeeding chapters, were all weighed against how these travelers saw the natural world and their place within it. Following two introductory chapters that establish the historical context and the motivations to travel, the ensuing chapters focus on each of the successive steamer stops—the initial passage out from Puget Sound ports, Fort Wrangell, Juneau, Glacier Bay, and finally Sitka. Since the travelers themselves hardly deviated from the set stopping points along the Inside Passage, this study follows their progress northward at these ports of call. This history unfolds in space.

The first chapter, "Continental Drift," links the far north with a wider field of imperial imaginings. Tracing the travels and writings of a young Englishman, the chapter ties Alaska to Africa, both through the particular experiences of this man and in a wider culture of surrogate adventurers transfixed with colonial exploits in the Congo and the far north.

Chapter 2, "Alaska with *Appleton's*, Canada by *Baedeker's*," highlights the era's obsessive interest in travel literature. Guidebooks helped scenic entrepreneurs to boost travel. Texts produced new readers and readers found new worlds of experience. Their subsequent travels, whether actual or imagined, helped conjure new cultural identities. Well-to-do Americans with increasing amounts of leisure and increasing spells of anomie sought the supposedly curative conditions of travel. Going outside into nature offered a timely antidote to the unstable environment of late nineteenth-century industrial society. Their travels were acts of differentiation, distinguishing the elite from the mass of middle-class tourists flooding more accessible sites. The salubrious sea airs and pleasing landscape vistas remedied the supposed trials of a life of urban ease.

Chapter 3, "Scenic Bonanza," considers the production of nature as an aesthetic object worthy of travelers' attentions and extended travels. Viewing nature became a critical part of wealthy Americans' cultural self-definition. The chapter details the Inside Passage's course, sailing out of Puget Sound ports north through the narrow channels leading past the British Columbia coast to southeastern Alaska. On this periphery we may consider what Henri Lefebvre has called "the global division of nature." "The earth, underground resources, the air and light above ground," he writes, "all are part of the forces of production and part of the products of those forces."[22] Scenic resources had come to exist in this curious tension as both producer and product of the forces of capital. In this circular logic, nature had come to represent a utopian alternative to the very forces that had produced wild nature as an idea in the first place.

Chapters 4 and 5, titled "Frontier Commerce" and "Totem and Taboo," respectively, trace an ex-Navy man's journey north to Fort Wrangell, Alaska. His experiences contrasted sharply with those of his wealthy counterparts, as different social constituencies reached different conclusions about the same circumstances with little consensus regarding their meanings. These chapters turn from the old sailor to a discussion of sexuality on the empire's fringes, to prostitution and Indian slavery, to the bourgeois tourists' observations on Tlingit women, to those native women's development of a thriving curio trade, selling souvenirs to the tourists who in turn take these trinkets home to their metropolitan parlors. Experience became a trinket, and the souvenir a hieroglyphic of their travels. Like the prostitutes who were both seller and sold, the tourists, likewise alienated from themselves, were both buyer and bought. Ending in the private spaces of the city, the analysis returns to the domestic interior where, as Walter Benjamin described, "the fictional framework for the individual's life is constituted in the private home. His living room is a box in the theater of the world."[23] Meanwhile, the outliers of the nation, those presumed unproductive citizens, offer a point of tension with the bourgeois travelers.

"Juneau's Industrial Sublime," Chapter 6, follows the meanings travelers attached to their visits to the Juneau area, site of one of the largest industrial gold-mining operations in the world for much of the late nineteenth century. The technological sophistication of the gold works seized these tourists' imaginations. They found little conflict between the extractive activities of the mine and the scenic wilderness they had come so far to see. There appeared to be enough resources of all kinds to go around. So transfixed were the visitors with the mine's industrial drama that they ignored the hundreds of native workers who helped keep the operation running.

In Chapter 7, "Orogenous Zones: Glaciers and the Geologies of Empire," travelers turned their attentions to Glacier Bay, the northernmost point of their passage.[24] Here tourists exercised their amateur geologic knowledge, interpreting and exploring the vast ice fields at tidewater. Earlier chapters have discussed nature's aestheticization; its supposed therapeutic qualities; its relation to imperial adventuring, social Darwinian ideologies, and industrial incorporation. In short, a concatenation of cultural, political, and economic practices constituted late nineteenth-century understandings of nature. Beneath these social productions and commodifications lay the bedrock of natural science. The chapter examines their geological discourse, a natural history that legitimated their culture's possession of nature. Geological strata and glacial deposits were historical formations. That is to say, for contemporaries the language of geology was a way of seeing nature that placed its substance in a great sweep of time. But this geological grammar was, too, a historical formation, the product of the era's particular economic rationality. Their science was unthinkable without their society's simultaneous endeavors to capitalize on nature.[25] This was especially true of geology, a science that allowed its practitioners the ability to read the land, its strata, and ultimately its value. Darwin and his interpreters had already given sanction to interpreting biological and social phenomena in the same structure of thought. The geologizing mind positioned human nature within a physical universe of natural laws, where those "races" most capable of controlling nature's resources were determined to rule over the others.

A concluding chapter, titled "Inside Passage," and a final epilogue, "Out of Alaska," consider the wider meanings of all this activity. Sitka marked the final stopover on the tourists' junket. At Sitka travelers enjoyed a final opportunity to acquire souvenirs and snapshots of their coastal transit. After considering the particular meanings of Sitka in the travelers' experience, the chapter wrestles with the wider meanings given the landscape and the region's indigenes. The discovery of gold in the Klondike in 1896 and the rush north in 1898 marked a series of changes in the far north. Other gold discoveries would follow at Nome, Fairbanks, and elsewhere throughout the region. These stampedes were built upon the foundation established by several decades of tourist travel. But this nineteenth-century story did not end simply with the discovery of gold in the Klondike. Nature, itself, as understood and as formulated in the late nineteenth century, survived into the twentieth century, and this colonial legacy continues to lie largely unrecognized beneath the surface of the present. Alaska took its turn in the frontier myth, that much celebrated movement from east to west, then turned north. The north has a meaning that is as clear today as when the word stood for a place not yet discovered.[26] Darkest Alaska joined its global counterparts. The utopian narratives of American pioneering, however, have hidden Alaska's conquest.

Chapter One
Continental Drift

"Less is known today of Central Alaska than of Central Africa," noted Charles Erskine Scott Wood during an 1877 reconnaissance of the Inside Passage. Wood went north to climb mountains, but also "to acquire information about the unknown districts lying nearest the coast, with a view to future explorations."[1] Acting as a military escort to Chicago adventurer Charles Taylor, the pair attempted an early ascent of Mount Fairweather and had their sights set on tackling Mount St. Elias. In the imperial drama of the late nineteenth century the image of Darkest Africa prevailed over the imaginative spaces of empire. And Americans, like Wood, reached intuitively for the image of the dark continent when confronting their own dark places. The northern landscape that emerged from the traveler's pen connected this far corner of North America with a global vision of colonial encounters, even as these same travelers Americanized the colonial encounter, distinguishing the push north from its supposedly more brutal analogues elsewhere. In the heyday of European colonial adventures in Africa and elsewhere, Alaska was not remote or removed, but cut from the same cloth. It was assuredly different in degree, but not in structure. The constant revolution of expanding capital, and the global flow of materials, resources, and people, also trafficked in ideas. And so Alaska joined Africa in the widely shared cultural shorthand of the era, a metonymic structure that linked the ongoing western fantasy of exploration to the institutions of imperial power. By the time of Wood's venture along the southeastern Alaskan coast, more than a decade of American adventuring had laid claim to the territory and its resources.

In 1864 the Western Union Company sought to connect North America and Europe. The company had recently established a transcontinental telegraph link. The following year the company sent an exploring expedition into Russian Alaska. Their goal was to survey the future route of a telegraph line up through British Columbia, across Alaska, under the Bering Strait, eventually connecting with the Siberian line across subarctic Asia to Europe. This ambitious venture unraveled when an even more audacious scheme succeeded. In July 1866 underwater cable laid across the floor of the Atlantic allowed for instant telegraph communications between Europe and America. The Russian-Alaska telegraph project was abandoned.

"The project of the Western Union Telegraph Company of an overland telegraph across Bering Straits was a failure," one expedition member would later testify. But if the expedition's original aim was a bust, then the interest generated by their explorations did not go unrecognized. "Its greatest result," the expedition member Henry Bannister added, "was the annexation of Alaska."[2] While he exaggerated, the expedition did encourage an awakening interest in the far north. The work of the expedition's scientists and surveyors helped to provide a baseline of information concerning the region.

If this initial exploration opened Alaska for the Americans, then this opening was accomplished through the efforts of the expedition members who turned their experiences into words. Figured in the explorer's pen, Alaska became not only an object of desire, a place to dream over, but also a new physical space capable of absorbing the nation's expansionist energies.[3] William Henry Dall's *Alaska and Its Resources* and English artist Frederick Whymper's *Travel and Adventure in the Territory of Alaska* published soon after the telegraph expedition and the subsequent Alaska purchase helped spur a widening interest in the North.[4]

These books straddled the expansionist impulse—on one side the discerning and scientific search for resources, and on the other, an itch for adventure. "Adventure and my love of roaming alone," as one of the expedition's members announced, "induced me to take the trip."[5] Adventure served imperialism as much as the pragmatic discovery of strategic minerals had promoted the incorporation of the new territory.[6]

But adventure needed cultivation. It relied upon its nurturing in narrative. Actual exploits induced surrogate experiences where a national audience of readers enjoyed a vicarious play of imagined exploration. "Virtually there was, and is, little known about it," Whymper wrote of Alaska's mysteries.[7] Hired as an artist-illustrator to accompany the Western Union Telegraph explorations, Whymper turned his two and a half years of travel in the North into a popular travel account. His work marked the beginning of a flood of travel writing following American purchase. "So little is known of the interior of Russian America, that I trust even this imperfect and meager narrative may prove not altogether uninteresting," Whymper wrote, characteristically downplaying his exploits.[8] Where the old West was gradually losing its so-called frontier atmosphere, Whymper stressed that in the new North, "the natives have been hitherto so isolated from civilization, that perhaps in no other part of America can the 'red-skin' be seen to greater perfection. In a few generations he will be extinct." Whymper marked the north as native and therefore savage. The expansion of the United States and its addition of the new territory of Alaska bode ill for the region's indigenous people. The inexorable force of natural law, Whymper and his readers believed, would extinguish the natives. The white men's coming into the country would proceed easily. It was their destiny, or so they believed.

The Alaska purchase also suggested a wider territorial appetite. "There are, however, many, both in England and America, who look on this purchase as the first move towards an American occupation of the whole continent, and who foresee that Canada and British America generally will sooner or later become part of the United States," Whymper predicted. "It is the destiny of the United States to possess the whole northern continent," he wrote. Whymper, echoing the sympathies of others, welcomed a contiguous United States extending to the Arctic. "Looking at the matter without prejudice, I believe it will be better for those countries [the United States and Canada] and ourselves [Great Britain] when such shall be the case. . . . Our commercial relations with them will double and quadruple themselves in value," he concluded.[9]

Canada "would always be a welcome addition," the ardent western booster Horace Greeley once announced.[10] Canadians did not share this enthusiasm for American jingoism. In the United States and Canada many believed that the acquisition of Alaska would make inevitable the annexation of British Columbia.[11] Canadian anxieties over the imperial desires of its southern neighbor helped to push through the British North American Act of 1867. Americans chasing gold in Cariboo and on the Fraser River had already filled the region soon to be known as British Columbia. The newly formed Dominion of Canada welcomed the subsequent inclusion of British Columbia in 1871 and stanched the American appetite for territory. Massachusetts native Abby Woodman Johnson, traveling the Inside Passage in 1889, reflected the enduring suspicion that the United States would soon occupy the Canadian West. "They are very like our people though as yet not of us, a mistake which time will rectify," wrote Woodman of her observations of the Canadians she met along the British Columbian coast.[12]

Americans have "an unequaled record of conquest, colonization, and territorial expansion," U.S. Senator Henry Cabot Lodge wrote in 1895. "From the Rio Grande to the Arctic Ocean there should be one flag and one country." William H. Seward, Andrew Johnson's secretary of state, who had negotiated the Alaska purchase, boasted to a Boston audience in 1867, "Give me fifty, forty, thirty more years of life and I will engage to give you the possession of the American continent and the control of the world." But the imperialist vocation ran across national boundaries. The reigning orthodoxy suggested racial affinities tying Canadians, Americans, and the English. Americans were the ones most often pushing this blood tie.[13] "There is apparently much truth in the belief that the wonderful progress of the United States, as well as the character of the people are the results of natural selection," Charles Darwin estimated.[14] And his interpreters added that "there is abundant reason to believe that the Anglo-Saxon race is to be, is, indeed, already becoming, more effective here than in the mother country."[15] In spite of the troubles among Britain, Canada, and the United States, consistent intellectual and cultural affinities linked the nations. The idea of Anglo-Saxonism bound national differences through the late nineteenth-century orthodoxy that believed in the so-called "patriotism of race." "Somewhere deep down in the heart of every Anglo-Saxon lies the predatory instinct of his Viking ancestors—an instinct that a thousand years of respectability and tax-paying have not quite succeeded in eliminating," the writer Frank Norris insisted.[16] Americans, sensing a coming crisis with the disappearance of new contiguous territory, looked north to Alaska to satiate the expansionist impulse. "When the supply is exhausted," Josiah Strong warned in 1885, "we shall enter a new era."[17]

At about the same time that Frederick Whymper prepared to head north to Alaska, his brother, Edward, struggled to the summit of the Matterhorn in the Alps with a party of seven climbers. Their climb in July 1865 was the first ascent of the sharp and iconic peak. On the descent, however, one climber fell and pulled three others to their deaths. The accident shocked Europeans and especially the British public, who were appalled by the "dilettantes of suicide." "But is it life? Is it duty? Is it common sense? Is it allowable?" the *Times* of London editorialized in the wake of the tragedy. "Is it not wrong?" Queen Victoria contemplated outlawing mountain climbing altogether. Edward outlived the controversy surrounding the accident. Like his Alaskan-bound brother, he too was a skilled engraver and artist. In 1871 Whymper published *Scrambles Amongst the Alps,* illustrated with more than one hundred of his engravings. Despite the earlier denunciations, mountaineering, helped along by the popularity of Edward Whymper's book, garnered a broad following.[18] No doubt Charles Taylor's own desire to summit Alaskan peaks had been spurred by Whymper's book and the controversy surrounding the alpinist's high-risk gambit.

Edward Whymper celebrated what he saw as the virtues of alpinism, particularly the "development of manliness, and the evolution, under combat with difficulties, of those noble qualities of human nature—courage, patience, endurance, and fortitude."[19] His Alaskan-versed brother might have agreed. Certainly the Whymper brothers' adventures exulted in these new terrains. For the Victorians the Matterhorn disaster ranked alongside Lord Franklin's disappearance in the Arctic and David Livingstone's death in Africa.[20] Whether at the vertical or horizontal margins of empire, these frontier spaces offered a rough crucible of masculinity in the minds of the late nineteenth-century leisure class. Supposedly pent up and frustrated in the domestic realms of society—"just as the boy shut indoors finds his scope circumscribed"—these men sought their supposed freedom outdoors. Instead of "the snug, over-safe corner of the world," or what Theodore Roosevelt would call "the soft spirit of the cloistered life," the empire wilderness provided a testing ground, or so they believed.[21]

Frederick Whymper's narrative of his Alaskan travels helped to encourage the growing fascination with America's new territory. Alaska was to be the counterpart of his brother's Alps, a draw to a leisure class of Americans interested in adventuring in new lands. Within a decade the American territory would be widely advertised as the "Switzerland of America." As Frederick's exploring colleague William Dall noted in his own Alaska book, "The field now open to Americans for exploration and discovery is grand. The interior everywhere needs exploration."[22] Whymper and Dall joined a now distinguished lineage of explorers who celebrated their ventures in print. The era seemed to have reached what Emerson had predicted earlier: "novels will give way, by and by, to diaries and autobiographies—captivating books."[23]

Travel writing spread with territorial ambitions. No need to invent stories when the romance of real life provided all the detail and drama that metropolitan readers desired. Henry Morton Stanley, sent to Africa by *New York Herald* publisher James Gordon Bennett, Jr., celebrated his own extraordinary but brutal travels. Stanley, a Welsh orphan, spent his adolescence in the 1850s along the Arkansas River. Living in a malarial zone was not new to him. Stanley published *How I Found Livingstone* in 1872, recording his journalistic scoop, finding the British missionary David Livingstone in central Africa. *In Darkest Africa*, another bestseller, sold one hundred and fifty thousand copies in English and was widely translated. Following its release in 1890, one reviewer noted that it "has been read more universally and with deeper interest than any other publication." The noted explorer Sir Richard Burton, in addition to having written a series of books on his African travels, also published widely read volumes on his visits to Arabia, India, and America. In Canada, Captain William Francis Butler also turned from the boredom of barracks duty at the margins of the empire. Captain Butler wrote two books describing his Canadian wilderness exploits, *The Great Lone Land* (1872) and *The Wild North Land* (1873).[24] Butler went on to chronicle his later African experience in *The Campaign of the Cataracts; being a personal narrative of the great Nile expedition of 1884–5.*[25] These became easy Victorian bestsellers. And numbers of other Victorian men and a few women turned their experiences into words.

In 1883, the U.S. Army sent Lieutenant Frederick Schwatka north on a military reconnaissance of Alaska. Like army officer C. E. S. Wood among the Tlingit, Schwatka became another in a long line of imperial officers who turned their soldiering duties into a series of books and articles. He was an obvious choice for the War Department mission, having spent two years as the leader of the American Geographical Society's search for evidence of the British Naval expedition led by Sir John Franklin that had disappeared in the Canadian Arctic in 1845. The enterprising Schwatka turned his experiences while on the military surveys of Alaska into several popular travelogues and influential government documents—*Along Alaska's Great River, Nimrod in the North; or hunting and fishing in the Arctic regions,* and *Report of a military reconnaissance in Alaska made in 1883.* Schwatka modeled his exploits on the successes of men like Stanley and Butler. His description of the summer heat on the Yukon River made this northern waterway another river of empire, "the dancing waters that made one feel as though he were floating on the Nile, Congo, or Amazon," Schwatka wrote.[26] He searched for (in his words) "hostile Indians" up the Yukon. In his way, Schwatka helped to open Alaska. His explorations added little new knowledge to the region that had long been traversed by Europeans and Americans (and before them ages of indigenes). Like his better-known contemporary Stanley in Africa, Schwatka's travel narratives advertised the hitherto little-known north to the metropolitan imaginations of reading Americans. Answering the charge that Schwatka's explorations were of no "practical value," a *New York Times* article countered, "This might as well have been said of the voyage of Columbus. It is not until regions as remote as Alaska have been brought to the notice of the public . . . that the commercial 'prospector' is stimulated to see what can be done toward developing the resources."[27] These "prospectors" were interested in more than just developing the region's resources, as Schwatka highlighted in his travel books that were slanted more to the tourist's imagination. "Among their number," Schwatka observed of a party of Alaskan miners, "was a young lawyer, a graduate of an eastern college, I believe, who had joined the party in the hope of finding adventures and of repairing his health, which had suffered from too close an application to his professional studies."[28] In opening up the country, adventurers hoped to blaze the trails for civilization, and to open up themselves to the empire wildernesses' supposed regenerative effects. In making Alaska into an American territory, these travelers remade themselves.

In 1883, as Schwatka headed north to Alaska, Edward James Glave quit his job in a London counting-house and left England.[29] Young Glave felt himself an outcast. He loathed office work, the indoor labor, the dreary months, hating, as he said, the "foggy London streets and the ways of city life." The physical presence of the unreal city had proved too much. London, then the largest city in the world with more than four million people, had closed in on him. Glave had become just a number among the anonymous crowds flowing over London Bridge on their way to and from work. His counting-house clerkdom left him perched above the lowest classes, but barely middle class, comfortably anxious. "I longed only for the time of my deliverance," he confessed.[30] He could have been one of Rudyard Kipling's imperial minions, who romanticized, "We were dreamers, dreaming greatly, in the man-stifled towns; We yearned beyond the sky-line."[31] For Glave, deliverance would require an adventure, one well beyond the gloom, "brooding motionless over the biggest, and the greatest, town on earth."[32]

It has been said that adventuring is intrinsic to human experience.[33] Every epoch has witnessed some sort of restlessness. And perhaps, late Victorian Britain encouraged a particularly energetic form of such world wandering, given that the Union Jack flew over so many colonial possessions. But if some general notion of adventure seems fixed, then the meaning of this wandering has varied. And each historical period has given its own peculiar stamp and form to the idea of adventure.

"Very early in life," Glave confided, "I made up my mind that I would some day see for myself the wonderful countries that I read of in books of travel and adventure that formed the whole of my schoolboy library."[34] "I lived in imagination in strange countries and among wild tribes," he recollected, "my heroes were all pioneers, trappers, and hunters of big game."[35] Yearning for some more intense experience than that offered by his London firm and city life, "I decided to myself that I would make my own way in the world, away from the beaten tracks of civilization."[36] In some primeval remove, Glave sought to make his own history. He might have agreed with Robert Louis Stevenson's declaration that "'real art' that dealt with life directly was that of the first men who told their stories round the savage camp fire."[37]

Travel narratives filled the presses. In *How the Poor Live* (1883)—a "book of travel," as he described it—George Sims wrote of a trip to "a dark continent that is within easy walking distance."[38] "This continent will, I hope, be found as interesting as any of those newly explored lands which engage the attention of the Royal Geographic Society," Sims wrote. Reformers and bourgeois voyeurs trekked into the East End slums of London. Social reformers published a widely read pamphlet, *The Bitter Cry of Outcast London*, that year, raising awareness of industrial England's social crisis. Faced with the awful evidences of the distress wrought by industrial capitalism, Glave and his cohort seemed to either flee, or live vicariously reading of the miseries of others. Wealth and

crushing poverty existed side by side. And the wealthy believed themselves to be overwhelmed by lower-class degenerates. Class distinctions
blurred into the racialist conventions spawned by social interpretations
of Darwinian evolutionism. In *Hard Times*, Charles Dickens had made
clear the analogue between the industrial city Coketown and its colonial
counterpart. "It was a town of unnatural red and black like the painted
face of a savage," he described. Similarly, Sims wrote, "The wild races
who inhabit it [London's East End] will, I trust, gain public sympathy as
easily as those savage tribes for whose benefit the missionary societies
never cease to appeal for funds." The empire's relationship to its
periphery, particularly Africa, became an interpretative mirror for the
more immediate, and potentially more unsettling relationship with
working-class others in the metropolis. Social Darwinism validated the
colonial order, just as it confirmed the industrial class order as natural.
The experience of empire served as an anodyne helping to explain metropolitan disorders. Cockneys and Congolese came to occupy similar
places in the minds of bourgeois observers regardless of their political
sympathies. They existed in their degraded condition because of *what*
they were, not what role they played in industrial civilization.

Glave read the magazines celebrating the lives of vagabond boys, traipsing after dreams of gold or imperial glory. Auriferous dreams—
Treasure Islands, King Solomon's Mines, El Dorado fantasies—drove
these escapist fictions, these fictions of capital. In England, Edwin Brett
pioneered a profitable penny-press empire, publishing a slew of cheap
titles, eagerly read for their violence and escapism. By the 1880s the
reaction to these "penny bloods" had set in and Glave would have had
to content himself with titles like *The Boys Own Paper*, published by the
Religious Tract Society. Instead of *The Wild Boys of London*, the society
pushed "anti-authoritarian impulses into an imperial channel."[39]

The print revolution had changed utterly the way people experienced
their world. The flood of printed information transformed how people
thought about themselves and others.[40] Reading let them temporarily
experience the lives of the various under-classes and exotic foreigners,
only to return with relief to the safety of their own parlors.[41] Not content
with his work-a-day life, Glave sought adventure. "The old spirit moves
us to migrate, we burn still with untamable, inextinguishable savagery,
abhorring walls, and roof—the entire house of civilized restraint," wrote
Canadian frontier veteran Roger Pocock. In *The Frontiersman*, Pocock
romanticized this imperial restlessness. "We ask, we adventurers, the
earth for our bed, the stars for our clock, the morning chill for our
reveille, the ends of the earth for our portion, and in the path of our
world-grabbing savagery the shuttles of Fate are weaving the fabric of
Empire."[42] The imperial adventure narratives of the period made their

indelible mark on young Glave's mind. And Glave's reading guided his next moves.

By any traditional measure of historical significance, Glave's youthful foray would not amount to any great shudder in the grand patterns of human history. Perhaps his departure might earn him citation as a passing anecdote. But Glave's life would soon touch upon the great themes of the late nineteenth-century world: imperialism with its insatiable quest for raw material; the germs of the Empire's mentality; the awful schism rent by evolutionism; the spreading power of print capitalism, communication technologies, and transportation; the era's profound anxieties driven by the divisions of class, race, and gender; and the tensions wrought by swelling urban centers. As Glave lived in the world, his particular history merged with the general patterns of the age. Karl Marx, a careful observer of late nineteenth-century change, emphasized that the "constant revolutionizing of production, uninterrupted disturbance of all social relations, everlasting uncertainty and agitation, distinguish the bourgeois epoch from all earlier times." This bourgeois epoch spurred Glave's anxiety and his nostalgic flight to the empire's ends, his search for deliverance, away from the beaten tracks of civilization. Through him we may seize that elusive place in which individual experience and collective experience merged.[43] And in the end Glave figures in the story of the tourists' opening of the north.[44]

Edward Glave, just shy of his twentieth birthday, wished to trade what one English urban critic termed the "terrible Darwinian drama of survival in the streets" for that of another wilderness, a "real" wilderness, not some artificial urban chaos, as he perceived it.[45] A reciprocal relationship formed between the urban and so-called wilderness spaces of empire. Where social critic Charles Booth stood aloof and saw in London "a rush of human life as interesting to watch as the current of a river," Glave only wished for the river itself, the real thing, an outlet. This new world of information and transportation offered Glave a route to the river.

Gazing over the map of the continents, Glave saw rivers with great estuaries traced on the charts for only a few miles into the interior and "then dribbled away in lines and hesitating dots; lakes with one border firmly inked in and the other left in vague outline; mountain ranges to whose very name was appended a doubtful query; and territories of whose extent and characteristics, ignorance was openly confessed by vast unnamed blank spaces." Glave, anticipating Joseph Conrad's Marlow, had a passion for maps—those dream-texts of empire—and would lose himself in the imagined glories of exploration, putting his finger on that "white patch for a boy to dream gloriously over."[46] He desired to fill in these blank spaces with places, names, lines of location.[47] And a great river would provide the pathway into this imagined blankness. He plotted his own story as surely as he would soon plot the lines of passage on the maps of his wanderings.

Glave arrived at the coast in preparation for heading up the great river into the heart of what was to him strange country. His employer recognized in the pale Londoner "those qualities . . . which were absolutely necessary in a pioneer. He was tall, strong, and of vigorous constitution, with a face marked by earnestness and resolve."[48] Character was marked indelibly upon the body, according to this nineteenth-century code. Their race logic saw in separate peoples the markings of species' superiority (or inferiority). Glave was expected to establish a trading station, deep in the interior, up in the forests, up river of the falls, three hundred miles above the pool. An outpost that, it was thought, might provide "a beacon on the road towards better things, a centre for trade of course, but also for humanizing, improving, instructing."[49] Colonialism's "three C's"—commerce, Christianity, and civilization—determined the conquest of this resource-rich region.

Moving up river, Glave confirmed his imaginings, finding in the landscape a perfect replica of authentic wilderness. Going up the river was for Glave like "traveling back to the earliest beginnings of the world."[50] "The surrounding scenery is as wild as the water it encloses, and changes with every turn of the river; . . . rounding another bend tall barren cliffs stand sentinel on either side, their heights worn by time into jagged pinnacles, their bases torn and shattered by the fierce flood perpetually assailing them," he pictured.[51] His sublime contemplation of the region's vast spaces accomplished an imaginative erasure. This *terra incognita*, emptied of its human inhabitants, became vacant land, a spatial *nullis* awaiting European settlers. In the minds of Glave and his employers, commerce would be just the thing to settle this wild place. In the beginning the natives generally accepted their small intrusions. The newcomers seemed ill suited to the place, since they died like flies. The traders followed the men with god and they brought guns and cloth and other things that were of use.[52]

Once at the station site, Glave and his native laborers hacked out an outpost from the black forest. In its broad leafy shadows, Glave erected the few rough buildings of this Inner Station. Nicknamed by his native neighbors, "Mwana Tendele," or "son of Stanley," Glave lorded over this outpost of progress, building the infrastructure for colonial rule, suppressing local control over trade, buying up the ivory, and supposedly bringing an end to the trade in human lives.

For you see, when Glave left England, he had signed on with the International Association of the Congo. His river was the Congo.[53] Young

Glave's employer was the mercenary explorer turned commercial imperialist Henry Morton Stanley. An inveterate self-promoter, the arrogant
Stanley recognized that fame sold books. His *Through the Dark Continent*
(1878) and later *In Darkest Africa* (1890) proved immensely popular.
These travel books became the model for the flood of writing following
on the heels of his exploits, as Europeans and their settler brethren
touched every place they could. Joseph Conrad would later write that
Stanley's exploits were "the unholy recollection of a prosaic newspaper
'stunt' and the distasteful knowledge of the vilest scramble for loot that
ever disfigured the history of human conscience and geographical
exploration."[54]

The people living along the river dubbed the impetuous Stanley,
"Bula Matari," meaning the "breaker of rocks" (or at least this was how
Stanley remembered it). Did they see in him some hostility to the forest,
a desire to conquer all nature? Stanley liked his new name.[55] But his conquests sought victims other than merely inarticulate nature. Working for
Belgium's King Leopold II, Stanley brought violence and brutal suppression to the river basin's people. His excesses earned him a new name,
according to the missionary George Grenfell, who noted that the people
on the upper Congo had begun to call him "Ipanga Ngunda," meaning
"destroys the country."[56] As Richard Burton charged, Stanley "shoots
negroes as if they were monkeys."[57]

These names may be apocryphal. The Africans of the region were not
of one mind, nor did they speak the same language. But Stanley's violent
reputation was not in doubt. Glave, however, fell under his spell. He
believed that in the minds of the "natives," Stanley's arrival served as
"one of the principal marks of time."[58] History began with Stanley, or
so Glave believed. Time began with the arrival of white men, according
to the colonizing Europeans.[59] Glave's history anticipated the provoca-
tions of the imperial historian Hugh Trevor-Roper, who much later
wrote, "Perhaps in the future there will be some African history to teach.
But at present there is none, or very little: there is only the history of
Europe in Africa. The rest is largely darkness, like the history of pre-
Columbian America, and darkness is not a subject for history."[60] The so-
called "rule of darkness" has hung like a spell cast over non-Western
spaces, whether in Africa or the Americas. At the 1884 Berlin Confer-
ence, the European powers partitioned much of Africa into new colonial
"states." For the next six years the white-suited clerk Glave would work
for the Congo Free State, the private domain parceled out to the Belgian
king. In 1886, Glave assisted the American Henry Sanford in his efforts
to investigate the region's resources, anticipating future U.S. investment. In the middle of the tropical rainforest near Luokolela, at the
mouth of the Sangha River, the expansionist and often-violent Stanley

tutored the young Glave. Glave could not have had a better teacher. Stanley instructed the young Englishman in the ways of conquest. Up river, great stores of ivory and rubber might be had. Stanley's nurturing earned Glave, his so-called "son" as the Africans recognized him, the Belgium Star of Service, awarded by King Leopold II himself.

Glave soon slipped out from under Stanley's shadow and earned himself a new title—"Makula," meaning literally "arrows," referring to his newly earned reputation as a hunter and provider of meat. He so enjoyed shooting hippopotami and Cape Buffalo that Stanley had to reprimand him. Glave had become the great hunting frontiersman of his schoolboy dreams. His self-fashioning found success in the recesses of the Congo. Though Glave thought he had left the counting house back in London, he had become its furthest extension. Imperialism, driven by capitalism, unified all space, spreading its wealth unevenly between societies. The accountants, as Herman Melville once observed, "have computed their great counting house the globe, by girdling it with guineas."[61] Money was the measure. Nevertheless, Glave's efforts were an act of differentiation. Leaving the city with its supposed clones, he made a new and separate identity in what Stanley called the "unpeopled country."

The anthropologist Claude Lévi-Strauss described the character of this repudiation of the social order, this flight from ordinary living, when he wrote, "A young man who lives outside his social group for a few weeks or months, so as to expose himself to an extreme situation, comes back endowed with a power which finds expression in the writing of newspaper articles and best sellers and in lecturing to packed halls."[62] The irony exposed by Lévi-Strauss and enacted by Glave was that "the conscious repudiation of the social order has as its final object the improvement of one's own standing within the order." Glave's quest for the unknown, to paraphrase Levi-Strauss, took place simultaneously as "an individual quest for power within the framework of an order that is already known intimately." Glave had fashioned a new identity for himself, but he did not do so outside of the cultural choices available to him.[63] It was in relation to the alien Africans (in Glave's mind they were so) of this terra nullus (only in rhetoric was the land vacant) that Glave, the adventurer, staked out a new self. He might learn their curious ways and interpret these exotics to the metropolitan millions. Ten years after his initial departure from London, Glave published his memoir *In Savage Africa: Six Years of Adventure in Congo-Land*. But by then he had already moved on to another endeavor.

Returning in 1889, Glave may have passed Konrad Korzeniowski—soon to be known as Joseph Conrad—on the streets of London. The as yet unknown expatriate Polish sea captain was then preparing to join the International Association of the Congo (he would dub it the "International Society for the Suppression of Savage Customs" in his fictional tale), to pilot a steamer up the Congo River. Like Glave, Conrad would turn his experiences into words, famously so.[64] Stanley was his Kurtz.[65] Conrad never mentioned the great river in his *Heart of Darkness*; instead, the place remained ambiguous. Empire was ubiquitous. With some shifts in scenery and situation it could have been any place. And this world of fiction—Conrad's novella—was Glave's world of fact, of empire and casual violence, where the banner of "free" trade brought exploitation. Destruction sprang from acts—slavery's suppression and commerce, but also from the written word—that heralded (at least in the minds of the European imperialists) progress toward human freedom.

In late summer 1889—Glave had returned from the Congo and Conrad was back from the East Indian Ocean—the Great London Dock Strike nearly shut down the city, and nearly every riverside worker had joined the fight. The metropolitan wilderness was changing too. "That immense haunt of misery is no longer the stagnant pool," Engels wrote of the strike, "it has shaken off its torpid despair, has returned to life, and has become the home of what is called the 'New Unionism'; that is to say, of the organization of the great mass of 'unskilled' workers."[66] Stanley's just-published bestseller *In Darkest Africa* attracted a phenomenal readership. William Booth published his popular evangelical tract *In Darkest England and the Way Out.*[67] "As there is a darkest Africa is there not also a darkest England?" Booth queried. The connections between the core and the periphery, the parallels between London's destitute and Africa's "primitives," wedded the colonies to the core. Resources ceaselessly transported from those colonies filled the docks and factories of the metropole. And the dislocating forces of capital undermined working lives in the capital as well as the colony.

Glave headed to the United States on lecture tour celebrating his African adventures, and earning a profit from the vicarious interest in his experiences. But in New York City, yearning for some new exploit, Glave joined an exploring expedition to Alaska and British Canada, sponsored by *Frank Leslie's Illustrated Newspaper.* He would serve as the expedition's executive officer and official artist. *Frank Leslie's* editor hyped the expedition, touting, "It is not unlikely that the result will be second only to that of Stanley's explorations in Africa."[68] Glave's tutelage under Stanley lent an air of authority to the expedition. As the editor anticipated, "We have every reason to believe that this exploring expedition will penetrate farther into Alaska than the feet of white men have hitherto trod."[69]

In the minds of these late nineteenth-century men, Africa and Alaska existed side by side, cohabitating the same space in their colonizing imaginations. A system of global representation could exert its discursive practice over the corners of the world.[70] "Opportunities for exploration in Alaska were as enticing as those in Africa," the editor enthused.[71] *Leslie's* editor W. J. Arkell also anticipated the rewards of increased readership tied to launching the exploring expedition. This technique for *making* the news had old roots. But given the stupendous rise in print culture—the enjoined surge in literacy and development of mass print technologies—publisher-sponsored expeditions could significantly boost sales. News editors knew the potential rewards to be reaped from the Stanley connection. After all, Stanley's "discovery" of Livingstone on assignment for the *New York Herald* led editor-owner James Gordon Bennett, Jr., to *make*, not simply report, the news. Stanley's scoop in 1872 resulted in record sales for *The Herald*. Leslie's publications, which had pioneered the use of illustrations, had profited from its adventure features over the years. However, *Frank Leslie's Illustrated Newspaper*, which had long been the weekly leader in scandal, thrills, and adventure, lost its sensational qualities and most of its widespread appeal after Leslie's widow sold it in 1889, according to historian Frank Mott.[72] In 1890 with Glave's Alaska expedition the weekly newspaper sought to recoup its lost market share.

Edward Glave, that "son of Stanley," might help conjure these increased sales. Americans, facing the U.S. census director's announcement that "There can hardly be said to be a frontier line," needed, it seemed, new fields for expansion, for freshening their democracy. Immigration and the emergent urban tensions fostered a need for an imagined safety valve, some release of the new population pressures that might be found in new territory. The readership thirsted for the sort of exaggerated adventure narratives that increased the store of geographical knowledge.

The observations of these sponsored explorers could not be separated from the imagined audiences who would read their texts. Their writings conformed to the expectations of the readers, as much as to the actual objective realities confronted on the frontier fringe.[73] Explorer Glave's individual experiences in Alaska would be marked by the expectations of his American audience and his own African years. The discursive practice of colonial power was linked to its material practices. The explorer relied upon his sponsors for his supplies and in the end the publication and promotion upon which he stakes his reputation. The adventurer structured his (or her) experiences to conform to the requirements of those sponsors. "The explorer testifies," historian J. K. Noyes writes, "to all those hidden eyes looking over his shoulder, acting on the form of his prose." Glave's articles, reported in *Frank Leslie's Illustrated Newspaper*, stretched over three months in nine illustrated parts.[74]

Before he headed west to San Francisco and then north to Alaska, Glave visited Tiffany and Company in New York City to have his watch reset to Greenwich Mean Time. He noted in his journal that it was losing a second a day. This diary detail suggested Glave's obsession with time. After all, a second a day would hardly seem to warrant concern. But for the explorer such accuracy was necessary. Glave's maps with their invisible matrix of latitude and longitude were constructed with respect to time, measured in minutes and seconds. And importantly the reference point for the maps and charts and for Glave's chronometer was Greenwich Mean Time—empire time. Greenwich, England, served as the temporal and spatial starting point for all locations.[75] For the explorer to fix himself in space, he would have to fix himself in time as well. Every place referred back to England. But for the time being Glave's watch setting would only serve to predict the arrival and departure of trains as he made his way across the American continent.

In the spring of 1890 the five-man party—three of whom were reporters or artists—headed north to explore the upper Yukon River. Two members were familiar with arctic and subarctic Alaska. One of these men, Jack Dalton, gave the expedition a particular sort of authenticity. He fit the emerging western stereotype of a gun-toting rugged individualist then celebrated in dime-novel fictions. Dalton was one of those itchy-footed migrants that seemed to leap-frog across the West, never settling for long in any one place. He was born in 1855 in the Cherokee Strip of future Oklahoma. He cowboyed in Texas, drifted westward from ranch to ranch, settled briefly in eastern Oregon, wrangling and logging in the Blue Mountains where he shot and killed a man at close range on the main street of Burns. Dalton escaped to San Francisco, shipped out for Alaskan waters on a sealing vessel, and was jailed in Sitka along with the rest of the ship's crew for poaching fur-seals. (The U.S. government had awarded a monopoly lease to the Alaska Commercial Company entitling the company to harvest fur-seals on the Pribilof Islands in the Bering Sea. Sealing by any other interests was illegal and the U.S. Cutter Service strictly policed the region's waters.) Once released from prison, Dalton prospected and worked odd jobs along the Alaska panhandle, before returning to San Francisco in early 1890. His frontier character, celebrated in Glave's reports, helped to sell magazine copy. But his particular knowledge of the coast north of Juneau proved an important asset to the expedition.

Frank Leslie's editor had set ambitious goals—"to traverse and, as far as possible map the interior of Alaska"—that seem all the more ambiguous when cast within the unspecific "interior." Since this interior lay beyond the careful lines of the U.S. coastal survey charts, this supposedly unmapped, and unknown zone afforded the expedition members considerable latitude concerning where they ventured. "The Intrepid explorers, with the assistance of from one hundred to one hundred and fifty natives, and others, will start on their march to the interior," according to Leslie's Newspaper.[76] Only thirty or so reluctant Tlingit porters from Chilkat could be convinced to join the party. Alaska's "surf-beaten coast-line has long ago been charted, and its navigable waters have been explored; but the great interior, unapproached by waterways, is almost unknown," Glave enthused.[77] The newspaper perpetuated the myth of first arrival, boasting that, "We have every reason to believe that this exploring expedition will penetrate farther into Alaska than the feet of white men have hitherto trod," echoing the rhetorical symbols of Africa's exploration, a expedition "second only to that of Stanley's explorations in Africa."

Arriving at the mouth of the Chilkat River, north of Juneau, Glave noted that the weather was "splendid." With twenty-four hours of daylight, the snow melted quickly off the hillsides. In summer, Glave enthused, "central Alaska looks almost tropical."[78] Glave transposed easily his African experiences to Alaska. Being harassed by local natives, Glave reverted to his African practices, "We informed them that if they continued to hinder us and to thwart our progress we would put them in irons and take them to the coast."[79] Glave's journal entries invoke a constant comparison with Africa, noting the recent practice of slavery by the Alaskan natives and the on-going trade in humans in Africa; the dependence on native labor in both Alaska and Africa. According to Glave, the Alaskan natives' general backwardness, thievery, filth, and conniving compared equally to the Africans' savage state. Alaskans and Africans fetishized and worshiped devilish shamans who held the people in their thrall, or so Glave thought. Glave's context for understanding these hyperborean people found fruitful comparisons through his recent tropical African experiences. His interactions with the Tlingit and interior Athapaskans mixed with his African experience: "Several of the Indians have returned sick and we are left quite busy dosing them with quinine, fortunately there is no medicine man in the village."[80] The poison quinine no doubt did little to help the Alaskans in this malaria-free zone, though the mosquitoes flew in thick clouds. These northerners shared with the Africans in Glave's mind the same tendency toward degeneration. "There are only a few of them left, applies to the Indian race, their numbers are gradually dying down," noted Glave in his journal.[81] Of the estimated twelve hundred Chilkats and Chilkoots, the expedition noted, "These twin-brother savages were formerly the most warlike natives in Alaska, but contact with the whiteman, and servile subjection to his whiskey are fast bringing them down."[82]

But Glave's observations of native disappearance stood in stark contrast to the other details he noted about native life in the north. He observed their work in canneries, packing salmon for worldwide markets; hunting seals whose furs would be finished in London factories; packing loads for expeditions like his own; piloting vessels through the narrow water passages of the coastal archipelago; and manufacturing curios for the summer tourist trade. "Moccasins, fancy bead and leatherwork are hung about," he observed, "and will be sent down to the coast, there to be exchanged to the summer tourists for silver dollars. At present most of them are out of funds, but are looking eagerly to the return of fat tourist pocketbooks."[83] Clearly the Tlingit were not disappearing. They in fact served as the principal labor force for the new resource economies along the coast—fish canning, mining, and tourism. Nevertheless, Indian lassitude and inefficiency were blamed for the region's backwardness. "Defective transport," the unfortunate reliance upon Indian carriers in Glave's estimation, was "the sole reason for the undeveloped and unexplored state of the land."[84] Glave sought to remedy this state of underdevelopment.

Glave and Dalton soon parted from the other members of the expedition and reconnoitered the headwaters of what they thought was the Alsek River, which they descended to the Pacific. The pair actually canoed down the Tatshenshini River, not the Alsek. A trip down the Alsek in a wooden dugout would likely have proved fatal to Glave and his three companions, Dalton, a native man called Shank, and a shaman. Turnback Canyon on the Alsek River has Class VI rapids, indicating the likelihood of drowning. Fortunately, they spent the first several days floating down the Tatshenshini before it joined the Alsek, fifty miles before the ocean. The Tatshenshini was not without its own excitements, as several rapids tested the paddling abilities of Glave's Tlingit guides.

In Glave's view, two otherwise remote geographies were brought into the single frame of his experience. Glave named the nearby mountain range—the Stanley Range—for his mentor. He had already named a lake after his editor, Arkell, and a glacier, the Leslie, after his sponsoring magazine. Passing down the upper braided channels of the headwater shallows of the Tatenshini, freely transposing African landmarks with new Alaskan ones, Glave called the confluence of the Tatshenshini and the Alsek, "the Pool," like the great backwater above Stanley Falls on the Congo River. "Throughout my letter I have retained the native names of geographical points," insisted Glave, despite his renaming a number of major features for his expedition's sponsors. "To destroy these by substituting words of a foreign tongue is to destroy the natural guides," he argued. But Glave retained the native identifiers only for the purpose of more effective navigation, recognizing that the local people—the coastal Tlingit and the interior Champagne and Aishihik—were, and would continue to be, instrumental in guiding the newcomers in their sup-posed discoveries in the northland. Names mattered.

The rivers of Glave's explorations could hardly be "discovered," since natives had known of the rivercourses, as had more recent European and American visitors. Cook and Vancouver had both noted the obvious valley of the Alsek River. La Perouse called the river "Riveirre de Beh-ring" in 1786, Tebenkof adopted the name "Alsekh" in 1849. During Frederick Schwatka's *New York Times* expedition to climb Mount St. Elias in Alaska in 1886, the newspaper proudly announced that Schwatka had discovered the "second Mississippi," a river "not thought to be rivaled by any Alaskan River" and named the river after the proprietor of the *Times*, George Jones, "in compliment to a gentlemen whose relations to the expedition justly entitle him to the distinction." Finally the United States coast survey dubbed the river the "Harrison" in 1890.

From June through January 1891 *Frank Leslie's Newspaper* published story after story covering the expedition. Glave's narratives suggested both the practical drama of figuring out what actually lay in the interior as well as a model of heroic venturing, realized particularly in his 1890 river expedition down the Alsek River. "Having covered several hundred miles of hitherto unexplored territory," Glave claimed right of first pas-sage down the mis-named Alsek River.[85] Not surprisingly, Glave's hired Indian guide, "Shank," who knew the entire river's course, had obvi-ously passed up and down the river that connected his interior people with the coast at Dry Bay. The explorer did not lead, but was led.[86] Glave noted his reliance upon native-drawn maps with "their scribblings of val-leys, hills, and lakes availed to keep us on our course to the far interior of Alaska."

Visitors to Alaska had long relied on local informants to help sketch the coast and interior. In 1869, the U.S. Coast and Geodetic Survey established a station near Klukwan on the Chilkat River in order to observe a solar eclipse. Chilkat chief Kohklux and his wife provided sur-veyor George Davidson with a detailed map of the route from the coast to the Yukon River, the same route that part of the *Leslie's* newspaper party would take to the river. "At his own suggestion Kohklux proposed to draw upon paper his route," Davidson later noted. "Kohklux started from his place at Klukwan and drew all around the paper and I gave him the back of an old map on which he and his wife drew their routes etc. in 1852."[87] The chief detailed the long-established trading route up the Chilkat River, over the pass, and through the Southern Tutchone trad-ing centers of Neskatahin, Hutshi, and Aishihik en route to the Yukon River. The Chilkat Tlingit had long maintained strict control over the trade in furs between the interior and the coast. Acting as powerful mid-dle marketers the Tlingit mediated trade relations between Russian and later Hudson's Bay Company and American maritime merchants. The route that Glave and his party "pioneered" had a long and well-trodden history. "Lying face downward the old chief and his wife discussed and laboriously drew on the back of an old chart the lines of all the water courses, and lakes with the profile of the mountains as they appear on either hand from the trail . . . and the limit of each of the fourteen days journey across to Fort Selkirk is marked by cross-lines on this original Chilkat map," as a *National Geographic* magazine writer, Eliza Scidmore, explained this episode of indigenous mapmaking. So accurate was the map, according to Scidmore, that "this Kloh-Kutz map was the basis of the first charts [*sic*]."[88] But the map was not only a relatively accurate representation of the topographical features of this critical trade route; the map was also a memory.

In 1852, Kohklux had led a party of Tlingit to rout the Hudson's Bay Company (HBC) permanently from its post at Fort Selkirk at the junction of the Yukon and Pelly rivers. The Tlingit burned the post and kept the HBC from continuing to interrupt the Tlingit's coastal control of interior fur trade. In 1869 Davidson noted the thorough control the Tlingit continued to exercise over the valuable fur trade up and down the southeastern Alaskan coastline. "The savages of the coast proceed about a hundred miles in canoes, and thence trudge away on foot the same distance to an inland mart, where they drive a profitable business, as middlemen, with neighboring tribes."[89] Scidmore called the Tlingit "relentless monopolists." Kohklux's map embodied a different set of relations, composed as it was out of the recollection of this strategic raid. The map suggested an alternative struggle and its representation.

The newcomers relied overwhelmingly on the traveling experience and cooperation of their indigenous guides. But the Europeans and the indigenes experienced these spaces in dramatically different ways. "The world of the journey furnished a symbolic text where each culture read its own intentions," Paul Carter writes.[90] The coastal Tlingit and the interior Athapaskans had their own stories for these rivers and mountains. In their memory, the Alsek had flooded in the 1850s, destroying whole villages along the river's course. Near the headwaters a glacial surge, the sudden movement of miles of ice, had dammed the river. These ice dams can be quite substantial, remaining for years. When the river ruptured the dam, the floodwaters burst with a volume greater than that of the Amazon, though only briefly, but catastrophically, flushing with a great wall of earthy water, wiping out aboriginal villages at the Tatshenshini confluence and well downstream at Dry Bay. A Southern Tutchone story recalled this history. The surge had been blamed

on the arrogance of a young Yakutat Tlingit visitor to the Yukon who made fun of an Athapaskan shaman because of his balding head. "Ah, that old man! The

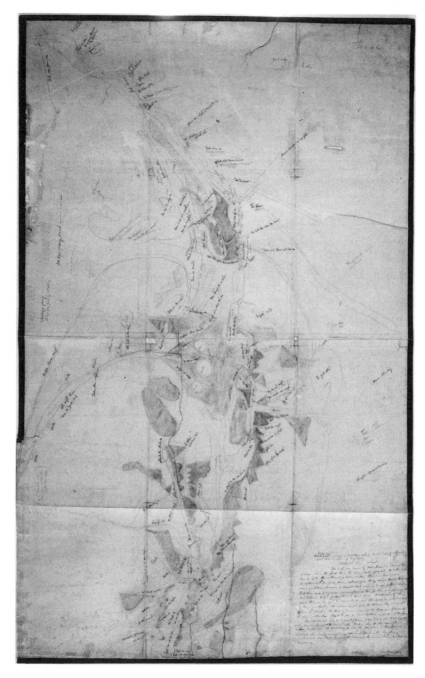

Figure 2. Sketch map showing route of the Chilkat chief Kohklux in 1852 in Alaska and the Yukon. Drawn by Kohklux in 1867 with place-names and annotations added by George Davidson, director of the Alaska coastal survey. (Image courtesy The Bancroft Library, University of California, Berkeley)

top of his head is just like the place gopher plays, a bare stump," said the visitor. Another older Tlingit man warned him not to behave so rudely, but the damage was done. To punish him and his kinsmen, the shaman sat on the top of Goatherd Mountain and called the glacier across the Alsek River. A lake formed behind the flank of the glacier. Then the shaman broke the dam, causing a flood that scoured the landscape and drowned those Yakutat Tlingit camped at the junction of the Tatshenshini and Alsek Rivers.[91]

The incidents and accidents of traveling that constituted the indigenous history of the country did not exist for their white clients. If Glave had inquired about the history of the river, then he did not elaborate this in his dispatches to the outside. And even if he had learned of the history that constituted the indigenous experience of this place, then it would have been unlikely that their explanations of cause and effect would have satisfied his European reason. The indigenous experience of place could not be easily incorporated into the Europeans' historical practice.

Frank Leslie's Illustrated Newspaper trumpeted the expedition's successes. "As much of the work was done in portions of the interior not previously visited by white men, a great body of fresh information has been obtained, by which blank spaces in the map can be filled out and the water-courses accurately outlined." The trip disproved the belief, bolstered by the opinions of prominent authorities, "that this vast stretch is nothing but one solid mass of ice."[92] In fact, the expedition—Glave and Dalton's navigation of the Tatshenshini and lower Alsek, coupled with the other party's crossing to the upper Yukon and descent to the Bering Sea—had added little new knowledge to the outsiders' understanding of the region's geography. Although the geographical and scientific results of the expedition were limited, the regular coverage by *Leslie's* did much to stimulate public interest in Alaska.

Edward Glave and his partner Jack Dalton became ardent publicists for Alaskan development. Following the 1890 trip, the pair planned a second venture, aimed at opening interior Alaska to travel. Glave noted that his first experience in Alaska had "assured me beyond doubt that defective transport was the sole reason for the undeveloped and unexplored state of the land. The Indian carrier was the only means of transportation; he controlled the situation, and commanded the most exorbitant pay. Moreover, his arrogance, inconsistency, cunning and general unreliability are ever on the alert to thwart the white man."[93] "Students of colonial discourse will recognize here the language of the civilizing mission," writes literary historian Mary Louise Pratt, "with which North Europeans produce other peoples (for themselves) as 'natives,' reductive, incomplete beings suffering from the inability to have become what Europeans already are, or to have made themselves into what Europeans intend them to be."[94] Non-capitalist indigenous societies and their subversive landscapes were depicted as degraded and primitive. As Glave found during his African sojourn, Alaska needed the civilizing methods of rational labor regimes, a money economy, and systems of transportation and property. The indigenous "failure" to exploit the region's resources signaled and legitimated the newcomers' entry into the country.

Leaving New York in March 1891 for his second trip north, Glave expressed some reservations about his walkabout life. "I realize that I have a big undertaking in hand in formally equipping and carrying out an Expedition to the Heart of Alaska, but thank God I feel equal to the occasion," Glave admitted in his journal.[95] Here again Glave's words adhered closely to his African experience. The spirit of penetrating the interior, to "the Heart," linked these otherwise disparate continental exploits. The region was not only an object of Glave's discoveries, but, importantly, an area for potential development, where gold might be found. Once in the interior, Glave duly noted that his expedition's arrival "with the pioneer band of horses is a most important event in Alaskan history, destined in the near future to receive due recognition."[96] The Chilkat had other opinions about this intrusion, of course. For a hundred years they had worked successfully to maintain control of the passes to the interior. The coastal Tlingit had ruled the trade in furs between the interior Athapaskan fur trappers and their middlemen, the Hudson's Bay Company. They had prevented the HBC from establishing their own direct trade with the coast. By the late nineteenth century this dominance was slipping. And so it was significant that Glave and Dalton's efforts to open a pack trail to the interior proved successful. Glave and Dalton, however, went over the passes with bigger goals than the establishment of a trail. After all, the Indian trail had been established for centuries.

Glave's second trip over the Chilkat Pass went for gold. "Gold has been discovered everywhere on the outskirts, warranting the supposition that the same precious metal exists in the interior . . . a fact which created in our minds the reasonable hope that we might strike the supply at its source," he fantasized.[97] Glave had difficulty convincing native guides to accompany their trek, being constantly warned of extreme obstacles, swamps, cannibalistic tribes, uncrossable rivers, anything to throw these white men off the mineral trail and to discourage them from upsetting the native trade relations. But with bribes of tobacco, the white men left with detailed maps of the region. "I cross-questioned them most fully," Glave related, "and learned of unmistakable landmarks and bearings; and when the natives refused to accompany us as guides, their scribblings of valleys, hills, and lakes availed to keep us on our course to

Figure 3. Former African adventurer Edward Glave on safari in Alaska. Glave's sponsor, *Frank Leslie's Illustrated Newspaper,* sought to enhance readership with vivid illustrations of the expedition's exploits. Tlingit porters haul Glave (African-attired in British pith helmet, tropical tunic, and knee-high leggings) from an improbable crevasse fall. "Progress of the 'Frank Leslie's Newspaper' Expedition Through Alaska—Crossing a Glacier—Rescuing a Member of the Party from a Perilous Position" (*Frank Leslie's Illustrated Newspaper,* July 1890). (Courtesy Sterling Memorial Library, Yale University)

the far interior of Alaska."[98] Glave and Dalton transformed local knowledge of the region into information to serve the expansionist energies of American, Canadian, and British capital. "It is not until regions as remote as Alaska have been brought to the notice of the public," the *New York Times* argued, "that the commercial 'prospector' is stimulated to see what can be done toward developing the resources."[99] Indeed, if advertising the region could achieve such ends, then Glave's efforts enhanced the new attentions focused on the north. Alaska was the drawbridge between America and Asia, as one contemporary observer noted.[100] Northern resources would, it was assumed, fuel the extension of the American commercial empire ever westward, expanding its Pacific horizon. And gold-seeking lay at the ideological and material heart of the region's transformation from the supposed "backward" and "vacant" native space to a realm not only inviting the vanguard of prospecting pioneers, but also of troops of curious tourists.

Dreams of mineral wealth drove Glave's expedition, legitimating the expense and effort. But Glave's treasure-seeking motives were entangled in a host of complicated emotions and relationships. The treasure sought could not always be so easily defined. Glave admitted in his journal that his years of "adventure seeking are now numbered. I will no longer seek wild and empty places simply for the gratification of facing the dangers which present themselves and of overcoming the difficulties and obstacles which one meets in travel."[101] The aggressive search for mineral riches could not explain Glave's wanderlust. "My ambition hitherto has been a selfish and insolent one. I will change before it is too late, before the fascination has got to strong a hold of me and has to an extent estranged me from my friends," he confided. Glave had never really turned his back on thoughts of home. Perhaps at those moments when he was most removed, up the Congo or halfway down the Alsek, he had been seized by the desire to return to the relative safety of old London. Once in the spare Alaskan tundra, he only wished to be back at home, back in the city. "My ambition now is to make a big fortune and marry the girl I love and then settle down and obtain as much happiness during my remaining years as possible, doing as much good as I can to help my fellow man and shaping my own road to prosperity so that so that my own rise will not mean others' fall, that my success will not be purchased at the expense of others' failure."[102] Even his admonition to help others was here couched in the inscrutable language of currency. "I have got the blues very badly. . . . Remembrances of old Africa make me feel miserable. The different events which occurred during my six years in Africa appear in panoramic." Glave wondered whether he would ever return and determined that "if I do it will be for some important work, not merely to say that I have been to Africa, but in some work with the sincere object of relieving the hideous misery of the curse of slavery, drinking the life blood of that country." He would not return as a mere tourist, "not merely to say I have been to Africa."[103]

In the end Glave returned to the exotic romance of his own fight to rid Africa of slavery. The fascination had gotten a strong hold of him. By September 1891 he had enough of Alaska. "I do not want to visit this part of the world any more. I have seen all I want of the interior of Alaska and the copper-colored rascals peopling it." But despite his failure to strike it rich, Glave concluded, "the journey is a wonderful benefit to the land. Prospectors can now visit the country and probe into the minerals of Alaska. We have proven the practicability of taking pack horses into a belt of unexplored territory, a land which gold hunters have been anxious to visit but the opportunity has been denied them for want of transport. The way is now open to them."[104] The discursive evidence of his trip certainly opened the way into the interior, as much as any actual trail breaking accomplished by Dalton and Glave. After all, native travelers had used the route over the Chilkat Pass to carry on trade between the interior and the coast for centuries.

Glave did return to Africa. Incapable of escaping his own fiction, he followed the paths taken by his schoolboy heroes—the tireless David Livingstone, Henry Morton Stanley, and "those pioneers, trappers, and hunters of big game." Glave imagined that he had in the end thrown off the city's tethers, that he had escaped the urban core into the wilds, to places of alternative experiences, open spaces capable of absorbing his romantic energies. But his imagined escape was only that—*imagined.* These wilds, Alaska or Africa, were not alternative landscapes. His frontier fantasies of self-reliance, separation, and isolation were just fictions. In Alaska, as in Africa, Glave served as a vanguard (and only a minor figure at that) for the commercial energies unleashed by the spread of new technologies of transportation, communication, and production. His travels celebrated in print did more to promote the rising tourist fascination with the north than in accelerating mineral development in the north. If capitalism built the city, then it also *made* the wilderness. Seeing nature as a utopian alternative to the city was (and is), as Raymond Williams reminds us, a historical illusion. "Capitalism is the basic process in the history of both."[105] Men such as Glave, armed with pens and paper, disappeared into the masculinized borderlands of empire. They reappeared in their travel narratives, recounting their ventures, justifying the presence of the white settlers, transforming raw nature into resources, and setting the stage for new forms of cultural conquest, charted in their fictions of capital.

Henry Morton Stanley, writing the introduction to Glave's narrative,

In Savage Africa: Six Years of Adventure in Congo-Land, highlighted the service such books performed to the wider reading community. Glave's travelogue contributed, according to Stanley, "to the pleasure of many stay-at-home readers in parlor and school, on the farm and at the counter, for as every one cannot go to Africa, why may not Africa be brought to them as is here done."[106] Print culture boomed with the unprecedented access to mass production and mass consumption. The textual traces of Glave's adventuring satisfied the desire for some alternative to the penury of daily life in increasingly mechanized and commodified industrial society. If men and women could not actually travel to the ends of the earth, then they could enjoy the voyeuristic experience of reading about other's adventures. Such vicarious experience gave the work of Glave and other travel writers a dual significance. The travel narrative provided descriptions and information that served material ends, perhaps enhancing access to a particular region, encouraging the actual extraction of resources. These narratives also worked their discursive magic over a wide readership, entertaining office- and parlor-bound men and women. Glave's written work contributed to the ways in which his readers thought about colonized landscapes and people, helping to define how Westerners should perceive and act toward the non-Western world. And this discourse played an essential role in tying disparate individuals to national and imperial identities. Those armchair adventurers could share a common national identity by reading travel accounts and perhaps visiting these newly opened regions.

What should we make of Edward Glave's wanderings? Does it matter that his exploits traversed the globe, joining in his own experience Africa and Alaska? His links to companies and governments suggest the spread of larger systems of economic and political control under widening capitalist rule. Under the racialist logic of the era, Europeans assumed static primitive societies in the subarctic and the tropics would disappear or perhaps naturally evolve into progressive capitalist orders. Western commercial culture would bring such stability into being, Glave assumed, by creating a new field for consumer desires. By establishing a range of conventions and ideas within which to consider these unincorporated regions, the era's travel writers developed a language for the unwritten landscape. These colonized spaces were new and exciting, even entertaining. And they were incorporated in the minds of imperial readers, as their lips silently mouthed the words of discovery.

Real or imagined, significant or minor, the explorations of this mobile agent of empire merged Africa and Alaska in Glave's own lived experience. Certainly the legacy of pith-helmeted Congo colonizers displaying the severed hands and heads of the colonized did not fit into the histor-

ies of Alaska and the Yukon's immediate past. If there had been violence, then it was the Russian promyshleniki who had perpetrated it at
least a half-century earlier, or so thought the newcomers. In the north
there were no Kurtzs, nothing resembling the violence that rent the
Congo interior during the last decade of the nineteenth century. In
America and Canada, and in their territories, there was no conception
of evil, not of the sort that Stanley exhibited and Conrad made infa-
mous. True evil was something that happened somewhere else in their
exceptionalist account of the American colonial encounter. The American experience was not even deemed colonial in character—in Africa,
in those savage zones, but not here, at least, not according to their narratives. Destruction arrived in more insidious forms—disease, whiskey,
and commerce. In the racialist evolutionary thinking of the day, indigenous people suffered these plights because of hereditary weaknesses.

The natives were destined to inevitable decline, or so it was believed.
And the resources that they left unused would then enter world markets,
justifying the newcomers' presence. When he wrote of Alaska, Glave's
rhetoric conformed to the language of pioneering, the utopian vision of
frontier white men settling the vacant lands of the north. He cast himself
and his accomplice, Dalton, as rugged frontiersmen overcoming natural
obstacles, bringing nature under their productive rule. Glave's northland narratives mirrored, unwittingly or not, the resilience of American—or rather North American—exceptionalism. His writing obscured
the realities of empire beneath the utopian rhetoric of settler expansion. To be sure the relative absence of state-sanctioned brutality in the
north could not begin to compare with the level of routine violence in
the Congo. To be sure the patterns of American manifest destiny or Canada's supposed benevolent expansion differed dramatically from the
brutal scramble for Africa. But these relative differences should not
elide the presence of institutional and cultural forces that eroded the
subarctic native hold on their lands and cultures. We should not so easily
exclude Alaska from the wider patterns and practices of empire in the
late nineteenth century. Once having recognized the differences, we
might then see northern expansion within the global spread of industrial capitalism.[107]

Glave's story touched upon the main streams of late nineteenth century history—imperialism and commercial power, the new technologies
of print capitalism, communication, and transportation, and the ideologies of white supremacy. His travels and his writing deserve attention
because together they reflect some of the central themes that arose from
this milieu. Glave was a peripheral character probing the borderlands of
empire. But he is central for what he represented. Glave traveled
between continents, a confusing national character, a Brit who comes of

age in the Congo, trained by the era's archetypical colonialist, Henry Morton Stanley; he leads an American expedition of exploration funded by a New York newspaper and nominally aided by the United States military, penetrates the northland of Canada, and "discovers" a major Alaskan river to which he applied the wrong native name. Like his protégé, Stanley who claimed himself as American, or English, or Welsh to suit his needs, Glave traveled between national identities. Glave's chameleon qualities raise important questions about the fungibility of national identities. Americans, Canadians, and the Brits were assumed to share the same racial characteristics. In Glave's border crossings we might recognize historical patterns that lumped the late nineteenth-century Anglo-Western world into a wider field of colonial practices.

Dreams of mineral wealth lay at the heart of this New World experience. When Glave trumpeted his opening of the Alaskan interior to gold-seeking prospectors, he confirmed the self-evident meaning of gold. He enhanced the treasure-seeking fantasies that were already on everyone's mind. The likely presence of gold and the means to find it validated the newcomers' fevered prospecting. In Alaska, the temporal and spatial last frontier, gold again served as a central myth for the expanding metropolis. Glave might as well have been leading Conrad's "Eldorado Exploring Expedition" in *Heart of Darkness*. "To tear treasure out of the bowels of the land was their desire, with no more moral purpose at the back of it than there is in burglar's breaking into a safe," Conrad wrote.[108] As the imperial adventure narratives of treasure seeking and conquest had made a strong impression on the young Edward Glave, so too did Glave's mature musings on the importance of his explorations encourage a resurgent quest for minerals. His trail-building efforts were but one aspect of his influence. His labor in words had its own history. Travel writing like Glave's did more than simply describe. This literature structured new forms of experience. Glave's and his contemporaries' words once read became their own reality. Their accounts helped to build a vision of the New North, what Charles Hallock embraced in his travel narrative as "Our New Alaska."

Chapter Two

Alaska with *Appleton's*, Canada by *Baedeker's*

In 1889, Rudyard Kipling suffered a breakdown. "My head has given out," Kipling wrote in a letter, "and I am forbidden to work and I am to go away somewhere . . . I can do nothing to save myself from breaking up now and again," admitting to thoughts of suicide.[1] His doctors advised a sea voyage and extended travel to ease the strain of his work life. Arriving in San Francisco after a rough Pacific crossing, Kipling could only marvel with disappointment at the place. "Recklessness is in the air," he noted of the Americans' habits. Everything seemed expressed in "dollar terms," he lamented, repeating the then-commonplace British criticism of the Americans' commercial ways. But if Kipling found Americans to be a strange lot, then they found him equally out of sorts. His 1889 passage from India to the states and onward to the east and finally to England inverted the assumed westward movement. The Americans' West was Kipling's East. The American's New World settlement moved relentlessly westward, their orientation fixed to eastern beginnings. "They could not imagine an Englishman coming through the States from West to East instead of by the regularly ordained route," he wrote.[2] Increasing numbers of American tourists took "the regularly ordained route," reenacting, as it were, the frontier thrust westward, now in Pullman railcar luxury, hoping to glimpse what Lewis and Clark had seen. "Eastward I go only by force; but westward I go free," Thoreau had written in 1863. The western journey implied freedom and autonomy for travelers.

Kipling dismissed such enthusiasms, viewing tourists, especially American ones, as "a crowd of creator-condemned fools." He rejected an American's pronouncement that "this running to and fro upon the earth . . . would draw America more closely together." Instead Kipling returned to serious strategic matters. Standing in Vancouver looking east and west, he put himself at the center of Britain's empire and mused over the geo-political implications of the Canadian transcontinental rail link, just completed in 1885. The Canadian Pacific Railroad would, he thought, "throw actual fighting troops into the East some day when our hold of the Suez Canal is temporarily loosened." Imagining the sweep of the North Pacific suddenly breached by the Russian fleet, Kipling analyzed, "All that Vancouver wants is a fat earthwork fort upon a hill . . . a selection of big guns, a couple of regiments of infantry, and later on a big arsenal. . . . It is not seemly to leave unprotected the head-end of the big railway; for though Victoria and Esquimalt, our naval stations on Vancouver, are very near, so also is a place called Vladivostock, and though Vancouver Narrows are strait, they allow room enough for a man-of-war."[3]

Kipling's celebration of machines, deep-sea cables, railways, steamships, and industrial engineering feats centered on his jingoist fixation with imperial strategy. He was "the literary aspect of the British Empire," as the writer Robert Graves would later described him. His travel writing merged with other forms of "research," fusing the urgency of military strategies—obsessed with military detail, carefully reviewing American and Canadian railway development, U.S. Army readiness and training—with the text of the bourgeois tour narrative. Though Kipling perceived himself as a self-appointed imperial agent, he was also a tourist. His North American reconnaissance afforded him an escape from the "fenced in, railway ticket, kind of life at home."[4] Like Edward Glave also traveling in the Pacific Northwest in 1889, Kipling sought some reprieve from the stresses of industrial society. But he hardly escaped the confinement of railway and steamer schedules, following the rails north to Vancouver, then across the Northern Pacific rail line to Yellowstone and the eastern United States. Kipling considered following the steamer route to Alaska. He might have chosen to head north to Alaska following in the wake of his compatriot Edward Glave who had steamed north a month earlier. Dismissing such a mere scenic venture, he headed instead to Yellowstone.

"To-day I am in the Yellowstone Park, and I wish I were dead," Kipling groused, not suicidal, just fed up with the American characters that he found so base.[5] Amidst a "howling crowd" of tourists, he asked a stage driver what all the commotion was about. "You've struck one of Rayment's [*sic*] excursion parties. . . . Aren't you one of 'em?" Kipling quickly replied, "I belong to T. Cook and Son." The company to which the driver referred was the Boston-based Raymond & Whitcomb Company. Founded in Boston in 1879, the company organized its first transcontinental excursion to California in 1881.[6] By the late 1880s, it had established a sophisticated full-service organization that depended upon a series of upscale Western hotels and agreements with rail lines and steam navigation companies, directing excursions to California and Alaska. The largest of the American tour companies, Raymond & Whitcomb sought to relieve their clients "from the ordinary cares, responsibilities, and petty annoyances of traveling." It offered a home away from home, what Henry James would dub America's "hotel-civilization."

Kipling traveled instead with the British-owned Thomas Cook and Sons. Cook had launched the modern tourist industry, organizing excursion trains with a British railway company to visit the Crystal Palace exhibition in 1851.[7] It expanded rapidly as a growing leisure class in England found time and money for extended forays to the Continent, Egypt, and the United States. Cook packaged tours to America in the 1860s and during the 1870s coordinated the guided excursions with U.S. railroad corporations, negotiating reduced rates and other perks, such as through service and more elaborate train accommodations. By the 1880s Cook and Sons operated some thirty branch offices from New York City's Broadway to San Francisco's Palace Hotel.

Raymond & Whitcomb and Thomas Cook and Sons were the two largest transcontinental companies among many smaller local outfits, catering to the sudden explosion of tourist travel during the 1880s and 1890s. Despite Kipling's own patronage of Cook and Sons, he had little good to say about the tourist throng. "The tourists—may their master die an evil death at the hand of a mad locomotive!"[8] Henry Morton Stanley echoed Kipling's intense dissatisfaction with the west coast tourist experience. Stanley touring the west described the hotels as "whitewashed Mugby Junctions . . . the proprietors of these establishments vie with each other for exorbitant charges and poor fare."[9] Kipling leveled his critiques at the tourists themselves. "It is not the ghastly vulgarity, the oozing, rampant Bessemer steel self-sufficiency and ignorance of the men that revolts me, so much as the display of these same qualities in the womenfolk," Kipling complained.[10] But worse, in his eyes, these tourists were "irreverent Americans" because of the abuse they inflicted on the nature that they had come to see in the first place. U.S. army units patrolled trails in Yellowstone Park in order, in part, to keep the tourists from ripping the place up. "Guarded by soldiers who patrol it with loaded six-shooters in order that the tourist may not bring up fence rails and sink them in a pool, or chip the fretted tracery of the formations with a geological hammer, or walking where the crust is too thin, foolishly cook himself," he observed.[11] Apparently tourists could be as much a threat to the scenery as the detested poachers and Indians whom the army pursued vigorously at the park's fringes. The American nation, he bemoaned, "very seldom attempts to put back anything that it has taken from Nature's shelves. It grabs all it can and moves on."

Tourism in Kipling's mind constituted little more than another extractive industry, selling a Barnumesque fascination with volcanic nature in Yellowstone. Natural scenery had become a commodity. As other forms of industrialized leisure emerged, elite tourists sought to distance themselves from low-brow tourists. They set themselves apart by embarking on extended and costly journeys in time and space. They confirmed their high-brow status in conspicuous leisure enabled by their wealth.

Increasing numbers of Mark Twain's "New Barbarians," garrulous American tourists abroad on the continent, turned their backs on Europe and instead headed west to California and north to Alaska. However, Americans did not abandon Europe entirely. These trans-Atlantic trips became ever more affordable and the burgeoning middle class partook of the Grand Tour. Henry James lamented the Grand Tour's increasing popularity during a trip to the Alps in 1873, "It's not so long ago that lords and nabobs monopolized these pleasures; but nowadays a month's tour in Switzerland is no more a *jeu de prince* than a Sunday excursion. To watch this huge Anglo-Saxon wave ebbing through Berne suggests, no doubt most fallaciously, that the common lot of mankind isn't after all so very hard and that the masses have reached a high standard of comfort."[12] And in the United States spur railroads and increased leisure offered the middling classes new opportunities to tour the traditional leisuring grounds of the wealthy. "These fugitives from heat and toil" swelled the cultured touring venues that became more accessible and affordable to more and more people. Bemoaning the arrival of even the working class in the former preserves of upper-class leisure, one writer noted, "During a portion of the hot season all available space had been packed with factory hands."[13]

Elites in their turn sought to separate themselves from these inroads made by middlebrow boors.[14] Travel writer Henry Finck advertised the Alaska tour as a more exotic locale, where "one is certain to find pleasant companionship . . . the passengers on the Atlantic steamers represent all classes of society, and even of the tourists not all are pleasure seekers in an aesthetic sense. But of the Alaskan passengers the majority are apt to be persons of refinement and taste, since the only magnet that can draw them there is the hope of enjoying fine scenery."[15] Cost effectively segregated out the undesirables, as wealthy travelers sought the status of this remote locale. With excursion fares running more than a hundred dollars for two weeks to a month of travel, most Americans could ill afford the cost, or the time away. The steamship itself was an instrument of trade, a floating hotel where the home and the market merged. Tourist numbers in Alaska rose from 1,650 visitors in 1884, to 2,753 in 1886, and by season's end in 1890, 5,007 sightseers had headed north on the Inside Passage route, a thousand miles of waterway running up the west coast from Puget Sound to Glacier Bay.

Like Kipling and Glave, the Methodist minister Stephen Merritt decided to tour the West and Alaska in summer 1892 but for health reasons. "This is the month that has turned aside the coming earthquake that

Figure 4. Pacific Coast Steamship Company promotional pamphlet (San Francisco: Goodall Perkins and Co., February to May 1896). (Courtesy Alaska State Library, Historical Collections)

most likely would have shattered my physical frame and wrecked my health and strength," he revealed in his diary of the trip.[17] "For I believe had I not taken this month and the next for relaxation, the bow that had not lost its tension for years and years would have snapped from over and long continued exertion and my prospects for life been blasted," Merritt wrote. At fifty-nine Merritt, who had occupied several Methodist Episcopal pulpits in New York City, was best known as a funeral director. He oversaw the arrangements for General Grant's funeral and a number of other notable figures. Merritt put himself through seminary school, working as a janitor to cover tuition. "The World-wide Known Undertaker," "Largest in the World," as his advertisements ran, had reached a level of financial security, but not without considerable effort. By the 1890s the Merritt household, like so many others, suffered an epidemic of nervous exhaustion. In addition to the minister's near collapse, his daughter had recovered recently from "her household sickness." The differential diagnosis of nervous disease most often directed a home cure for women, where as men were directed to travel. Ironically, Merritt and his wife were freed to travel west and north to prevent his "earthquake," following their daughter's isolated recovery in their home.

Kipling and the Merritts shared this condition of nervous strain with countless others.[18] Physicians in the industrialized countries had begun to recognize a spate of widely observed symptoms of nervous disease. "These conditions . . . constitute a family of nervous diseases that have developed chiefly during the last half century," observed New York physician George Beard in 1879.[19] This new family of nervous disorders was prevalent particularly in the northeastern United States, England, and continental Europe, according to Beard who researched and defined what he called "neurasthenia," then assailing "our brain-working classes." The one great cause, he reasoned, was "civilization." Beard advanced his theory of the causes of nervous disorders by "studying the habits and diseases of savages and barbarians of all climes and ages, and of the lower orders about us."[20] Pathological nervousness did not appear to affect these others, but rather the disease limited its attacks to the bourgeoisie, those "brain workers" trapped in the office or home. "The chief and primary cause of this development and very rapid increase of nervousness is *modern civilization* which is distinguished from the ancient by these five characteristics: steam-power, the periodical press, the telegraph, the sciences, and the mental activity of women."[21] Railroads with their attendant industrial growth were no longer what Emerson rhapsodized as "the whistle of the locomotive in the woods . . . that music . . . the voice of the civility of the Nineteenth Century."[22] Instead, as Beard described, "the West, formerly a wilderness, but, presently there is a cloud of steam in your eyes, and when it is blown away there is no more log cabin or buffalo on the scene." Now there was "a city of factories and churches and palaces that hides the earth from view . . . the Arcadian farmer who has been lulled to sleep by the hum of his wife's spinning-wheel is awakened by the shriek of the locomotive."[23]

Beard suggested a number of curative steps, important among them physical activity, while neurologists recommended long summer vacations, "outdoor life," and "particularly outdoor air." The well-known neurologist S. Weir Mitchell went further. "The man who lives an out-door life—who sleeps with the stars visible above him—who wins his bodily sustenance at first hand from the earth and waters—is a being who defies rain and snow, has a strange sense of elastic strength. . . . Some such return to the earth for the means of life is what gives vigor and developing power to the colonist of an older race cast on a land like ours."[24] Here Mitchell confirmed several dominant patterns that arose from the perceived crisis of overwork and nervousness. Just as men might mine the ground for riches, so too did these "natural" men, "a few generations of men living" off the land "in such fashion store up a capital of vitality." Drawing loosely from Darwinian evolutionary think-ing, Mitchell and others perceived that instinctual drives had been diminished by the clutter and noise of the new industrial era. The vitality stored up by "an older race," Mitchell believed, was passed on as a tangi-ble inheritance. It accounted for the "prodigal activity displayed by their descendants, and made possible only by the sturdy contest with nature which their ancestors have waged," according to Mitchell. Urging the medical equivalent of the frontier thesis, he insisted that the continua-tion of this contest "serves to keep up our pristine force and energy." But opportunities to renew this vital capital earned in the frontier con-test with raw nature were waning as civilized men and women increas-ingly turned their lives indoors and inside the dense urban haunts of the industrial cities. Once sturdy Anglo colonists, endowed with racial vigor through their historical contest with nature, bred vital spawn, or so it was believed. But that earlier generation's investment had been over-drawn and nervous disorders multiplied among the upper classes. Ideas about race and class commingled with emerging medical ideas. Space itself, Beard believed, was responsible for nervousness: "little account has been made of the fact that the old world is small geographically [and therefore not prone to nervous disorder]. The discovery of America, like the invention of printing, prepared the way for modern nervousness," increasing "a hundred-fold the distresses of humanity."[25] "The newspa-per is his sole literature," Mitchell lamented.[26] The "sorrows" of any one remote part of the world were, according to Beard, "made the sorrows of individuals everywhere."[27] Tourist promoters proved selective readers of the physician's researches. Wide-open space was both cause and, according to the Alaska tourist promotions, cure to this malaise.

Marc Cook in his 1881 book, *The Wilderness Cure*, described his own experience with the curative powers of the outdoors. Suffering from a "deathly cough," his physicians administered a series of supposed reme-dies—"three or four bottles of cod-liver oil, a gallon or two of rye whis-key with rock candy, and an amazing amount of good advice"—that had been applied within the space of just three months, but all to no avail.

In New Hampshire with a view of Mount Washington, Cook applied the wilderness cure. "In the dry bracing atmosphere of that region, where the sandy soil sucks up the moisture, and no foul odors pollute the air, he gained steadily," Cook wrote of his own recuperation.[28] On return to the city, "hemorrhages of the lungs returned," and Cook returned to the wilderness, "where he is cured by the environment, and though he was at death's door, he enjoyed a complete recovery."[29] "I am persuaded," Cook urged, "however, that there are in this country to-day ten thousand persons who, fighting the weary fight for health, would find cause enough for thanksgiving if they could penetrate this vast wilderness and breathe in the life-giving air day and night the year round."[30] But Cook warned against impatience. "When Nature is called in as a physician, she is often dishearteningly slow in her process and cure. . . . She exacts unquestioning belief in her powers, and a patience which endures with the duration of life." As enhanced machines and new inventions became the measure of progress, so too had nervousness become a measure of civilization. To have suffered from neurasthenia was to have signaled one's social status. Merely to have afforded the cure, both in leisure time and money, attested to one's financial power.

What are we to make of this digression into late nineteenth-century nervous pathologies? What has this to do with Alaska? Rudyard Kipling and Stephen Merritt, along with perhaps thousands of others of their class, suffered from a disease linked by contemporaries to rapid societal changes. Their extended touring figured as part cure for their physical and mental conditions, suicidal by Kipling's own description. Kipling's touring and writing, and the diagnostic texts of late nineteenth-century physicians, offer a window into a more complicated understanding of late nineteenth-century tourism. Though it might seem risky to propose a coherent and comprehensive interpretation of tourist motivation from these medical texts and reflective travelogues, individual psychology was (and is) a social product. And inasmuch as Kipling or Merritt the individual reflected his society, we may gauge what motivated others to embark on lengthy and expensive excursions. Before turning to Alaska, we need to consider the range of conventions and ideas that emerged concerning late nineteenth-century tourism. These practices and ideas proposed new forms for understanding wilderness, the out-of-doors, the gendered nature of these spaces, and the rationalization of leisure time. After we recognize the cultural roots of these conventions, we may then appreciate the more complicated experience of travel in the late nineteenth century.

Fears of howling wilderness had within a half-century or so been substituted with a new terror of the urban spaces wrought by industrialization.

This urban fear was not simply a response to environmental stimuli—the noise, the speed, the mental activity—but fear of mass urban unrest, fueled by the massive railway strikes of 1877, the Haymarket Square tragedy in 1886, the Homestead violence in 1892, and thousands of other strikes and lockouts. The Darwinian wilderness of the summer streets in the great swelling ghetto centers of the late nineteenth-century city fueled the seasonal flight of the well-to-do. "Freedom—delicious, absolute freedom—from dust and noise, and the roar of the city streets," Marc Cook cheered on his escape from the city.[31] Cook blamed his maladies and state of mind on "the poisoned air of crowded cities and unventilated rooms." "Slowly, very slowly, as the walls of the dungeon closed in, inch by inch, on the wretched prisoner, until the great apartment has become a tomb," he wrote.[32] "It is neither hot nor cold air, damp nor dry air, but *pure* air which is necessary to diseased lungs," precluding the presence of "Telluric or miasmatic poison," supposedly prevalent in the pestilential cities. Cook and his contemporaries believed that trees, in particular evergreens, filled the air with their "resinous odors which they exhale." "While balsamics, which are also disinfectants," Cook reasoned, "purify the atmosphere." The atmosphere of forested regions became "heavily laden with ozone in a natural sequence . . . nature's choice for counteracting atmospheric impurities," he concluded.[33] Northern evergreen forests offered the perfect palliative to civilization's perceived ills.

The upper classes identified the impurities of the city especially with the new immigrant populations. This flood of new aliens threatened the body politic as well as contributing to the ills of individuals, or so it was believed. "Let but Law lift its hand from them for a season, or let the civilizing influences of American life fail to reach them," Charles Loring Brace had warned, "and if the opportunity offered, we should see an explosion from this class which might leave this city in ashes and blood."[34] This fear of class warfare had only grown since Brace had warned his nervous bourgeois readers in 1872 and spurred a new cohort of travelers to flee to imagined restorative wilderness. Indeed, as Marc Cook stressed, "A return to the invigorating, out-of-door existence of the savage is Nature's antidote for a disease, which is almost an outgrowth of civilization and its enervating influences."[35] No surprise then that the leisure class headed north into its supposedly empty spaces, free of the social encumbrances of the immigrant masses.

The Alaskan traveler Stephen Merritt worked incessantly. "For fifteen years I had lost but seven Sundays out of my own pulpit, and for the last year had hardly been out of the city for twenty-four continuous hours," he wrote in his diary. Merritt described how his various duties had reached a natural break, allowing him to pause in his missionary and temperance work, "and so for the first time in my life the way was opened, and so we came, and therefore write."[36] For Merritt writing was inseparable from the activity of traveling. His diary writing served as a productive outlet for an activity—touring—that stood so incongruously outside his regular regime.

Minister Merritt and his family hoped to partake of the Alaskan excursion's "hygienic value"—"a delicious mixture of ocean and mountain air."[37] Merritt also imagined the west and north as his heritage, claiming, "For many years it has been my desire and design to see 'the land I fondly call my own.'"[38] What could he have meant by such a claim to ownership? Did he recognize his own inheritance of what a generation earlier William Gilpin had called the "Heredity line of progress" that swept westward to the Pacific? Another Alaskan tourist noted that this stretch of territory was "the pride of every native of the United States."[39]

In order to see this native patrimony the Merritts joined a package tour organized by Raymond & Whitcomb Company. The Merritts, like their touring peers, believed that civilization had advanced so far as to leave only a few corners of the globe open to true wilderness trips. The tourist, according to one travel writer, "who would seek the 'wilds of America' will only find them in Alaska."[40] Ironically, these tourists revolted against the commercial face of industrial society, but they were in fact steeped in its commercialism—buying rail and steamship tickets, hotel accommodations, restaurant meals, special clothing, and guide books.[41] As well a troubling paradox of cause and cure arose from the very instruments of their travel, the railroad and steamship. Nervous sufferers sought their cure in the very technologies that had according to their medical science caused their afflictions in the first place. "The perfection of clocks and the invention of watches have something to do with modern nervousness, since they compel us to be on time, and excite the habit of looking to see the exact moment, so as not to be late for trains or appointments," Beard diagnosed.[42] And yet the tourists eagerly jotted down departure times in their diaries, disparaging the ship or rail company for any delay. Their fastidious diaries, too, were affectations of their schedule-obsessed, day-counting lives. Additionally, the physician found that the "molecular disturbance caused by traveling long distances . . . would have an unfavorable influence on the nervous system."[43]

The very wealthy, such as William Seward Webb, author of *California and Alaska over the Canadian Pacific Railway*, Vanderbilt in-law, and owner of the custom railway car manufacturing company, the Wagner Palace Car Company, could overcome some of the clinical hazards of high-speed travel. As he plotted the three-and-half-month excursion by private train and reserved steamship to California and Alaska, Webb stressed that their trip was "to be entirely independent of time-tables . . . under such a scheme the party would be relieved of any anxiety they might otherwise have had in regard to making connections."[44] And Alaskan traveler Carter Harrison insisted that "Motion is nature's first inexorable law," giving sanction to his extended travels with his lay interpretation of the entropic theories then under scientific scrutiny. Apparently, Harrison felt that the average tourist should not resist the natural tendency toward wandering about as confirmed by science. "The summer outing is urged by honest doctors, with the admission that change of air and scene is often times worth more than all the nostrums doled out over apothecaries counters," Harrison reasoned.[45] He added that aside from health, extended summer outings served as "brain food." These were not idle passages. Their touring was an educational affair. Travelers might also transform themselves in the strenuous environs of the north. In 1886 the explorer Frederick Schwatka recommended that tourists indulge in an "Alpine journey to the head of the Yukon river . . . the trip could be made between visiting steamers and I will guarantee the persons will come back with more muscle than they took in."[46] The Chilkoot Pass, soon to be celebrated as a will-breaking obstacle on the route to interior gold fields, was here touted as a rugged, but leisurely foray, a curative adventure.

Some of the era's social critics took a dim view of such conspicuous consumption. Tourism, according to Thorstein Veblen, served primarily to demonstrate "one's own or one's society's ability to dispose of time and energy for no immediate practical purpose." And if this leisure was spent out of sight as it were, well removed from the metropolitan public spectacle in the case of the Alaskan tour, then the gentlemen and women of leisure needed to "find some means of putting in evidence," their unseen idleness, Veblen observed. Through their prolific published travel narratives, these late-nineteenth century tourists both demonstrated their economic positions to a wider audience, as well as proffering evidence of productive activity in their labor of words. Not all contemporary observers cast such a disparaging light on the emergence of this new leisured traveling class. The physician George Beard argued in support of the leisured classes, proclaiming leisure as virtuous. "The moral influence of such a class scattered through our society must be, on the whole . . . salutary and beneficent," Beard argued, "by keeping constantly before the public high ideals of culture for which wealth affords the means; by elevating the now dishonored qualities of serenity and placidity to the rank of virtues, where they justly belong."[47] During several decades of often-violent strife between labor and capital with the casual displacement of workers as a matter of industrial management, distinctions concerning non-productive pursuits became increasingly important. Tourism was made "virtuous," while vagabondage was made "vicious."

How was one to reconcile traveling idleness with demands for masculine vigor, Protestant activity, and productive labor usually associated with Victorian Americans? To be sure the days of travel were crowded with details, packing and unpacking, menus to be read, choices to be made, sights to be seen. All their shuffling about gave them the appearance of industrious activity. But the packaged, guided tours disguised their constant consumption. Pre-paid travel, meal tickets, and group rates freed the excursionists from the constant exchange of cash. They had already paid of course, but at least the constant reminder of their continuous consuming slipped into a past moment of exchange. Tourism appeared steeped in dilettantism, sentimentalism, a seemingly feminized activity of passive observance and self-indulgence. And yet journal writing seemed to have given some sanction to this otherwise unproductive waste of time. For as Webb rationalized, "It was something more than a trip of pleasure, as, indeed, it could not but be to any business man."[48]

Tourists were inveterate scribblers. Kipling had noted as much when he wrote derisively, "The congregation returned to the hotel to put down their impressions in diaries and notebooks which they wrote up ostentatiously in the verandas."[49] The diligent recording of their experiences offered stay-at-homes access to a vicarious moment in reading. "A beautiful or grand scene is doubly enjoyed when one feels he may through a letter have hundreds see what he sees and as he sees. They become his companions and hold sweet communion with him, though thousands of miles lie between them."[50] The influence of travel spread widely through this shared, vicarious experience, as the travel book and their dutiful recording served as practices of conspicuous consumption that maintained their class status.

Recalling his opportunity to tour the Inside Passage of Alaska, Rudyard Kipling had a more jaded perspective on Charles Harrison's "brain food" offered along the way. Merely crossing Puget Sound from Victoria to Tacoma he had discovered that the route was "surfeited with scenery." He would have agreed with the early Alaskan traveler R. W. Meade, who concluded that the scenery was "so continuously magnificent, it becomes monotonous."[51] "When you have seen a fine forest, a bluff, a river, and a lake you have seen all the scenery of western America," Kipling decided. "Sometimes the pine is three hundred feet high, and sometimes the rock is, and sometimes the lake is a hundred miles long. But it's all the same . . . I'm getting sick of it." En masse,

Kipling found the scenery overwhelming, redundant. "Men said if I went to Alaska I should see islands even more wooded, snow-peaks loftier, and rivers more lovely than those around me. That decided me not to go to Alaska."[52]

Unlike his English counterpart, the naturalist John Muir perceived "in this web of scenery embroidering the northern coast . . . such indefinite expansiveness, so great a multitude of features without any redundance . . . so varied and at the same time so similar, their lines graduating delicately into one another in endless succession."[53] Such endless sameness that drove Kipling to distraction raised Muir to rhapsodic epiphanies. Traveling on a mail steamer in 1879, he wrote, "The forests and glaciers are the glory of Alaska, and it is not easy to keep my pen away from them."[54] Indeed, Muir's writing enthusiastically promoted Alaska's natural scenery and helped to launch tourist ventures northward. "Day after day we seemed to sail in true fairyland, every view of islands and mountains seeming ever more and more beautiful . . . I never before had scenery before me so hopelessly, over-abundantly beautiful for description . . . this enchanted land of lake and fiord, forest and waterfall, mountain and island, begins to appear in full force just below Departure Bay, and ends far north if it ends at all. It seems as if surely, following this shining way, we should finally reach heaven," Muir beamed.[55] Given the time and resources, who could resist the temptation to venture north given Muir's published ecstasies? For Muir, it was not simply travel, but wilderness itself that served as the medicine for the ills of industrial civilization. The northern argosy along the Inside Passage inoculated sojourners with the protective medium of Muir's wilderness ideology. "While we sail on and on through the infinite beauty enchanted, hard, money-gaining, material thoughts loosen and sink off and out of sight, and one is free from oneself and made captive to fresh wildness and beauty, obeying it as necessarily as unconscious sun-bathed plants," he described.[56] Muir encouraged wilderness wandering as a tonic to ward off "what the great Dr. [William] James had called the habit of inferiority to the full self."[57]

These Alaskan ventures were not, however, voyages of self-discovery. They were quite the opposite. The *experience* of Alaskan travel may have been perceived as one of enhanced freedom and autonomy, where the participants imagined themselves loose of the fetters of their over-civilized existence. But the need to escape, to return to a more "natural state," could only have been imagined from within the cultural conventions of urban, industrial life. And the ability to partake in such flights from civilization was borne by the utmost efforts of their society's most sophisticated and technologically advanced systems of transportation and communication. Northern tourists were caught in their own self-fashioning embrace of experiences they imagined would free them of certain qualities. The wilderness scenery they believed to be the nostrum for their nervous lives was instead the product of their worrying. Viewing the Alaskan wilderness as an edenic alternative to the city disguised the role of capitalism in fixing the meanings given to the oppositional poles of industrial life. Their travels and their writings were more about fixing identities and social status than about any corrective to the ills they suffered living in modern society. These were voyages of self-creation.

During a lengthy period managing his valuable fruit ranch in Martinez, California, Muir lamented, "I am losing the precious days, I am degenerating into a machine for making money. I am learning nothing in this trivial world of men. I must break away and get out into the mountains to learn the news."[58] Repeating the concern that men had become machines, Muir worried about his own susceptibility to nervous prostration. "My weariness of this hum-drum, work-a-day life has grown so heavy it is like to crush me. I'm ready to break away," he wrote in 1888 before escaping to Alaska for the summer.[59] But it was the very contrast with industrial civilization that had shaped Muir's wilderness yearnings in the first place, and his personal financial fortune that allowed him to continue to view the world in the way that he did.

The romantic retreat into wildness had enjoyed a privileged place in American thought. Muir, who toted well-read copies of Ralph Waldo Emerson's and Henry David Thoreau's works with him on his Alaskan sojourns, echoed Emerson's insistence that "cities give the human senses not room enough." Though his formulations were not new, Muir seemed to stand at the divide between the gradual rejection of sentimental and aesthetic modes of nature appreciation and an increasingly naturalistic and masculine emphasis on strenuous activity and open contest with nature. While Muir never adopted the rhetoric of nature's conquest that came to dominate some quarters of the national imagination, he did mold for himself an identity that balanced aesthetic appreciation with active and masculine engagement with the natural world. Early on he saw himself as a romantic adventurer in the image of Alexander von Humboldt.[60] "I wish to be a Humboldt!" Muir pronounced in 1866. With this claim, Muir resolved one of the fundamental tensions of his wandering life: how, like the tourist, was he to explain a passive, idle, and nonproductive existence alongside society's expectations of productive work? William James described the era's tension over gendered behavior, writing that "Sick souls [are] more often feminine than masculine, and young than old, whose soul is of this sky-blue tint, whose affinities are rather with flowers and birds and all enchanting innocencies than with dark human passions."[61] Muir's Sierra colleague, the geologist Clarence King, had resolved these contradictions by identifying himself as

both an aesthete, capable of sublime contemplation of nature's wonders, and a rugged mountaineer carrying out the productive work of the
survey. He had found refuge from "nervous disease" in his mountaineering ventures. But Muir's inclinations drew even closer to the ques-
tionable affinities "with flowers and birds" to which James referred. And
yet he earned respect and authority for having found in his writing the
means to blend the tropes of the bourgeois travel narrative with more
rigorous and presumably productive forms of research: geological science, his obsession with glaciers, and natural history more generally.
He shared with his British counterpart Rudyard Kipling an ability to create a productive turn from his travels, legitimating, in the words of writer
William Stowe, "what might otherwise have seemed the sinful self-
indulgence of travel."[62] Though Muir expressed a nascent ecological
worldview borne of his careful observation of the natural world, especially along the Alaskan coastline, his ecological vision necessitated a
proper steward and therefore assumed similar imperial ambitions to
that of Kipling, albeit without the bravado. Muir's accounts of his solo
exploits in the forests and mountains of Alaska and the Sierra displayed
a studied nonchalance. His writings demonstrated an understated risk-
taking that betrayed its opposite.

In Muir's Alaskan travels we may also recognize the merging of secular
travel and religious observance, what his contemporary, economist
Thorstein Veblen, would soon criticize as "honorific expenditure."[63] In
addition to offering what Minister Merritt termed "hygienic value," specific natural spaces became for Muir places of pilgrimage that accorded
a site of spiritual revitalization.[64] At the same time, Muir's Alaskan writings, first published in newspapers and magazines, also boosted the
emerging tourist industry that connected east coast cities by rail to west
coast ports, and to steamer routes along Alaska's Inside Passage. "Since
I made my first excursions and called attention to the wild scenery of
Alaska through the newspapers," wrote Muir, "a bright and lively stream
of tourist travel has been developed through the midst of the more
accessible portion of it, and fortunately the most accessible is also the
most interesting portion of Alaska as to the grandeur and novelty of the
scenery."[65] Muir clearly laid claim as dean of Alaskan promoters. But his
writings also served as proof, as Veblen insisted, of his quest for his own
cultural capital and the ability to spend time in nonproductive activity.
Tourism represented a calculated expression of "pecuniary culture,"
putting one's wealth and status on display, in Veblen's contemporary critique of leisure. "The rituals of 'decent' expenditure and divine service," in William Stowe's analysis, "are parallel ways of using the surplus
time and money generated by a booming bourgeois economy to create a
stable, 'respectable' society."[66] Muir, who had married into a prominent

California family and was a wealthy agribusiness man in his own right, sought an alternative identity in his Alaskan ventures. These northern escapes freed him as it were from his "hum-drum, work-a-day life." His visible, public, and conspicuous connection to the natural world also signified a spiritual grace, or so he assumed. Higher learning and an educated appreciation of the natural world during these wilderness forays indicated not idle mental excursions, but rather, in Muir's own words, the "very foundational truth we had been to church and seen God."[67] It separated him continuously from his touring counterparts, whom he frequently disparaged. "The best things and thoughts we get from Nature we dare not tell," Muir revealed to a friend. "To lay out all his [God's] delicate treasures for the coldly critical eye of an unimaginative world seemed a kind of betrayal," Muir wrote with little recognition of his own advertising. "Why should I take to trouble to coin my gold?" he continued, borrowing from the metaphor of monetary standard to describe his wilderness observations. "Some will say it is Fool's Gold. It cannot be weighed on commercial scales. There is no market," he wrote.

Yet Muir found quickly the alchemic power of his pen. "We are going to write some history, my boy," Muir proclaimed to his Alaskan travel partner and Wrangell minister, S. Hall Young. "Think of the honor! We have been chosen to put some interesting people and some of Nature's grandest scenes on the page of human record and on the map. Hurry! We are daily losing the most important news of all the world."[68] Muir went on to build his career through writing, an activity he had also contemplated as a betrayal. In doing so, he simultaneously evoked and exploited the appreciation of landscape as a legitimate object of passive contemplation. He simultaneously reveled in publishing his aesthetic renderings of the landscape and found it impossible to capture Alaska's natural splendor with his words.

John Muir's activities did not exactly parallel those of the world-wandering Kipling. But Muir, like Kipling, recognized the power of information. New knowledge about the remote reaches of empire helped unite the globe's peripheries, as Thomas Richards writes, "not by force but by information."[69] Their interests reflect their individual predilections, and it hardly seems proper to consider them under the same discerning lens. And yet Muir, like Kipling, served as an agent of empire. Muir, who had inherited Thoreau's call to live deliberately and outside the promptings of modern industrial civilization, became paradoxically a principal proponent of northern expansion. Instead of seeing the tourists who followed in Muir's wake as somehow escaping civilization into the liminal spaces at the margins of empire, we should recognize that tourists were an incorporating arm of that empire, both

consuming and producing the new reach of national power into the new
northern territory.[70] Travel writers such as Muir and Kipling, and the
era's guidebooks, such as *Baedeker's*, re-made the Alaskan scenery into
an object of consumerist fascination. Such popular literature created an
imaginative space into which prospective travelers might delve during
the winter months in anticipation of summer's excursions.

As Karl Baedeker's guide enthused, "The *Scenery* passed *en route* is of
a most grand and unique character, such as, probably, cannot be seen
elsewhere at so little cost and with so little toil or adventure."[71] During
the mid-nineteenth century, Baedeker's became the standard authority
on travel. First published as a guidebook series for German tourists, Baedeker soon contracted books in French and English and spread his publishing empire to cover much of the globe, including Alaska in the
1890s. The published travel guides, travelogues, and magazine articles
expanded the tourists' world. *Appleton's Guide-Book to Alaska* and *Baedeker's Guide* filled the growing desire for facts about the north. This latter
work provided a spate of details for eager travelers, intent on taking in
the new and fashionable excursion. "My sole object is to put on paper,
for the benefit of others," Septima Collis wrote in her travel book, "the
impressions made upon me by the voyage, and to explain how this
delightful excursion can be enjoyed without the slightest fatigue or discomfort, and at a trifling expense."[72] What amounted to a trifling
expense was, of course, relative. But as one excursionist admitted, these
books performed a key role in preparing travelers for their future visits.

"Spent a greater part of the day in reading Miss Skidmore's book on
Alaska," Mrs. Wood wrote in her diary, "improving on the time to read
now as I imagine later, I shall want to use my eyes for another purpose
[*sic*]."[73] In 1885 traveler Eliza Scidmore wrote the first complete Alaskan
guide book intended for the then-growing tourist interest in the territory, and a whole series of travelogues and additional guides followed.
These guides provided information on the more mundane aspects of
the travel regimen, hotels and restaurants, what to wear, the average
temperature, and the average price for certain curios. Travelers like
Eliza Clendenin went north to Alaska well informed about the possibilities for seeing glaciers and tree-clad islands, for shopping for curios—
"best obtained at Sitka"; for buying furs—"at Juneau"; for visiting the
largest gold mine in the world, also at Juneau; and for viewing "the best
collection of Totem Poles he is likely to see" at Wrangell.[74]

Eliza Clendenin's 1891 Alaskan Inside Passage tour would have been
inconceivable to traveler's more than two decades earlier, soon after the
American purchase of Alaska from the Russians in 1867. *Appleton's Hand-
Book of American Travel,* published in 1872, did not spend much time on
Alaska. "Though it is not likely to prove very inviting to travelers, a brief

Figure 5. Cover of Alexander Badlam's popular travel account, *The Wonders of Alaska, Illustrated* (San Francisco: Bancroft Company, 1890). (Courtesy Yale Collection of Western Americana, Beinecke Rare Book and Manuscript Library)

sketch seems necessary," the guidebook writer had noted. At the outset, the guidebook writer helped to establish the rhetoric of native erasure when he noted of Alaska, "whose wilds the foot even of the savage has never wandered! The eye fairly wearies of the endless monotony and death-like stillness of these primeval forests, and seeks for more peaceful landscapes, but in vain."[75] Movement in space paralleled an imagined movement backward in time, back to the "primeval forests." "Nothing," according to the Appleton's guide, "disturbs the dreary loneliness." In 1872 this description hardly encouraged tourists to spend weeks on the southeastern Alaskan coast.

The profusion of travelogues and contemporary guidebooks formed a crossroads of sorts between the face-to-face exchanges through which elites corresponded and the mass tourist culture that took shape during the last decade of the nineteenth century. In some ways the Klondike Gold Rush might be considered the event that marked the maturation of mass tourism in the north. With their published advice, guidebook writers replaced what historian Dona Brown identifies as "a service that had always been part of the tourists' personal network of acquaintances and obligations."[76] But the testimonials provided by travelogues only exaggerated the bourgeois network of advice, offering a wider network of travel recommendations that might attract the growing leisure classes in the United States, Canada, and Europe.

"For the benefit of such of your readers," wrote Lieutenant Beardslee, moonlighting as a travel writer, "with adventurous turn of mind, fondness for travel, and who may be bothered every summer with the great question, 'Where shall I go?'"[77] Beardslee answered "Alaska," knowing perfectly well to whom he was writing. The high cost of the Inside Passage tour policed the borders of class participation, determining largely who could join what one traveler called the "Happy Family."[78] The traveler's comment referred jokingly to P. T. Barnum's American Museum with its "Happy Family," an odd collection of animals—kittens and rats, monkeys, pigeons, and porcupines—living in domestic bliss. This traveler's note juxtaposed such mass amusements with the well-heeled diversions on the Inside Passage tour. These casual references to Barnum condensed a whole host of complicated social meanings. The "Happy Family" allusion performed a sort of cultural shorthand, associating Barnum's base amusements with an expensive and select leisure. The comparison was rejected, even as it was being made and the satiric parallel helped to firm up leisure-class consciousness. The so-called "Happy Family" was an invitation-only affair. "The gracious companionship of Nature," argued the author of *The Wilderness Cure*, "that is something at once so subtle and exalted, that all mankind are not permitted to enjoy it."[79]

These touring elites were not so much the passive victims of new advertising manipulation as they were participants in these new industries of movement and observation. Their travels and their writing helped to promote the Inside Passage tour. For the well-to-do leisure set an Alaska trip became the thing to do. First promoted by word-of-mouth, the reputation of the tours' scenic excellence spread. "Were the attractions of this north coast but half known thousands of lovers of nature's beauties would come hither every year," wrote one travel writer. "Without leaving the steamer," he continued, "one is moving silently and almost without wave motion through the finest and freshest landscape poetry on the face of the globe."[80] Indeed the Inside Passage catered perfectly to what Henry James dubbed as America's "hotel civilization." Tourists could travel without ever leaving the security of their floating islands. The tourists replaced the material cargoes and in a way became cargoes themselves. Home and market merged. The boats were themselves instruments of trade. The passengers were products, commodities embodied as people, what Henry James called "commercial persons."

The travel report, both the published travelogues and the private journals, may be understood as a form of writing in which the travelers' subjectivities projected outward.[81] Part of this subjective experience

Figure 6. "Cruise party, *S.S. Queen* for Alaska, June 1897," Oliver Family Photograph Collections. (Courtesy The Bancroft Library, University of California, Berkeley)

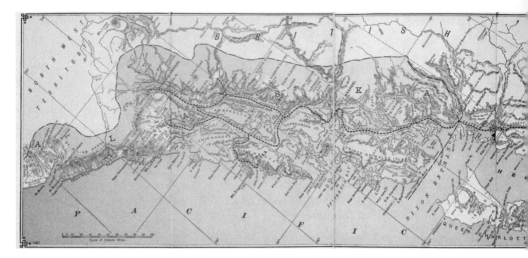

Figure 7. Map accompanying Eliza Ruhamah Scidmore's *Appleton's Guide-book to Alaska and the Northwest Coast* (New York: D. Appleton and Company, 1899) detailing the coastal Inside Passage route. "The Route of the Alaska Excursion Steamers" (Chicago: Poole Bros., c. 1891). (Courtesy Yale Collection of Western Americana, Beinecke Rare Book and Manuscript Library)

exposed the close affinities of landscape and advertising. Glaciers, totem poles, natives, prospectors, Russian forts, mountains, and forests all became tempting items that tourists expected to see. And their experience of seeing was something that they bought. The commodification of scenery as resource could hardly have been more thinly veiled. Traveler Charles Gates dubbed Alaska "the scenic store-ground of the world."[82] A week-long trip along this "great salt-water river" was a "genuine American Switzerland," offering sights of "the highest snow mountain in the world," "islands and forests—Indian Traits—Alaskan villages—glaciers—an iceberg factory."[83] Mixing the metaphors of gold mining, writers minted their own currency with their published words, joining the ranks of an ever-growing group of professional travel writers. "In voyaging past the unbroken wilderness of the island shores the tourist feels quite like an explorer penetrating unknown lands," Eliza Scidmore surmised.[84] And John Muir echoed this experience of discovery, indicating that the traveler was as likely to also make important self-discoveries. "While we sail on and on through the infinite beauty, enchanted, hard, money-gaining, material thoughts loosen and sink off and out of sight, and one is free from oneself and made captive to fresh wildness and beauty," extolled Muir of the virtues of travel.[85] "Perhaps no territory of equal extent on the globe," *Appleton's Guide* pronounced,

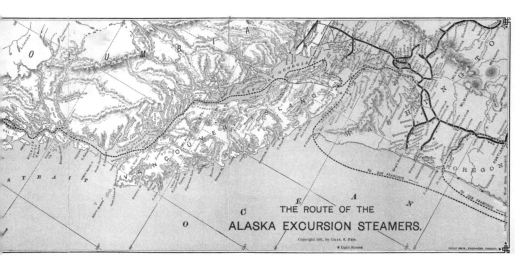

THE ROUTE OF THE
ALASKA EXCURSION STEAMERS.

"except Central Africa, is so little known."[86] Exploration marked the pedagogy of the travel guide. "Each arm of the sea and the unknown, unexplored wilderness that lies back of every mile of shore continually tempt the imagination," wrote Eliza Scidmore.[87] The conjuring of the exploration narrative suggested the relationship between the tourists' power and the metaphorical power of the explorer, and though perhaps set out playfully, they ended up revealing the way the one—exploration—serves as a model for the other—touring.[88]

In the minds of the traveling elite, the far north came to represent forms of consciousness that resisted the social fragmentations characteristic of the late nineteenth-century cities. To be sure, these northern spaces were themselves the sites of their own dramatic social dislocations, as the following chapters will show. But these local fragmentations were understood and contained within the closed rhetoric of the frontier. The urban leisure class sought new travel sites, ones that might distinguish their adventures from those increasingly crowded and now routine middle-class excursions to accessible western American locales. "Fashions differ for different classes," Georg Simmel wrote, "the fashions of the upper stratum of society are never identical with those of the lower; in fact, they are abandoned by the former as soon as the latter prepares to appropriate them."[89] The now well-trodden destinations in the states necessitated this upper-class search for new locales.

The Inside Passage offered such a trip. The newness of the north added to the cultural capital extracted from such travels. Their tourism became an act of differentiation. This new leisure-class identity rested, according to Thorstein Veblen's analysis, upon "conspicuous consumption." Bourgeois identities relied upon consumption, not occupation, in order to define themselves. But more than that, the bourgeois travel writers helped to refine the aestheticization of nature, claiming nature as "an empty, wild place where humans could connect with their souls and their nation."[90] In their writing, bourgeois travelers searched for a language that might bring all things into relation. This effort worked in part to arrive at an understanding of these new (to them) regions, but also to result in control. Nature, as they constructed it in the north, provided the model for the ideal social order.

Alaskan travel writer Henry T. Finck celebrated the Inside Passage as "a scenic bonanza" in his travel guide, *The Pacific Coast Scenic Tour*.[91] By the eve of the Klondike find in 1896, "An Alaskan trip, as we make it, is a summer tour *par excellence*. The very word 'Alaska,' spoken on a midsummer day, with the mercury verging on the nineties, conveys to the tired brain of the business man, immured in heated brick and mortar, to the man of law, the teacher, artist, actor, or invalid, visions of cool retreats fanned by glacial breezes, that revivify life like an iced champagne."[92] In their northward travels bourgeois tourists found solace from the ailments of affluence in Alaska's salubrious airs. "Nothing truly wild is unclean," Muir stressed. Contemporaries saw the wild Alaskan coast as a geography of health.[93] "In God's wilderness lies the hope of the world," Muir rhapsodized. "The galling harness of civilization drops off, and the wounds heal," he prescribed.[94] The curative powers of travel linked the nature of the land, sea, and air to the body's interiors. "The charms of Alaska," one writer insisted, "cannot be described; it must be felt."[95] The nature within commingled with the nature without. And the tourists' romantic vision of their leisured passages hid their voyages' carefully packaged materialization of feeling. Successful and overworked, they fled the summer city heat and their own neuroses and "recuperated in health by a fortnight's tour amongst the island and mountains of the North Pacific."[96]

Chapter Three

Scenic Bonanza

Gazing at the green archipelago from the deck rail of the steamer *Queen*, Minister Stephen Merritt stared into the "inky blackness . . . the water deep, blue and clear." He had found respite from the rigors of his city life in the "matchless scenes of indescribable beauty . . . the islands, the coves, fjords . . . strangeness and beauty; the calmness continues . . . more and more sublime." Merritt could hardly contain his enthusiasm. "We are now sailing through a scene of unparalleled splendor. . . . Oh it is gloriously wonderful," he wrote in his journal, describing the Inside Passage route to Alaska.[1] In June 1892, Merritt and the hundred-odd tourists aboard the steamer churning northward on the coastal passage had grown accustomed to this scenic procession. After three thousand miles or more of transcontinental rail travel, their seeing had been trained, so to speak. Like the passing landscape seen through the railcar window, passengers selected images from the whirr of their speedy transit. The view from the steamship deck offered a panoramic sweep, a continuous horizon not available from the confines of the railcar window. Nor could scenic tourists always gush about the beauties seen during their cross-country train trips. The rail lines sought out whenever possible the straightest route and the easiest. For the scenic traveler this search for topographical efficiency often meant visual tedium as mile after mile of unrelenting plain and semi-arid steppe passed the railcar windows. The Canadian Pacific Railroad line and the Denver and Rio Grande lines had sought to alleviate this scenic boredom, routing their respective railroads through difficult and scenically exciting mountainous terrain.

But the Inside Passage waterway followed the natural lines of the coast, seeking out calmer waters, avoiding the open swell and storm-bent seas of the open ocean. This natural route required the least capital to exploit. It was safe—relatively—and it was scenic. The coastal route north wound between thousands of islands through often-narrow canyon passages, "like a river," delivering a nearly constant "picturesque" visage. The ship passage north wove through spectacular watery chasms and rain-forested island chains. Framed views seen from the train window became the more expansive scene from the deck of the steamers as they plied their way northward and westward along the circuitous waterway. "A panoramic and kaleidoscopic picture is continually presented," Merritt rhapsodized in his diary account. On the hurricane deck, scanning the island-dotted horizon, late nineteenth-century tourists such as Merritt were overwhelmed, often confused: "it was constant change, with a wonderful sameness," he noted. Another artifact of the touring mind-set may be found beneath the stylized rhetorical conventions of the picturesque, their almost mawkish descriptions in these diary and journal entries. Merritt reckoned his daily accounts as an accurate record of his trip, of what he had seen. He would likely have agreed with John Muir, who described the passage north, where "New scenes are brought into view with magical rapidity."[2] Even the scenery had been "arranged" for the excitement of the mountainous landscape grew in scale as the sightseers proceeded northward.[3]

Steam travel, while by no means new in the 1880s and 1890s, nonetheless still had the capacity to produce a certain inspired rhetoric. "The advantage of travelling in this lazy manner," Edward Pierrepont wrote of his northern travels, "passing one's time in luxurious idleness is very great. Each morning our eyes feast on new wonders; for, while we are spending the nights in sleep, one hundred and eighty miles farther north in this strange country makes a change of scene."[4] Space had been annihilated by time, according to contemporary analyses of the effects of mechanized movement. "Capital by its nature drives beyond every spatial barrier. Thus the creation of the physical conditions of exchange—of the means of communication and transport—the eradication of space by time—becomes an extraordinary necessity for it," Karl Marx wrote.[5] Movement in effect deterritorialized the landscape through which these tourists traveled, collapsing space and time. The old localisms that had characterized American society prior to the advent of the railroad were broken. "The old transport technology . . . permitted the traveler to perceive that space as a living entity," Wolfgang Schivelbusch writes.[6] But the new technologies of travel blurred such organic relationships. The steamers were scenery machines making pure objects of the view.[7]

Tourists observing the northwest coastline from the steamer deck enjoyed a comfortable separation from the supposed wilderness they surveyed in their sweeping gaze. If they had actually been forced to travel over the terrain, then it could not have been picturesque—in fact, far from it. "The shores are clothed with forests and undergrowth dense and impassable as the tangle of a Florida swamp," observed the travel writer Eliza Scidmore in 1888.[8] And when William Pierce prospected along the coast in the 1880s, he found "very hard traveling, for it was raining almost continuously and the growth of underbrush was so dense as to be in places almost impenetrable. Here grows a shrub called Devil's Club. It grows very dense and is covered with thorns. These thorns are strong and sharp, and long enough to penetrate your clothing. They are slightly poisonous and cause inflammation. In some places are great tracts of fallen timber, and the streams were high and difficult and dangerous to ford."[9] Prospector George Ogrissek echoed Pierce's disgust with the hazards of cross-country travel. This country was decidedly not picturesque if one had to actually move through it. In his search for gold, Ogrissek noted in his diary, "I started up the mountain to investigate a cliff of rocks and had a horrible time of it. Good god so wild and devilish a country I have never met before! Giant trees blown down by storms for a hundred years lie piled about one over the other in indescribable confusion—at some places 30 to 50 feet above the rocks below with a dense confusion of a growth of cactus thistles, black alder, pines and etc. Why it threatened my existence every step I laboriously made— the bushes being wet and being compelled to crawl over through and under it—got thoroughly soaked, dripping wet, and hurt my sore hand so often that the pain was almost unbearable."[10] With unrelenting alder thickets and carpets of devil's clubs—"used by the Indians as an instrument of torture, especially in the work of correcting witches," according to Muir—travelers intent on doing more than just looking found the region uninviting or worse.[11] Tourists celebrating the picturesque virtues of the British Columbian and Alaskan coasts proved themselves profound spectators. They could cherish the aesthetic drama of the coastal theatre revealed during their ocean-going transit. But their means and method of passing freed these men and women from having to interact with the landscape that from a distance appeared so remarkable.

"Picturesqueness is the offspring of the viewer's orientation," Paul Carter writes.[12] Freed of any organic relationship with the land and its people, these tourists could merge their Victorian aesthetic and Christian pieties. Merritt and the other tourists conjured a new aesthetic order for the region. They had in their private jottings and in their published travelogues conjured new "facts" about Alaska. Earlier guidebook writers noted that Alaska "is not likely to be much frequented by travelers," that its uniformity, its "endless monotony," and "death-like stillness" could hardly serve as legitimate objects for the touring imagination. But by the 1880s travel writers fixed on the visual panoramas afforded by Alaskan travel. Within a decade and a half of Alaska's purchase from Russia in 1867, tourism promoters had found the new territory and its visual resources titillating to the anxious bourgeois urbanites with money and time to spend on lengthy forays. "Were the attractions of this north coast but half known," John Muir noted, "thousands of lovers of nature's beauties would come hither every year."[13] By the mid-1880s the burgeoning power of print capitalism had spurred a new market in northern travel. Tourism brought mass culture and nature together.

Muir celebrated the ease with which travelers might enjoy the coastal panorama, "the finest and freshest landscape poetry on the face of the globe," without ever having to leave the steamer.[14] "The discomforts of a sea voyage are not felt," Muir advertised, "nearly all the long way is on still inland water. It is as if a hundred Lake Tahoes were united end to end, with banks and backgrounds multiplied in the same ration as to sculpture and extent of range and refinement of waterlines." Merritt, Clendenin, Muir, and the innumerable others excursionists believed that they were merely "reading" the landscape poetry that revealed itself along the passage north. But their "readings" revealed as much or more about the viewers' subjectivities as it did about the actual seen landscape. The nature that they saw was the nature that they had been taught to see. As spectators they assumed that what they viewed were "facts." The forests, islands, glaciers, and ocean passages were absolutes, objects of nature, there to be discovered by their inquiring eyes. In the elaborately illustrated *Picturesque Canada,* George Grant enthused that "British Columbia is so vast in extent, so rich in material resources, of the sea, the forest, and the mine, and in scenery."[15] Grant *made* the visual material. The scenery, the salmon, the timber, the gold—all could be had in the new province. But while these physical realms certainly existed, the sightseers gave their observations the certitude of fixed meanings, what Carter calls the "unquestioned convention of the all-seeing spectator," the "illusion of the commonplace." While the northern attractions may not have been ordinary to the touring newcomers, these sights were quickly incorporated into the language of the picturesque and thus made familiar and comprehensible. Their sightseeing voided alternative meanings.

Late nineteenth-century tourists continued to rely upon the interpretative framework built by more than a century of artistic activity—romantic poetry and landscape painting—that emphasized the emotional experience engendered by aesthetic appreciation of supposedly nonhuman spaces. The romantics had lifted the strict reportorial style of earlier travelogues, emphasizing instead the travelers' emotional responses to the visual experiences of touring. This sensibility, in the words of Percy Shelley, relied on "the immediate impression of the deep and powerful feelings excited by the objects which it attempts to describe; and as an undisciplined overflowing of the soul, rests its claim to approbation on an attempt to imitate the untamable wildness and inaccessible solemnity from which those feelings sprang."[16] While Shelley's description begins to touch upon the other principle descriptive convention of the nineteenth century—the sublime, which we will discuss shortly—his words expose the heart of the romantic sensibility. Romanticism provided an ongoing rhetorical premise for fixing individuals in relation to the places through which they traveled. Recognizing beauty in nature served as a rejuvenating experience of pleasure, the antithesis to the polluting environs of the industrial cities that these tourists had recently left, though their experiences were bought with the profits generated by the productive labor of those same cities.

The key feature of the picturesque hinged on its relationship to the representational strategies of landscape painting. Tourists' abilities to recognize the picturesque in nature were tied directly to landscape elements they had been trained to recognize and interpret through painting and literature. As such the picturesque had a simplified and formulaic quality. Raw nature was too chaotic. Instead, the picturesque convention gave sightseers an interpretative strategy through which they might make sense of the sudden newness of this northern coast. British art critic John Ruskin, writing in his multivolume work of the 1850s, *Modern Painters,* enshrined in the critical vocabulary of the nineteenth-century bourgeois traveler what he termed the "Turnerian Picturesque."[17] Analyzing the paintings of J.M.W. Turner, Ruskin described the compositional elements of "Turnerian topography" and "Turnerian light." Ruskin's picturesque typology—five volumes in all—was widely read and influential. The picturesque conventions delineated by Ruskin and others endured through the nineteenth century and can be found at play in the travel writings, both in vernacular diaries and published travel literature. Alaskan travel writer Eliza Scidmore, writing about the Inside Passage in 1885, located her observations firmly within the established conventions and compositional strategies of landscape painting discussed by Ruskin. Borrowing the rhetoric that recognized in nature representational styles drawn from the artifice of landscape painting, she wrote,

The Scenery gains everything from being translated through the medium of a soft, pearly atmosphere, where the light is as gray and evenly diffused as in Old England itself. The distant mountain ranges are lost in the blue vaporous shadows, and nearer at hand the masses and outlines show in their pure contour without the obtrusion of all the garish details that rob so many western mountain scenes of their grander effects. The calm of the brooding air, the shimmer of the opaline sea around one, and the ranges of green and russet hills, misty purple mountains, and snowy summits on the faint horizon, give a dream-like coloring to all one's thoughts.[18]

This word picture advertising the Alaskan scenic landscape could have as easily substituted for a compositional study for a properly picturesque painting with its attention to subtle color, horizon and contour, depth of field, and pleasing situation. This attention to artistic renderings could at times invert the experience of observing "nature." The exterior and physical world became the perfect mirror of an artist's image in Henry Finck's description of the coastal scenery. "Not only has Alaska the third highest mountain range in the world," he insisted, "but if the greatest landscape artist had been consulted, its members could not have been arranged in a manner more continuously impressive to the tourist. Beginning near Victoria with a moderate altitude and mere patches of snow on the sides, they daily grow higher and whiter until the climax is reached in the St. Elias group."[19] Like Ruskin before them, Finck, Scidmore, and many others found in mountains "the beginning and end of all natural scenery."[20]

The trip along the Inside Passage offered a continuous series of views, discrete scenes that might be distinguished from one another through the interpretative conventions of landscape art. It was not possible, given the constraints on their imaginative responses, to see or interpret the land and water in any alternative manner. Because nature appreciation, like the appreciation of fine painting, required effort, erudition, and an educated eye, it was an experience that tourists desired. Such experiences, and the ability to describe them, confirmed one's class status. Because recognizing the picturesque confirmed one's status amongst other travelers, the autonomy of the landscape aesthetic was unlikely to be overturned. In fact, the picturesque scene, once taken from its context, could lead to startling reversals. One diarist noted that "after dinner the majority of the passengers congregated on the bridges over the paddle boxes, the better to see the view which was extremely fine . . . toward evening the shores drew closer together."[21] Here the passivity of the sightseeing experience reversed the order of things, insisting that the shore itself was in motion, not the ship's passengers. A whole host of elements resulted in this inverted series of relationships whereby these travelers imagined, as Muir said, "new scenes [that] are brought into view with magical rapidity." The magic of steam-fired locomotion freed the tourists of having any direct hand in their movement up the coast. And this position freed them from having to relate to the coastal environment in any direct fashion. This separation allowed for other indirect relationships with the environment through which they passed, but especially the tourists' abilities to see these spaces as a series of disconnected images, enframed by the contours not of the land itself, but rather the artifice of paint, pen, and increasingly the camera lens; and, in turn, the ways in which these practices of seeing translated into actual sight.

The enforced leisure of shipboard life, the daily monotony of ocean travel, had long been an occasion for reflective journal-keeping. For Stephen Merritt and innumerable other late nineteenth-century tourists the experience of travel was inseparable from the activity of writing. "I would never tire of writing and viewing," Merritt insisted in his Alaska diary.[22] Merritt's diary prose, its saccharine aesthetic, borders on the unbearable. But aesthetic renderings, seeming excessive to an early twenty-first-century reader, likely impressed late nineteenth-century readers steeped in the verbose conventions of the picturesque. The written word, like an artist's paint, transformed space into fixed and plotted meanings. Sailing up through the "green archipelago," Muir unveiled the islands "like extracts from a fine poem . . . each seems a finished stanza." He made a careful distinction between just any poem and "a fine poem," one that mirrored the cultured status of its readers. And Muir, too, had schooled himself in the romantic poetry from earlier in the century. "We both loved the same poets," Muir's friend and Alaskan traveling companion S. Hall Young remarked, "and could repeat verse about many poems of Tennyson, Keats, Shelley, and Burns. He took with him a volume of Thoreau and I one of Emerson, and we enjoyed them together."[23]

In order to read this landscape Muir assumed a certain cultural literacy, not much of an assumption given the elite audience that paid thirty dollars for the complete volume of *Picturesque California,* in which Muir described in detail the Alaskan trip. Tourists' reading, like their travels, helped to confirm their upper-class status. Taste and literary appreciation functioned as markers of class status. These armchair sightseers— for the volume was filled with photogravure illustrations of Western American and Alaskan sights—like their actual sightseeing counterparts, understood Muir's metaphor. One need not even travel to Alaska to enjoy the visual thrill of the picturesque, albeit vicariously. After all, the actual sightseers such as Merritt were busy interpreting what they saw through the increasingly elaborate visual technologies of the picture. The spread of printing technologies and the distribution of landscape imagery established an ever-growing national audience and market for scenic nature. The spread of scenic landscapes through the technologies of word and image gave new territories like Alaska a national context. Translating space into the written word or stylized picture served as a form of capture. Words and pictures, spread widely, confirmed the region's national possession first in the minds of the citizen elite and gradually amongst the wider public.

Shipboard passengers on the Inside Passage, gazing at the passing terrain, divided what they saw into a series of scenes. The exotic forested islands and glaciated mountains presented objects from which the tourist might choose to compose pictures in his mind's eye. And increasingly their compositions were captured in photographs. The handheld Kodak had become available in the early 1890s and tourists recorded their journeys with snapshots. So prevalent was photography that the traveler H. W. Seton-Karr wrote in his Alaska travelogue of the utilitarian virtues of picture taking. "Such a book does this profess to be having the merits, if it has the defects, of an instantaneous word-photograph, rather than of a carefully elaborated work of art," he wrote.[24] Travel writing now aspired to record and mimic the new image technology, rather than the earlier traditions of artistic display.

Tourist Septima Collis, on first sighting the Stikine River delta near Fort Wrangell, Alaska, saw "a beautiful picture." But clouds prevented her from getting "a Kodak copy." Her fellow tourists turned their cameras on each other. "The Kodak fiends were at work everywhere preserving as best they could the counterfeit presentiments of each other," she remarked.[25] In her own way, Collis suggested the unreality of the photographs she and her friends took. She was disappointed in her own efforts to take adequate photographs, but admitted that "many of our photographs of the scenery" were "perfect gems in their way." "Gems," a figure of speech, or something more? The photograph confirms the taker's presence at the moment of the picture's taking. It served as a certification that she had been on site. Photographs trumped other forms of representation because of their claim to mimicking reality. The tourists' photographs substituted for the actual moment of their taking. Like gems, Septima Collis's snapshots held value both for what they were—desired—and for what they represented—a form of social status.

"Careless, half-educated persons," Alaskan travel writer Maturin Ballou insisted, "are sent upon their travels in order, it is said, that they may 'learn'." Ballou had turned from a career writing sensationalist literature and adventure stories. He was widely credited as the father of the dime novel.[26] "Such individuals had best first learn to travel," he urged. Responsibility for improving "the modern facilities for seeing the world" fell to the educated and trained observer. For it was these elite travelers who possessed "the trained and appreciative eye . . . like the object-glass of the photographic machine," Ballou observed in his Alaskan travelogue, *The New Eldorado*.[27] Ballou noted that the trip to Sitka and back (he assumed an East coast departure) was easily made in three months, clearly indicating who could afford not only the expenses of the trip but also the extended time away from work. Chronicling his own trip, Ballou advertised the cross-country pleasures of the Northern Pacific Railroad and his return via the recently completed Canadian Pacific Rail. On board the steamer *Corona*, he mingled with the upper-class clientele of a Raymond and Whitcomb excursion numbering some eighty travelers. Ballou, nearly seventy years old, had made a career of

Figure 8. Advances in technology made photography accessible to travelers, particularly with the advent of the Kodak camera with rolled film. "You press the button, we do the rest," inventor George Eastman advertised his snapshot camera in 1888. "Amateur photographers on deck of S.S. *Queen*, Alaska Route." Photograph by I. W. Taber, San Francisco, n.d. (Courtesy of The Bancroft Library, University of California, Berkeley)

travel writing—describing his ventures around the world. Writing about leisure was work for Ballou.

Instead of focusing on what these touring photographers and writers recorded, we should turn to what point of view, what unstated perspective was suggested by the pictures they made. These working travel writers did not merely report what was *seen*; rather, they constructed images based upon the conventions of the picturesque.[28] These writers turned scenes into words and with the help of technological advances in image reproduction, added simulacra that enhanced the veracity of their textual translations of the Alaskan coastline. The supposedly "unexplored" quality of the region enhanced these travel writings' commercial value. As travel writer Ernest Ingersoll lamented in the guide *To Alaska, by the Canadian Pacific Railway*, "the world now seems a very small, and pretty well-known sort-of-place." "Regions that a few years ago were considered beyond civilization, not only, but outside of knowledge," he continued, "have been described, photographed, and mapped in so rapid succession that little seems left to reward a tourist in search of novelty."[29] Ingersoll helped to conjure an image of dwindling scenic resources whose cultural value was enhanced by their "unknown" aspect. In a shrinking world, the novelty of the unknown was vanishing and readers' were sure to desire Alaskan views all the more for their fashionable and fleeting newness. Ingersoll, a noted naturalist, had made a career outlining the tourist routes in the continental United States and Canada. *Knocking Around the Rockies* in 1883, *Crest of the Continent* in 1885, *Yellowstone* in 1889, and *Canadian Guide Book* in 1892 established his reputation for accurate and informative travel books. But the transcontinental rail routes and their associated tour sights suffered from advertising overload. One correspondent indicated the excessive attention to cross-country ventures, writing, "I do not know of any traveler who has visited San Francisco without writing a book."[30] Other tourists, less intent on writing of their appreciation for the scenic beauties of the west, simply documented their itineraries. The Shepard family, traveling west and north from New York to Alaska and back, comprised a substantial entourage, including Elliott F. Shepard's wife, her maid, their daughter and her maid, six other family members, a conductor, a chef, a butler, and a porter. Elliott Shepard itemized his completed itinerary: "Time, 4 months, 17 days. Total Travel, 14,085 miles. 38 hotels. 26 different railroads."[31] Shepard had reduced their travels to a numerical series, quantifying the extent and expense of their movements and signifying the family's elite social status.

Perhaps responding to the well-traveled tour sights, or more likely to the glutted market for transcontinental travel writing, Ingersoll turned his attention northward. He was not alone in his new northerly wordsmithing. His brother T. W. Ingersoll joined him in extolling the visual splendor of the Inside Passage, publishing *Picturesque Alaska* in 1890.[32] But the fixation with publishing one's travels soon overwhelmed the Alaskan coastal tour. "Tourists were just beginning to learn of Alaska and to wish to explore it," Alaskan missionary S. Hall Young noted of the 1880s coastal tours.

Many writers, mostly women, made trips from Portland to Fort Wrangell and Sitka and back, on the same steamer, and they *wrote books on Alaska*. Only two or three of them deigned to stop off between steamboats. Dall's book and a few of the earlier publications on Alaska, all of them full of mistakes, were copied by these tourists, and their own imagination added to the errors. To write a book on such a country as that, after having made only this one hasty trip, would be like publishing a volume descriptive of the Metropolitan museum when the author had only scanned the building from the outside and turned back at the entrance. Only one or two of these books survived more than a year or two.[33] (italics in original)

We may forget too easily while reading these descriptions that they were written by women and men sitting at typewriters or with notebooks often far distant from the scenes of their descriptions. As such, travel writing became a peculiar sort of labor. The reproduction of visual experiences allowed for new experiences of "seeing," but ones disassociated from the sites. And perception was transformed by the ability to experience these places quite removed from the visual spaces so described.

Septima Collis suggested that the new technologies of representation had not determined new modes of seeing. "No camera, no pencil, no vocabulary," she wrote, "can do more than produce a desire to see for one's self. I can only say that it has been my fortune to behold much that is grand in nature and in art at home and abroad."[34] These technologies had not created the new visual culture. Instead, images in paintings and photographs, and words in poems and travelogues, accelerated the spread of mass visual culture centered on "nature." Visual images became increasingly standardized through the new technologies of mechanical reproduction. The consumers of these images, increasingly mass consumers, came under a broad process of "normalization," whereby each aspired to "own" the images of scenic attraction through direct experience or indirect image possession.[35] Tourists then came to represent part products of the new industries of mechanical reproduction and part consumers of that industry. And as Collis suggested, it was her and numerous others' travel writings and photographs that helped to "produce a desire." Natural scenery had become a commodity. Like gold money, picturesque words and nature images served as symbols, representations of scenes severed from their source.

The economy of desire, unwittingly intimated by the tourist writers such as Collis, sought the exchange of these images for the real thing. Importantly, the spread of this print culture helped to spread this "desire to see for oneself." Merritt confirmed this exchange value. "It is *worth* the cost and hardship of the journey to witness the sight" (italics added)," Merritt wrote, as he looked out at the setting sun on the Inside Passage. Merritt coupled the economy with the exaggerated significance of time as something that could be wasted.[36] The travelers' leisure was organized and rationalized in the same manner that their capital and other peoples' labor was valued.

The "nightless day," the aurora borealis, "the mighty glaciers . . . the thundering iceberg plunging into the sea and floating off in its glory of inimitable splendor," "the placid waters," "the biggest quartz mill ever constructed," "the queer customs of the natives"—these were the recurring sights found on the Inside Passage itinerary and recycled in the travel books and magazine articles beginning in the early 1880s. The Pacific Coast Steamship Company's advertising pamphlet *All About Alaska* suggested that these novelties might "well make the trip the object of a life-time. There is nothing like it. Without doubt it is 'The Biggest Show on Earth.'"[37] Echoing P. T. Barnum's trademarked circus, "The Greatest Show on Earth," the steamship company claimed Alaska as a spectacle comparable to the master showman's elaborate entertainments. This reference to Barnum offered a cultural shorthand, a sign suggesting a much-condensed meaning quickly understood by late nineteenth-century readers.[38] For the wealthy clients of the nascent Alaska travel industry, the reference to Barnum's supposedly low-brow spectacles emphasized how different the direct experience with Alaskan nature was from the contrived circus spectacles arranged under great tents for thronging urban masses.

Alaska came to be represented as a natural zone, purified and set apart from society. Nature's objects were "real," unlike the theatre of assembled animals performing for the circus. But it was not so easy to distinguish between artifice and nature. Nature tourists believed that they communed with authentic versions of the natural world on their trips north to Alaska. Turning nature into aesthetic objects accomplished a sort of sleight of hand, a deceit whereby the objects of nature—a mountain, a glacier, a native, a seascape and island—became utilitarian objects of capital. Journeys to Alaska, costly and time consuming, buttressed elite cultural identities and helped create a field of activity that generated a particular status. Alaskan tourists thought they were escaping industrial culture through their travels into nature. In fact these tourists' flights from civilization were borne by the technological advance and capitalist advertising that brought them into "nature." Nature existed both *through* and *for* the visitors' eyes.

Alaskan tourism promoters recognized that in order to make the most of market potential, they needed to marshal the full power of capital investment, advertising, and integrated organization. Captain George S. Wright led a group of tourists, perhaps the first organized tour, up the Stikine River in 1878, at the height of the Cassiar Gold Rush in interior British Columbia.[39] In the succeeding years, steamship companies supplying industries along the coast added the coastal tour to their operations, accommodating tourists along with their other freight. The Pacific Coast Steamship Company (PCSC), formed in 1874, had been running the side-wheel steamer *Ancon* on the coast routes since 1877. The PCSC added additional steamers to the route and dominated the coastal tourist trade until after the turn of the century. In 1888 the PCSC ran the screw propeller *George W. Elder* in addition to the *Ancon*. The increased popularity of the Alaskan summer excursions encouraged the company to add new ships to its schedule. In 1888 the PCSC added the side-wheel steamer *Olympian* to its fleet, highlighting that the ship "will carry no steerage passengers, and none but first class, and will carry no freight."[40] Tourist traffic now made possible the segregation of wealthy travelers from the migrants who headed north to work in the seasonal resource economy. Steerage rates still allowed for working-class travelers to gamble on northerly job prospects, with prices running $20 from Portland to Fort Wrangell, and $25 from San Francisco, half that of the cabin rates. The Canadian Pacific Navigation Company had been formed in 1883, acquiring the coastal steamers of the Hudson's Bay Company fleet.[41] Oregon Railway and Navigation Company added the side-wheel steamer *Olympia* to the northern route in 1884. PCSC, consolidating its hold on the coastal tour, took it over in 1887.[42] In 1888 a roundtrip excursion from New York City cost $233, from San Francisco, $130.[43] The steamship companies arranged for ticket sales through the transcontinental lines—Northern Pacific, Union Pacific, Canadian Pacific, and later Great Northern. And in turn, these rail corporations marshaled the publishing and nationwide distribution resources at their disposal to advertise travel to Alaska. "In the coast-region of Alaska exists a vast area of novel scenes, glorious landscapes, and infinite opportunity for sport and adventure as yet unmarred by the contact of civilization," Ingersoll urged on behalf of the Canadian Pacific Railway.[44]

"If," as Eliza Clendenin hoped in her travel diary, "the numerous

Figure 9. Steamer *Ancon* in Glacier Bay, Alaska, in *Alaska Souvenir Photographs* (Boston: Partridge Photo, 1887). (Courtesy Yale Collection of Western Americana, Beinecke Rare Book and Manuscript Library)

guidebooks tell us the truth, we are going to see the grandest sight of our lives."[45] If guidebooks guaranteed superlative sightseeing, then they also helped to relieve the terrors of travel. Protected within the secure confines of the ship, the northern trip had been advertised as particularly open to women travelers. "Ladies without Escort can make the trip," Charles Gates noted, "without experiencing the slightest unpleasantness or being in any way oppressed by the doubts and difficulties to travel in the ordinary way."[46] In her popular travelogue Eliza Scidmore commented on the ease with which women like herself could enjoy the Inside Passage route. When a man aboard the *Idaho* remarked to Scidmore about the hazards of a woman traveling alone, she shrugged off his concerns. " 'You ladies are very brave to venture up in such a place. If you only knew the risks you are running—the dangers you are in!' And the pioneer's voice had a tone of the deepest concern as he said it," Scidmore recorded. "We received this with some laughter," she wrote, "and expressed entire confidence in the captain and pilot, who had penetrated glacial fastnesses and unknown waters before."[47] "We are favorably impressed by the Captain and other officers," wrote another woman who examined the ship and crew at the wharf in Seattle, "and make careful notes regarding proper clothing, tobacco, medicines, chairs, photographic supplies and the hundred other things that come up in planning a trip of this kind." Scrutinizing her fellow passengers, she seemed satisfied; "the outlook is promising," she wrote of her future companions, "and we return from our hour of investigation quite satisfied with the conditions of our prospective expedition."[48]

These well-to-do travelers expected the right kind of people to accompany them on their northern circuit. The early mail steamers of the late 1870s and early 1880s with their rough comforts would no longer satisfy these now discerning and demanding clients. Captaining such a trip became an exercise in entertainment as well as navigation. The steamer captains were expected to recognize the distinctions of their new and wealthy clientele. The wealthy tourists carried themselves as if wearing uniforms of entitlement. "The ship is a yacht, of which the Captain is the host, the passengers his guests," Septima Collis announced in her popular travelogue. "The object of the cruise," she wrote, was "the pursuit of pleasure; and if I succeed in inducing my country-women to follow my example and postpone Paris and London, Rome and Vienna, the Rhine and the Alps, to some future day, they will always have reason to be grateful to me, and I shall always have reason to be satisfied with my effort."[49]

The expectations of wealthy travelers, accustomed to having things their way, often met with sudden resistance from ship's captains, unaccustomed to being directed by anything other than the weather and the

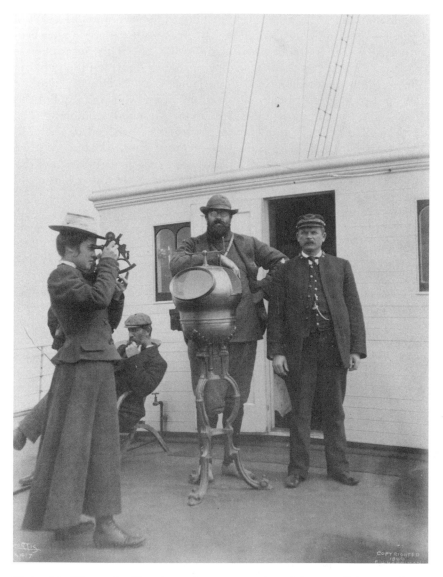

Figure 10. Woman looking through sextant on board the expedition vessel
George W. Elder, with two men and Captain Peter Doran during the Harriman
expedition to Alaska, 1899. Photograph by Edward Curtis. (Courtesy Library of
Congress)

seas. In summer 1894, the passengers aboard the steamer *Queen* signed a petition requesting the captain to stay over another night in a particular port along the Inside Passage. A wealthy dowager in the seat of honor next to the captain at the first seating at dinner delivered the petition. After reading the document, Captain James Carroll replied, "My dear madam, I regret very much to disappoint you and your friends, but this steamship is not run by petitions. We sail on the scheduled time."[50] The chummy confidence of the leisuring bourgeoisie proceeded, generally unperturbed by such blunt refusals to acquiesce to their assumed privileges. Theirs was a tight circle of word-of-mouth prerogatives and distinctions, ruled by sets of cultural markers that determined who could belong to their comfortable clan.

If the excursionists could not dictate directions to the captain, then at least they knew how to change things to their liking. Passengers had long complained about conditions aboard the steamers in the 1880s. These steamships were, of course, working boats carrying supplies and mail to the communities dotting the coastline. But as the tourist market grew, so too did the steamer companies' attempts to accommodate and attract new passengers. The world-traveling Englishwoman E. Katharine Bates compared the Alaska trip unfavorably to other sea-borne excursions. Bates complained about the quality of the steamer *G. W. Elder*'s accommodations. "The cabins are extremely small, and when three passengers are packed in each cabin, like herrings in a barrel, it is easily understood that there must be considerable drawbacks to a purely pleasure excursion," she wrote.[51] "The Alaska expedition has much novelty to recommend it," she reasoned, "But so long as the world lasts, mental impressions must and will depend to a great extent upon physical conditions, and I think the Pacific Coast Steam Shipping Company might materially improve these."[52] "Doubtless the steamers at present are crowded," Bates noted, "but then Alaska just now is a novelty."[53] Any traveler in steerage could have confirmed Bates's estimation of the comforts, or rather lack of comforts aboard ship. "The accommidations on this ship are very poor," wrote steerage passenger, literally lower-class traveler, Oscar Bike, on his trip north. "Quite a bit worse than camping out, there is lots of kicking on board and likely to be trouble before long [*sic*]."[54]

Shipboard travel thus offered a condensed mirror of society with its strict divisions of class rank and priorities. The ship served as a floating microcosm of the wider society. The upper-class vacationers recognized as much and increasingly demanded separation from those passengers traveling for reasons other than leisure. With the new pressures of their wealthy clients' demands, the PCSC announced in 1887 that "the increased popularity of the Alaska Summer Excursions and the demand for fine and fast steamers have induced the Company to secure and specially fit up for the purpose the new and magnificent side-wheel steamship Olympian . . . she is fast and makes the trip from Tacoma, W[ashington] T[erritory] to Alaska and return in about eleven days. She visits Glacier Bay and other interesting points in Alaska." But most important to attracting passengers of the "better class," the company announced "the *Olympian* will carry no steerage passengers, and none but first-class, and will carry no freight, except perishable and Express freight . . . and thus afford a splendid opportunity of viewing the wonders of this Wonderland."[55] The steamer company priced the roundtrip from San Francisco to Sitka at $130 and ticket sales were coordinated with railroads that serviced the ports of embarkation at San Francisco, Portland, Tacoma, Seattle, and Vancouver, British Columbia.[56] Ticket prices ranged from as little as $95 at a budget rate and as much as $240, depending upon the arrangements of berth and meals. But the total costs of an Alaska trip ran much higher, if one considered first-class travel from East Coast cities and the sundry expenses of extended travel. "Alaska is a valuable possession," C. E. S. Wood wrote, "Go and see! The round trip from New York will cost you about six hundred dollars, which does not include hotel expenses."[57] Steamers like the *Queen* and the *Olympian* might take as little as twelve days to two weeks from the Puget Sound ports of Seattle or Tacoma. Other steamers that carried tourists as well as cargoes and stopped frequently might take eighteen to twenty days for the roundtrip north to Glacier Bay and Sitka and back to northwest port cities.

The cities of the West became tourist destinations in their own right. Alexander Badlam, among other travel writers, wrote whole chapters—"Cities of the Great Northwest"—locating them as destinations, not simply as staging points for departures. "The cities of the extreme northwest—those products of phenomenal growth—have surely, a claim upon our attention . . . these pushing towns."[58] Seattle's population surged from just 3,533 people in 1880 to 42,837 in 1890. This phenomenal growth was largely the result of the extension of the Northern Pacific line and the completion of the Great Northern railway. And after 1885 and the completion of the transcontinental Canadian Pacific Railroad, Vancouver and Victoria (via ferry connections) became advertised ports of call. The trans-Canada rail service linked with ocean steamships that traveled to China, and in the words of one travel writer, "the interests of the whole British Empire are closely interlocked."[59] The western metropolis stood as fact and symbol for the nation's progressive expansion. And visiting travelers marveled at these instant cities even as they embarked upon their nature voyages that held a decidedly antiurban bent.[60] Boosting the West had for some time wedded settlement promotion with tourist advertising. As one settlers' guide boosted the West, "In the following pages we have briefly outlined its resources and capacities for sustaining a large and prosperous population, and directed attention to its wonderful attractions for the tourist and health seeker."[61]

If these travelers were observers, then they were equally consumers (and therefore observed carefully). And what they saw and experienced was conjured more by what they had been prepared to see than what they actually saw on their travels. Tourism relied (and relies) on the pre-imagining of an experience by its subjects. Tourists traveled by virtue of having already traveled, in their minds. And in order to have imagined a future touristic experience they relied on a body of literature and image that laid out the terrain of their future experiences. The wide circulation of written and visual images helped to replicate the normalizing desires of future consumers. As they were told—shown—what to expect, so they too conformed to consistent and uniform, homogenous and easily marketable needs. Scenes were lifted from their organic context and used to replicate homogenizing signs. These signs in their turn inspired individual desires to travel and see these now abstracted sights. And in this lay the predictable trap that left the tourist with expectations to be filled or unfulfilled and the dilemma that there could be little "real" experiences, but only those that were mediated by their anticipations. They were told what they saw, even before they saw it. Even their science told them this was so. "Every perception," as William James wrote, "is an acquired perception without pre-vision, . . . there can be no perception—we must have some idea of what we want to see before we can see it." The world was not transparently evident for them to see. They did not control their sightseeing experiences. New and powerful marketing arrangements helped to determine the capacities of these touring observers. While what they saw on their excursions up the Inside Passage could never be entirely determined, neither could these travelers behold the world as transparently evident.[62] People themselves had become products.

But travelers need not actually venture to this remote (to them) coastline. The desire to see for oneself could be satisfied in a vicarious fashion. New technologies of reproduction—lithographs, chromolithographs, photogravure—offered images for mass consumption. Catharine Beecher in her widely read home improvement manual *The American Woman's Home* recommended the display of chromolithographs. "Surrounded by such suggestions of the beautiful," the domestic scene was trained in "correctness of taste and refinement of thought."[63] She recommended Albert Bierstadt's *Sunset in the Yosemite Valley* as the perfect addition to the parlor. Bierstadt, veteran of the Hayden survey, seized the opportunities afforded by the new print technologies, "publishing versions of his paintings with every medium available, from wood and steel engravings, to chromolithography to the new photomechanical processes (collotype, photoengraving, and photogravure)," according to Bryan Wolfe.[64] His aggressive marketing strategy made him a wealthy man and helped establish a role for Western American images in the articulation of a new national landscape. And the spread of "chromo" technology brought art "within the reach of all classes of society."[65]

Stereographic images too proliferated in the later decades of the nineteenth century. Two images viewed alongside each other with a special magnifying glass produced a three-dimensional appearance, a similitude of the actual scene. American western scenes, including Alaskan views, became quite popular. In an early version of virtual reality, Oliver Wendell Holmes, the stereograph's inventor, predicted that stereographs would make travel unnecessary. "The sights which men risk their lives and spend their money and endure sea-sickness to behold, these sights are offered to you for a trifle, to carry home with you, that you may look at them at your leisure, by your fireside," he wrote.[66] A half-century later this belief in the evocative power of the photographic image had grown in power. "The traveler seeks experiences of places, not places themselves," Albert E. Osborne wrote in 1909. "Stereographs can give such experiences. If it is the experience of a place, and not the place itself, which we seek in traveling to it, if we seek the real place only as a means of giving us experiences of it, then we are prepared to see, that, if a substitute for the place can give us the experience, the place itself is not essential to us," Osborne concluded.[67] Examining a photo reproduction or reading a travel book was in itself the symbolic attaining of travel. It was while they were reading that they were traveling, and we may assume that the great majority of readers never actually made any serious attempt to make these expensive journeys themselves. Traveler Carter H. Harrison recognized as much when he wrote, "A beautiful or grand scene is doubly enjoyed when one feels he may through a letter have hundreds see what he sees and as he sees. They become his companions and hold sweet communion with him, though thousands of miles may lie between them. This is sympathy and sympathy makes the joy of life."[68] The lure of the travel book resided in the fact that the reader, while reading, lived in the aura of travel.[69] Most did their travel easily.

The travel literature and imagery generated by two decades of interest and activity along the Alaskan coast validated the region as culturally significant. "I would fain divert a portion of the travel which habitually goes to Europe to this new field of commerce and adventure. I would popularize home excursion among our votaries of fashion . . . as the primary and proper thing to 'do' before attempting the Old World Tour," wrote traveler Charles Hallock.[70] Appealing to Americans' sense of patriotism, he categorized an Alaskan trip as a sort of corporate-training jaunt for aspiring European travelers, urging, "so make it incumbent upon every American citizen, who would claim consideration abroad, to be duly accredited at the home office as competent to travel."[71] Septima Collis made no claims to producing a scientific or historical work, but rather she transformed the coastal cruise into a highbrow entertainment. "I want them to know, as I know, that the ship is a yacht, of which the Captain is the host," Collis insisted. She hoped to convince her "countrywomen" to postpone trips to Paris, Rome, or London and instead opt for the Alaskan venture. General William Tecumseh Sherman, twenty-odd years after the Civil War, touted Collis's travel account. Extolling the virtues of far northern tourism, he predicted in the foreword to Collis's travelogue, "I am sure it will influence thousands of tourists to visit our own sublime regions in America before going to Europe."[72] And because these newly described regions came to characterize the nation, travel to the north became a civic duty, at least among the privileged class. A railroad promotional brochure trumpeted as much, insisting, "Travel, for business or pleasure, is now almost a fine art . . . the patriotic American is just awakening to the fact that the United States and its possessions contain a greater diversity of climate than any other nation on the face of the globe."[73] The relationship here between climatic variety and patriotism might seem obtuse, but to the late nineteenth-century American the national embrace of the latitudes extending from the near tropics to the arctic confirmed the imperial magnificence. And what better way to recognize such national greatness than to visit these regions. Alice Rollins's travelogue *From Palm to Glacier* indicated this fascination with the extent of the national domain. And Kipling would soon admonish the Americans to take up the "White Man's burden," to spread civilization's dominion from "palm to pine."

But these travelers' attentions were directed at more than simply the extent of the new national possessions. John Hyde, writing an advertising brochure for the Northern Pacific Railway, fixed progress as an object of tourist desire.[74] History in the north was not about the past, of which most concluded there was very little. Instead history was a future task, to settle and to spread civilization's dominion.

While, as the present writer has elsewhere observed, old-world armies have been contending for the possession of narrow strips of territory, in kingdoms themselves smaller than many single American States, and venerable savants have been predicting the near approach of the time when the population of the world shall have outstripped the means of subsistence, there has arisen, between the headwaters of the Mississippi and the mouth of the stately Columbia, an imperial domain more than three times the size of the German empire, and capable of sustaining upon its own soil one hundred millions of people. What the United States is to the world at large, this particular region is, in may respects, to the Great Republic itself; and its scenic attractions have this additional advantage over those of other parts of the country, that, traveling to them as he does, through the vast wheat fields of Minnesota and Dakota, the gold and silver ribbed mountains and rich pastures of Montana, and the forests, wheat field and hop gardens of Washington, the tourist sees something of a section of country whose extraordinary productiveness has drawn upon it the attention of the whole civilized world, and led to the most remarkable movement of population witnessed in modern times.

Here in the West tourists might witness the nation's progress in the productive settling of the continent. Hyde noted that this spectacle of progress turned north to Alaska, where Americans were "engaged in subduing the refractory powers of Nature and despoiling of its vast and varied riches one of the greatest of her treasure houses."[75] The spectacle would be found not in relics, nor solely in the West's and North's monumental natural features, but in change itself, transformation, evidence of progress. On their journeys to Alaska, travelers highlighted the sudden cities—San Francisco, Portland, Seattle, and Tacoma—that had grown phenomenally in just several decades. And in turn these cities launched a thousand and more schemes for raiding the riches of "the greatest of her treasure houses": Alaska.

Indeed, the American tourists possessed the new north, or at least believed themselves to own the vast territory. "An American would not be quite himself if he did not experience some glow of feeling in coming into a region, however distant, that belongs to his country, and in part belongs to him," enthused the travel writer Henry M. Field in *Our Western Archipelago*. "Every man in the United States is owner of Alaska, to the extent of one seventy millionth part of it," he continued, "wherefore it becomes him to look sharply at his new possession, with the interest which comes from a feeling of proprietorship."[76] Alaska became part of a perceived American birthright. Of course, who met the qualifications for proprietorship was a question under much debate in the 1880s and 1890s.

While well-heeled tourists and travelers sought out the visual wonders of the new north on their summertime cruises, other Americans fought for wages and control over the conditions of their labor. And occasionally, the bourgeois pleasure seekers confronted the "unpleasantries" of the laborers' struggles. In summer 1894, according to one account, "scores were prevented from coming by the strikes which had just broken out, and that were especially violent in the western coast. A party from San Francisco, that succeeded in getting through, had a pitiful tale to tell of a blockage so close that not a train could move, and they had to take to the sea on the Walla Walla, in which they were so crowded that eighty-five had to sleep on the cabin floor!"[77] Aylett Rains Cotton, recently graduated from Stanford University, also traveled throughout the West during summer 1894. He recorded a confrontation between strikers and soldiers on the Northern Pacific line. The armed standoff ended peacefully when the soldiers advanced on the workers en masse with fixed bayonets.[78] Other travelers complained of this violent state of affairs, interrupting their carefully arranged touring plans. "The strikes of the summer were nowhere more violent than on the Pacific coast," wrote one traveler, "and the railroads were tied up so that it was impossible to move. A gentleman and his wife from New York, who came on with us, had been shut up in Portland for a month. Another passenger, who was from California, told me that it had taken him twenty-two days to get to Portland! . . . As soon as a train was made up, the strikers would uncouple the passenger cars from the engine. This paralysis of communication might have continued for months, had not the Government put forth its strong hand. But as soon as the bluecoats were distributed along the lines, the strikers began to see things in a new light."[79] The tourists, on the other hand, had little interest in seeing things in a new light. In order to preserve the magic of leisured movement, they did not connect the workers' battles to their own travels, except that the strikes disrupted their schedules. These tourists were unwilling or unable to recognize the labor that lay beneath their sightseeing.

After having arrived at a West Coast port—San Francisco, Portland, Tacoma, Seattle, or Vancouver—these travelers embarked on steamships that plied the coastwise trade, touching at various ports of call along the west coast of British Columbia and southeastern Alaska, usually ending their northward transit at Sitka before returning south along the same Inside Passage route. Freed of the inconveniences that occasionally plagued their transcontinental train travel, susceptible as it was to the remonstrations of striking industrial workers, the northward travelers breathed a sigh of relief. "At last," exclaimed one writer, "we are on the waters bound for Alaska."[80] The seasonal labor force in Alaska had yet to organize, and though occasional strikes disrupted travel, the corporations' reliance upon native Alaskan laborers kept the labor question at bay.

"Free from the worry and turmoil of a busy world," J. A. Zahm lectured his audiences on the healthful benefits of an Alaskan trip, "and breathing an atmosphere that seems to possess all the invigorating properties attributed to the Elixir of Life, of the alchemists of old."[81] "At the end of five or six weeks, having passed through a succession of fairy-lands and wonder-lands one can be back in Chicago and ready to enter again, with renewed vigor, upon the duties of life," Zahm insisted. Sailing out of Puget Sound, men and women of Zahm's ilk enjoyed a cruise comfortably removed from the crises that rent the United States during the last two decades of the century. Their voyages north were as much an escape from the threat posed by these usually summertime battles as they were a venture into nature.

Nevertheless, northern travelers recorded the working lives observed from their shipboard positions. Edward Pierrepont, son of the former U.S. attorney general, noted that the longshoremen at Nanaimo, a coaling station on the inside coast of Vancouver Island, were principally native men. "The Indians in loading or unloading here (the whites being scarce), require just as much pay as white men, while the Chinamen receive less; the Indians being found much better workers from the fact of their greater strength."[82] These wealthy travelers were not blind to the basic functions of the western economy. But they did routinely fail to recognize the fact that their leisure had been earned at the expense of a fantastically exploitative wage system—both at home and on their travels to the north.

Landscape was certainly a pictorial notion. But in Alaska, before it was a scene viewed by tourists, the landscape was a strategic point of reference. Before it was an aesthetic resource, the view was a strategic one. The earliest Alaskan touring excursions merged landscape aesthetics and military surveillance. The tactics of reconnaissance and tourism were linked in the close cultures of the nation's military and social elite. In summer 1868, the photographer Eadweard Muybridge obtained a commission to join General Henry W. Halleck's reconnaissance trip to Alaska. Halleck also invited an entourage of wealthy and well-connected elites to join his coastal survey. Muybridge had followed Californian landscape photographer Carleton E. Watkins in documenting the scale and beauty of Yosemite. He would later experiment with time-stop photography, successfully capturing the movement of animals and people in time and space. In 1879 he invented the Zoopraxiscope, a precursor to a motion-picture machine, the Kinetoscope, later developed by Thomas Edison. But early in his career, Muybridge's photographs for the 1868 Alaska expedition aboard the steamer *Pacific* indicated the close correspondence between the genre of landscape study and the medium of the military field of view. Spatial relationships captured by a map or a chart might also be claimed strategically with a photograph. As with the use of a map or chart, landscapes were understood as an orientation. Such an orientation implied a relationship between the viewer and the viewed. It constituted not only what was at a distance, but also the most appropriate point from which to view the scene. As an artistic genre, landscape representations relied on carefully defined lines of linear perspective and horizon. Military planners relied on these same lines of comprehensive viewing to achieve a single point of command. Muybridge easily mixed these similar lines of sight on his northern transit. His presence aboard this early reconnaissance signified the conjoining of the imperial connections between strategic sites and aesthetic sights. "I have to acknowledge the receipt of copies of your photographs of forts and public buildings at Sitka and other military posts taken for use of War Department and also views of scenery in Alaska," General Halleck wrote after the expedition. Halleck was the former general-in-chief of the Union armies during the Civil War and the author of *Elements of Military Art and Science,* first printed in 1846 by the New York publisher Appleton and Company, the publisher of later Alaskan travel guides. Halleck's study served as the main text at West Point for a generation.

The general recognized the critical overlay of art and science afforded by photographic technologies. "These views besides being beautiful works of art give a more correct idea of Alaska and its scenery and vegetation than can be obtained from any written description of that country," Halleck acknowledged of Muybridge's photographic work.[83] The photographs served the dual functions of surveillance and scenery, of

Figure 11. "Entrance to Grenville Pass," 1868. Photograph by Eadweard Muybridge. Lone Mountain College Collection of Stereographs. (Courtesy The Bancroft Library, University of California, Berkeley)

Figure 12. "Fort Tongass, a view from the Fort," 1868. Photograph by Eadweard Muybridge. Lone Mountain College Collection of Stereographs. (Courtesy The Bancroft Library, University of California, Berkeley)

military science and art. His aesthetic views could not be separated from the strategic views that sought to maintain control over the region's indigenes. The act of seeing the scenery was profoundly political.

It is difficult to identify the first purely tourist ventures northward. Some travelers, such as John Muir, sailed the Inside Passage, traveling on the regular mail and supply steamers that connected the early resource ventures to commercial hubs in Vancouver, the Pacific Northwest, and San Francisco. During the 1870s attention had focused increasingly on the scenic qualities of the southeastern coast of Alaska and British Columbia's west coast. R. W. Meade described the scenic values of the coast in an early article in *Appleton's Journal* published in 1871. But like many others, Meade, while admitting that the "traveler from Alaska may enlarge a good deal on scenery," nevertheless found the view "so continuously magnificent, it becomes monotonous."[84] By 1878 specially organized touring trips had been arranged on the Stikine River, where the visitors gawked at the valley's hanging glaciers and at the influx of gold seekers trekking in to the interior mines of the recently developed Cassiar gold fields.[85] Northern touring ventures always mixed natural scenery with the views of progress, the labor of resource extraction.

Another early junket to Alaska was organized by the U.S. Department of War, at least in an unofficial capacity, in summer 1881. General Nelson A. Miles, then commander of the Department of the Columbia, led this seemingly unlikely strike northward. General Miles's professional life had been preoccupied with frontier fears of Indian attack. He carried these concerns northward on his northern inspection tour, preoccupied with documenting the potential threats supposedly posed by native Alaskans. Miles had earned fame (or infamy) as a decorated Civil War veteran, as the field commander in the Red River War (1874–75) against the Kiowa, Comanche, and Southern Cheyenne, as winter campaign leader against the Sioux on the Northern Plains in 1876–77, where he earned the name "Bear's Coat" and imprisoned Crazy Horse, and as the general who intercepted Chief Joseph's Nez Perce and forced the chief's surrender some forty miles from the Canadian border and safety in fall 1877. Miles had been at the forefront of American expansionist policies, enforcing conquest with brutal repetition upon the Native peoples of the American West. Following his tour of duty in the northwest, he would achieve even greater fame (or again, infamy) in his dogged pursuit and eventual capture of Geronimo and the Chiricahua Apache in 1886, and as overall commander at Wounded Knee in 1890.

Alongside these engagements, Miles's several-week trip to Alaska must stand as an anomalous side-show. But during his service in the Northwest, Miles had taken a special interest in Alaska. According to Henry Villard, president of Northern Pacific, "the first Alaskan excursion party, numbering eighty, including General Miles, then in command on the Pacific coast, and a military band, went over the coastwise route, under my administration on the steamship Idaho in 1881."[86] Villard credited Miles with having launched the region's tourist industry. The *Idaho* and other steamships would thereafter regularly serve tourists on the Inside Passage route. General Miles's interests were broader than simply invigorating a nascent excursion business up the coast. Concerned about the limited government presence in the region, then administered by Treasury Department revenue cutters and a Sitka-based naval vessel, the general urged more thorough investigations of the coast and particularly the interior. "Whatever its treasure," he emphasized, "they are beyond the reach of private enterprise."[87] Again the metaphor of treasure helped to conjure an image of future riches awaiting discovery. But more than simply exploiting solely Alaska's worth, the expansionist Miles suggested even greater territorial claims. In a letter to General Sherman, he prophesied, "I think it too soon to occupy the boundary line now, when we are ready for that the North Pole may be the boundary," Miles wrote in 1881. Imagining an extension of American sovereignty from the Canadian-U.S. boundary line at the forty-ninth parallel to the pole, the general expressed an attitude that had some widespread appeal. He believed that force might not be necessary to claim British Columbia and the British Northwest Territory since "a majority of British Columbia would vote for annexation tomorrow."[88] Tourism in the north was not a benign presence. "The beauty and grandeur of these scenes is equal to anything that I ever witnessed," the general exclaimed.[89] His sentiments carried nationalist implications. His scenic pronouncements, his contemplation of the region's picturesque qualities bore the mark of the general's imperial world, a world he had taken an instrumental role in shaping. This whole world of "scenes" was available to Miles's transvaluing imagination. Because he could compare Alaska to other conquests, Miles and his contemporary excursionists actively incorporated the scenic resources of the northwest coast into their inventory of picturesque possessions. Their aesthetics were in no way free of their imperial imaginations. In fact, these ideologies of the picturesque pretended that what was seen had transcendent value, instead of the truth, which was that they had, in their aestheticizing grip, given the land its worth.

Like Miles, Alaskan tourists held the whole world sublimely in their minds' eye. "And when the dazzling peaks, rising at a bound far above the wooded hills around them, and the frozen rivers, wide and long, are seen," one traveler confided, "the admission can easily be obtained that Alaska is par excellence *the scenic store-ground of the world*, its inlets rivaling the fjords of Norway and its glaciers those of Switzerland" (italics added).[90] The Inside Passage tour compressed all the equivalents of the world's wonders into one easy voyage. "For all such surprises," Frederick Schwatka advised, "must the tourist be prepared on this singular voyage."[91] Like Miles, Lieutenant Schwatka's supposed military reconnaissance touted the scenic route's features as well. He likened aspects of the route to other well-known tourist landmarks, ones likely known to the worldly clientele reading these travel books. Schwatka compared sights along the passage to the canyon of Yellowstone, the streets of Lisbon in Portugal, the Argentine Pampas, the Hudson River at West Point, the Swiss Alps, and the Delaware Water Gap.

By the late 1880s northern steamer traffic increasingly accommodated tourists' needs, adapting schedules and shipboard comforts to bourgeois desires. Travelers embarked at Puget Sound ports—Tacoma, Seattle, Port Townsend—making connections via San Francisco or joining northbound cruises at the Canadian Pacific Railroad terminus at Vancouver or at Victoria. British Columbia's provincial capital, Victoria, and the nearby coaling station at Nanaimo served as points of contrast from the rambunctious American ports of departure. As one writer observed, Victoria with its well-kept gardens and orderliness was "one of the prettiest and most engaging colonial towns," contrasting markedly with "the fever and activity of American trade and competition."[92] With the arrival of trans-Canadian rail service and connecting steamers to China and other Asian ports, the "interests of the whole British Empire are closely interlocked," according to another visiting writer. And Victoria stood as "a colonial town," part of a British imperial geography, one that contrasted with the so-called "fever" of a peculiarly American capitalism. Observers noting the English prettiness often chose not to describe other aspects of Victoria. The ethnographer Franz Boas visiting in 1889 described a strikingly different Victorian capital. He noted that native people far outnumbered Europeans in British Columbia—an estimated 38,000 lived in the province, with most living along the coast. "The stranger coming for the first time to Victoria," he wrote, "is startled by the great number of Indians living in this town. We meet them everywhere. They dress mostly in European fashion. The men are dock workers, craftsmen, or fish vendors; the women are washerwomen or working women." And like every colonial town, a shadow village inhabited by the displaced indigenes lay just out of sight, close enough to afford workers for the colony's industries, far enough away to be an invisible presence. "Certain Indian tribes have already become indispensable on the labor market, and without them the Province would suffer a great economic damage," Boas insisted.[93] Walking around the suburbs of Victoria, Boas noted, "We come to that part of the town exclusively inhabited by Indians. They live in miserable, dirty wooden shacks or even in light tents."[94] The pretty colonial town with its mimicry of an English village also mimicked the careful barriers of class and race, where the workers toiled behind the hedgerow, discreetly out of sight.

Sailing north from Victoria on the southern tip of Vancouver Island, steamers churned through Canadian waters up Haro Strait and into the Strait of Georgia, passing between the protecting mass of Vancouver Island and the British Columbian mainland. Stretching for more than a hundred miles, the twenty-mile-wide strait narrowed into distinct channels separated by a series of islands. While the northern passage up the coast was generally protected from the open Pacific, the route was not without navigational hazards, some of them quite significant. Midway up the length of Vancouver Island the open waters of the strait narrow and pass through a series of tight passageways. The tide that flows through these constrictions generates incredible forces and attracted the attention of the northbound travelers. "Up a piece above Vancouver we came to Seymour Narrows," one writer recalled. "I'd heard about it being a dirty piece of water, so I stayed on deck to study it. It's got to be run when there is slack water, on account of the strong tide." The tide stream reached speeds of 15 knots, with the south setting flood and opposite ebb tides. And when the winds ran counter to the tide a tremendous steep sea could erupt in the matter of minutes. George Vancouver, the first European to chart this passage, commented in 1792 that the tide rushed "with such impetuosity as to produce the appearance of falls considerably high."[95] Coastal sailing directions warn that when the tides run, "the eddies and swirls are extremely heavy, and when opposed by a strong wind, the races become very dangerous to small vessels."[96] In the nineteenth century, navigators imagined even worse. "There's a sucking whirlpool. . . . It's just like pulling the plug and letting the water run round and round. Then it gets just like a funnel with all the water pushing and shoving to get into the whirl."[97] Others elaborated on these Odyssey-like hazards, one describing an English man-of-war that was "caught in the whirl. He went around faster and faster, until he was sucked down clean out of sight . . . even the masts went down in that hole. It was just the end for every soul on board."[98]

Given the often-hazardous sailing conditions along these coastal waters, mariners were not resistant to relying upon superstition in order to safeguard their passages. Not unlike the shamanistic faith of the Tlingit seamen, ships' captains relied upon ritual practices fixed in the ancient traditions of their maritime culture. Piloting relatively sophisticated machines did not stop these moderns from believing in mystical relations, omens, and good-luck charms. Sailing north in the bark *Legal Tender*, the German ethnologist Aurel Krause noted that the vessel struggled against serious head winds. Krause, then heading north to study the Tlingit and their supposed primitivity, wrote in his journal, "the captain thinks there is a witch aboard. The first mate thinks the loss of the horseshoe, which the captain had thrown overboard, is to be blamed for the steady head winds. The captain never wants to sail this ship again." Two days later the captain, in ritual fashion, stood on deck with his back toward the ocean and "again throws an old horseshoe overboard to attract good winds."[99] Krause did not elaborate on whether the winds ever came.

The strong tides, peculiar currents, and mercurial winds along the coastal passage had long plagued visiting ships. Captain George Vancouver's flagship *Discovery* struck a reef while navigating the west coast in 1792. Negotiating the narrow island channels under sail proved extremely hazardous. A lack of charts and an understanding of the tide patterns made early navigation extremely difficult. The steamer *Geo. S. Wright* sank in winter 1872 off the Queen Charlottes along the appropriately named Cape Caution. With the advent of steam-driven vessels and with more thorough charts, the coastal passage had been made safe, but only relatively so.

Despite these advances by the mid-nineteenth century, the Inside Passage's labyrinth of overfalls, tide rips, fog, and hidden reefs cowed even the most confident mariners. These waters gave no leeway to overconfidence. Tides could range up to fifteen feet above or below mean levels. At constrictions like the Seymour Narrows, billions of gallons of seawater squeezed through the narrow shots of granite mustered suddenly huge forces. "As we approached these narrows," one tourist described, "the water presented a most turbulently fascinating appearance twirling around furiously in hundreds of little whirlpools, while large portions of the surface appeared to be several feet higher than the adjoining parts, as if a submarine earthquake had raised some places and thus made the water run down hill."[100] Add a sudden wind to the scenario and sudden steep-walled waves could erupt as if from the depths, as the collision of opposite forces, the tide running hard at five knots or more and the wind blowing against the tidal river, ebb or flood could prove disastrous to waterborne craft. "The fury of their tiderips is beyond imagination," ship passenger Bernard Bendel wrote, "and their roaring noise is heard many miles."[101] Some of the narrow channels, mostly avoided by larger craft, have tidal currents that reach as much as sixteen knots. Navigating these narrows could be safely made only at slack tide, ten or maybe twenty minutes at Seymour between the incoming and outgoing tide flows. It was not always easy to determine precisely when those few minutes would fall during the twice-daily pause between ebb and flood.

Seasoned pilots salted their stories with well-timed exaggerations set to tease the newcomers. Passage from the open waters of the Georgia Strait into the channels leading north and west required vessels to pass through one of several rapids. While the Seymour Narrows may have afforded the most open channel for large ships, the pass demanded skill and timing if a ship were to avoid grounding or sinking. Ripple Rock, the tip of a submerged ridge, lay just below the water in mid-channel. Tales of death at sea were a constant for late nineteenth-century travelers. And the memory of recent disasters along the northwest coast no doubt reminded seasoned mariners and sightseers alike of the hazards found in the dark and cold waters. In June 1875, the side-wheel steamer USS *Saranac* ran afoul of the Inside Passage's dangerous tides. In preparation for the Philadelphia Centennial exposition, the 2,150-ton, three-masted gunboat with a crew of 300 had been dispatched from San Francisco to Sitka on a collecting voyage, gathering curios and ethnographic artifacts. But on the morning of June 16 the *Saranac* fell victim to the Seymour Narrows. "Here," a travel writer noted, "the contending currents take a vessel by the nose and swing her from port to starboard, and from starboard to port, as a terrier shakes a rat." The *Saranac* swung to and fro, tearing open her steel hull on the submerged ridge. All hands abandoned ship as the captain drove her bow into the nearby shore rocks in an attempt to save her from the depths. In a desperate effort to save the huge vessel, heavy hawsers were fastened from the ship to nearby trees. But as the tide ebbed, the stern sank, the ship filled and plunged to the bottom, uprooting and dragging the enormous trees with her. The ship's crew was later rescued from their rocky perch and amazingly no lives were lost.

Mariners navigating the narrows were not always so fortunate to get away with their lives. The steamship *Grappler,* originally a British gunboat serving the British Columbia coast, may have been the doomed ship disappearing into a whirlpool referred to above. She had been refitted as a freighter, supplying the canneries up the coast. In April 1883 the ship caught fire and was swept on the 15-knot tidal river into the maw of Seymour Narrows with more than a hundred passengers, mostly Chinese cannery workers, jumping overboard to swim or drown. One of the few survivors painted a horrific scene at the official inquest: "As the heat became unbearable men were jumping and falling in the water everywhere. The last ones to leave couldn't stand the shock going from searing heat to ice cold water, and their faces could be seen in the red glare before they disappeared."[102] Earlier, in summer 1881, the USS *Wachusett* ripped open her hull as she spun in the tide current. If supposedly well-trained U.S. naval vessels could meet with disaster, then what could the scores of busy freighter and passenger vessels hope for?

Tourists knew of these hazards and of the navigational difficulties encountered on their passage northward. "This Pass," Mrs. Wood wrote in her travel diary, "is only navigable at a certain stage of the tide and in daylight. The current rushes through at a furious rate, and the wind also blows very hard—the narrow passage acting as a funnel." And even at the most provident timing of the passage, perhaps ten or twenty minutes at the slack tide, "the water boils in smooth eddies and deep whirlpools, and a ship is whirled half round on its course as it threads the narrow pass between the reefs. At other times the water dashes over the rapids and raises great waves that beat back an opposing bow, and the dullest landsman on the largest ship appreciates the real dangers of the run through this wild ravine, where the wind races with the water and howls in the rigging after the most approved fashion for thrilling marine adventures."[103] Another writer emphasized the sublimity of these experiences, where the most profound truths could only be found in the intense emotions conjured by exciting, even death-defying experiences. At Seymour Rapids, the water appeared to run downhill in a rapid as if a submarine earthquake had struck, "the spectacle," the traveler enthused, "was as exciting as the Niagara rapids, and more sublime, because of the fact of being on the water, and the knowledge that there were hidden rocks all about, added just that slight suspicion of danger which stimulates the feeling of sublimity."[104] In the travelers' imaginations the experience provoked sensations of authentic living, direct contact with active nature beyond the serial events of their urban lives. Here was adventure. This was what they had come for, those approximations of authentic existence that could be found outside the ordinary redundancy of the everyday.

Their vacations were a retreat back into an imagined past. The refined effect generated by feelings of the sublime arose from overwhelming emotion. The sublime experience represented the experience of the real, that kind of precious experience that pretended to transcend the historical situation and instead allowed individuals to enter into a supposedly unmediated interaction with the natural world. And because it is supposedly timeless, the experience itself touched upon the transcendental and in keeping with an established American genre: sublime experiences were theological, where one might have touched God. The sublime relied upon the arousal of dread or a glimmer of terror. Edmund Burke, writing at the end of the eighteenth century, identified the sublime as "whatever is fitted in any sort to excite the ideas of pain and danger; that is to say, whatever is in any sort terrible, or is conversant about terrible objects or operates in a manner analogous to terror, is a source of the sublime." "That is," Burke added, "it is productive of the strongest emotion which the mind is capable of feeling."[105] "To fill the mind with that sort of delightful horror, which is the most genuine effect, and truest test of the sublime," Burke concluded. Once faced with nature's infinitude, its vast natural powers, travelers touched upon their own insignificance. Too much terror, however, would break the spell. The sublime, like the picturesque, was still the experience of observers who could stand apart; they were not full participants in nature's "delightful horrors."

Elizabeth McKinsey in *Niagara Falls: Icon of the American Sublime* insists that by the late nineteenth century, ideas about the sublime had gone out of use. "Changes in the image of Niagara Falls after about 1860 indicate a profound shift in attitude toward nature," McKinsey writes. "Both the actual scenes of the Falls [marred by excessive tourism] and the aesthetic assumptions of artists who journeyed there reveal the eclipse of the sublime as a motive force in American culture."[106] And Anne Hyde in her study on nineteenth-century tourism in the American West adopts a periodization that denotes the end of the sublime in the post–Civil War years. According to these analyses the meaning of tourist objects of the sublime became "overdetermined," and therefore lost their sublimity. But these authors' foreshortened periodization misses the enduring quality of the sublime representational style, a style that had suffused American and Canadian culture, enduring well after its supposed end. Perhaps it was this thirst for new and as yet undetermined natural objects that attracted so many travelers to the north during the last decades of the nineteenth century. The sensation of the sublime relied upon the vague sense of terror. The etymology of the word *terror* may be related to *terrain*, and hence, related to *territory* itself. And while such an etymological link appears obscure, it does suggest terror as a threat to sovereign boundaries. In the case of the sublime sensation of terror the threat was manifest as a challenge to an individual's sovereignty over self and soul. Confronting the experience of the sublime was then a reassertion of one's own sense of self-control, a sign of one's sovereignty.

The rhetorical virtues of the sublime thus served wider social purposes for those who could speak its language. Being able to speak the language of the sublime served as the imprimatur of one's upper-class status. By mastering the vocabulary tourists claimed their elite status, their social distinction. Their representations of experience along their Inside Passage tours signified the structure of social relations, and their supposedly natural positions within the social order of the era. "One venturesome traveler after another," wrote travel writer Henry Jacob Winser, "to the surprise, and not infrequently against the advice and remonstrance of his friends, ventures forth to put the claims and pretensions of the railroad and steamship companies to the test, and return to be the hero of the social circle in which he moves."[107] Travel carried a social cachet, and to have traveled came increasingly to serve as a mark of prestige. And this prestige derived significantly from the enduring aesthetic conventions of the sublime and picturesque. Winser confirmed as much when he characterized Alaskan travel as "the rapid succession of one sublime and unlooked-for spectacle after another kept the mind in a state of perpetual tension." For those who had "the means and the leisure," one travel writer boosted, "the scenic wonders of the Northwest, though discovered only within the last few years, have already made the region in which they lie as famous among lovers of the sublime and beautiful in nature, the world over, as the recent marvelous development of its agricultural and other natural resources has rendered it in the world's markets and exchanges."[108]

If tourists felt elevated socially by their conspicuous consumption, then they felt equally uplifted spiritually and individually. For Stephen Merritt the experience of the sublime was given even more significance by virtue of its perceived religious import. "The scene is sublime and had we not been almost surfeited with grand scenery it would be enrapturing," the Methodist minister wrote. "Oh the wonderful works of God! Cloud and mountain meet and blend so it is difficult to tell where the one commences or the other ends. Heaven comes down to earth and earth reaches up to heaven. Sublimity of grandeur,—quiet but immense . . . the view is indescribable—the quiet seems almost oppressive. Oh the eternal solitude of these mountain fastnesses! Wonderful! No one could

look upon the sublimity of this sunset scene and say, There is no God."
Merritt's Methodism exhibited the mark of Wesleyan discipline and self-
control. His experience of the sublime rested on what Max Weber had
recognized at the heart of the protestant impulse, the "denial of the
spontaneous expression of undisciplined impulses."[109] While Merritt's
exuberant emotionalism may have simulated a certain spontaneity, it
was anything but sudden and unstudied. His diary account reveals a consistent and thoroughly structured encounter with wild nature. Far from
absorbing the anarchic possibilities of wild nature, Merritt and his
cohort contained its chaotic potential and by association their own anomie. Instead of an undisciplined overflowing of the soul, what Percy Bysshe Shelley had called the "attempt to imitate the untameable wildness
and inaccessible solemnity" of nature, Merritt revealed his deep religious conviction. Instead, he was intent on seizing upon the transcendent qualities of the relationship between himself and God in the form
of nature.

Ironically fear, in the general sense, did not generate a sense of the
sublime. The "delightful horror" found in awesome nature could not
also be found in the social chaos and danger of the Victorian and Gilded
Age cities. The upper-class anxieties generated by a supposed excess of
democracy were displaced onto empty nature. Sublime terror was intimately class bound and rooted in those upper-class comforts and privileges. It relied upon those bourgeois benefits that afforded them their
leisure and their far-flung travel, and which allowed them to find titilla-
tion in the presence of a near terror.

In contrast to their military predecessors, tourists' aesthetic representations did not seem to dwell on the great ideological issues of the era.
Blissfully musing on the qualities of the glittering sheen of their watery
passage north, their travels seem without political content. But the
absence of any political content in their northern musings was in fact a
confirmation of their ideological bent. Their aesthetic pieties served the
moral and political counter to what they saw as a surfeit of democratic
anarchy.[110] Traveling outside of history, the bourgeois tourists retreated
from fundamental questions into a selective nostalgia.

Once through Discovery Passage and the Seymour Narrows, Alaska-
bound ships steamed west along the north coast of Vancouver Island,
passing through the Johnstone Strait and into Queen Charlotte Sound.
The Inside Passage protected shipping from the brunt of the open
Pacific Ocean for most of its nearly thousand-mile length. Instead of the
cold, salt running hills of the Atlantic that harried tourists traveling from
North America to Europe, the Alaska trip enjoyed generally sheltered
waters.[111] "You will realize," one writer encouraged, "by the compass of

your appetite, that you are obtaining all the advantages of a sea voyage without being obliged to wrestle with that much-dreaded monster, sea-sickness."[112] "Oh! it was a landlubber's paradise in which to go to sea," another pronounced.[113] These were not idle advertisements to tourists likely also considering an Atlantic crossing for the European Grand Tour. But the Inside Passage was not entirely free of open crossings exposed to the full fetch of the eastern Pacific. The coast seas were rough even in summer. And once past the north end of Vancouver Island ships crossed the forty exposed miles of Queen Charlotte Sound. Passengers on the Alaskan steamers could get their first glimpse of the Pacific's power as their ships entered the sound. They wrote less frequently of the ocean's fury. Fear and queasiness had a habit of stilling their pens and their appreciation for the undifferentiated sea. If the weather was foul, then great shrouds of white-capped swells rolled in a constant chain toward the dark shore. The conifers studding the shore would appear black, and the sea, in between the white wave crests, would look black too, and above it all gray scudding storm clouds raced. A ship's rigging would whistle and shake in the winds. "The sea was running high now and the boat," one writer recalled, "it seemed, would almost go over on its side, then back again. The sensation to me was as if I were in a giant swing, swinging the wrong way at the wrong time and often it seemed as if I were standing on my feet, then on my head."[114]

Another wave-tossed passenger noted that at "about three o'clock Thursday morning, we had reached Queen Charlotte Sound, the only rough water encountered on this inward passage, for we were really out to sea." The passage could be navigated at night, what little night there was during the long summer days, and the more scenic landscape of the inside route might be saved for daytime viewing. But passengers could not avoid the sudden swell of sea-sickness brought on by a horizon-less rise and fall of the ship. "We have had one run of 6 hours on the open sea and about 1/3 of the passengers took advantage of the fact and paid their respects to Neptune by heaving overboard, I was not among the number," one thankful traveler recorded.[115] Another fell victim to the condition, writing, "I am utterly disgusted with myself on this trip and shall not be likely to flatter myself again that I am anything of a sailor. However, this illness was short lived, for as soon as we reached the Islands again it was perfectly quiet." Turning in to Fitz Hugh Sound the steamships pressed into calm waters and for another two hundred and fifty miles enjoyed the protected but tight route up the Inside Passage. The ocean and its rollers were soon lost behind Calvert, Hunter's, and Bardswell Islands. The narrow channels were so close that a ship's spars sometimes brushed the overhanging trees. A quick dash across the twelve-mile open bight of Milbanke Sound left vessels with a stretch of

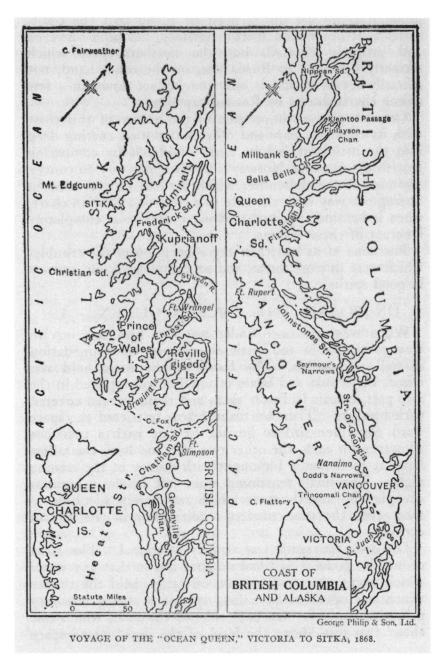

VOYAGE OF THE "OCEAN QUEEN," VICTORIA TO SITKA, 1868.

Figure 13. "Voyage of the 'Ocean Queen,' Victoria to Sitka, 1868," in *A Journey to Alaska in the Year 1868: Being a Diary of the Late Emil Teichmann,* ed. Oskar Teichmann (Kensington, England: Cayme Press, 1925). (Courtesy Yale Collection of Western Americana, Beinecke Rare Book and Manuscript Library) long inside passages behind Princess Royal, Pitt, and Packer Islands, before debouching again into Dixon Sound. The run up to the open ocean at Dixon Sound presented passengers with "the arrowy reach of Grenville Channel, which is a narrow cleft in the mountain range, forty-five miles long, and with scarcely a curve to break the bold palisade of its walls. In its narrowest part it is not a quarter of a mile in width."[116] "So straight," according to Schwatka in characteristic military swagger, "that it almost seems to have been mapped by an Indian."[117] Schwatka either did not know, or chose not to recognize, that native people were often employed as pilots and were valued for their intimate knowledge of the coast's complex hazards. Dixon Sound marked a return to American waters. Aside from a stop at perhaps Victoria, Vancouver, or Nanaimo for coal, American vessels ordinarily avoided Canadian ports of call as they steamed through Canadian waters en route to Alaska. "As soon as the fifty-fourth parallel is crossed, he is conscious of a strange new feeling toward the scenery he is passing," one travel writer noted, "the same picturesque shores, the mountains, the forests, the waterfalls with thrills of admiration. The waters of Dixon Sound are very like those of Arthur passage or Chatham Sound [in Canadian territorial water], but when an American knows he is in that inlet, his heart swells with a sense of proprietorship. He has entered into Alaska, his own country."[118] "With a new sense of ownership he contemplates the vastness of the province which he has planned to explore. It is really harder to conceive an idea of the titanic size of Alaska than to grasp its beauties as they crowd one upon another," the writer recounted.

The open reaches were not always storm tossed. The crossing of Dixon Sound in the summer travel season could be as still and smooth as an inland lake. The relatively warm ocean currents and the cold mountain air combined under calm conditions to blanket the coast in fog. As Scidmore described in her popular guidebook, the coast could be "a stilled expanse on which fog and mist eternally brood. The Kuro Siwo [Kuroshio], or Black Stream, or Japan Current, of the Pacific, which corresponds to the Gulf Stream of the Atlantic, touches the coast near this Sound, and the colder air from the land striking this warm river of the sea produces the heavy vapors which lie in impenetrable banks for miles, or float in filmy and downy clouds along the green mountain shores."[119]

The powerful Japanese current circling in a huge clockwise coriolus gyre brought warmer equatorial waters from the western Pacific into the north Pacific and eventually along the Alaskan and British Columbian coasts. The "black stream" flows like a river fifty miles wide and more than one thousand feet deep along the northwestern Pacific. The Kuroshio Extension then threads a path across the northern Pacific, dividing and diminishing in strength. But this powerful force exchanges the hot waters of the tropics with the cold subarctic waters, regulating the earth's temperature. The northwest coast owes its sweep of temperate rain forests and rich biodiversity to the effects of this current. So strong was this current that Japanese junks blown off course had been found wrecked on Attu Island in the Alaskan Aleutians, and others had been discovered disabled, floating belly up, their exposed hulls serving as wooden islands for resting gulls, drifting with the current far out at sea, and capsized sealing schooners would occasionally drift up along the coast, "unlovely as the corpse of a man."[120] It is not improbable that Japanese castaways had at times in the past settled with native North Americans along the coast. "The pulse of the Pacific is no little thing even in the quieter moods of the sea," Kipling noted.[121] Some of his contemporaries believed that the current was responsible for a warm inland sea at the North Pole. August Petermann, a respected geographer and an advocate of the theory of an ice-free polar sea, incorporated the theories of the American oceanographers Silas Bent and Matthew Fontaine Maury. He concluded that if the thermal current known as the Kuroshio (the "Black Stream of Japan") were followed through Bering Strait, it would lead to a hole that it cut in the "paleocrystic sea, a great ring of pack ice around a warm polar basin that was formed by the meeting of the Kuro Siwo and the Gulf Stream."[122]

The warm ocean current—only relatively warm, given that ten minutes or so would render most humans hypothermic—supported a stunningly rich marine life. "The Whole Sea is on Fire!" one apparently panicked tourist shouted in warning, as the steamer cut a swath through the surface plankton.[123] "The water around us," she says, "was thickly starred with phosphorescence, and at a short distance the million points mingled in a solid stretch of pale unearthly flame." Awash in the steamer's bow wave, phosphorescence sparkled with a sudden flashing glow as the ship cut through the living sea, bright with microscopic light.[124] This strange phosphorus of life revealed the nutrient-rich waters brimming with plankton visible only through the agitated glow of their phosphorous-rich frames.[125] This bioluminescence suggested the even wider range of marine life borne by this tiny life in the coastal waters.

The abundance of salmon formed the base of the region's indigenous subsistence. So rich were the annual salmon runs that the Tlingit and other coastal people organized their societies around the annual salmon migrations. Predictable runs of spawning salmon ensured a reliable and rich food supply. If ever there were a people of plenty, then the native Alaskans were such a people. "I have read about the fish in these waters," wrote a traveler, "but you can imagine nothing about it until you see them jumping up out of the water in every direction."[126] The travelers described a great living ocean of mammalian abundance, as well. Muir once noted watching "a school of porpoises, a square mile of them" from the steamer deck. And whales—periscoping orcas, migrating grays, breeching humpbacks, and lone minkies—were a common sight as they gamboled in the wind-pushed waves. Whales alongside the steamship were often inexplicably targets for men with guns, bending over the rail, firing crazily into the soft gray bodies, their broad backs arching and slipping beneath the surface.[127] The glacially obsessed Muir described the whales with "their broad backs like glaciated bosses of granite heaving aloft in near view, spouting lustily, drawing a long breath and plunging down home in colossal health and comfort." It was unlikely there was much shooting on any steamer on which Muir was a passenger. But passengers and crew fired their weapons from the decks of these ships with some frequency, often at birds. Usually gulls were the intended target, but sometimes less common birds such as eagles were killed. Eliza Scidmore described the captain aboard the *Idaho* shooting a bald eagle and displaying the dead bird on the deck. "The out-spread wings measured the traditional six feet from tip to tip, and the beak, the claws, and the stiff feathers were rapidly seized upon as trophies and souvenirs of the day," she noted.[128] Steamer passengers collected anything, even the most transient of nature's displays. Observing the intense phosphorescent sparkle, the tourists wished to possess it too. "A bucket was lowered and filled with the water, and the marvel of the shining sea was repeated in miniature on deck," Scidmore wrote.[129] But the beautiful effect was shorter lived, and like a shiny river stone, the seawater lost its luster when reduced to the tourists' bucket. They could not possess the sea's sparkle.

The sea's wealth corresponded to the dense green life of the land. "To the casual observer there appears to be timber enough in that region," one writer estimated, "to last the whole country for ages, until the forests of Maine, Michigan and Wisconsin shall grow again."[130] Another traveler likened the verdant shoreline to "such a tangle of exquisite ferns and mosses as you would expect to find only in a tropical county."[131] On the narrow passage north, travelers noted evidence of the spread of frontier settlement. In this utopian vision, hardy pioneers pushed the borders of civilization on into the northern wilderness. "On either side the shores are very rugged," Wood wrote in her journal, "and everywhere covered with timber. All through the day our view had been obstructed by the forest fires which are burning every where—probably settlers making a clearing."[132] It was far more likely that native people had started the fires. Natives had long used fire as a method for managing their environment. The tourists' romantic vision of sturdy pioneers settling the land hardly fit with the general patterns of development in the north. The steep, timbered mountain slopes of the coast were not promising agricultural locations. The expected stages of development from resource extraction to farming did not follow here along the far northwest coast. "There is no land, it is all mountains, forest, and water," advised a Haida man from the coast.[133] Settlements hugged the shoreline. The rivers and the sea provided the only reasonable means of travel. But nevertheless these travelers held to the idea of the wilderness as a stage on the way to eventual settlement, a future of farms and travelers' hotels and conveniences. Their optimism was as unimpeachable as it was blind to the realities that any permanent resident, white or native, could have set straight. The sights along the Inside Passage contained "such a large number of attractions, each of which would make the fortune of a village and a dozen hotels in Switzerland."[134] The same might eventually be true of Alaska.

Along their Inside Passage, travelers such as Stephen Merritt believed that they had found an aesthetic alternative, a place more real than the difficult urban industrial landscapes that they had temporarily fled. Travelers invested Alaska with transcendent possibilities. The experience of the sublime aesthetic led to an inchoate experience where diarists betrayed their own inability to capture an experience in words. "The average tourist has no disposition to resist the spell; he surrenders unconditionally. Lord Dufferin has pronounced the scenery of Alaska to be the sublimest he has witnessed in all his travels."[135] The overwhelming emotional experience broke an individual's ability to rationally perceive their environment. Or at least so these writers relayed in their words. "The sunset, too, is almost certain to be of such indescribable grandeur that pen and brush will be thrown down by the despairing author and artist, who will alike resign themselves to the ravishing beauty and splendor of the scene."[136] Tourists felt completely taken by their visual experiences. This was what they had come for. Their written words, claiming the uselessness of words to define their feelings, completed their experiences.

Here along the northwest coast they might experience a form of moral uplift only possible through a direct engagement with active nature. And as emphasized above, these supposedly unmediated experiences were translated thoroughly with the language of landscape painting. As the writer Eliza Scidmore explained, "The scenery gains everything from being translated through the medium of a soft, pearly atmosphere, where the light is as gray and evenly diffused as in Old England itself. The distant mountain ranges are lost in blue vaporous shadows, and nearer at hand the masses and outline show in their pure contour without the obtrusion of all the garish details that rob so many western mountain scenes of their grander effects." The muted effects of the fog-begirt coast gave, in her view, "a dream-like coloring to all one's thoughts." Given the railroad and steamship publishers' goal of boosting their tourist trade, the difficulties of the voyage, with its sometimes-constant rain, did not often make it into print. Scidmore did suggest gently that indeed the Canadian and Alaskan coasts differed from the operatic drama of the Rockies and Sierras, so oft repeated in the enormous canvases of painters such as Thomas Moran and Albert Bierstadt.

The painter Albert Bierstadt, hoping to reinvigorate his lagging career, went north in 1889.[137] But his trip afforded him few opportunities to explore the majestic possibilities of the coastal scenes. It rained every day. At Loring Bay, an isolated fishing post and cannery north of Ketchikan, Bierstadt's steamer, the 266-foot side-wheel *Ancon*, ran afoul of a submerged reef. When the tide fell, it broke the steamer's back, stranding the passengers and crew.[138] Here romance met reality.

Bierstadt and his fellow travelers confidently viewed the scenic world through sets of preestablished categories. So too did this world stubbornly resist their easy comprehension. Gazing supremely from the height of the ship's hurricane deck, they might confidently embrace the view with their own imaginative renderings. But with the huge ship marooned on a jagged reef, its keel snapped in two, the casual travelers were turned into anxious castaways. "It was a narrow escape," Bierstadt wrote of their abandoning the stranded vessel. For five days he and the other passengers lived in "Indian huts" before being rescued by another passing coastal steamship. "I was busy all the time and have 60 studies in color and two books full of drawings of Alaska . . . I am doing good things and it will pay," he reassured his wife. "This scenery is fine and also quite certain that it will pay me well," Bierstadt emphasized.[139] Scidmore in her guidebook echoed the famous painter's assessment of the surrounding landscape. Near another cannery just to the south of Ketchikan, in the Revillagigedo Channel, Scidmore exclaimed, "Of all the lovely spots in Alaska, commend me to the little land-locked bay, where the clear green waters are stirred with the leaping of thousands of salmon, and the shores are clothed with an enchanted forest of giant pines."[140] It is unlikely that the wrecked steamer's former passengers shared much enthusiasm for the scenery. Nearby Ketchikan's thirteen feet of rain each year meant a soggy experience, even though the 200 passengers and crew had escaped from the *Ancon* to the near shore without incident. Forced to bivouac in the cannery, the tourists had to endure a string of odiferous days and nights. And if the smell did not get to them, then their hosts were not the sort that these well-heeled travelers were accustomed to meeting on equal ground. "A fearful smell, a big greasy cannery," John Muir had written of these fish factories. Unable to contain his own racial views, Muir added that these canneries were full of "unutterably dirty, frowsy, Chinamen. Men in the business are themselves canned."[141] The financially independent Muir had little trouble condemning those who had to work to survive. A large number of native Alaskans staffed the Loring Bay operations, with the men fishing and the women performing most of the indoor canning labor. In 1890, at Loring men earned a dollar fifty per day for preparing salmon and women earned the same.[142] A guidebook noted as an aside that two or three fish canneries and trading stations are visited before Wrangell was reached.[143]

The visual stage of western expansion ignored the nitty-gritty labors that made the opening possible. Bierstadt personified a tradition of western landscape painting that represented the region in grandly exaggerated style.[144] He painted, like his contemporary Thomas Moran and others, in dramatic colors on enormous canvases, celebrating unambiguously the country's conquest. In his best-known paintings, human figures, if they appeared at all, were cast as tiny figures on a landscape filled with theatrical sunlight, illuminating gigantic mountains and colossal clouds. When human efforts figured in these paintings, such as the railroad cresting the Sierras, it was a plain acknowledgement that the West was synonymous with progress itself.[145] These were huge romantic art works, intended to convey the West's monumental features as icons to a nation in search of a symbolic heart. Bierstadt's works and that of his peers were widely exhibited and reproduced with the newest print technologies. This work played a significant part in helping to fix the idea of America as nature's nation. However, by the 1880s artistic tastes had changed. Realism supplanted the exaggerated romanticism and allegorical style of Bierstadt. Once the toast of the metropolitan art scene in America and Europe, Bierstadt now found his work rebuffed. No longer in favor, prices for his work plummeted. *The Last of the Buffalo* (1889) was rejected at the Paris Exposition of 1889. Perhaps he had headed north hoping to recoup his losses and to find new dramatic landscapes, a fresh view for his audience. Could the North supply new scenery capable of rekindling the drama of the romantic West? Whatever the specific reasons for Bierstadt's northern turn, he seemed certain "that it will pay me well." His northern venture, cut short by the wreck of the *Ancon,* yielded a number of sketches, but only two small oil paintings. Of the two, *The Wreck of the Ancon* was significant, in that it seemed to mark a distinct break with the progressive optimism carried by his earlier work. Here nature held none of the grandiose poise that figured in his earlier canvases. Where before machines had served in his work as powerful symbols of unstoppable progress, here the *Ancon* lay broken and useless. Where his earlier work displayed vast spreads of contrasting light and dark, here the light was diffuse. Clouds obscured the scenery. Everything

Figure 14. The Inside Passage posed considerable hazards to navigation, as the renowned landscape painter Albert Bierstadt found on his own ill-fated voyage north. Albert Bierstadt, *Wreck of the "Ancon" in Loring Bay*, 1889. (Gift of Martha C. Karolik for the M. and M. Karolik Collection of American Paintings, 1815–1865, 1947. Museum of Fine Arts, Boston)

appears slightly out of scale. The alders on shore seem large and unlikely, adjacent to the large steamer snapped in two on the submerged reef. The cloud-filled sky and the water appear fused, their colors nearly the same. The horizon vanished in an opaque blur of green gray and brown. In the foreground nothing fills the canvas, save the murky shadow cast by the ship's hulk, an unlikely shadow given the conditions. In the distance there was little to take a bearing on, a distant tree-studded island, the vague outlines of mountain slopes, but nothing more. In the middle ground, the stranded steamer dominates the painting with the stern facing the viewer. The rigging leans counter to the smoke stack, signaling that the ship's keel had indeed snapped, leaving the vessel's stem and stern askew. The *Ancon*'s paddlewheel covers shine oddly in yellow, the only sign of brightness in this otherwise gloomy scene. Bierstadt understood through experience how precarious his transit north had been. Here his attempt to rejuvenate his flagging career ran aground, both literally and figuratively. It could have been worse. Plenty of ships had met with disaster on these waters with considerable loss of life. Once castaway, the fairy-tale theater of Bierstadt's previous work withered in Alaska's relentless rain. The imperial gaze so characteristic of his earlier work seemed to have lost its perspective in the fog. Bierstadt's Alaska trip and the work it generated was hardly noticed. Certainly the dismal painting attracted little of the attention that his magisterial canvases had once garnered. There was little room for reckoning with accounts of loss and failure in the triumphalist tourist narratives.

Bierstadt's experience was unusual. Despite the occasional hazards and inconveniences sometimes experienced along the passage, most tourists returned from the north with their untarnished romantic notions intact. The traveler Stephen Merritt penned his own more characteristic satisfaction in his trip diary. "We are so comfortable, so nicely situated. The Raymond and Whitcomb Excursions are a decided success-there is no lack of anything in any way. . . . This is the Perfection of Travel. It is the heaven of rest. We enter upon the tenth day of our excursion-it seems like a month, we have seen so much, and every moment has been full of comfort and recuperation. A blessed trip."[146]

Chapter Four

Frontier Commerce

Not all travelers headed north pursuing the same scenic rewards. Though the leisure set exerted its persuasive powers over the representation of the north, and the transportation companies and advertisers marketed a particular regional aesthetic, the North and its meanings were broader and more complex than the prevailing sentiment. As powerful individuals and companies incorporated Alaska into a national network of capital, others boarded northbound steamers with different futures in mind. Workers heading north for wages, outcasts and outlaws escaped from their pasts, hopeful prospectors, women and men from all walks of life trooped northward with a world of expectations. Others awaited the arrival and uncomprehending stares of all these newcomers.

The Tlingit and other coastal people resisted the custodial attitudes that came with these onlookers. These distinct constituencies held different and often conflicted views of the so-called scenic wonderland. Holding divergent views on northern opportunities, these groups betrayed the influences of class, gender, and racial subordinations. These other travelers and their native and often reluctant hosts reached markedly different interpretations of the same spaces that the well-heeled passengers wrote of so prolifically. A lost history of gesture and unspoken words no doubt communicated the positions of these hard-bitten, or sexually suspect, or darker-skinned passengers. Occasional traces of these other lives endured alongside the records of the wealthy and well-connected leisure class.

In August 1896, Philip Van Buskirk traveled north. He had thought that this passage would be different; he'd been at sea for nearly a half century. At that moment somewhere in the heart of the Yukon a Tagish man named Keish scraped fantastic gold nuggets from an overgrown creek bed, tributary to the Klondike River. Outsiders such as Van Buskirk would not learn of this discovery for nearly a year. But Van Buskirk had little interest in the region's mineral possibilities. Nor did he venture north to see the sights. "I am not going on a trip to Alaska for the enjoyment of the grand and sublime scenery and all that," he confided to his diary.[1] His bonanza would be different. With no luggage, save that which he could cram into the pockets of his gray great wool coat, bearded and military in his posture, Van Buskirk stood apart. He made an odd figure alongside the tourist throng, crowding the deck of the steamer *Al-Ki* as she churned away from the Seattle pier that summer afternoon. "The steamer receives on board mules, horses, cattle, sheep and hogs and departing from Seattle at 3:20 p.m.," Van Buskirk noted in his careful handwriting, much practiced, having penned his daily journal for a half-century. The northern steamer routes were also trading ventures. With sufficient freight to drop off or pick up, the steamers would stop briefly at the canneries and mining supply points that dotted the coastline— Loring, Burroughs Bay, Kassan, Salmon and Red Bays, Killisnoo, Chilkat, Chilkoot, Pyramid Harbor, Tolstoi and Boston Bays, as well as the regular ports of call—Fort Wrangell, Juneau, Sitka, and during the excursion season, Glacier Bay.

Van Buskirk's bachelor life had little to compare to the bourgeois privileges enjoyed by the sightseers. He shared more with the migrating laborers who used these steamers on their seasonal parade north to summer wages, hauling fish from the sea, mineral ore from the gold-streaked veins, or ancient logs from the forested coast. But at sixty-two, Van Buskirk's working days were done and he enjoyed the slim luxury of a military pension. On the steamer deck that afternoon, he might have seemed a misplaced confederate, clad in gray, returned from that war just over thirty years earlier. And such a suspicion would have been correct. The Virginia-born Van Buskirk had fought for the South during the Civil War. In fact his military career spanned five decades. In 1846 he had enlisted in the Marine Corps at the age of twelve. Serving as a drummer, he joined U.S. forces at Vera Cruz during the Mexican-American War. He later sailed with the East India Squadron accompanying Commodore Perry's expedition to "open" Japan in 1853. A year later he fought alongside British forces in Shanghai during the Taiping Revolt. He killed a man that time. When the American Civil War began, Van Buskirk sided with the Confederate States and joined the Thirteenth Virginia Volunteers. Following his brief stint as a Confederate infantryman (he served only a few months before being captured), Van Buskirk reenlisted in the U.S. Marine Corps. He would later lament that the corps was "a huge mobilized penitentiary." He transferred to the navy and in 1869 was appointed a mate, serving another twenty-five years.[2] His Zelig-like journey through the wars and expansionist enterprises of the nineteenth-century United States had been little more than a drummer's daily grind.

When he thought of marriage the veteran mariner had been out of the navy for only half a year. His seafaring life had placed him in the

Figure 15. Philip C. Van Buskirk, undated photograph. (Courtesy University of Washington Libraries, Special Collections)

midst of far-flung American military endeavors and national civil war. A half-century of maritime military life had left an indelible imprint on the now elderly Van Buskirk. Having followed the sea all his life, he lived always on the threshold between ship and shore. A military bachelor, Van Buskirk had long rejected the social codes of domesticity and bourgeois acquisitiveness.[3] His was a life in between. And when finally free of his military duties, he entered into the less predictable realm of civilian society, settling in the Pacific Northwest.

"I avail myself of 'cut rates,' and make the trip as far as Wrangel," Van Buskirk noted in his journal. The one-way steerage fare to Fort Wrangell, Alaska, the usual first stop on the steamer passage north as far as Sitka, cost just $7. Seattle offered few hopeful prospects. "The panic of 1893 had hit it hard. A more run down at the heels and out at the elbows place I had never run across," another northern sojourner wrote of the city. It was a city of planked streets, ever-present muddiness, cow paths, and stumps.[4] Just northeast of the hardscrabble town Van Buskirk had bought a farm. But owning little more and having few connections he got itchy feet and the urge to follow the sea again.

Van Buskirk traveled lightly. He had traveled lightly all his life. He went north, as he explained to himself, "mainly to get a sight of and come to know something of the Thlinget race of Alaskans, for the chance I may have to come across a young woman of that race fit and willing to become wife or concubine to such a man as I am," he admitted in his diary. But he was not without some baggage from his previous life.

"Such a man as I am." Van Buskirk had reason enough to figure his manhood in self-consciously qualified terms. As a former military man, an officer, but one who rose up from the enlisted men's ranks and who never enjoyed the entitlements that often accompanied more well-connected and more senior appointments, and now an elderly bachelor with a stump-filled farm on the rain-soaked banks of the Snohomish River to manage, indeed, such a man as this might have reason enough to question his own marriageable attractions. But there was more. It had to do with his first loves.

Drummer George Schultz was one. "A genius of a young boy of twelve summers, good build, and size not exceeding four feet," Van Buskirk gushed over the child he met while serving in the East India Squadron. But there were others—fifer Ned Rodgers, Caravallo, a Portuguese boy also in the marines, James Keenan, Jared Mundell and the "wild" William Dagenhart, and more.[5] "I . . . have successively consummated with a vagrant, a soldier, a sailor-boy, a petty-officer of a ship and (over and over again) myself," Van Buskirk admitted in his diary.[6] Decades after Ishmael's and Queequeg's appearance, Van Buskirk's presence insists that like his fictional predecessors, men's sexuality ranged free within a ship's same-sex society.[7] But this ex-sailor's proclivities carried a burden. Van Buskirk was wracked with guilt for his homoerotic excursions and his pedophilic tendencies. He was also drawn to young boys and occasionally young girls. "My title is to a cell or crevice in the bowels of Hell,"[8] he concluded.

In the navy Van Buskirk worked and lived with men. After entering the marines as a twelve-year-old boy, young Van Buskirk came of age under the tutelage of seasoned mariners and rough recruits. In this exclusively male environ he enjoyed the camaraderie and sexual satisfactions then found on ships and in the world's ports. "There is no school of vice comparable to the navy. . . . Certainly ninety per cent of the white boys in the navy of this day . . . are, to an extent that would make you shudder, blasphemers and sodomites," Van Buskirk observed in his diary.[9] The ship's homoerotic spaces, the crowded adolescent carnality of the fo'c's'le and mid-ship hammock, or unobserved standing a night watch on the foredeck, afforded lonely men sexual adventures. Not taunted or despised, Van Buskirk's sexuality and that of his shipmates was ignored as long as their erotics remained in the background. Men such as Van Buskirk enjoyed the muscular male fellowship of the nineteenth-century navy. His intimate ties in the relative freedoms aboard ship appears to have been quite commonplace. Within this particular male subculture a code of manliness held to a spirit of mutualism that countered the rising possessive bourgeois individualism of the age.[10] The sailor had come to symbolize in the wider cultural imagination a certain sexual freedom, potently dangerous to some, suggestively liberating to others. But Van Buskirk, while certainly admitting same-sex desires, did not figure himself a member of any self-conscious subculture. Historian George Chauncey highlights that the sailor was "usually not 'of' that culture, since he typically declined to identify himself as other than normal."[11] And so it was with Van Buskirk.

These bonds permitted a variety of expressions of masculine desire. Van Buskirk's erotic life did not betray a singular nature—that of the homosexual. He did not consider himself a member of some subculture in late Victorian America. Rather, his sodomies weighed on his conscience as habitual sins for which he excoriated himself in his diaries. It was his behavior that he struggled with, not his being. Having once destroyed diary pages with evidence of his homoerotic play, Van Buskirk admonished himself, writing, "I hope I may forget what the expunged notes contained. But let no suspicion cross my mind in time to come that I am now striking from my diary some entry that would reflect disgrace upon me. No—no—no. I am my own severest judge," he concluded. "My *guiltinesses never* pass unrecorded. My crimes are all written here," he wrote.[12] Van Buskirk felt ashamed for what he did, not for who he was, at least as long as he remained in the navy.

Once separated from the military's intense camaraderie, Van Buskirk found himself cast into the more strict regimes of late nineteenth-century civilian culture, with its emphasis on respectability. He now found himself and his now peripheral sexuality at odds with an increasingly rigid sexual rule, one that determined same-sex desire as antithetical to what was considered normal heterosexual desire.[13] His same-sex forays were made illegitimate in the prevailing mood of late nineteenth-century bourgeois respectability. Sodomy had long been a forbidden act, but by the late nineteenth century such acts became the marker of a medical perversion.[14] Navigating the strictures of an increasingly normalized sexual existence posed a challenge to the old sailor's social habits. In the first month out of the service he clumsily proposed marriage to a woman, who apparently took Van Buskirk's uxorial desires as a joke. In the words of the contemporary sex theorist Havelock Ellis, "A man is what his sex is."[15] If this was the prevailing truth, and "a man's sexual constitution is part of his general constitution," the stamp of his individuality, according to Ellis, then the elder landsman Van Buskirk found himself once again at sea.[16]

"Such a man as I am," wondered Van Buskirk. Van Buskirk's notion of what his manhood meant suggested an allowance for his flexible desires. But his words also recognize that "such men as he" lay somewhere at the margins of bourgeois acceptability. Van Buskirk's self-professed qualification of his manhood served as a register of the disciplinary reach of society. Above all, Van Buskirk's sexuality served as a model for his relations to himself. He may have transgressed the gendered conventions of the day, but his transgressions were not free.

With the statement, "Such a man as I am," Van Buskirk hints at a deficient masculinity. And his anxiety over what he considered his aberrant sexuality evident throughout his early journals demonstrated the thoroughness with which this policing of bodies penetrated to the innermost psyches of the era's citizens and soldiers, whereby individuals policed their own bodies and their own desires. Ironically, Van Buskirk's half-century of military life at sea personified precisely those virile characteristics that politicians such as Theodore Roosevelt valued, men who "took up the white man's burden" in an imperial pursuit of global mastery. This ironic twist was lost on the elder sailor as he cast about the far northwest trying to fit into civilian life. In an era pervaded by Darwinian concerns about racial fitness and potential diminishment, procreative sex became socialized as the only natural sex act, even an act of patriotic duty. "Someday we will realize," Theodore Roosevelt stressed, "that the prime duty, the inescapable duty, of the *good* citizen of the right type is to leave his or her blood behind him in the world."[17] Van Buskirk struggled to become that "good citizen of the right type." "Unquestionably, no community that is actually diminishing in numbers is in a healthy condition," Roosevelt wrote, "and as the world is now, with huge waste places still to fill up, and with much of the competition between the races reducing itself to the warfare of the cradle, no race has any chance to win a great place unless it consists of good breeders as well as of good fighters."[18] "Survival of the fittest" had been replaced, in the words of eugenicist Karl Pearson, by the "survival of the most fertile."[19] Of course, fears concerning the nation's declining native-born white birthrate had been broached before, but never with as much fervor. The white birthrate had been gradually declining for nearly a century, but never before had native-born whites faced the presence of so many sudden immigrants. Roosevelt's and others' alerts to the potential ruin of race and nation figured substantially on the sexual practices of individuals.[20] And these anxieties hinged not on opinion, but rather carried the force of natural laws, biological facts that they believed to be fixed and immutable. "The sex is perverted," physician George Beard warned in 1884, "men become women and women men, in their tastes, conduct, character, feelings, and behavior." Everything seemed to be up in the air at this time.

"Such a man as I am." Van Buskirk applied the exclusionary principles of his society upon himself, at least to a degree. He applied the imperial dictates to himself, policing his own body and its desires. And of course this was how such power enforced itself, through the ongoing interior frontiers of each individual mind, placing oneself, or being placed within the strata of a national society. This life of Van Buskirk's was tied to the life of the species. But even this broad sense of inclusion—species—meant something much narrower in the late nineteenth century. "Good citizens of the right type," to borrow Roosevelt's meaning, were necessarily of northern European origin. Species then meant "white" and preferably of the better classes. Hybrids, that is, the progeny of sexual relations between the races, or even between classes, resulted in degenerate offspring as understood through the era's racial style of biological analysis. "Its successors will not resemble the healthy, normal type of the species, with capacities for development, but will form a new sub-species, which, like all others, possesses the capacity of transmitting to its offspring, in a continuously increasing degree, its peculiarities, these being morbid deviations from the normal form . . . [and] is soon rendered sterile, and after a few generations dies out," wrote the popular degeneracy theorist Max Nordau.[21] Such miscegenation led to racial degeneracy and the hereditary decay of the supposedly purer form of human development that was whiteness. But merely being white did not secure an individual from the degenerative influences resulting from deviations in the era's standards of normality.[22] And men like Van Buskirk struggled mightily to adhere to these intimations of normalcy. He engaged in a strenuous self-monitoring and had thus internalized otherwise distant relations of power, giving them a hold over his actions and thoughts, even as he believed those actions and thoughts were his own. Van Buskirk, like his fellow travelers, scribbled his thoughts into his daily journal entries. Journal keeping served as a rough technology of the self, a practice that carefully maintained the illusion of the writer's individuality, all the while complicit with the lines of power that surrounded him.[23]

Van Buskirk was an enthusiastic bachelor, at least up to the point of his northern sojourn. In the months before his August trip to Alaska, he had toured the Puget Sound barrooms and taverns, apparently enjoying the masculine camaraderie he found in these havens. Here he found a close approximation to the all-male society of the navy. And here within the precincts of a bachelor subculture based in the transient seasonal cycles of northwestern working-class life he learned of the easy availability of native women found in the shoreside towns along the northwest coastline. And so in August Van Buskirk struck out north in search of a wife or concubine.

The Alaskan coast offered for some a frontier escape into a host of fantasies. Lust for gold drew many northward; for others the draw was high wages, and for others literal lust pulled them northward to the supposedly loose fringes of the colonial frontier. Such frontier descents into sexual fantasies were common at the edges of empire. C. E. S. Wood, the young army lieutenant on leave, took refuge in a Tlingit village during his travels around Glacier Bay. Introduced to a young Tlingit woman, "young, plump, good looking (as the round faced Thlinkit Indian are good looking after their fashion," Wood took advantage of the sexual openness he found during his stay. "I was then 25 and wore sky-blue army trousers," he later wrote, and "the 'princess' after the simple frank fashion of her sex among her people made love to me."[24] Wood chose not to mention the sexual liaison in his 1882 *Century Magazine* article, "Among the Thlinkits in Alaska." Recounting his exploits to his late Victorian audience did not permit any open discussion of his sexual exploit, even though the image of the Indian maiden had been a mainstay of European-American cultural constructions assuming the sexual availability of native women. Empire provided sexual opportunities for Victorian men when those prospects were often controlled at home. And while the port cities of San Francisco and Seattle were certainly no havens for Victorian prudery, towns such as Fort Wrangell afforded possible liaisons with native women. Men like Wood and Van Buskirk followed the imperial romantic model of the lone male on a sexual adventure.

Native bodies were eroticized, as the oft-noted "Indian Maiden" in nineteenth-century travel texts suggested. And this eroticization stemmed from the reach of imperial power into the very commingling of bodies here in Wrangell and elsewhere. For like the critic Edward Said's nineteenth-century Orient, the north too took perverse shape as a "male power-fantasy" that sexualized a feminized native for Western power and possession.[25] But frontier sex came close, here, to being no more than a metaphor for other, more important (that is, male) dynamics played out in what Said calls "an exclusively male province." Sex was a trope for other power relations within the matrix of imperial power relations.

Out here on the periphery American newcomers found themselves released from the libidinal constraints of more established Victorian communities. Within the late Victorian culture of supposedly restricted sexuality, sex in the rough settlements of the northwest coast hinged on redirection, not repression. And while missionaries certainly strove to chart a new Victorian sexual discipline over the region, their early efforts were more often in vain. "Empire unquestionably gave them an enlarged field of opportunity," Ronald Hyam wrote of the relationship between empire and sexuality. Rudyard Kipling suggested the advantages of more libertine colonial sexuality in his popular verse, "The Ladies," from *The Seven Seas*:

"Now I aren't no 'and with the ladies,
For, taking 'em along,
You can never say till you've tried 'em,
An' then you are like to be wrong.
There's times when you'll think that you mightn't,
There's times when you'll know that you might;
But the things you will learn from the Yellow an' Brown,
They'll 'elp you a lot with the White."[26]

For Kipling the colonial frontier afforded a rough and acceptable school in sex. Thus educated, frontier men—soldiers and workers mostly—might return eventually to the domestic confines of the metropolis with a worldliness that served as a virtue rather than a vice. On the fringe, the invitation to guilt-free sex was made possible through the stark divide of the savage and the civilized, a divide that explicitly sexualized the colonial spaces of the globe. The sex of native women was made use of by imperial visitors. The Americans were not somehow exceptional in this capacity. The increasing bourgeois regulation of sexual behaviors may have incited sexual desire at the margins of bourgeois control in towns such as Fort Wrangell.[27] Sex reigned free, or at least with less restraint, in the outposts where native women met newcomers. Western cities and towns, fish canneries and timber company camps, mining settlements and military stations all tolerated prostitution to a degree. Some passed ordinances making sex work illegal, but then did not enforce these regulations, or did so selectively. Other government officials and company managers sought to segregate the sex trade from other commercial affairs.[28]

Transient northern work cycles followed the ebb and flow of resource booms and busts and the turn of the seasons with the long days of summer followed by the equally long, rain-soaked nights of winter. The sex trade in the North catered to these mobile workers. The well-established maritime links between coastal ports such as Fort Wrangell and Juneau connected these local hubs to San Francisco, Portland, Tacoma, Seattle, Victoria, and Vancouver. And these cities in their turn were tied to international prostitution networks that paralleled the equally wide reach of late nineteenth-century labor movements.[29]

Native women helped staff this coastal sex trade. "The women of the tribe were in the habit of going to Victoria, BC, to Fort Wrangell, and to other points, where the miners from various parts of British Columbia congregated during the winter season," one traveler observed of the coastal sex trade.[30] They led lives of "indiscriminate prostitution," according to this writer, "with the consent, and often under the escort of their husbands, fathers, or other male relatives, until they had accumulated as much money as they desired, when they returned to their village and resumed their ordinary domestic relations." Many native women traveled to Victoria, "the El Dorado for large earnings," to take advantage of higher wages for sex work.[31] It was reputed that they could earn twice as much in the cities as in the brothels and dance houses of the north coast.[32] But the hurly-burly of the sudden mineral rushes, first on the upper Stikine River just interior from Fort Wrangell in 1862 and later in the Cassiar region in 1875, accelerated the pace of coastal economic life. Fort Wrangell served as the entrepot for these gold rushes. The sex trade expanded to service the thousands of prospecting men who trooped north and through Fort Wrangell on their way up the Stikine River into the interior.

Sexual exchanges between Europeans and the coastal indigenous people had a history long antedating the Alaskan purchase by the United States. While Captain James Cook's expedition's initial contacts proved disappointing to his men, just a few years later George Vancouver's visits along the coast in 1792 were noted for his crew's sexual forays with native women.[33] This customary expression of hospitality quickly broke down into more business-like prostitution, coerced sex, and lucrative marriage ties between locally powerful natives and the newcomers.[34] Sexual liaisons with the newcomers proved economically and politically valuable as indigenous groups navigated the sudden changes wrought by the European arrivals.[35] These liaisons took many forms. Along the Northwest coast slavery was practiced, though actively suppressed, until the late nineteenth century. Slave women, usually women captured in raids on neighboring groups, often facilitated initial trade contacts between British, Spanish, French, Russian, and American shipping. The Spanish left little more than names—Malaspina, Valdez, Cordova, Rivillagigedo, Bucareli—during their brief visits along the far northwestern coast between 1774 and 1790. The French passages were even more fleeting, a single expedition under the leadership of Comte de La Pérouse in 1785. Further French activity fell victim to the Revolution in 1789 and to the loss of twenty-one sailors at the entrance to Lituya Bay north of Sitka along the Alaskan coast. "Nothing remained for us but to quit with speed a country that had proved so fatal," La Pérouse concluded of his efforts in the north.[36] Persistent Russian interest in the North Pacific and points south spurred Spanish settlement in Alta California. And Russia, or more precisely its fur-trading companies, built Fort Ross on the northern California coast in 1812. Their persistence led to a more enduring presence in Alaska. The Russian companies helped supply the Spanish with manufactured goods and established a long-term presence in Alaska, even though their California base remained understaffed and was abandoned in 1840. The Russian *promyshleniki*, the fur traders and trappers, gained a well-deserved reputation for their brutal sexual exploitation of Aleut women in Russian America during the early decades of the nineteenth century.

Native prostitution spread with the expanding fur trade, both on the coast among Russian fur traders, Hudson's Bay Company (HBC) vessels, and the Boston men, which resulted from increasingly frequent visits by American ships sailing from New England ports. In the interior where the HBC expanded its trading posts into the far reaches of the northland, close liaisons between trappers and native women became accustomed practice. Native elites profited by selling their female slaves' services as prostitutes.[37] Both native men and women profited from prostitution. While the profits helped to provide some native women with financial independence, the sex trade did little to upset the rigid hierarchies separating native elites from low-caste and slave members of their respective societies. Female slaves remained important in prostitution through the 1860s.[38] Indeed, into the final decades of the nineteenth century prostitution fueled what remained of the slave trade.[39] And, though slavery disappeared, its impact lingered on, with former slaves occupying low-caste positions within local native societies and continuing to sell themselves as sex workers in the predominantly male towns and work sites settled by incoming Americans and Canadians. While higher wages pulled many native women south to the cities, the north coast sex trade also prospered. In Sitka Russian Creole observer Stephen Ushin lamented the prevalence of alcoholism and its attendant "corruptions." "The other epidemic which rages here no less than drunkenness," he wrote, "is prostitution." "Prostitution is rapidly spreading and because of it our social life lost its former regularity based principally on accord in family life," he recorded.[40] Ushin was a member of a well-established Creole community, the result of a century of liaisons between Russian men and native women in the north. Speaking in defense of his Creole lineage, Ushin complained of the invading presence of American soldiers in the former Russian Alaska. "Until the arrival of the Americans," he wrote, "there was here some kind of balance in this respect, but with the raising of the American flag, the entire life of Sitka has been refashioned to the detriment of the entire population."[41]

In 1867 when the Americans assumed "ownership" of Alaskan territory from the Russians, an estimated 500 Europeans and European Americans lived in the entire region, while approximately 1,200 Creoles called Alaska home.[42] But if the local Creole recalled an era of sexual balance in the Russian colony, he did so with a rosy nostalgia. His was a selective recording of Russian activities in Sitka and elsewhere along the coast. Since the establishment of Sitka in [1804], then called New Archangel, Russian fur traders and workers—*promyshleniki*—enjoyed a monopoly on the coastal fur trade and its attendant sex trade, a trade that extended beyond the Aleut. Khlebnikov reported that the Tlingit, called Kolosh by the Russians, prostituted their female slaves to Russian officials and settlers in the early part of the nineteenth century.[43] In fact the spread of venereal disease among the Tlingit and Russians became so severe that Lieutenant P. N. Golovin noted, "Almost all the women who are engaged in clandestine debauchery in the area around New Arkangel [Sitka] are afflicted with this disease. At one time syphilis was so widespread among the workers and soldiers . . . that when the present Chief Manager arrived in the colonies he had to resort to forcefull measures in an attempt to wipe it out."[44] The manager ordered the scattering of brothel huts destroyed and established a central prostitution venue whereby he might control the local sex trade.

By the early 1800s the Russian fur traders, consolidated under the monopoly charter of the Russian American Company in 1799, were spread thinly over a wide coastal territory. From the sealing grounds of the extreme northern Pribilof Islands at the edge of the Arctic Ocean to the thousand-mile Aleutian Island chain to Cook Inlet and Kodiak Island, Russian interests expanded southward under the direction of Baranov, the savvy director of the company between 1791 and 1818. Baranov established New Archangel, later Sitka, in 1804, after a protracted and violent struggle with local Tlingit. In 1818 the outpost had grown in size and became the capital of Russian America. More than a century of coastal trade, principally in furs, had firmly established the practice of intermarriage. The coastwise sea otter and the interior fur trade prompted close relations between native people and the Russian American Company and Hudson's Bay Company traders as well as "Boston men," who were Americans trading independently along the Inside Passage. These liaisons produced a creole culture along the northwest coast, part Russian and part indigene, whether Tlingit, Aleut, or any number of other native groups who intermarried with Russian promyshleniki, Hudson's Bay traders in the immediate interior, or other visitors, including increasing numbers of U.S. citizens and Canadians. Where the Russians tended to accept these interracial liaisons, the American society that developed after the purchase was not nearly so accepting. Men who lived with native women came to be known derisively as Squaw men or Siwash men.

At Fort Wrangell, the Stikine Tlingit had traded with Russian American Company vessels as early as 1811. Like the other Tlingit clans further to the north, the Tlingit protected their own fur-trading enterprise, strictly controlling the movement of the trade between the interior Athapaskan groups and European traders on the coast. During the early years of Russian rule, the Tlingit resisted successfully any complete Russian dominance of this trade and their territories. Unlike their far northern counterparts, the Aleut, the Tlingit maintained more independence in spite of the Russian presence. The Russian America Company established Fort Saint Dionysius on Wrangell Island, near the outlet of the Stikine River, in 1833.[45] The river afforded access to the interior Hudson Bay trading posts and an outlet to the fur company's western network. The Russian company built this fort to help contain HBC traders then working into the upper Stikine watershed, ever nearer the then Russian-claimed coast. In 1840 the British leased the coastal port from the Russians, took possession and renamed the post Fort Stikeen. The HBC also established a post at Fort Taku near present-day Juneau, though this station was only briefly occupied. The fur-trading company quickly found it to be more efficient in terms of cost and manpower to conduct their coastal business from the mobile base afforded by their steamships. Thus, Fort Stikine was mostly abandoned by 1847.

Prostitution served as only one form of sexual liaison between newcomers and natives in Russian Alaska and elsewhere along the long coastline. In Sitka and the other Russian forts, including Redoubt Saint Dionysius (later Fort Wrangell), promyshleniki made a variety of arrangements with native women. "Some of the laborers and soldiers," according to Golovin, "who are afraid of becoming infected [with venereal disease] buy women slaves from the toions [chiefs], keep them at their own expense. It is quite expensive to support a Kolosh [Tlingit] woman; it costs from 25 to 30 paper rubles a month, which not everyone can afford. As a result, most of the laborers and soldiers look for easier alliances, and there is no possible way one can watch over them."[46] These "easier" arrangements ran the gamut from informal unions to formal marriage. But most marriages were à la façon du pays, or of the custom of the country that allowed for such intimate intercultural relations. Prostitution was not the usual sexual relationship between the natives and newcomers within fur-trade society. Many of these relationships endured as long-lasting unions.[47] And, these relationships were often initiated by native people. "The Indians," Sylvia Van Kirk writes, "initially encouraged the formation of marriage alliances between their women and the European traders . . . a marital alliance created a reciprocal social bond which served to consolidate his economic relationship with a stranger."[48]

Concubinage was the dominant domestic arrangement through the nineteenth century in the region, while prostitution flourished in the garrison and boom towns that grew up on the coast. "At present there are no marriages in the country, though plenty of concubinage," Church Missionary Society Bishop Bompas wrote from his post on the upper Yukon River.[49] But the so-called "tender ties" that marked concubinage also betrayed an often-darker side. As the regional economy moved to broader resource development, these relationships no longer served the same purposes that they had in the earlier fur-trade society. These relations, while facilitating reciprocal social, economic, and sexual ties, also revealed patterns of violence where native women suffered from abuse. Bereft of the importance these alliances carried during the heyday of the fur trade, unions between white men and native people became increasingly prone to violence and exploitation.[50]

Many of the early prospectors pursued liaisons with native women. Joseph Juneau, who staked one of the first claims near the future town site that would bear his name, lived like many of his compatriots, spending much of his time with local women. "Joe Juneau was always getting fascinated by some new squaw, and between hootch and squaws he never had a cent to get away on," an Alaskan miner wrote.[51] Amongst the male traders on the upper Stikine it was common practice to live with a native woman, called a *kluch* in the coastal Chinook patois. In winter 1895, near the Telegraph Creek trading post on the upper Stikine River in British Columbia, an Indian woman was discovered frozen to death. "The Bull Frog," as she was nicknamed by the local whites, "was lying on the trail about ³/₄ of a mile from his house dead." Apparently having left her white partner late one night, "she had started to go home and fell on the trail from drunkenness and froze to death," according to a trader's journal.[52] Local whites held an inquest the following day, but waited another day so that "the body could be thawed out." It had been 20 degrees below zero the night of her death. Her blanket-covered rigor had softened enough after a night alongside a glowing wood stove so that they could investigate. "Finished holding the inquest," the trader Callbreath wrote, "and came to the conclusion that the woman was smothered by being held down by standing on the back of her neck, by whom unknown." The investigation into the woman's murder ended as soon as her body had thawed. Callbreath's journals indicate that many, perhaps a majority, of the white men who worked as packers, trappers, traders, and miners kept native women as *kluch*. And though it would be impossible to generalize about the nature of these relationships, the casual disinterest in investigating this brutal violence suggests the inequities at the heart of these sexual liaisons. That they made so little notice of the woman's murder indicates how little her life registered in this transient and sometimes violent society.

Such violence was not limited to rough-neck frontier workers. American soldiers and sailors stationed up and down the coast following Alaska's purchase in 1867 brought their own penchants for violent domestic relationships to the native communities. At Sitka in 1874, twenty-three-year-old Mary Elizarovna Lebedev "was unmercifully beaten in the garden by her lover, an American soldier." "The beating was so cruel," according to one observer, "that since yesterday she has been unable to walk, has had to go to bed and has been given last minute communion by Reverend N. Kovrigin who noticed that her brain was evidently injured."[53] Lebedev, a Creole woman of Russian and Tlingit heritage, had a three-year-old daughter, Anna.

Such violence was not unusual. The relations between the newly arrived American soldiers and the influx of other Americans, increasingly prospectors, raised the tensions between Tlingit communities and the newcomers. "Though preserving law and order along the Alaskan coast," one traveler noted, the American military "had not tended to improve the moral condition of the Indians."[54] The Russian Creole viewed the American newcomers with distrust, especially given the condemnation that these newcomers registered in their observations of Russian America. "The meaning of truth and honesty is incomprehensible to these degraded wretches," wrote William Dall. "Life among the natives is far preferable to being surrounded by white men of such a despicable class," he wrote.[55]

Though to be sure the social conditions found along the coast with the arrival of the Americans were far from stable. Most observers highlighted what to Victorian mores appeared to be utter destitution and immorality. "It seems quite evident that a very low state of morality reigned in the colony previously," fur trader Emil Teichmann observed during a business visit in 1868. He noted that the Alaskans seemed "to live together without regard to age or sex."[56] Sexual orientation appeared to enjoy an open liberty in the rough Alaskan coastal villages where European, American, Native Alaskan, and Creole bodies mixed freely. "There came to light almost every day some scandal not unlike those which have become familiar in the *demi-monde* of Paris . . . in some cases [men] even openly promoted it [prostitution] in order to gain a profit for themselves," Teichmann sermoned.[57]

The U.S. Army had occupied six posts in Alaska between 1867 and 1869, with Sitka and Fort Wrangell the principal military sites. The newly purchased territory was administered initially as a military and a customs district, though it was not clear which division should exercise authority over coastal governance. This division and the lack of an organized civilian territorial government led to haphazard administration and law enforcement during these early years. Alaska officials noted consistently the widespread effects of the uncontrolled liquor trade, mostly locally distilled *hootchenoo* or molasses rum, also known as hooch. "One of the direct evil results of this detestable vice has been the debauchery and degradation of the native women by a licentious soldiery," lamented Treasury Department agent William Gouverneur Morris in an 1878 report.[58]

By fall 1870 the army had pulled its garrisons from all its posts but Sitka. But the discovery of gold in the Cassiar region in the upper Stikine River drainage area in the early 1870s brought the army back to Wrangell. Having routed the gold in the south at Fraser and Cariboo, prospectors turned northward. In the first year of the Cassiar rush several thousand miners hustled through Wrangell and then up the Stikine River into the interior gold country. Other strikes at Sitka and Sum Dum Bay scattered eager gold seekers throughout the region's exposed quartz outcrops and alder-thick creek beds. Prospectors crowded up the Stikine River in spring 1873, traveling upriver to the HBC post at Glenora, then overland to Dease Lake. They returned to the coast in the late autumn carrying their gold, and they did this until the gold and their endurance ran out. Those first two years they brought out more than two million dollars in soft nuggets and dust. In the winters the white population increased, with several hundred miners waiting out the cold drizzle on the coast and heavy snow in the high country until spring, when they would sled up the frozen rivers before the ice broke up. Native Alaskans congregated here as well. "The Indians belonging to this place (the Stickeens) number about two hundred and fifty," George Bailey reported. "At the same time, there are upwards of two thousand about the place, consisting of Chilkats, Tahkos, Sundowns, Kakes, and Hydas, during the summer and fall, employed in transporting goods and stores up the Stikeen river to the gold mines. These Indians quarrel among themselves, but have little, if any, trouble with the whites, and the people of Wrangel consider themselves in no danger from them, claiming that if the white people (miners who winter here) behaved as well as the Indians, it would be a quiet community [sic]," Bailey described.[59] But by 1879 the gold had mostly played out. Hundreds of Chinese miners took over the claims, "being of a persevering nature, satisfied with small returns for their labor," according to Canadian geologist Warburton Pike, who, passing through the region in the late 1880s, noted the shift in the diggings' population.

In 1877 the Army withdrew its garrisons from Alaska and the lone artillery company that had occupied Fort Wrangell retreated to the south, finding action in the wars against the native people of the continental West. A scattering of customs collectors and vessels of the revenue cutter service provided the only formal U.S. government presence, until the fear of an uprising in Sitka in 1879 spurred the U.S. Navy to again patrol the coastal archipelago. In 1884 the U.S. Congress passed the territory's First Organic Act, establishing Alaska as a "district" and providing for civil government. Civilian government did not mean local rule, as the new district was effectively governed through the federal appointment of officials, most importantly the district court judge and the governor.[60] Given the inadequacy of this civil governance, Wrangell's residents and the rest of this vast district were left largely to their own devices. "The state of the law is uncertain," Alaska authority William Dall lamented as late as the mid-1890s, "the seat of authority is obscure, divided illegitimately between naval officers, the revenue cutter service and a powerless governor."[61]

But in the boom years of the 1870s, towns such as Fort Wrangell seethed with fevered Argonauts. "Following in the steps of the troops, come the miners, who seem to have emulated the sons of Mars in the prosecution, performance, and mad riot of the quintessence of vicious enjoyment," one government agent reported.[62] In addition to its casual and tolerated violence, the sex trade carried other devastating consequences for the native Alaskans. "A whole race of prostitutes have been created, and the *morbus incessens* of the Latins, which the Roman doctors declined to treat, is found in full feather and luxuriant blossom," the agent continued. "Today there is not a single surgeon or physician in Southeastern Alaska, and when a victim becomes infected with the *lues venerea*, his fate can be predicted. Syphilitic diseases are the great bane of the country; but few of the women who indulge in promiscuous intercourse are free from the poisonous taint."[63] Characteristically, the agent represented the white clients as the victims of this epidemic. Tlingit women, and undoubtedly a few white women as well, were portrayed as poisonous temptresses. Judging by the notations in the journal of the HBC trader at Telegraph Creek, up the Stikine River from Fort Wrangell, the disease spread into the interior with the miners' sluicing. The trader John C. Callbreath noted the then-accepted treatment— "Injection for Gonorhea, 10 [unreadable] zinc, 3 "sul morphine, 4 oz. Water," making certain that he had the plenty of the much-requested remedy on hand.[64] And when imported supplies ran out, the infected resorted to local sources, "2 table spoons full balsam . . . 1 tin cup water soft-mix with 4 spoon full Cat[?] wood ashes, pour off when it settles and mix with the balsam. 3 tea spoons a day taken one hour before meals," according to Callbreath's treatment notes.[65]

The wages generated by the sex trade ensured the presence of native brothels in the small towns dotting the coastline, and especially those such as Fort Wrangell that became supply centers for gold seeking and salmon factories. The perceived need to control white men's frontier sexual adventures and the supposed profligate corruptions of the region's native people spurred the early efforts of missionaries. The Russian Orthodox Church and the Roman Catholic Jesuits had been active for some time, but had relatively little success in converting native Alaskans. Both churches had more success with more northern native groups along the Bering Sea and up the Yukon River drainage area. It was the Presbyterian Church that enjoyed substantial government support and established its missions and schools in Wrangell, Juneau, and Sitka and grew to hold the most influence over native and newcomer sexual relations.

The missions targeted specifically prostitution's "wages of sin" in their efforts to redeem Tlingit. Missionaries exerted their efforts on Tlingit children, especially girls, and created a system of schools through which they might inculcate their foreign ideas.[66] In Wrangell Amanda McFarland established a school for Tlingit youth in 1877 with the support of the Presbyterian Church. Presbyterian home-mission organizer Sheldon Jackson followed the example set in Wrangell. The so-called "Apostle of Alaska" set up the Industrial Boarding School for native Alaskan children in Sitka the following year.[67] Schools also appeared subsequently at Chilkat and Juneau.[68] Within a year McFarland had received funding for a boarding school for girls, intending to rescue them from the regional sex trade. "It was a very necessary step in order to rescue them from the temptations with which the new order of things now surround them," one observer wrote, echoing the general belief among the coastal missionaries.[69] The missionaries strove to domesticate the rough features of southeastern Alaskan settlements. "The town of Wrangell is a mud-hole and a wharf," described one missionary, "at least, it must have been only that before the missionaries made it a home also."[70] Missionaries, but particularly female religious workers such as McFarland, created new moral territories for themselves in this wider public world.[71] Within five years, Jackson and his fellow missionaries had helped to establish six schools in the region, three of which were boarding schools. The zealous newcomers did not hesitate to claim a superior status for themselves, likening their efforts to a wider world stage, but particularly to Christianity's rescue of Africa. "The Church of God has ever been the conservator and the pioneer of true science and of discovery," wrote an Alaskan missionary. "No Stanley would have flung wide the doors of the 'Dark Continent' had not a Livingstone and a Moffat gone before," she concluded.[72] Transient observers such as John Muir were less sanguine about the supposed civilizing virtues of the mission efforts. "It is too often found that in attempting to Christianize savages," Muir concluded, "they become very nearly nothing, lose their wild instincts, and gain a hymnbook, without the means of living, being capable of taking nothing more. They mope and doze and die on the outskirts of civilization like tamed eagles, in barnyard corners, with blunt talons, blunt bills, and clipped wings."[73]

In southeastern Alaska Tlingit women were "sent to the mines, while the husband lives in idleness at home on the wages of their immorality," Sheldon Jackson noted in his widely read *Alaska and Missions of the North Pacific Coast*.[74] Jackson toured the nation, lecturing to congregations on the dire need to save Tlingits from their own "barbaric" institutions and the onslaught of civilization. The "Indians regard their women as slaves," Jackson insisted.[75] "When they arrive at the age of twelve or fourteen years, among the Tinneh, the Thlinkets, and others, they are often offered for sale. For a few blankets a mother will sell her own daughter, for base purposes, for a week, a month, or for life. Sometimes they are traded off by the husband for something he may desire," Jackson wrote.[76] Amanda McFarland's mission became the keynote in Jackson's public appeals for financial assistance to the northern mission efforts. "It will be borne in mind at that time she was the only Christian white woman in Wrangell," Jackson emphasized. "Mrs. McFarland felt from the very commencement of the mission, the need of a 'Home' into which she could gather such promising girls as were in danger of being sold, and train them up to be the future Christian teachers, wives, and mothers of their people." Jackson's text highlighted the oppositions

between the Tlingit and the Americans, emphasizing their native barbarism against white civilization, native darkness contrasted by the European American lightness, Tlingit irrationalism and superstition
alongside the newcomers' reason and science, the indigene's marriage
to nature and the Christians' cultural dominion over that nature. Their
colonial discourse fixed native Alaskans as a population of racial degenerates and thereby justified their conquest and legitimated their systems
of administration and instruction.[77] But a paradox lay at the heart of the
natives' objectification. Attempts to domesticate the Tlingit relied upon
their primitive otherness and the possibility that they might be remade
as Christian westerns. Missionaries in particular could not admit the
unconvertible nature of natives; they had to assume that their complete
assimilation was possible. The colonized native Alaskans could not be
completely different from the newcomers, because to admit such would
undermine the very legitimacy of their assimilating project.

Prospectors, northern merchants, and the beachcombing rabble pop-
ulating northern settlements such as Fort Wrangell met the missionary
vanguard with distrust. These northern workers understood their sexual
intimacies with native women in a slightly different light. "The Indians
here do not withdraw from white people; they rather actively seek contact with them," a prospector recalled. "Traders and miners speak the
language of the Native more or less. It is easier for them to learn Indian
because many of them live with Indian women whom they purchase
according to local custom. Fifty dollars is the usual price," he remembered.[78] A *San Francisco Chronicle* reporter went so far as to characterize
the relations between missionaries and local nonnative Alaskans as a
war. "I do not say that all the men who have come to Alaska as missionaries are all schemers, but still they do have that reputation. They are
adept at antagonizing. Every settler distrusts them. . . . There is a war
between the settlers and the missionaries," the reporter commented.[79]
While this may have been more hyperbole than fact, the so-called settlers, mostly transient prospectors, were coming increasingly under the
moral control of the missionaries. They were especially upset over the
missionaries' efforts to end their relationships with native Alaskan
women. Long-time trader Callbreath recorded the travail of prospector
Jake Johnson, who was "hauled up for living with his woman or wife without the formality of marriage. He was fined $15.00 or one week in jail."[80]
Further north, along the Bering Sea coast, more formal arrangements
presided. "The white [fur seal] hunters are generally married to Creole
or Aleut women. The law prohibits the killing of any fur-bearing animals
in Alaska by any but natives, and the regulations of the Treasury Department recognize as natives white men who have married native women,"
one-time Alaska governor Alfred P. Swineford wrote.[81] "This is a new fad

of the missionaries to force the people to marry their squaws," Callbreath complained of the Fort Wrangell Protestants' social control. The actual legal status of these marriages remained in question, as did many legal technicalities in the loosely governed district of Alaska. "Altho Jake was married according to the tribal rules and had been living with his woman for over 20 years. It will create some stir among Indians and whites [*sic*]," Callbreath predicted. Another Alaskan miner visiting Juneau noted the changes exacted by the religious missions. "I was fortunate in arriving in 1895 for I saw the last of the old regime in Juneau. Society was changing, men bringing in their wives and social lines beginning to be drawn," William Johns reminisced.[82] "In the spring of [18]'96 the white girls forced out the Indian women from the dance halls where they had danced on an equality with them and the Indians opened a dance hall of their own in the Indian Village down the beach, but could not compete with the white girls uptown though some of the old-timers and squaw-men went down occasionally," Johns wrote.[83] Johns's recollections indicated that white prostitution began to assert control within the frontier demi-monde, even as the Protestants sought to control sexual relations between white men and native women.[84] The Christians' controlling impulses sought to direct lower-class whites' behavior, as much as that of the native Alaskans.

The Protestant attack on frontier sexual practices would achieve some eventual success. More than a decade later a published study of the Tlingit indicated that sex work among the native people had diminished in importance. "While prostitution is practiced, it is not advertised and fostered as it is with civilized races," Livingston Jones noted in his study of the Tlingit in the 1910s. "Women are debauched but are not willing parties to the transaction. . . . There are a few native girls who imitate their fallen white sisters. They barter their virtue, and some of them, when they find themselves trapped, resort to abortion . . . while there may be yet a few native girls who lead a fast life, the number is small as compared with those who were once given to it," he observed.[85]

When Philip Van Buskirk traveled to Fort Wrangell in 1896 the region was on the cusp of change. Missionary control over native-white sexual liaisons helped mark the shift from a sex trade that employed native women toward an emerging prostitution economy staffed by white women sex workers tied to wider regional and national networks that extended to cities such as San Francisco, Seattle, and beyond. But it should come as little surprise that Van Buskirk sojourned northward believing that he might find a Tlingit wife or concubine. For several decades the supposed sale of native girls and women, or the ease of fixing a marriage through cash transactions, pervaded the commonplace understandings of late nineteenth-century European-American north-westerners. "It is a common practice for Indian parents to sell their daughters, or husbands their wives, for a blanket or a few pounds of tobacco, to the white miners for the season, at the end of which the women return to their homes, to be disposed of in the same manner the following year," one observer wrote.[86] "Theoretically, every man is in favor of missionary work," Alaskan expert William Dall wrote on the missionaries' efforts at reform, "but when, as in the present case . . . [they] teach the Indian . . . on no account to sell his young daughters to white men, as was formerly the practice."[87] The anthropologist Franz Boas, studying the Northwest coast native peoples in the 1890s, explained how easy it was for outsiders to misconstrue native marriage customs along the northwestern coast. Writing of the Tlingit's southerly neighbors, Boas observed, "Marriage among the Kwakiutl must be considered a purchase." But, he stressed, "the object bought was not only the woman but the right of membership in her clan for future children of the couple."[88] "The charge of selling girls was," according to historian Douglas Cole, "erroneous in the sense of a father profiting commercially, except in the very short run, from the 'sale' of his daughter." On the other hand, the affair did have the air of a transaction, whether material, religious, or ceremonial, because of both the initial bride price and the repayment, made in goods and, more significantly, through the bestowing by the bride's side of rank, privileges, and names upon the groom's.[89]

Such transactions did not imply a "sale." Clear distinctions existed between the transfer of wealth connected with acquiring a bride and ordinary buying and selling.[90] Wealth was group, not individual, property, according to anthropologist Philip Drucker.[91] The practice of polygyny, often involving the marriage of Tlingit men to interior Athapaskans, also suggested the formality of a business transaction. The Tlingit guarded access by outsiders to interior fur-trade routes and through these marriage alliances helped to secure extended business arrangements between strangers.[92] But among outsiders, these native marriage practices still held the appearance of a purchase. No doubt the prevalence of prostitution strengthened white men's impressions that native women could be bought. Too close contacts with the indigenes prompted fears of sexual regression among whites. It was their own lusts, real or imagined, that they feared, particularly working-class white men who might, it was believed, succumb to the supposed uninhibited sexual energy associated with the so-called savage.

Native practice of marriage alliance and a tradition of freer sexual relations conflicted with bourgeois Western sexual ideals. In the contrast between these traditions, the newcomers stigmatized the natives as given over to degraded savage behaviors. "The women are often very pretty . . . I have even seen girls who in form and features possess a beauty and grace which would be acknowledged anywhere," one traveler remarked. "Their sense of morality is, however, not very great; for, true children of nature, as they are, they follow the desire of the heart without hesitation."[93] How different were these views on native women from what either bourgeois or working-class European-American society practiced at that time? "The Victorian institution of marriage," Anne McClintock writes, "as it stood was no more than the symbolic and contractual surrender of a woman's sexual, property and labor rights into the hands of a man."[94] Though this may exaggerate the social experience of late nineteenth-century marriage practices, McClintock's observation exposes the legal structure of European-American marriage rites. And while bourgeois white men and women looked upon Tlingit sexual relations as utterly alien, commenting often on the unfortunate treatment accorded native women, they seldom noted the patriarchal streak that ran through their own bourgeois marriage practices.

Frontier towns such as Fort Wrangell were realms apart, realms of sexual disorder in the eyes of bourgeois visitors and missionaries. The prevalence of prostitution and "mixed-race" liaisons evidenced, according to their world view, the degenerate fringe of empire. Again McClintock notes the provocative and symbolic message passed between bourgeois visitors and native prostitutes. These women were seen as especially atavistic and regressive. "Inhabiting as they did, the threshold of marriage and market, private and public, prostitutes flagrantly demanded money for services middle-class men expected for free," McClintock observes. "Prostitutes visibly transgressed the middle-class boundary between public and private, paid work and unpaid work."[95] And while the tourists who visited these roughshod towns were unlikely johns in this coastal harlotry, they were nevertheless critical observers. As the missionaries fixed their attentions to domesticating native homes, the excursionists set their sights on improving the view.

Sightseers toured Tlingit homes as thoroughly as they scanned the natural landscapes for sublime views. Touring Tlingit households, "the white visitors made themselves at home, scrutinized and turned over everything they saw with an effrontery that would be resented, if indulged in in kind by the Indians," travel writer Eliza Scidmore observed.[96] "The one door gives entrance to an interior, often twenty and forty feet square, and several families live in one of these houses, sharing the same fireplace," one traveler noted. This domestic communalism violated the revered conjugal ideals of the visitors. Victorian sexual discipline necessitated the privacy of the separate sphere. Sex was a private affair. And the nuclear family was the foundation for setting out bourgeois identities. Late Victorian domestic life set strict libidinal constraints, or at least the premise of constraint. Eroticized racial others living in open communal situations could hardly be expected to take up the controlled sexual lives and individualistic ambitions of property ownership demanded by bourgeois society. Native sexual deviance stemmed from the absence of what was then deemed the proper domestic arrangement of the supposedly natural reproductive social unit.[97]

In the territories like Alaska, late nineteenth-century anxieties regarding the fate of the nation and race converged around the family.[98] A community's sexual practices were tied closely to ideas about the nation and the economy. If native peoples were to acculturate, their supposedly savage ways needed to bend to bourgeois mores. "A Christian Indian," wrote missionary (and later Alaska territorial governor) James G. Brady, "properly . . . feels that their own safety is in having a separate house, where they can have the privacy of family life. . . . To meet this increased expense the Indians . . . must be put in the way of earning more money. To Christianize the Indians without helping them to new industries and new methods of earning money is to impoverish and make them more wretched. The work of the church is only half done in giving them the gospel; she must also assist them in their efforts to live a Christian life."[99]

A less harsh brand of social evolutionism allowed that native peoples might endure (where eugenics proponents predicted only native demise as a weaker race in a losing struggle for survival), if only they could be encouraged to take up rationality over instinct.[100] "Indeed American civilization," Septima Collis inveighed, "is doing a great deal for the Siwash. It reminded me of the story told me by an officer who accompanied Commodore Perry's expedition to Japan, to the effect that when they first arrived they could drop a five-dollar gold piece in the street and find it there the next day, because no man but the owner would dare lift it; but in a month or two the growth of American civilization had been so rapid that, at the sound of the fall of a quarter, a dozen Japs would madly rush at it to put foot upon it, each roundly protesting that it was his."[101] "Siwash" was the common term adopted by white visitors for the coastal people, derived from the French *sauvage*, or savage. The wonders of progress, thought Collis, were soon to spread over the "newly caught, sullen" peoples of the far Northwest. Native Americans, it was believed, needed to be spurred by envy to desire what the newcomers desired, to imitate their wants, to be on the road to European-American progress and civilization.[102] Their careful attentions to native domestic lives mirrored the visitors' own position that the solution to social disorder lay within the family.[103] Sex and its control was a thoroughly political affair.

Van Buskirk would not have been aware of all of this history. But it was there nonetheless, there in the taverns and shabby hotel lobbies of the rough towns fringing the Puget Sound, there in the timber camps, fish factories, and mining outposts, there in the white consciousness of what was possible, of what could be had for a few dollars or more, of what one's skin color might entitle him to. His decision to head north searching for "a wife or concubine" was founded upon this unthought past. Van Buskirk's moves were determined in their way by all the secret affinities that linked him to this region's sexual past; a chance conversation over beer about sex.

And curiously, Van Buskirk, who had earlier considered his seaborne life as one of imprisonment, found new shackles in the supposed freedom of civilian life. He was free, but not free. Free of his past life subject to the rigid discipline and hierarchies of the state's military might. What appeared to be a severe and regimented life in the marines and navy— those institutional extensions of the state—had been, paradoxically, the most free with respect to his sexuality. But in civilian life he found new strictures. Going into what would seem to have been the most free and celebrated realm, that of the frontier, that realm of self-definition outside of the reach of societal controls, was in fact the most un-free. Here he felt more acutely the pressures to conform and police his sexual proclivities. As his contemporary Oscar Wilde wrote, "Under the little tent of blue which prisoners call the sky."[104] Where Wilde's imprisonment was the jail itself, Van Buskirk's gaol was out in the open, in civilian society.

The body had become a site of more systematic political attention. While governments passed new laws controlling directly what men and women might do *with* their bodies, it was not the juridical categories of control that effected the most sustained surveillance of citizens' activities. Rather, new scientific categories of definition, discipline and disease, normalization and regulation achieved far more thoroughly what laws sought to suppress. Individuals such as Van Buskirk monitored themselves, and thus internalized the relations of power. His self-surveillance in effect constituted his self. Sexuality possessed the soul of each individual, because identity came to be seen as emerging from sex itself. Controlling one's sexual instincts implied a kind of sovereignty over oneself. Claims to territorial sovereignty complemented the social strategies of self-government. The technologies of the self—journal-keeping, even travel itself—worked as tools to hone individual identities. Van Buskirk made himself into an object to be seen and judged, and in so doing allowed in all those forces of society then propagating new forms of discipline, agencies for social control that might optimize certain bodies' capacities, and thereby improve the racial qualities of future generations. The great strategies of geo-politics hinged as much upon the little tactics that controlled the habits of men such as Van Buskirk, or the women missionaries, virtually anyone, as it did on the swing of military and political power. Techniques for disciplining individual bodies were followed by the emergence of the "population" as an object of control. And in administering the life of society, careful statistics were gathered to document the native population of the region.

And yet, Van Buskirk was still drawn to forbidden fruit. His earlier admissions to having had "irregular concupiscible thoughts" in the presence of children shadowed his travel north.[105] He filled his diary with copious notes about the children he met during his trip—notations that must be considered in the context of his admitted sexual relations with five-year-old Harriet and eleven-year-old Julie, and with innumerable boys.[106] (There is a danger here. When considering Van Buskirk, we should be careful to reflect on his sexuality and the disturbing dimension of his pedophilia within the context of his personal and individual history and what it might suggest about nineteenth-century tensions. But we should not understand his homosexuality and brief pedophilic inteerest as necessarily linked or determined beyond the scope of his own particular history. That is, we ought to reject presentist judgments that see the one implicated in the other.) Upon meeting Stikine Tlingit clan chief John Kadashan, also traveling in steerage, Van Buskirk spent more time describing his daughter "Elizabeth, a very nice, gentle, good natured, good looking, well dressed girl of fourteen who speaks English fluently." Of another young passenger, "Eola Elgro Miller—a sweet little girl, I am already on the best of terms," he wrote. After arriving in Wrangell, Van Buskirk befriended another child: "Have already a little Thlinget child friend, a girl of about six years, bright and gleesome, whom I meet on the long plank walk." Later he spends the day with seven-year-old "Sandy Clark (quarter Indian)." "Sandy and I go hunting for wild strawberries this afternoon . . . but if we miss the berries, we have at least a bathe in Sawmill Creek," Van Buskirk chronicled of his first full day in town. In the following days, the old sailor amused himself by strolling the town with a precocious twelve year old, Charles Cagle, son of the town's store clerk, "a bright white boy." But of the Tlingit he developed a less hopeful opinion, noting, "My dignity ruffled this afternoon by what appears to be saucy deportment on the part of a young Indian girl." Van Buskirk's libidinal currents flowed in many directions. Despite his impulse to marriage, his visit to Wrangell seemed more intent on revisiting other fields of desire.[107] However, there is no indication that he followed his child interests further than seeking youthful accompaniment during his brief stay. Were these rapturous swoons over children, neatly penned in his diary? Or were they merely innocent expressions of an old man enjoying their youthful presence? Does it matter?

Van Buskirk was not free from exercising the power of his race and gender. And though his possible persecution (even that of his own punishing guilt) as a peripheral sexuality may have cast him as an outsider, he too enjoyed the power of the markers of his white manhood. Van Buskirk's travel north is not just a prescient example or a telling anecdote. His life, recorded in his own hand, is a trace. Van Buskirk's knowledge about himself implicates not only the peculiarities of his existence as an individual, but also the constitution of his identity through all the hidden lines of social arrangement, lines that tied him inextricably to the question of sex, a question whose answers lay not only within Van Buskirk, but also outside in the late nineteenth-century naturalization of social, economic, and political concerns.

Arriving on an unusual southeastern Alaskan morning, "the sun out, breezes light, and air balmy," the old sailor strode across the stone shore wreathed in seaweed red and brown. Stumps and logs, moss covered, blocked the town's two crowded streets. The ground itself was "a degraded bog, oozy and slimy, too thin to walk in, too thick to swim in." And the village itself was "a moist dragglement of unpretentious wooden huts and houses that go wrangling and angling along the boggy, curving shore of the bay for a mile or so."[108] Panning his gaze along the sweep of the ramshackle waterfront, the newly arrived Van Buskirk jotted down the pertinent details, a studied practice for the military mariner, who had carefully eyed the world's ports. "I stand at the end of the long wharf and count 139 houses averaging, I think, three rooms each. They are mostly well built houses and those occupied by the Indians differ in no respect as to general style from those of the whites: they all look alike outside," he recorded in his journal. "These Indians, however, are in their domestic habits, so far as I can see, quite as untidy as the Irish," he compared.[109]

Here at edges of American and Canadian territorial expansion the construction of bourgeois white racial identities relied on familiar divisions. Van Buskirk easily assumed the discourse of empire, dividing colonizer from colonized, but also separating the upper classes (and those who desired such a status like himself) from their subaltern counterparts. And why not compare the immigrant Irish, who one contemporary had called the "White Indians of Ireland"?[110] "Indian-ness" had long occupied a symbolic position in the social landscapes of the New World and the Old.[111] These images of domestic degeneracy were a stock feature of bourgeois critiques of racialized others, whether on this far northern periphery or in the urban immigrant metropolises. Skin color served as an imprecise marker of superiority.[112] Instead the iconography of domestic life served to represent the status and hierarchies of the colonized and colonizers. Comparison of natives with foreign immigrants justified the exploitation of natives *and* the domestic repression of immigrants as urban savages likened to their colonized brethren at the margins. Class inequalities had been naturalized through the ubiquitous grammar of race. And these inequalities became more entrenched by virtue of these ongoing comparisons between the hinterlands and the centers of power.

Society explicitly positioned its lower classes alongside "savage" others in the discourse of the day. The working poor, "persistent paupers," prostitutes, criminals, revolutionists, and anarchists all carried the "stigmata" of "race degeneration," even though they might be white. Sexual deviants, as a prominent degeneracy study by nineteenth-century sociologist Eugene Talbot highlighted, were representative of a "still blacker phase of biology."[113] The metaphor of race suffused all levels of social differentiation. Explicitly linking race, biology through gender, and sex, late nineteenth-century theorists relegated all forms of degeneracy to the overarching frame of race difference with its hierarchy of color marked on the body itself. Degenerates need not be identifiable by skin color alone, though their degeneracies, once discovered, marked them as black. The supposed collapse of native Alaskan society hinged as much on outside influences as on the presumed evolutionary weaknesses of the so-called primitive society. "The result of the '*devil's* missions' to Alaska," wrote missionary Carrie Willard, "prosecuted by the whiskey dealer, the license vender, the dance-house proprietor, and by men who, having forsaken the teaching of good mothers and prostituted their own God-given instincts, have, instead of making pure and happy homes with women of their own race and intelligence, taken advantage of the native custom of marriage to build a domestic structure which cannot endure and which works ruin to all concerned." Making Indians into white men and women did not include blurring the lines of race and class. Bourgeois critics of this sexual frontier sharpened their attacks as often on the degeneracy of the working-class white men living in and around the Tlingit coastal villages. Debates about sex served as focal points for struggles over power, uneven struggles where lines of race and class became blurred. Careful attention to the domestic details of native life, what Willard called "the daily recurring scenes in those 'dark places of the earth' that are 'full of the habitations of cruelty'" might eventually reform dangerous primitives.[114]

If some Alaskan visitors lamented the Tlingits' presumed barbarisms, others had more positive impressions of these native Alaskans. "I do not hesitate to say that if three-fourths of these Alaskan Indians were landed in New York as coming from Europe, they would be selected as among the most intelligent of the many worthy emigrants who daily arrive at that port," wrote Vincent Colyer, Special Indian commissioner to Alaska.[115] Regardless of these outsiders' perspectives—positive or negative—on Tlingit villages, the figures of comparison were most often reminiscent of the urban savages in the hot summer cities from which these tourists and other visitors had escaped. Travelers used their experiences in Alaska and other frontier locations to help them think about questions of race and gender, nation and citizenship. By the late nineteenth century, workers too were savages.[116]

How can we explain the coincidence of Van Buskirk's homosexuality, alongside his patriarchal heterosexism, which had little to do with actual sex and everything to do with power, the peculiar powers of masculinity and whiteness. Just as Van Buskirk had criticized Tlingits and the Irish, another observer might have seen the old sailor's sexual deviance as the marker of a savage, the stamp of blackness. But Van Buskirk's sexual proclivities, though deemed degenerate, did not occur outside of their own unequal, power-determined oppositions. His homosexuality had not been practiced as an adversarial politics, and in many ways, as Alan Bray has written, such same-sex behavior "merely repeated prevailing patterns of dominance and subordination in cultures characterized by gender polarity."[117] And so his search for an Indian wife seemed to reflect unselfconsciously patterns of customary power. In order for Van Buskirk to maintain his new standard of living he needed to enlist the labor of a woman, or else hire workers to help maintain his newly acquired homestead in the Snohomish River valley.

Van Buskirk seemed entangled in contradictions. In an age of considerable gender anxiety, here we have the sea-roving Philip Van Buskirk, an avowedly homosexual sailor now turned homesteader and looking for a wife, a Tlingit wife, hoping to take advantage of "the native custom of marriage." The confusions provoked by his sexual turns posed few conundrums for the sailor-turned-landsman. And Van Buskirk's innocent wanderings appeared unfettered by the gendered conventions that shaped the outlook of those other tourists who pressed north to see more than the forests and icescapes of the far northwestern coasts. Is his story an irrelevant historical note, a random life leaving little effect wider than his own lost relationships, or something more? Something, a life in history, he strode flesh and bone across the kelp-strewn seaside at Fort Wrangell, walking the edge of a system of relations representative of his time.

What becomes of this life? He drifts out of our picture as surely as he drifted in. In the sweep of history, Van Buskirk's peripatetic life caused no great wave of change, not even a ripple. His life has meaning, if it does, because his presence illuminates a historical economy of power where each individual was touched by contemporary hierarchies of nation, gender, race, and class.[118] Van Buskirk, as an individual historically constituted within relations of power, offers a route into a wider engagement with sociopolitical phenomenon. Because power was (and is) manifest everywhere, then its general features may be found in even the most mundane and minute details—a single life, Van Buskirk's life.

Van Buskirk's appreciation for the natural beauties of the far northwest differed from that of his genteel companions aboard the steamer *Al-Ki*. The neuresthenic tourists, alongside Van Buskirk, strolling the steamer deck and plank walks of Wrangell, feared men like him. They would have agreed with physician George Beard, who pronounced in cases such as Van Buskirk's that "the sex is perverted . . . men become women and women men, in their tastes, conduct, character, feelings, and behavior." Their sex-disciplining rejected the errant sexualities of homosexuals, prostitutes, and the working class. But their discipline, the new techniques of sexuality, or rather its control, were, as Foucault insists, applied first by the bourgeoisie to themselves.[119]

What of "the monotonous nights of the Victorian bourgeoisie"? What entanglements were engaged during the short summer nights in the steamship staterooms rolling with the sea swells? Enclosed in their private spaces, segregated from the steerage mongrel marriages, their compartments mirrored the domestic arrangements of home, safe to reproduce among themselves. "As small in number as pug-dogs on this earth, the ship immobilizes and gathers them, and constitutes a temporary 'reservation' where an ethnographic curiosity as well protected as a Sioux territory will be kept and, with luck, increased," as Roland Barthes wrote of the "Blue Blood Cruise."[120] But, given the cramped quarters aboard many of the ships, it was unlikely that these travelers found much space for sex. "The cabins are extremely small," E. Katherine Bates complained in her travelogue, "and when three passengers are packed in each cabin, like herrings in a barrel, it is easily understood that there must be considerable drawbacks to a purely pleasure excursion."[121] Their excursions, unlike the recollections of Van Buskirk, recorded nothing explicit regarding their sexual lives, no apparent commerce in the cramped staterooms. This absent record may say as much through its silence. "Sexuality," Foucault insisted, "must not be thought of as a kind of natural given which power tries to hold in check, or as an obscure domain which knowledge tries gradually to uncover. It is the name that can be given to a historical construct: not a furtive reality that is difficult to grasp, but a great surface network."[122] This great surface network spread into the far corners of empire.

Chapter Five

Totem and Taboo

When Stephen Merritt, recovering from his depressive episodes, reached Wrangell in July 1892, he relished the chance to investigate "this strange, and to me, intensely wonderful place." The town seemed to have changed little since the American takeover. The occasional boom of a gold discovery somewhere in the interior crowded the outpost, but it soon fell back into its sleepy corner of the world. C. E. S. Wood's description in 1877 might have easily passed for Merritt's view more than a decade later. "A few sick or bankrupt miners were hanging about the American town," the visiting Wood wrote. "One ragamuffin, almost picturesque in tatters and dirt, was seated on the shoe-box steps of the 'Miners' Palace Home and Restrent,' playing an asthmatic accordion to an audience of half-naked Indians, wearing yellow headkerchiefs and cotton drawers" [*sic*].[1]

On a mild overcast morning, Merritt marched through the village, noting carefully the details of the native presence. "The Alaskan is of the Esquimau type, not given to much work; lives in squalor, idleness, and shut out from the world has no refinement or culture. . . . They are idolaters and pay worship to their curious gods made by men's hands, carved out of wood, in hideous forms, 30 feet high, all moss covered by age, and smaller ones in their homes." Merritt went on to describe the particulars of Tlingit village life as he understood it. "They live very plainly. . . . They are very indolent, and sit down, men, women and children as if there was nothing to do. . . . The Missionaries are not very successful in their work, and some intelligent citizens of this territory say, no good is done—rather evil, from the effects of rum, tobacco and nameless evils," the visitor wrote.[2] Traveling with his wife and daughter, Stephen Merritt found the indigenes' habits unspeakable, "*nameless evils*," as he wrote. Merritt, as representative of the bourgeois family— "the legitimate and procreative couple," according to Foucault—"laid down the law." Here Merritt wandered through the Tlingit village passing judgment upon the local habits. "The couple imposed itself as model," Foucault wrote, "enforced the norm, safeguarded the truth, and reserved the right to speak while retaining the principle of secrecy."

A single locus of sexuality, according to Foucault, "was acknowledged in social space as well as at the heart of every household."[3] And here Stephen Merritt, his wife, and daughter placed their observations regarding the Tlingit within the narrowed dictates of the Merritts' own metropolitan culture. Behavior that fell outside strict norms was deemed a threat, and as such Merritt recognized the Tlingit as degenerate idolaters, their actions "unspeakable." Here Merritt and others like him extended their social space beyond the domestic interiors of the metropolis, beyond the public spaces of the immigrant cities, and into the territorial fringes of American empire.

"We purchased a few curios, saw much, learned some, and had our hearts deeply moved and strangely drawn toward this dark, benighted, idolatrous people of our own land who need and would take, I believe, the gospel of our Lord Jesus Christ," Merritt wrote. The question of ownership—"our own land"—was assumed and Christianity deemed the cure for the native peoples' apparent social pathologies of indolence and idolatry. Capitalism and Christ would make Alaska into an American territory and Alaskans into American citizens, or so Merritt and his cohort believed.

While Philip Van Buskirk had noted that most of his upscale traveling companions, men and women such as Merritt, journeyed north for "the enjoyment of the grand and sublime scenery and all that," he hardly noticed that this leisure class too was interested in the region's native people, though for quite different reasons. "Many, probably the majority of you," wrote one guidebook writer, "will be more interested in hearing something of the people, than of the country itself. It is the people the tourist wishes to see when he visits a new country; and their peculiarities attract probably more attention than the country's scenery, however beautiful or grand it may be."[4] Another writer noted that "the chief amusement in which the visitor can indulge, is to watch the Indians as they lounge along the store fronts, or saunter leisurely through the straggling town."[5] "Meeting an Indian on the path now and then only increased the romance," tourist Mrs. Wood described in her diary, though she added that "had they been in blankets and war paint it would have been more interesting." Regrettably, she noted on her visit to another Tlingit village, "The steamer's whistle blew before we were more than half way back, to warn us the time was nearly up, consequently we saw nothing of Chilcat. I was sorry afterwards as we learned the Indians there were living almost in their barbarous state—so that it would have been entertaining to see them and look into their houses."[6]

Fort Wrangell afforded an ideal vantage for travelers interested in viewing native Alaskans. "Opportunities for work at wages, which were small but seemed large to the Natives, as well as the gathering of a number of merchants to Fort Wrangell with supplies of new, strange and attractive goods, drew the attention and presence of the Indians from eighteen to twenty different tribes and from distances ranging from sixty to four hundred miles," the missionary S. Hall Young wrote of Wrangell during the 1880s.[7] Wrangell could boast of "a concentration of a larger number of Indians than any other trading center of this region," according to an 1879 article in the *Alaska Appeal.* "Some 2,000 Natives can at times be seen swarming about the place, especially in the spring of the year, before the annual exodus to the mines. Another means of attracting the Natives and their trade is the employment of hundreds of their young men in freighting by canoe, woodchopping, and various kinds of labor . . . even the Indians pay indirectly for the development of their country's resources."[8] The coastal entrepot followed the seasonal cycles of northern industries and at one season would be a hub of activity, while at another almost vacant. When the tourists arrived at the height of the summer work season, the town was hardly as crowded as it might be during other times of the year, but it was ideal for their sightseeing, its rough plank walks crowded with Tlingit women selling curiosities to the visitors.

Where Van Buskirk sought access to Tlingit women, or so he said, these other travelers felt less comfortable in close proximity to the native Alaskans. A missionary recounted his visits to "every cluster of Indian lodges," and he advised "the lovers of the picturesque to content themselves with a distant view." Dirt, he proclaimed "prevails over all."[9] One might have expected John Muir to raise up native lives as examples of "natural men," living close to nature. But Muir felt little enthusiasm for native lifestyles. "Most Indians I have seen," Muir concluded, "are not a whit more natural in their lives than we civilized whites. The worst thing about them is their uncleanliness. Nothing truly wild is unclean."[10] These traveling writers appeared obsessed with cleanliness. And seeing the Tlingit as "filthy in the extreme," these writers confirmed the picture of Alaskan natives' brutish, depraved lives. Their discourse secured an image of the Native Alaskans as existing in a completely primitive, degenerate state. Even Tlingit hygiene offended visitors. Their hair was often dressed with grease and the smell was offensive to American noses. A lifetime spent outside required other protective practices not easily understood by more pampered visitors. The dark paint or charcoal used to protect their faces from sunburn and from mosquitoes was regarded as dirty. Tlingit ethnographer George Emmons noted that Tlingit had used urine as a solvent for grease. "As late as 1885 I saw at Klukwan large tubs of urine just within the doorway that were used for washing the body and clothes, tanning skins, and fixing colors used in basket weaving," Emmons wrote. But he observed, "In habits of personal cleanliness, the Tlingit have unquestionably improved, and soap has taken the place of urine." Emmons added that Tlingit frequently used sweat baths and relied on local hot springs "in case of disease, as a tonic or luxury." "Washing the face and hands," according to Emmons, "was generally practiced upon rising." And women took great care of their hair, "which was considered a feature of beauty." But instead of recognizing habits of cleanliness, transient observers, like the summer tourists, only noted disarray and dirt. And this state of social chaos evidenced in "some of their habits being so utterly disgusting they cannot be mentioned" seemed to necessitate civilized intervention.

The tourists found particular difficulties adjusting to the odorous whiff in the air around Fort Wrangell. Their discomfort arose from what nearly every traveler remarked as "a superior Siwash perfume" or the "les Odeurs de L'Alaska." "It is difficult to surmise what Wrangel would be without the Indians," wrote one traveler, "but even the most ardent admirer of the red-men would not dare to assert that life is made more pleasant by their presence. They lumber up nearly every foot of available space, squatting, crouching, or lying at full length; they carry with them an atmosphere of unpleasant odors."[11] Another prayed that "the smell of salmon may never come back to me; may the lasting smell of the Siwash Camp never come back to me."[12]

Dead sea life and rotting salmon stank. At least it did so for these newcomers. "We went into some of these houses, and saw how the Indians lived. Owing to the large number of dogs and quantities of bad-smelling fish, we were very glad to get away from that neighborhood," Charles Gillis wrote of his olefactory experience in a Tlingit village.[13] But the reek of salmon that the tourists found so unbearable was a scent the coastal natives associated with life itself. Salmon smelled of wealth, of money. It even held the essence of copper, a useful metal long traded between coastal peoples. The anthropologist Claude Lévi-Strauss in his twentieth-century studies of Northwest coast cultures noted that among the Tlingit's southern neighbors, the Kwakwaka'wakw (Kwakiutl), the word for the smell of salmon was the same as the word for the smell of copper. The equivalence between copper and salmon was also in evidence among other North Pacific coastal peoples.[14]

Smell served for the sightseers as a guide to sensory perceptions that held the certainty of universal human experience. The supposedly putrid smell of fish marked the Tlingit as unclean and therefore uncivilized. But there was no universal natural sensory perception, no common agreement regarding odor, or even sight, taste, and touch. Even "nature" itself, cultural geographer Henri Lefebvre insists, "as apprehended in social life by sense organs, has been modified and therefore in a sense produced."[15] Different groups within a particular society, and between different cultures, could have remarkably different experiences of physical nature. Even the "smell" of money held different meanings, as the phrases "filthy lucre" and "filthy rich" suggest. If the bourgeois travelers had reflected upon their own exchange relations, then they too might have recognized the close affinities between money and excrement. "It is possible the contrast between the most precious substance known to men and the most worthless . . . has led to the specific identification of gold with faeces," Sigmund Freud wrote.[16] But such recognitions ran subliminally below the surface features of bourgeois life and would not have been immediately recognizable, thus allowing for the easy condemnation of cultural and racial others like the Tlingit.

Men such as Van Buskirk, or the so-called squaw men, found little disagreeable about the Tlingit, save that the old sailor resented one girl's "saucy deportment." These white men eroticized native bodies. Many bought sexual access. Their exercise of power was connected intimately to the body. But their intimacies did not segregate the colonized from the colonizers.[17] The well-heeled travelers, who shunned these sexual intimacies as unspeakable, conjured their own landscapes of the colonial body, making a commodity of Tlingit cultural landscapes, even as they found the native Alaskans' physical presences offensive.

The travelers' offence at local odors was only one aspect of a complicated mix of repulsion and attraction that characterized bourgeois reactions to Tlingit society. "The Indians of the West have always been an attractive sight to tourists. The Indians of the southeastern Alaska are far more interesting than any of the Western aborigines," promoted one writer. "The Southeastern Alaska Indians have quaint and unique customs," he added.[18] And so, like the mountains and glaciers, the native people themselves became conventional sites of attraction for the tourists. The travelers filled their writings with descriptions of the Tlingit, ones that implicitly fixed their own superiority in relation to the objects of their gaze.

The visitors' descriptions resorted to animal metaphors in an effort to articulate the distance between the Tlingits' supposed primitiveness and the tourists' own claims to civilized status. "These natives have broad faces, small pig-like eyes, and high cheek bones, not very nice to look upon, yet not without a certain expression of real intelligence gleaming through the accumulated dirt," Maturin Ballou wrote in *The New Eldorado*.[19] Travel writer Septima Collis described Tlingit women along the town's boardwalk, "stretched upon the ground like as many seals."[20] Even the travelers' occasional glimmers of generosity hinged upon a certain element of surprise and wonder, as if they had gazed upon another species. Other writers confirmed as much, characteristically casting their interpretations through the relatively new lens of Darwinian evolution. "Philosophers who tell us that the proper study of mankind is man," one wrote, "may feel a scientific curiosity in inspecting this division of the race. It is a new variety of the human species, which may at least serve as a study in anthropology."[21] He continued, noting that "to judge from the specimens presented to us, that they are not attractive, as they seem to be stunted in their growth—squat in figure, short-bodied, short-legged, and low-browed, and at the first look present no signs of physical or mental activity. . . . We judge of races a good deal from the way that they live."

Others confused the randomness of Darwinian selection with that of the evolutionist Jean-Baptiste Lamarck, who theorized that an individual's development mirrored the inheritance of characteristics acquired from the immediate environment over the space of just a few generations. Traveling observers, practicing the pose of amateur gentleman naturalists, attempted to explain the physical appearance of these other bodies. "The constant life of the Tlinkits in their canoes when procuring food or at other occupations on the water has produced, in conformity with the doctrine of natural selection and the survival of the fittest, a most conspicuous preponderating development of the chest and upper limbs over the lower, and their gait on land, resembling that of aquatic birds, is scarcely the poetry of motion as we understand it," wrote another traveler.[22] Another writer linked apparently stunted or arrested physical development to this same environmental evolutionism. "They are usually of low stature and ill formed. The legs of both sexes are bowed by constant sitting in their canoes, where half their lives are spent. Their legs are scraggy, hands and feet small, but toes turning in— making them walk parrot-like," the visitor reported.[23] The traveler's gaze reduced Tlingit individuals to the status of specimens, bits of knowledge, to an animal-like state.

For the bourgeois travelers their descriptions helped to fix their assumed superior status, for if they were not in fact a separate species higher on the evolutionary ladder, then they were certainly, in their own minds, superior among the broad range of human races. John Muir's detailed natural history of the Tlingit's physical appearance echoed the extent to which this racial mapping flowed out of imperial discourses. "They are pale copper-colored, have small feet and hands, are not at all negroish in lips or cheeks like some of the coast tribes, nor so thick-set, short-necked, or heavy-featured in general," wrote Muir.[24] Here Muir's comments reflect the dominant discourse of racial difference that constructed racial others according to the fundamental division between black and white, as well as the evolutionary anthropology of the great

Chain of Being.[25] "These Indians are very sensitive about their copper hue, and blame a woman, an Eve, for it. . . . The Tsimshean's are not nearly so dark as other Indian tribes, and it is probably largely for this reason that they consider themselves superior."[26] Muir's categories led him to contrast the Tlingit with Africans, a comparison that recognized "negroish" as a negative physical trait within the racist discourse of the day. Racial difference was fundamental to the narrative of colonial encounters. Racialism functioned through "'degrees of deviance' from the white norm."[27] To this grammar of opposites, Alaskan travelers added the metaphorical split between themselves as human and Indians as animal. By this means, constructed racial differences served as identifiers for other forms of difference and control. Visitors rigged an understanding of the human body that fixed race in a series of observable and heritable corporeal differences.[28] Great distances had been spanned. And geographical separation had been eliminated, only to be replaced with the invented internal distances of racial separation.[29]

Hierarchies of race as understood on the frontier of the nation-state translated easily into hierarchies of class difference elsewhere. "All along the main street . . . the Indian women were assembled in little groups of four and five squatted in the shadows of the houses, admirably counterfeiting with their olive skins, bright black eyes, and showy colors the Italian peasants," Collis wrote.[30] Immigrants, lower-class whites, sexual deviants, and alien others became synonymous with contamination and degeneracy. "Savage Indians," the "Black Irish," Jewish "White Negroes," and others whose class status marked them as well, the prostitutes, whiskey traders, menial laborers—all were fixed as beyond the pale. Along with prostitutes and homosexuals, working-class trade-unionists and anarchists, Tlingits represented a threat to civilized norms, clear evidence of the degraded effects of a "race" given over to their primitive idolatries and desires. Bourgeois whiteness, with its sexual self-control and social rules, had been normalized as the defining American characteristic. The flood of reportage from the frontier periphery not only reflected this assumed dominance, but it also helped to create this position.[31]

Desire, like smell, was a social product. These visitors betrayed their own virile imaginations, even as they denied any attraction, in their written renderings of the Tlingit. "These women are hideously ugly at their best and their blackened faces and their labrettes do not increase their charms," A. E. Browne wrote.[32] Quite accustomed to sexualizing the view of native women, these male visitors inverted their own fantasies, as they found Indian women not alluring but repellent. "They are generally much inferior both in stature and form to the white race . . . it would require an exceedingly fertile and romantic imagination to discover among these people a single specimen of the beautiful Indian maiden, we have all read about, but whom so few have ever seen," one traveler lamented in a common refrain.[33] Even the steamer companies advertised repugnant aboriginal features as a source of attraction. The Pacific Coast Steamship Company's 1887 brochure "All About Alaska," highlighted the draw of the steamship arrivals for the locals. "You will be amused to see the squaws on the arrival of the steamer . . . dressed in their best raiment, and many of them with a portion of their face blackened—sometimes their teeth—which, added to their natural ugliness, makes them look like the very old Nick himself."[34] Now while these upper-class travelers to the far North were hardly sex tourists, they nonetheless felt compelled to register their observations regarding the so-called "Indian Maiden." And this imaginary "maiden," they discovered, was not a virtuous and celibate young woman, as they had idealized, but instead a willing sex partner, or sex worker, a complement to "an exceedingly fertile and romantic imagination." The virginal Indian maiden, as they had conjured her, could not be found. Instead, they found only what they imagined as degradation and sexual savagery, another stereotype that fit into their interpretation of native sexuality. The white men's aversions were marked by the equal pull of their desires. But they found no savage beauty, save that which they saw in the glacier-draped mountains.

Not only did wealthy white men find in Wrangell an inverted sex fantasy; so too did their wives. Writing copiously of their travels, these women often reinforced their roles as guardians of domestic virtue, as they naturalized the degraded state of their native counterparts. "The native women are very ugly, and to their natural homeliness they add a smearing of seal oil and lard black," Matilda Lukens noted in her journal.[35] Lukens, of course, did not recognize that these blackened faces were often signs of mourning. The constant reference to Tlingit women's blackened faces should have reflected ominously on the high mortality rates, but to the tourists this blackface seemed only a curious primitive attribute, not a marker of recent death. And these supposed primitive practices only helped to confirm a hierarchy of culture in which these white wealthy women stood alongside their husbands, earnest matrons holding in check their men's impulses, setting in their discourse domestic examples at the uppermost link in the "chain of being."

The travelers' doubts as to the moral sense demonstrated by Tlingit women were reinforced by contemporary psychological theories. "We should certainly not expect," Freud would soon write in *Totem and Taboo*, "that the sexual life of these poor, naked cannibals would be moral in our sense or that their sexual instincts would be subjected to any great degree of restriction."[36] Their lack of restraint served as yet another marker of their primitive atavism. In contrast to the presumed coastal savages, touring women positioned themselves as custodians of bourgeois respectability, a distinction that rested upon class and racial ideas, and to psychological theories that were premised upon interpretations based upon the contrast between bourgeois society and its supposed savage opposite.[37]

Tlingit men too came under the travelers' dominating gaze. Tourists filled their writings with punishing judgments regarding the laziness of native men. Tlingit men wasted time, did not know the value of money, and forced Tlingit women to do much of the work. Of course, the tourists' fleeting views of the native economy encouraged inaccurate snapshot pictures of men's labor. The resource economy required men to work far from the town centers that attracted the tourists. And the seasonality of this work meant that many men and women were absent during the summer tourist season. As a result, the scribbling tourists feminized native men, characterizing them as indolent and unworthy family men.

Does it matter that these travelers figured the Tlingit as fascinating objects of their sightseeing and as depraved counterparts to nineteenth-century bourgeois sexuality? Fears of degeneration and lost fecundity stalked the late nineteenth-century American bourgeois conscience. While these travelers may not have spelled these anxieties out in so many words, they did situate themselves within a broader imperial context of expansion with its consequent concerns over race mixing and the supposed dilution of racial purity. Perhaps this was why the so-called "squaw men," those white men, mostly prospectors and vagabond laborers who took up with native women, were viewed with such contempt. Sexuality appears as "an especially dense transfer point for relations of power," Foucault wrote.[38] And here, on the fringes of American empire, sexuality was manifest through its supposed suppression by the twin forces of the missionaries and their bourgeois traveling supporters. But in its very suppression sex was everywhere present as an "unspeakable" thought. A closeted sexuality was at the unconscious base of the new political economy.[39]

Taught to see the world through the new lens of anthropology, many late nineteenth-century travelers, when faced with Tlingits in the flesh, reverted to comparisons with the only interpretative situation they knew and understood: the exhibition. At the Chicago World's Columbian Exposition and other world's fairs, Americans viewed an Alaska Indian village that showcased the "fast-developing resources" of "our vast territory."[40] But the exhibition attendees also learned to connect the histories of Western civilizations to other peoples and races, though these connections served only to mark the evolutionary differences that separated the civilized from the semi-barbarian, the primitive, and the savage.[41] "The most interesting things," one traveler wrote of his visit to Wrangell, "were the Bear Totem Poles, mossy with age, and the old Siwashes. One old Siwash, was, except for his dirty unkemptness, the image of the Japanese manager of the Japanese exhibit at the World's fair in Chicago in 1893 and a noted Japanese merchant baron, and gave me the first inkling that the Siwashes on the British Columbian coast and Alaskan coast were the descendents of Japanese. And I later found them to have many of their characteristics; cruelty, treachery, utter lack of gratitude no matter what one had done for them, including their own people."[42]

The traveler's observation found a similar, though more objective, interpretation in the notes of Franz Boas, who was traveling the northwest coast, measuring skulls, searching for an answer to human variation and the question of race. "While I was so occupied it suddenly occurred to me that Haida and Tlingit did not have the structure of Indian languages, but that of the Asiatic. You can imagine that this thought caused me a great deal of excitement because that would be an important discovery," Boas wrote in his diary during a summer research trip in 1888.[43] "They remind us so strongly of the east Asiatic peoples that throughout British Columbia there is the indisputable opinion that they are descendants of Japanese sailors," Boas noted of the local interpretation of the physical resemblances.[44] This link suggested to some the possibility that the Tlingit and other coastal cultures had degenerated from an originally higher Asian civilization transplanted to the eastern littoral of the Pacific rim.

John Muir, for one, saw a strange world vanishing. "The moss-grown ruins of the deserted village seem to foreshadow too surely the fate of the Stikeen tribe, and perhaps of all the allied tribes of this portion of Alaska. . . . Like snow in sunshine they are passing away. Will they perish utterly in this land of abundance."[45] The Canadian explorer Warburton Pike also saw inevitable extinction. "What other fate can be in store for a native race when the hunters leave the woods to work for wages and drink, while the women live in luxury on the proceeds of their immorality."[46] And Eliza Scidmore saw native demise as rooted in the prevalence of a wide variety of diseases. "Consumption is the common ailment and carries them away in numbers, yet they have no medicines or remedies of their own, trust only in the incantations and hocus-pocus of their medicine men, and take not the slightest care to protect themselves from exposure."[47] Scidmore noted that "great epidemics have swept these islands at times," citing specifically the devastating effects of the smallpox epidemic of the 1840s that by some estimates halved the coastal native population. "The tribes never regained their numbers after that terrible devastation, and since black measles and other diseases have so reduced their people that another fifty years may see these tribes extinct," she concluded.[48] There could be no easy transition between tribe and state. The evolutionistic idea that tribal entities were forerunners to state-based societies helped to explain the rise of civilizations predisposed to success by superior racial stocks. But the rhetoric of native erasure here assumed their eventual disappearance.

Natural biology had deemed these lesser races unfit in the assumed struggle for survival. "If the primitive races of Alaska are doomed to extinction," wrote a visiting missionary, "being incapable of surviving in the struggle for life, why not allow the course of nature to extinguish them, and forbear to anticipate the catastrophe by injustice or cruelty? It ill becomes a brave and magnanimous people to seize lands and confiscate the scant resources of a depressed and vanishing race. Let us preserve as relics of a prehistoric past our predecessors on this continent. . . . They are decayed families, but they remember their ancient respectability, which, though they know it not, we know is coeval with that of the Teutonic and Gallic nations, the Scottish clans and Saxon hordes."[49] Relying on a long tradition of degradationist anthropology, Lindsley recognized an internal cause of the Tlingit's decline—"decayed families." In the exhibitionist impulse, he urged preserving a remnant. His museum imagination fixed the Tlingit as another display in the fantasy landscapes of empire, there for the travelers to gaze on. The colonial pavilions and native villages of the exposition grounds could now be found in place, authentic remnants of the past.

The Tlingit present was suggested to offer an approximation of the European past. Travel to the territorial periphery then implied not only a movement in space, but also a movement back in time.[50] And the Tlingit presence helped illustrate this temporal shift, in the travelers' minds. "Visitors to Alaska will often hear," wrote traveler Henry Field of what was then considered the popular view of the natives,

on the steamer, a loud-mouthed talker, who thinks himself very wise, expatiating after this sort: "What are we going to do with these miserable natives? They are a bad lot. Indians are not good for much anyhow. They are lazy, dirty, and shiftless. We shall have to get rid of them some way. But we need not trouble ourselves about it; only let them alone, and they will get rid of themselves. Whiskey will do the business better than fighting. We have only to let the whiskey come in freely, and in this way we shall civilize them off from the face of the earth. It is only carrying out the law of the survival of the fittest, which is the great law of nature. The Indian must go, as other feeble races have gone before him. It is the will of the Almighty."

Field reasoned, "There is a certain brutal frankness in this—in the avowal of a purpose of extermination of a whole race; but only a cowardly hypocrisy will in the same breath talk of Divine Providence and the survival of the fittest . . . they are believers in witchcraft as much as the natives of Darkest Africa."[51] Field, borrowing and turning around the commonplace colonialist comparison to Africa, recognized that the dark places of the earth could also find space in the minds of so-called civilized men, men who, in Field's estimation, applied their own witch-craft, posing as God and science to advance their own desires. Confusing history with schemas of evolution, theories of organic development, and the supposedly divine progress of racial types, expansionists and their excusers advanced on the north.

Alaskan travelers often chose not to connect what they imagined as fact with what they saw all around them. Noting the diverse inhabitants of Fort Wrangell in the late nineteenth century, George Wardman admitted as much when he wrote that "Indians, and transitory miners, and Chinese far out number them [white settlers] but do not count as population."[52] Estimates of the region's native population varied widely, with some estimates in the mid-1880s suggesting a total population of between forty and sixty thousand across the entire territory.[53] The census of 1880 cited a total native population of 30,178, with more than 5,000 native people living along the southeastern Alaskan coast.[54] Regardless of the actual number, visitors rarely failed to note the low number of whites and Creoles living amid the obvious native majority. By 1887, Territorial Governor Swineford's annual report to Congress enumerated a population of "27,500 natives (uncivilized)," 2,500 natives "(civilized and more or less educated)," along with 5,000 whites, 1,800 creoles, and 3,000 Aleuts.[55] Swineford's report, however, more inclined to providing a comprehensive view of the territory, noted that "a large part of the labor employed at the various industrial establish-ments is drawn from the native population. The natives work in the mines and in the fisheries, in the digging of ditches, and construction of trails and wagon roads, and are, as a whole, as reliable as the ordinary class of white laborers."[56] Other observers went further, suggesting that, in the words of one, "along the coast the various industries in operation are largely dependent" upon native labor.[57]

The discourse of native extinction voiced by those travelers who had secure economic stakes elsewhere neither reflected the realities of northern work, nor the rhetoric of local white capitalists who had come to depend upon native workers. But the Tlingit had their own apprecia-tion of the value of their labors. "They understand," according to an observer, "the value of their services and are not infrequently inclined to emulate the example of their white brethren and go on a strike for higher wages, or because of some real or fancied grievance." Despite their comparisons to white workers in terms of reliability, the Tlingit still represented a separate population in the eyes of the Americans. They copied their white working-class counterparts in attempting to arrest a fair wage from their employers. But the colonial imagination could not admit that the Tlingit or any native people were in fact the same.

In general travelers and writers saw the Alaskans selectively, choosing to ignore that which was right in front of them, the obvious and confusing presence of so many native peoples who had failed to simply disappear. Sometimes the outsiders' constructions of the alien Tlingit existed in tension, as administrators such as Swineford identified certain characteristics, while transient visitors saw something else entirely. But regardless of their differences, what all of these observers shared was a consistent objectification of the native Alaskans and the assumption that these people were the rightful object of their administrating and sightseeing. To these late nineteenth-century observers these activities were not points of self-reflection. It was to them a matter of commonsense that they engage in classifying, administering, and more generally knowing the Tlingit and other native peoples of the north.

The travelers' longing to see vestiges of the primitive past on their coastal tours transferred easily into an appetite to possess some token of their brief visits. "The red natives of this North Pacific coast become familiar *objects* to the tourist" (emphasis added), concluded an advertisement for the Canadian Pacific Railway.[58] But the wealthy tourists, unlike Philip Van Buskirk, had no interest in taking anyone home.

In Wrangell the most obvious objects of the arriving tourists' attentions were the significant number of totem poles arrayed in front of the stretch of Stikine Tlingit long houses fronting the Wrangell waterline. "Wrangel is very interesting for its score or more of totem poles," one visitor wrote. "These show surprising ingenuity, wood carving ability and religious imagination of a stolid race of barbarians in portraying in this unique way out of the material at hand their tribal legends of the origin of their tribes," he continued. In spite of the "surprising ingenuity," he, like other nonnative visitors, nevertheless saw these people as "Children of nature-not very greatly higher in the order of intelligence than their companions of the woods, sea and air whose portraits they carve on their totems and whom they claim as ancestors." Of course, to the self-consciously civilized visitors the failure, as they saw it, to separate the human from nature served as the marker of an essential primitivism. And while the curious visitors "wished we had the heraldic ability to read them," the essential mystery bound up in these totems remained. These opposed cultures—as they were constructed in the social observations of

Figure 16. "Indian Village, Fort Wrangle [Wrangell]," 1868, Photograph by Eadweard Muybridge, Lone Mountain College Collection of Stereographs. (Courtesy Bancroft Library, University of California, Berkeley)

the visiting travelers—were incommensurable. The travelers felt no need to justify their presence, their right to be there as they saw it, and the right of the missionaries, gold seekers, and timber-mill and cannery owners was assumed. And this assumption lay within the motivating ideas of inherent racial superiority and progressive destiny. Such thinking was not just an idea; it was accorded the power of fact by their evolutionary discourse, a natural fact. And no amount of human meddling could alter, in their minds, the eventual results, that the totem poles "will doubtless survive the last of the vanishing races of barbarians that so picturesquely established their claim to art and religion," as one traveler predicted.[59] The certainty of native extinction rested upon the analysis of the most recognized intellectuals of the era. "In America," British sociologist Herbert Spencer insisted, "we have the fact that none of the aboriginal peoples, if un-coerced, show capacity for industry: in the North, cut off from his hunting life, the Indian, capable of no other, decays and disappears."[60] The information backing Spencer's assumptions drew upon the copious, but often random and unsystematic observations of travelers and gentlemen ethnographers, some of whom wrote back from the southeastern coast of Alaska.

The context for understanding and interpreting the native north lay in the wider metropolitan culture of popular expositions and museums. And so period travel writers slipped easily into the ubiquitous metaphor of the world-as-exhibition.[61] Africa, Asia, and now Alaska all received the generalizing discourse of the West meeting the other. The travelers' northern excursions were no less celebrations of presumed civilized progress than were the world expositions that placed marvels of technology in opposition to the "native village." A steamship's arrival at an Alaska port marked the same contrast of industrial supremacy and native stasis. "Everybody in town is on exhibition" on steamer days, Frances Knapp recorded during his mid-1890s travels along the southeastern Alaskan coast.[62] The expositions superimposed a framework of meaning over the world's peoples and territories.[63] Alaska was placed alongside Africa and other alien locales on a geographical ladder of difference. These representations ordered what people saw in the world; the exposition instructed them how to see and to recognize their necessarily superior relationship to that world through the exercises of their abstracting definitions and hierarchical orderings. "If—as Marx said— 'the wealth of those societies in which the capitalist mode of production prevails presents itself as an 'immense accumulation of commodities,' then world's fairs are the temple in which this merchandise loses all real contact with its value in use." Things became signs, stripped of any direct relationship to their origins. In an increasingly disenchanted modernizing world of rational science and industry, mystery and enchantment still had the power to excite the thousands of travelers who crowded coastal villages such as Wrangell looking for authentic evidence of native totemism.

"They are like large trees with the tops cut off and they are all carved in as toads and frogs, reptiles and birds and men life size, maybe half a dozen on a pole. We've seen some at the World's Fair just like them," Wrangell visitor Alexander Whyte recalled in a letter to his wife.[64] An earlier visitor went on to note that the monstrous faces carved on the poles had an "idolatrous air about them," and that the resident missionary was having them removed as fast as possible. "In a short time they will all have disappeared and carried with them whatever of traditional meaning they may have for the Aborigines, who will also disappear in a few generations."[65]

John Muir, during one of his early visits to Fort Wrangell, described the removal of one totem pole. Muir overheard chopping at the north end of the village, "then a heavy thud, as if a dead tree had fallen." An "archaeological doctor" had cut down one of the village's totems, sawing off the figure of a woman measuring more than three feet across. The thief and his accomplices, according to Muir, "conveyed it aboard the steamer, with a view to taking it on East to enrich some museum or other." Muir noted that the "sacrilege" nearly caused a violent row, and had it not been for the fact that the pole in question belonged to a Tlingit member of the Wrangell Presbyterian Church, the incident might have ended in violence. Nonetheless the pole's incensed owner confronted the thief, pushing home the question, "How would you like to have an Indian go to a graveyard and break down and carry away a monument belonging to your family?"[66]

Muir had seen the barbaric side of such collecting. During his cruise north aboard the *Corwin* in 1881, he observed the pervasive effects of epidemic disease and death along the Bering Sea coast. Landing at one village, he interviewed a survivor and inquired as to where all the people had gone. "He led us a few yards back of his hut and pointed to twelve or fourteen skeletons lying on the brown grass, repeating . . . 'Dead, yes, all dead, all mucky, all gone.' Muir noted that some two hundred people had perished at this village alone. With the natives nearly all dead, one of Muir's shipmates set about collecting what was left. "Mr. Nelson went into this Golgotha with hearty enthusiasm, gathering the fine white harvest of skulls spread before him, and throwing them in heaps like a boy gathering pumpkins. He brought nearly a hundred on board, which will be shipped with specimens of bone armour, weapons, utensils, etc." These relics would be shipped to the Smithsonian Institution and other museums for display and study, documents of what Muir believed to be a vanishing people. "In a few years at most every soul of them will have vanished from the face of the earth." [67] "There is no document of civilization," Walter Benjamin would later write in his oft-quoted observation, "which is not at the same time a document of barbarism. And just as such a document is not free of barbarism, barbarism taints also the manner in which it was transmitted from one owner to another."[68] Of Wrangell one travel writer remarked of this sort of barbaric transmission, "The city of the dead hold small terror for the curio-seeker who will wrest, in perfect equanimity, portions from tombstones that were probably placed long before his great-grandfather was born."[69] The acquisitive visitors culled their cultural treasures with a blind detach-

Figure 17. While visiting the uninhabited Tlingit village at Cape Fox, the 1899 Harriman expedition looted the clan houses of their heirlooms and ritual objects. "It was the most curious place," an expedition member wrote, "The tribe had moved away apparently, about 8 or 9 years ago leaving houses in good repair, others in bad decay, but also a lot of remarkable totem poles and head gears—masks, boxes, etc. (tho' all the necessaries were gone) which [we] have been bringing aboard most of the afternoon and evening, and shall do more tomorrow." "Relics," Harriman Expedition *Souvenir Album*. (Courtesy Yale Collection of Western Americana, Beinecke Rare Book and Manuscript Library)

ment, capable of contemplating such looting without an attendant horror.

Aggressive collecting by "archaeological doctors," amateur collectors, museum curators, and well-heeled travelers had led by the 1880s to a wholesale looting of the cultural artifacts of the Tlingit. By 1895, Alaska expert William H. Dall concluded that "The day of the ethnological collector is past. Southeastern Alaska is swept clean of relics; hardly a shaman's grave remains inviolate."[70] But the Tlingit were not defenseless against this sweep of their material culture, the objects of which ended up on display in metropolitan museums, world expositions, and private parlors. Many prospective collectors found recalcitrant Tlingit reluctant to part with totem poles and other valued belongings. When Charles Emerson toured Wrangell in early June 1890, he concluded that the totems "were formerly worshipped by the Indians, and are now to a certain extent, believed by them to be vested with the power of protection, so much so that it is almost impossible to get a totem pole at any price. I was shown one pole that it is claimed the owner was offered $10,000 in gold for, but the Indian laughed at him."[71] Perhaps the Tlingit saw into the white men's fetish, the fantastic valuation of gold in exchange for Tlingit cultural capital. The Wrangell clan leader Kadishan had long resisted offers to purchase the two dramatic poles that stood directly in front of the two-story Victorian home he had built in 1887.

It was here in this model of bourgeois domestic architecture that Philip Van Buskirk had tried in vain to convince Kadishan of the validity of the ougee board. Ultimately, though, Kadishan rejected Van Buskirk's witchery. The Tlingit chief knew that wooden boards and mumbled incantations could not raise the dead, despite Van Buskirk's best efforts. But Kadishan still placed his faith in the cultural power of his totems. With increasing incomes many Tlingit invested their earnings in con-

Figure 18. "Totem Poles, Chief Kat-a-shan's [Kadashan] House, Fort Wrangel [Wrangell]," Winter and Pond Collection, c. 1895. (Courtesy Alaska State Library, Historical Collections)

structing new totems. Applying new tools and adding elaborate painting, new poles were erected at Fort Wrangell through the 1890s, replacing those that had been stolen or sold.[72]

Traveling visitors found in the totems a valid representation of Tlingit culture. When these appeared at expositions and museums, they stood as stand-ins, signs for all of Tlingit culture. These artifacts were deemed authentic, for they represented the "real" context of the collected objects and the society that produced them. Since these societies were seen to be fast disappearing, the role of the collector and the museum served to rescue and preserve these last vestiges of soon-to-be lost peoples.[73] Along the beachfront at Wrangell, the totems served the same purpose for the tourists' gaze. And while the poles had not been physically stripped from their cultural context, the visitors were not capable of seeing these Tlingit objects as anything more than relics and artifacts of some deeper mystery they could not, or did not care to, penetrate.

Unable to purchase the real thing, tourists turned to other offerings. Tlingit carvers made "miniature representations" of their totems during the winter and sold them to the tourists in the summer, according to traveler Septima Collis during her brief stopover in Wrangell. She relished the opportunity to purchase the curios offered by Tlingit women who sometimes gathered in the hundreds, arranging the souvenirs along the wooden boardwalks of the town. Collis purchased a miniature totem pole and "a very grotesquely carved effigy of an Indian shaman." Facsimile shamans and miniature totems became popular items and the Tlingit quickly recognized what visitors wanted, spending "their winter evenings manufacturing imitation ones . . . to sell to summer tourists."[74] A travel brochure even went so far as to advertise the typical scramble to buy, pilfer, or photograph the artifacts of Tlingit manufacture. "Upon the first trip on the 'Spokane'—it is so upon every trip—there was a scramble to see the totems," the Pacific Steamship Company noted. "The cameras were turned loose upon these monuments at every opportunity. Slices of venerable totems were secured by the souvenir hunters, and toy poles, strangely carved with gargoyle heads or monster frogs and crows, were bought, to find their places later in the heretofore peacefully ordered homes of Vermont, Massachusetts or Connecticut."[75] Collecting souvenirs of their travels became an integral part of the tourist experience and the major steamship lines turned Tlingit material culture into new objects of desire alongside the more transient experience of the visual landscape.

By the early 1880s articles of traditional use had been bought up and the Tlingit shifted into this production of small-scale souvenirs specifically for the summer tourist season. What had once been original relics, that is, items of considerable practical or ritual use to the Tlingit themselves, were now copies reproduced en masse by native factories that worked overtime during the dark winters in anticipation of sales during the peak summer tourist season. At Wrangell, often the first extended stop on the steamer junket north, the Stikine Tlingit did their utmost to push their wares on the desirous tourists who were eager to find some supposedly authentic relic to validate their having traveled. "With all its rickety appearance there was no small amount of business doing in Wrangell," Lieutenant Frederick Schwatka noted as he passed through in 1883. "Indian curiosities of all kinds were to be had, from carved spoons of the mountain goat at 'two bits' apiece to the most elaborate idols of totemic carvings," he wrote. "A fair market is found for these articles among the few visitors who travel in this out-of-the-way corner of the earth, and when the supply is exhausted in any line the Natives will immediately set to work to satisfy the demand."[76]

However, the earliest visitors often had difficulty finding these curiosities for sale. When Sophia Cracroft visited Sitka in 1870, more than a decade before the start of a regular tourist route, she found it difficult to purchase souvenirs from the locals. A Sitkan Tlingit resisted her requests to sell household objects. Cracroft persisted in her search of the Sitka rancheria, but discovered that "there were so many away, who had locked up their houses that few things were offered to us for purchase, & the walk was fatiguing as well as fruitless."[77] At a time when the U.S. military punished Tlingit shaman for practicing what the Americans considered their dramatic primitivity and confiscated their fetishes, the tourists "caught in the spirit of the trade" bought up these rarities, practicing their own unconscious fetishism.[78]

Baskets from Yakatat, argillite stone carvings from the Haida villages on the Queen Charlottes, silver bracelets and teaspoons from Kasaan, bear-claw necklaces, rare mountain-goat blankets from Chilkat, miniature totems from Wrangell, toy canoes from Sitka, spoons, salad tongs, jewelry, even bones and the occasional skull raided from grave sites, shamans' rattles, capes fringed with puffin beaks, halibut hooks—every village along the coast seemed to have added curio manufacture to their local economy. Everything was shrunk to the scale of a bourgeois amenity.

"Men of the seventies and eighties," Nietzsche observed, "were filled with a devouring hunger for reality, but they had the misfortune to confuse this with matter—which is but the hollow and deceptive wrapping of it. Thus they lived perpetually in a wretched, padded, puffed-out world of cotton-wool, cardboard, and tissue-paper." To this clutter, tourists added an accumulation of artifacts. Contemporaries understood this passion for ownership as another manifestation of superiority, the move-

Figure 19. Tlingit with baskets and woodcarvings, c. 1893. Photograph by Frank La Roche. (Courtesy University of Washington Libraries, Special Collections)

ment of the invisible hand that propelled economic man out into the world. "Wherever civilization rises, the collecting taste lifts up its head and asserts itself. The acquirement of wealth is but a commonplace manifestation of the same spirit," wrote the editor of *The Curio*, a magazine devoted to collecting in 1887. The magazine went on to link this acquisitive spirit with Alaska, noting in a later issue, "It is only within the past few years that the wonderful resources of Alaska have become known to the public." Herein the idea of a "resource" had been extended from fish, furs, and minerals to include the native reliquary. The self-regulating effects of the market would, it was believed, extend its ministering hand to the far north.

Trade in Tlingit curiosities had attended the earliest visits by Europeans to the North Pacific coast. But with the purchase of Alaska by the Americans in 1867 new interest and activity sprung up. American and European collectors bought up as much of the products of Tlingit and other coastal peoples' material culture as they could. The increasing number of visitors spurred new arrangements between local white traders and Tlingit. Stores featured and advertised curios for sale at an early date. In 1870 Sophia Cracroft visiting Sitka stopped in "a shop where Indian curiosities are sold, and bought some." Her shopping spree extended into the neighboring Tlingit village where, venturing into Tlingit homes, she searched for baskets and "other queer things."[79] By the mid-1880s tourist demand had driven up the price of native artifacts. According to one museum collector the wave of tourists each summer had spiked the costs some 200 to 300 percent over the previous years.[80] Douglas Cole, a historian of the Alaskan curio trade, describes this as the "scramble for Northwest Coast specimens," spawned by the emerging museum culture and tourism. John Muir disparaged this obsessive scramble among museum collectors and tourists, noting that in Wrangell by 1889, "there was a grand rush on shore to buy curiosities and see totem poles. The shops were jammed and mobbed, high prices being paid for shabby stuff manufactured expressly for the tourist trade."[81] "Fort Wrangle," noted another observer, "is the El Dorado of the tourist."[82]

Summer demand for curios became so great that during the first seasons of the emergent tourist industry, the available souvenirs sold out. In summer 1882, the prominent collector James Swan observed that the tourist rush had "cleaned out the Indian market entirely and the agents of foreign Governments have swept away what the tourists have left."[83] Tlingit mass production quickly remedied these inventory problems, recognizing the need to overproduce simulacra to satisfy the intense seasonal purchasing demands. Travel writer Ella Higginson would later acknowledge that she had accumulated so many souvenirs that she reserved "an extra berth for our Indian baskets."[84]

"Everyone went wild over the Chilkat blankets," wrote one traveler.[85] Ceremonial Chilkat blankets, woven by Tlingit women in observance of strict ritual restrictions—abstinence from sexual intercourse and fasting—had become prime targets of the tourists. "The last are made of the hair of mountain-goats and colored with native dyes," according to one writer. But he lamented that by the 1890s "genuine examples, worth $60–$100, are now rare, and most of those offered for sale are of wool and stained with aniline dyes."[86] Indeed, blankets made with solely local materials had become difficult to find at least a decade earlier. A "genuine" blanket required three goatskins and the tourist demand led to more intense hunting pressure on regional mountain goat populations. Tlingit weavers also dropped the customs associated with preparing the blankets. Abandoning the labor-intensive gathering and treatment of local dyes—marsh mud, wolf moss, oxides of copper boiled in urine, hemlock, and red cedar bark—native weavers found it quicker and easier to rely on inexpensive imported dyes and wools to turn out a volume of blankets for the strangers. These literal heirlooms also quickly lost their customary ties to clan lineages as the traders and travelers bought up blankets both old and new. "An old blind man," travel writer Eliza Scidmore wrote, "with a battered hat on his head and a dirty white blanket wrapped around him, sat before one bark hut, with a large wooden bowl filled with carved spoons made from the horns of the mountain goat. These spoons once in common use among all these people, are now disappearing."[87] No doubt the mountain goats that provided the horns had also disappeared. And Tlingit craftspeople turned to deer antlers and other more readily available materials to meet the steadily rising demand for curios.

Photographs bought in the local curiosity shops in the coastal towns were another form of souvenir. Professional photographers made a thriving business of this trade in images, particularly supposedly authentic pictures of the indigenes. Tourist postcards, photograph albums, and illustrated books all offered broad access to bona fide Tlingit. The images marketed well beyond Alaska to a national audience expanded the reach of Alaska as an exhibition space of nature and natives. One need not venture to Alaska to obtain the view.[88] In Wrangell, Juneau, and Sitka photographers sold their images to the sightseers. By 1888 preloaded and easily portable Kodak cameras enabled the tourists to record their own souvenir images. Relatively inexpensive at $25, not including $10 for developing, picture taking came into the hands of the wealthy coastal travelers. With the invention of the Kodak "Brownie" in 1900, for the cost of one dollar nearly anyone might become a picture taker. But taking images of the local people represented an invasion, and as the picture taken by a tourist in Juneau suggests, many Tlingit resisted such outright intrusions by turning away in the case of this photograph, or in other instances by demanding some payment for what the tourists assumed was their right. "If not paid," Eliza Scidmore wrote, "the [Tlingit] family seems ready to tear the camera fiend to pieces."[89]

Tlingit material culture of all forms found new value in this market. "Stone-age implements are being rapidly gathered up in this country, and a trader, who has received and filled large orders for eastern museums and societies, threatens to bring up a skilled stonecutter to supply the increasing demands of scientists, now that the Indians have parted with most of their heirloom specimens," Eliza Scidmore noted.[90] At Wrangell and Sitka, and elsewhere along the coast, missionaries organized their schools to instruct young Tlingit to manufacture miniaturized Tlingit cultural icons and new items of bourgeois usefulness. "We feel the necessity of their becoming an industrious people, that they may become a good people. I intend to design some things for them after a while, and to offer rewards for designing among themselves," missionary

Figure 20. Tlingit avoiding the "stare" of the tourist's camera. "Indian Women and Children on Wharf—Indian Village, Juneau." (Courtesy Bancroft Library, University of California, Berkeley)

Carrie Willard wrote of her efforts to encourage Tlingit curio manufacture.[91] "We would like to have an outlet for this work," she continued. "There is an almost endless variety. They are very quick at copying. The large basket which they use for carrying water makes a good waste-paper basket." Simulacra filled in for the departing artifacts. The army explorer-cum-travel writer Frederick Schwatka designed the popular "Alaska totem spoon," and Eliza Scidmore noted in her guidebook that "the spoon mania has always flourished in Alaska."[92] Baskets, spoons, and toy totems filled the summer boardwalks of Fort Wrangell and the other coastal stopovers, as the Tlingit adapted to the new arrivals' acquisitive ways.

The expanded curio production exerted new pressures on the region's ecology. In addition to more extensive mountain goat hunting, other species came under attack. Native peoples increased their direct sales of furs to visiting travelers. Sea otters, even land otters, were hunted out in many locales. Bears' claws were collected and sold. Bird species—eagles, puffins, and other waterfowl—were hunted and sold. "The Indians used to kill many [eagles]—easy enough—as they perched in the dead trees over the wastes—put a glass ball in the claw and they dry it to sell to tourists as a curio. It is reported that they are fast being exterminated as actually competing with fishermen who want all the fish to be in cans!" one visitor recorded.[93]

Tlingit initiated much of this curio industry themselves. The Sitka Tlingit woman known widely as Mrs. Thom or "Princess Tom" was said to be the wealthiest person in the region, and much of that wealth, according to the traveler William Webb, had been generated by the sale of furs and "curiosities" to visiting Americans. Her total worth was estimated at between $10,000 and $20,000, though one visitor noted that the enterprising Tlingit business woman had amassed $100,000. Gadji'nt, her Raven clan name recorded by John Swanton, was also noted for having two brothers as her husbands. She organized curio purchasing trips up and down the coast, outfitting "a large boat well stocked with provisions and articles that she knows will be appreciated by the Indians; these she trades away for rich furs [sea otter] and curiosities which she knows she can readily sell to the Americans who visit Sitka. These journeys sometimes keep her away for three months at a time," the visiting Webb recorded. Gadji'nt (or Kaajint as it is sometimes spelled) cornered the intercoastal market in souvenirs. The owner of the schooner *Active,* she sailed to the coastal Tlingit communities, organizing craft producers, particularly women, throughout the region. A consummate entrepreneur, she put together far-flung connections with the interior, relying on ancient Tlingit connections with the Athapaskans.[94]

Tlingit women like Gadji'nt organized much of the regional tourist trade, producing, promoting, and selling trinkets for the strangers. "Most of the Indian men were at work in the mines but the squaws sat in rows on the pier or in front of their houses, offering for sale" the range of facsimile goods. "We went into numerous cabins in search of curios, and were impressed with the eagerness of the natives to make money," another traveler noted in her diary. "They offered us the spoons they were eating with, the ear-rings from their ears, . . . even the charms which hung about their necks . . . we came to the conclusion that there must be a Trades Union here, for the uniformity of prices was remarkable, and there was a positive firmness in the market," Matilda Lukens recalled.[95] A steamship guide counseled travelers to beware of bargaining with Tlingit along the boardwalk in Wrangell. "They will offer you furs, silver bracelets, little carved images, canoes and various nick knacks for sale, but, as a rule, they have a high appreciation of their wares, and you can do better to buy from the white man's store in Sitka or Juneau."[96] The curios themselves represented an imagined productive process, but the real lives and labor of the trinkets' producers was not revealed.

The sudden rise of a regional tourist industry allowed many Tlingit, particularly women, to take advantage of new opportunities, alongside the wage labor increasingly available in the region's salmon canning,

Figure 21. "Indian Merchants at Treadwell Mines," c. 1894. Photograph by Frank LaRoche. (Courtesy University of Washington Libraries, Special Collections)

timber harvesting, and mining enterprises. Curio production was primarily women's labor. Native craftspeople shifted their designs and products to attract the seasonal flood of consumers. Ready-made kitsch, put together sloppily compared to those objects crafted under strict ritual guidance, represented imitation miniatures of little or no practical use value.[97] Stripping objects of their original contexts, the Tlingit cottage industry satisfied the strangers' desire for icons of authentic native manufacture. The Tlingit, in a reversal of the stereotype of acculturating "natives," forced tourists into certain patterns of behavior, in a sense controlling them in their way. "It is a funny sight to see the whole ships passengers filing off the boat as soon as she came to the wharf and walking in a long string up to one street and pouring into each store in turn to search for bargains or curios, and they lose their heads and pay prices for the verriest trash which is perfectly absurd," one traveler observed of his touring comrades.[98] Traveler James Teackle Dennis seconded this cynical view of his fellow traveler's naiveté, noting of Fort Wrangell, "its chief business is to cheat the innocent traveler."[99]

"The real entertainment of the day came after we had bought our baskets and spoons and carvings at the traders' stores, and were enjoying

Figure 22. European-American merchants exerted increasing control over the profitable souvenir business, shifting the focus of trade from Tlingit-controlled boardwalks to white-controlled stores. "Native Curios, Sitka," c. 1900. (Courtesy Alaska State Library, Historical Collections)

a few dry hours in the cabin," Eliza Scidmore wrote. "Then the Indian women came tapping at the windows with their bracelets, and the keen spirit of the trade having possessed us, we made wonderful bargains with the relenting savages."[100] The *spirit* of the trade possessed the travel writer and her cohort. Here the travelers engaged in their own mystifications, that of the naturalized market. The market and nature were the same in their secular spirit of the trade. Consistent with the free trade ideologies and the scientific legitimacy they found in Herbert Spencer's social Darwinism, the tourists easily believed the market and nature to be one and the same, that their instincts reflected such an internal and naturalized human logic. As such their purchasing was another facet and form of labor. They dispelled their leisure class unease, and "spent" their time engaged in productive consumption. "Each squaw seems to have the shrewdness and business instinct of a Jew and a Yankee rolled into one. In their own language they comment freely on the tourist,—tit for tat,—and appear to find their [the tourists] doings rather ludicrous, which, no doubt, they sometimes are," writer Henry Finck noted in the era's racial vernacular.[101] Haggling for a better price served as the mock work of the tourist shoppers. It helped them to legitimate their leisure as they engaged with the penny-wise Tlingit saleswomen.

Provisioning tourists with the requisite bibelots was lucrative business. And the selling culture required proper displays to attract customers. Nonnative shop owners were hard pressed to out-compete the authentic displays of native women clustered along the boardwalks and Tlingit villages. The tourists' streetside barter with Tlingit women formed a part of the moment of the exchange to be later recounted, as much a memento as the ornamental swag they spirited home to their parlors. But white Alaskan merchants recognized and took advantage of the intimate relationship between museum and store display. The traders' stores "are perfect museums of Indian curiosities, furs, and oddities of Alaskan production," wrote one travel writer.[102] The late nineteenth-century museum and the study of anthropology had sanctified certain objects as authentic and therefore invested with particular value. Behind the museum's protecting glass these objects were out of reach, valued but not for sale. These museum displays found their counterparts in musty curio shops of southeastern Alaskan villages. "At the traders' stores in town," Eliza Scidmore wrote of Wrangell, "we found whole museums of Indian curios, and reveled in the oddities and strange artworks of the people."[103] Curio collecting imitated the ethnographic collecting activities of experts along the northwest coast and in subarctic and arctic Alaska. It was in the museum and the exposition that these travelers first discovered "natives." And once in touch with the "real thing," travel writers such as Scidmore and the others made a commodity of Tlingit cultural landscapes.

Tourists mimicked this obsessive collecting of late nineteenth-century ethnography and anthropology. Their mementos, later to be studiously arrayed in bourgeois parlors, mirrored, at least in a small way, the museum displays. Visitors aped the systematic collecting habits of the anthropologists and ethnographers who had granted an authentic and traditional air of rationalistic science and legitimacy to the late century obsession with the supposed primitive.[104] Caroline Frear Burk, writing in G. Stanley Hall's popular psychology journal *The Pedagogical Seminary*, identified the development of a collecting impulse rooted in childhood. For Burk this impulse was what she termed "the collecting instinct."[105] The wonder and curiosity evoked by the museum display could now be satisfied in the act of purchasing the very same objects.[106]

"No home is complete now-a-days without a neat and artistically arranged Indian basket corner," a steamer travel guide noted, reinforcing the shopping possibilities available to their passengers in the shore-side towns. "The fad of collecting these beautifully woven gems—the handiwork of the North American aborigines—is one which is fast finding favor with those who journey northward," the guide encouraged. For the tourists, the "baskets, odd carved totems, and fine bead work" preserved "one of the most interesting phases of Indian life," which the guidebooks predicted would "ultimately find their way into thousands of well-ordered homes." Even if the objects were not in fact the real thing, they were at least close approximations. The American strangers, in keeping with the contemporary spirit of P. T. Barnum, appeared happy enough to pay to be fooled, if they were fooled well. As one tourist wrote satirically, "'Wanted: An Alaskan tourist who has not secured a curio of some sort.' Address P.T. Barnum."[107]

These souvenirs served as authenticating signs of the tourists' fleeting experiences, their brief transits across the stony beaches separating their floating hotels from native Alaska. "The charm of having purchased such souvenirs on the spot forms half their value," a traveler noted.[108] For the tourists, the curios served as totems to their having been there, icons of their original purchase, the moment of acquisition where possession drew one into association with a unique and therefore more valuable experience. Curio commodities were representations of representations. These souvenir suggested things that might have had use value in their native cultural context. But their real use value was symbolic and locked in the closed cultural loop of the bourgeois' fascination with native labor, the hands of the craft worker whose efforts were etched or woven into the wood, wool, fiber, or stone, even if the original meaning of the object could not escape its own culture.[109] The souvenir helped to summon a lost world of "a fast dying race" and intimacies with nature conjured by the totem tchotchke. These souvenirs became magical things, incarnations of human labor and myth in which the social character of Tlingit labors and Tlingit myths became caricatures fixed in objects. Their curio purchases were decidedly second-hand experiences.

Experience itself had no materiality. And yet experience was what the tourists bought. The heavily marketed tourist experience acquired the form of a commodity.[110] And the tourist was a traveler, but also as a passenger, a commodity caught in an industry of transport and experience.[111] Their northern tours elevated the person to the level of a commodity; the tourist, to paraphrase Walter Benjamin, "surrenders to its manipulations while enjoying his alienation from himself and others."[112] But to have come to such self-consciousness would have broken the spell of the staged authenticity of their travels and of the bric-a-brac's magic for which they scoured the coastwise villages.

The curio once captured and returned home to the metropolitan parlor became the point of origin for a narrative, a story of purchase. But the meanings of these things proved circular. Travelers understood the things that they saw through the metaphors of the museum and the exposition. What they found and bought on their excursions already contained interpretations, ones framed for them in the cultural entertainments of the metropolis. They ventured to the periphery searching for things they already knew.

A dual play was at work in these exchanges, where traveling consumers were directed in their purchases by the signs of native authenticity. In fact, the world they bought was one remade for them by indigenes intent on raising the slim capital necessary to exchange for a wider world of goods manufactured by the industrial metropolis. Travelers placed greater value on those objects deemed to be most authentic. As the tourist trade made inroads into actual objects of Tlingit use and encouraged the manufacture of replicas, the value of "antique" goods was enhanced. The search for Tlingit baskets, in particular, became an expected routine on the passage. "It now takes a vigorous search of the Indian quarters in the fishing villages to produce any of the old baskets. Many have been cast away as worn out, but the collectors readily seize upon them, paying the natives exorbitant prices," the steamship travel guides noted.[113] The guides encouraged visitors to "poke your way into the countless huts and igloos in search of the rare and curious relics," thereby sponsoring countless untoward invasions of Tlingit homes.

"We of the highly educated classes (so called)," wrote William James, "have most of us got far, far away from Nature. We are trained to seek the choice, the rare, the exquisite, exclusively, and to overlook the common. We are stuffed with abstract conceptions, and glib with verbalities and verbosities." The psychologist James recommended that the best remedy under such conditions was to descend to what he and his contemporaries viewed as a more profound and primitive level. While expecting native extinction and supporting the eradication of supposedly savage customs, newcomers fixated upon traditional native practices and objects. Yet, while white men and women sought an escape from their over-civilized existences, they also bridled at the supposedly savage, instinctual lives of natives. This contradiction lay at the core of their imperial imaginings. Evolutionary stages, they had come to believe, had led certain races, certainly the Anglo-Saxons, out of the primitive near-animal state. This primitive authenticity linked bourgeois men and women to the savage, even as it separated them as civilized.[114] As a contemporary argued, the narrative of history enabled such a balance of opposites, evolution determined that "all our life had a history, that nothing happens disconnectedly, that everything we are or do is part of a current coming down from the remote past;" a current that maintained the barbarian "pugnacity," as James called it, flowing out of the past into the present, a biological determinism that made culture an inheritable trait that went by the name of race.[115] Civilized travelers occupied a privileged position in this historical tableau. They assumed their status as superior, while at the same moment they claimed their primordial ties.[116] The curios they purchased and photos they took confirmed the evolutionary progress they had made and helped to order their understandings of their imperial encounters.

Along the southeast Alaskan coast in the mist-enveloped region of a native religious world, the touring strangers revealed more of their own subjectivities in their habits and souvenir collecting. But, the tourists did not recognize their own mystifications, their beliefs masquerading as universal reason. The things they carried home reverberated with meanings, ones largely hidden from them. They took their souvenir buying to be a commonsense practice. But collecting *these* commodities was hardly so straightforward. Any commodity, according to Karl Marx, is a mysterious thing, "abounding in metaphysical subtleties and theological niceties."[117] The bourgeoisie accordingly saw products as having no relation to the conditions of their production. Or as Walter Benjamin summarized, they saw "no relation to the expropriation of wage labor that erased goods' identities as the historical product of communal labor, clothing them instead in the abstract guise of commodities from *nowhere* and *no-time*" (italics added). Social relations, Marx insisted, assumed "the fantastic form of a relation between things." But the tourists' souvenir commodities reversed this capital animism that made humans into things.[118] The tourist curios were signs that made things human again, or so they believed. That is, where industrial society produced commodities by alienating these products from labor, the curios represented the supposedly authentic productions of human hands. These souvenirs were incarnations of native labor, according to the tourists' view. These objects appeared transparent and the work of native craftspeople could be recognized as immanent in the thing itself. Strange, then, that the tourists sought to capture some sign of the work of Indian bodies, even as they found these same bodies repugnant and ultimately doomed to extinction.

The tourist curios were commodities that symbolized a lost world of totems. The fractured connections between humans and nature were restored. A primitive and presumably fast-disappearing phase of human history was fixed in a symbol, a sign of artisanal and presumed precapitalist production. These curios were very much in the guise of commodities from *somewhere* and *sometime*. But the animism of space and time was only a representation. The strangers could not hope to capture the Tlingit meanings bound up in what the tourists called totemism. Travel writer Ella Higginson described totemism as conventionally understood, comprising "a class of objects which the savage holds in superstitious awe and respect, believing that it holds some relation to, and protection over, himself."[119] The manufactured Tlingit curios were mass-produced miniatures that were representations of representations. The Tlingit and visitors' worlds were incommensurable, even though they might exchange objects between them.

The great divide supposedly separating the savage from the civilized hinged, according to Eurocentric reason, on the limitations of the former's abstract thought. "A savage cannot conceive of anything," wrote a white interpreter of the Tlingit, "that is not visible and material."[120] Hence they relied upon fetishes and totemic practices, according to the visitors' worldview. They believed that the native world was one fraught with unreason and superstition. Turn-of-the-century anthropologist James G. Frazer's massive study *The Golden Bough* filled several volumes with accounts of this primitive irrationality.[121] "The Thlinkeet Indians," he recorded, "have been known to attribute stormy weather to the rash act of a girl who had combed her hair outside of the house."[122] "A totem," Frazer wrote in 1887, "is a class of material objects which a savage regards with superstitious respect, believing that there exists between him and every member of the class an intimate and altogether special relation."[123]

Searching for an appropriate analogy to describe the bourgeois faith in their commodities, Marx turned to this "special relation," as recognized by contemporary anthropology, borrowing a related term from then-current ideas of totemism. "This I call the Fetishism which attaches itself to the products of labour," Marx wrote in the first volume of *Capital*. Inverting the categories of knowledge and power, he identified the "social hieroglyphic" of primitive culture as also belonging to industrial society. "We try to decipher the hieroglyphic, to get behind the secret of our own social products," Marx wrote.[124] But the tourists accepted the meanings that they gave to their mementos with little perceived need for plumbing the hidden meanings of their commodities. Their purchases performed an unthinking form of therapeutic self-fulfillment.

An enormous stream of writing poured from the territories and colonies during the closing decades of the nineteenth century. Nineteenth-century analysts such as Sigmund Freud and William James engaged in a systematic comparison of travelers' accounts, relying upon a collage of recorded facts and impressions. Cultural practices widely interpreted in these texts had been stripped of their local and specific contexts and instead applied to broad societal interpretations. Armchair anthropologists and social scientists pored over this travel literature, accumulating data rather unsystematically from the edges of empire. It was not by coincidence that James Frazer drew on Tlingit material in his enormous compendium of "savage traditions," or that Karl Marx found his most profound metaphor—the fetish—in the spate of mid-nineteenth-century writing on so-called primitive cultures; it was no accident that Thorstein Veblen, ever the contrarian, identified his age's conspicuous consumers as leisure-class barbarians. Nor was it an accident that physician George Beard diagnosed the ills of industrial civilization through his comparisons to the primal societies, or that eugenics originator Francis Galton spent his early career writing travelogues of his wanderings among what he presumed to be prehistoric peoples. "The social and political life of foreign nations offers a wide field and changing surface for examination;" Galton urged, "newly discovered objects for the yearly tide of vacation travelers, are of constant occurrence; scientific tours offer an endless variety of results; while narratives of adventure never fail to interest."[125] Race thinking and travel enjoyed a certain intimacy. It was not happenstance that sociologist Herbert Spencer, social critic Walter Bagehot, and psychologist and philosopher William James all began their considerations of human nature through the lens of the primitive. And it was certainly not a rhetorical convenience that led Sigmund Freud to subtitle his work *Totem and Taboo*, "On Some Points of Agreement between the Mental Lives of Savages and Neurotics." Along the southeastern Alaskan coastline the supposed savages and neurasthenic tourist confronted one another.

They were guided by the Darwinian insistence upon a struggle for existence that presented as a matter of scientific fact that "when civilized nations come into contact with barbarians the struggle is short."[126] Darwin, Freud, Marx, Spencer, Beard, Veblen, James, Bagehot, and others drew freely from the period's travel literature. The Western mind on which these formative thinkers and their intellectual peers centered their attentions was constantly referenced within the theoretical edifice of late nineteenth-century colonialism and in particular with the drama of contacts recorded in nineteenth-century travel literature. The travelogue helped in its small, but important way to help form the characteristic structures of late nineteenth-century Western thought. Bourgeois identities were created through an opposition to supposedly savage others. "In the mental life of the individual," Freud wrote, "the Other is quite regularly involved, as model, as object, as helper, and as adversary."[127] Walter Benjamin self-consciously employed the global meanings of Northwest Coast symbols. "Picture puzzles, as schemata of dreamwork, were long ago discovered by psychoanalysis," Benjamin wrote. "We, however, with a similar conviction, are less on the trail of the psyche than on the track of things. We seek the totemic tree of objects within the thicket of primal history. The very last—the topmost face on the totem pole is that of kitsch."[128] Totem poles, once belonging to local communities, now served as variable metaphors for metropolitan observers. On their visits to native Alaska, tourists, like their traveling contemporaries around the globe, constituted themselves through these Tlingit others. What they recorded and published would help to inform the wider intellectual practices of the fin de siècle.

If, through capitalism, the tourists practiced the same, supposedly "savage," fetish worship, then what remained of the difference between their and the Tlingit's worldview? Aurel Krause, after spending winter 1883 in a Tlingit village, concluded, "Their power of understanding is limited; the outlook which they have on their environment and which is best expressed in their myths is childishly naïve. The tales of the origin of things are full of lively imagination, but lack all sensible understanding and scarcely show any comprehension of the universe."[129] The visitors determined the Tlingit to be children of nature. And, of necessity, the newcomers believed that they brought the enlightenment to these endarkened peoples. Their confidence in the universality of their worldview appeared unflappable. The visitors set the fields of understanding and possible action. They presumed to possess the knowledge that the indigenes could not possess themselves.[130]

In reality, these tourists helped to inaugurate the further extension of a universal marketplace into the territory. And this was only natural to them. Everything, it seemed, could be bought and sold. Tourists posed a most effective form of power and capital's extension. They believed themselves to be only observers, casual passers-by, but in their transience they instituted a new order without association to any presumed formal institutions—the territorial government, the mission, the army or navy. They were not obvious parts of the apparatus of the state of which they were assuredly instruments. The navy's occasional bombardments of native villages were temporary intrusions when compared to the steady influx of tourists who insinuated their purchasing habits into the coastal communities. The travel writers and guidebook authors wielding the written word rivaled the actions of military commanders.[131] The outsiders' power thus worked less on the menace of death than through the constant refashioning of ordinary and everyday actions and relations. Native bodies and possessions were managed in myriad ways as they were directed by outsiders and organized themselves into the new tourist economy.

The travelers carried words and things home with them and what they wrote and bought helped make Alaska into an American territory. But the meanings latent in the things they carried home were more difficult to read. "After each visit [ashore] the cabins and state rooms are littered with ferns, mosses, wild flowers, clam shells, bits of mineral, slippery kelps, Indian curios, and souvenirs of all sorts brought on board," recalled traveler Charles Hallock of his trip north.[132] Nature and natives were reduced to collected bits of flotsam and jetsam, bits of knowledge represented in miniature, stowable amenities. The white wealthy visitors traveled with symbolic systems that, if we follow the analogies of contemporary analysts such as Marx, Spencer, or Freud, resembled Tlingit totemism. They too were engaged in a fetishistic relationship to reality. Savages, neurasthenics, and neurotics shared their mental lives, though neither would have recognized any similarities. Europeans, according to Freud, had abandoned totemism as a religious and social institution; it was "replaced by newer forms . . . it has left only the slightest traces," he wrote. But these slight traces were significant. The "newer forms" proclaimed civilized society to be free of the unreasoning superstitions and barbaric practices of primitive culture. And yet beneath the surface ran an uncomfortable taint betraying the so-called savage traces latent within the modern identity.

Such reckonings surfaced throughout the period, evidenced in the thinking of innumerable writers. "We must look to the savage portions of our nature if we would really understand ourselves," wrote H. Rider Haggard. Social anthropologist James Frazer alluded to this "subterranean" force of primitivism as "the volcano underneath," a savage trace laying permanently "beneath the surface" of civilized life.[133] "The Indian is to this day but little understood. By some he is looked on as an animal, by others as almost a hero of romance," Alaskan traveler Frederick Whymper wrote. Alaskan visitors such as Whymper saw little to celebrate with respect to the so-called barbarian virtues. "The ideal Redskin, the painted and much adorned native with lofty sentiments," Whymper wrote, "is certainly, as far as my experience goes, a very rare being at the present day, if indeed his existence at any time is not to be considered mythical. A creature, half child-half animal, a mixture of simplicity and ferocity, certainly exists; but though a partial civilization may have varnished his exterior, beneath the thin crust the savage nature lurks, ever ready to break forth, like those volcanic mountains whose pure snows only hide the molten lava within."[134] Like Frazer, Whymper and others sensed the explosive potential of this subterranean volcanic inner savage world. Freud would spend his career elucidating this latent savagism supposedly at the heart of the bourgeois psyche. "Such is our view of those whom we describe as savages or half-savages; and their mental life must have a peculiar interest for us if we are right in seeing in it a well-preserved picture of an early stage of our own devel-opment," Freud believed. For the casual visitors along the summer coast of southeastern Alaska, they too believed that they witnessed a "well-pre-served picture" of their own more distant pasts on display. But here they confused what they saw outside with what they thought lay inside as a part of an individual's mental development, in Freud's and other con-temporaries' view. Widespread understandings of human development determined that vestiges of primitivism were evident in civilized child-hoods, but that proper upbringings extinguished this savage "trace." "Primitive men," according to Freud, "on the other hand, are *uninhib-ited*: thought passes directly into action." Freud used the term "prehis-toric" to describe repressed childhood pasts. The psychologist's analysis drew parallels with the nineteenth-century theory of recapitulation, also called biogenetic law. Ontogeny recapitulates phylogeny, it was said. The development of the individual, according to this theory, repeats the evo-lutionary history of the entire group. This line of thought rested on a belief in the psychic unity of mankind. Freud had equated primitiveness with children and he believed that one might "deduce the original meaning of totemism from the vestiges remaining of it in childhood." Freud and others argued that primitive patterns of thought and behav-ior were recapitualted in the minds of children. Social analysts had adopted the key concepts of the sciences. And given the importance of reorganizing biological reproduction through the family, it should come as little surprise the extent to which prevailing biological concepts had been incorporated by sociologists and psychologists. But late nine-teenth-century psychology also developed out of the steady stream of information flowing from the colonial peripheries. Freud's and other's interpretations rested on the assumptions drawn from their readings of a wide travel literature, of which information from the Alaskan coast formed one small part. Regardless of the particulars of the then-evolving interpretations of human psychology, nearly all understandings of civi-lized society built upon the contrast with the so-called primitive.

The travelers' feelings about this thin divide between the savage and civilized were fraught with ambiguities. One contemporary article of faith celebrated the strenuous life and instructed bourgeois men to maintain their ties to their barbarian pasts. "It is the nature of the Anglo-Saxon race to love those manly sports which entail violent exer-cise, with more or less danger to limb if not life," wrote one late Victo-rian. "This craving for the constant practice and employment of our muscles is in our blood, and the result is a development of bodily strength unknown in most nations and unsurpassed by any other breed of men."[135] Other strains of thought counseled against such indulgence, fearing the release of unrestrained desires. These moderns longed for what they understood as reality, for authentic experiences believed available only outside of industrial culture on the wilderness periphery. But their anxieties were also grounded in deterministic laws of nature and biological bases for human behavior. Opening the door to unbridled primitive desires posed particular hazards to a class of Americans fearful of the weakening of their own racial stock, their economic markets, and the nation. Their survival of the fittest ideas indicated the necessity of a certain elemental sex drive, but those ideas also determined a strict observation of certain taboos.

Alien peoples such as the Tlingit personified all that was taboo. The native domestic realm revealed all that was dangerous, disordered, degenerated, and unclean. It was a forbidden space. Native social disorder, like that of the immigrant urban masses, seemed in upper-class eyes to be rooted not in political or economic inequities, but grounded in individual character. The solutions to social disorder then lay within the family itself and within the conforming possibilities of individuals themselves.

And though heredity was understood to determine individual character as a set of fixed racial traits, any improvement, they believed, must begin with the smallest social unit. Contrasts like those observed at Wrangell were instructive. The Tlingit longhouse stood in contrast to the Victorian parlor. These architectures told as much about the arrangements of their particular societies as about the spaces themselves. The picture of primitive disorder served to reinforce the wealthy visitors' own domestic order. While mission work and territorial governance might rescue the native family, the visitors spent their brief passages through native Alaska with their own domestic realms ever in mind. Social reorganization, as missionary Sheldon Jackson recognized, would necessitate a reconfiguration of Tlingit space. Tlingit kin would be segregated into Tlingit nuclear families, just like those of the visitors. The visitors themselves kept their minds ever fixed in relation to their own domestic spaces. "It may not be out of place to devote a few pages to the average tourist," wrote travel writer Ella Higginson. "To the one who loves Alaska and the divinely blue, wooded, and snow-pearled ways that lead to its final and sublime beauty," she continued, "it is an enduring mystery why certain persons—usually women—should make this voyage. Their minds and their desires never rise above a whale or an Indian basket; and unless the one is to be seen and the other to be priced, they spend their time in the cabin, reading and playing cards, or telling one another what they have at home."[136]

The *home* served as the mental center, the site of reproduction, both actual and social. The parlor, the center of the Victorian household, was the site for creating the bourgeois family's own sexuality. Centered on a

Figure 23. "The Thlinket [Tlingit] Indian" (sitka, 1887), E. J. Partridge
Collection. (Courtesy University of Washington Libraries, Special Collections)

narrowing of the family, the late nineteenth-century bourgeoisie
demanded individual discipline and restraint. Primitive sexual urges
needed to be held at bay. This class "must be seen . . . as being occupied
from the mid-eighteenth century on, with creating its own sexuality, and
forming a specific body based on it, a 'class' body with its health,
hygiene, descent, and race."[137] There was no universal sexuality; there
were only class sexualities. The bourgeoisie first applied its repressive
techniques upon themselves. And afterward assumed the rest of humanity should come under its imperial supervision. The tourists' accent of a
native-born Protestantism figured their view of the alien native world.

The travelers' society possessed two quite contradictory beliefs: that
they might be both driven by primitive desires and completely free, as
civilized beings, of such conscious or unconscious drives. Their understanding of history as a progressive movement from the primordial to
the civilized present enabled such a balancing of opposite extremes.[138]
The travelers' society in turn held contradictory impulses to both preserve and transform native culture.

The Tlingit, according to guidebook writer Eliza Scidmore, were
"almost too quick to lay aside their old ways. . . . It is the Thlingit's aim
to dress and live as the white man, and he fills his home with beds,

tables, chairs, clocks, lamps, stoves and kitchen utensils, and even buys silk gowns for his wife."[139] The Tlingit, she believed "were no longer picturesque, distinctive, or aboriginal." Even as they became domesticated in the eyes of the newcomers, they could not help but lose those attributes that constituted their very Indian-ness, according to the sightseers.

The travelers' written observations of native familial demise confirmed the superiority of their own particular social class. While the tourists' eyes gazed on fresh scenes, their minds were set on home. These imperial contrasts helped bolster bourgeois identities. "The private individual, who in the office [and on tour] has to deal with realities," Walter Benjamin wrote, "needs the domestic interior to sustain him in his illusions . . . from this derive the phantasmagorias of the interior—which, for the private individual, represents the universe. In the interior, he brings together remote locales and memories of the past. His living room is a box in the theater of the world."[140] Imperial contexts were instrumental in helping to fix bourgeois identities in the imperial metropolis. They never left home too far from their thoughts.

The words and things that they carried home provided the evidences of their having traveled. Their published travel books, their journals and diaries passed among family and friends, Kodak snapshots and lantern slides, and their curios neatly displayed in their parlors all stood in for their fleeting experiences. Their admitted pleasure in possessing native objects depended upon others. The gratifications associated with ownership relied upon others' acknowledgements.[141] All social relation was based upon its representational value. As traveler Ella Higginson wrote, "you will bring home with you not only Atka baskets, ivories, kamelinkers, bidarkas, virgin-charms, and dozens of other curios that will make your friends die of envy."[142]

"As the home, in its loveliness and in its sanctity, grows up and obtains permanency and durableness," a writer for a late nineteenth-century collecting magazine noted, "the collector's genius presides over its beautifying operations and coordinates the treasures scattered about by past and present generations."[143] Psychoanalytically speaking, fetishism was a strong, mostly eroticized attachment to a single object. The fetish was an object supposed to be inhabited by a spirit. It was anything that was exaggeratedly reverenced or loved, an object rousing undue interest by its sexual association. The tourists' carefully arranged curios filled the mantles and tables of their parlors, taking privileged positions. Strange figures from remote locales and memories past transformed the parlor space into a theater of the world. Looming over these domestic scenes the primordial objects represented a world of unrestrained and unconscious desires. And yet the parlor scene was the supposed center of repressed Victorian sexuality. The phantasmagoria of the domestic interior was the ambivalence of the bourgeois mentality that exhibited a constant fluctuation between wanting one thing and its opposite.[144] The travelers' totem collecting was hardly stripped of a certain sexuality. Returning to these scenes of domestic security, where life was safe from the market, the homebound tourists filled this space with totems of primordiality. Here at the center of their own elaborately sexualized space, the Victorian parlor, the returned travelers constituted their distance from savage desires, but also their close proximity. "The physiological side of collecting is important," Benjamin wrote. "In the analysis of this behavior, it should not be overlooked that, with the nest-building of birds, collecting acquires a clear biological function."[145] While at once repudiating native bodies as utterly other, the returned travelers simultaneously filled their most intimate private spaces with the artifacts of these same native bodies. The final meanings of their curio displays will probably always recede from comprehension, filled as they were with all the complicated lines of late nineteenth-century ideas and feelings. But if, as Benjamin suggests, their collecting had a "biological function," then this utility emerged from the supposed contrast between the savage sexuality represented in the native fetishes and the evenly controlled behaviors of the civilized travelers. The curios indexed bourgeois society's strength, its ability to expand its political horizons, to control, and to understand these native others.

Connecting everything to everything they sought a language that might bring all things into relation with one another. If they seemed uncomfortable with the wider exposure to different cultural meanings, they do not reveal this in their writings, so secure do they appear. This security may be found in the surety of their understandings, in the firm structures of thought found in their observations, in their social Darwinism, and in their rough anthropology. If their travels were redemptive, then they were so because they confirmed what they thought they already knew about the world. The civilized visitors' assumed biological vigor; their race superiority, often unspoken, presided over their visits and lingered in the presence of the curio fetishes long after their returns home. These supposed laws gave cover to a moment of high imperialism where science gave sanction to hierarchies and dominations that were ordered in history and reflected the contingencies and historically relative structures of perception underpinning the power of this particular social class.[146]

When John Muir and the missionary S. Hall Young paddled out from Fort Wrangell in autumn 1879, they planned to stop over on another northern island. Muir had heard rumors "that there was a Harvard graduate, bearing an honored New England name, living among Kake Indians on Kouyou Island." Young recounted their attempt to contact their countryman. "On arriving at the chief town of that tribe we inquired for the white man and were told that he was camping with the family of a sub-chief at the mouth of a salmon stream. We set off to find him. As we neared the shore we saw a circular group of natives around a fire on the beach, sitting on their heels in the stoical Indian way. We landed and came up to them. Not one of them deigned to rise or show any excitement at our coming. The eight or nine men who formed the group were all dressed in colored four-dollar blankets, with the exception of one, who had on a ragged fragment of a filthy, two dollar, Hudson Bay blanket. The back of this man was towards us." After speaking to the chief, Muir crossed to the other side of the fire and saw his face. "It was the white man, and the ragged blanket was all the clothing he had upon him! An effort to open conversation with him proved futile. He answered only with grunts and mumbled monosyllables. This the most filthy, degraded, hopelessly lost savage that we found in this whole voyage was a college graduate of great New England stock!"[147] Muir likely agreed with his literary mentor Henry David Thoreau, who wrote in *The Maine Woods* that "There is, in fact, a remarkable and unexpected resemblance between the degraded savage and the lowest classes in a great city. The one is no more a child of nature than the other."[148]

The late nineteenth-century nostalgia for the pre-industrial past did not include completely turning one's back on civilization. There could be no therapeutic return if there was no return. Too close a communion with the frontier communities brought forward the threat of contamination. Unlike this Harvard graduate gone native, the tourists never really left the home places they carried around in their heads. Like Muir, the tourists clung to their bourgeois identities, rejecting the Tlingit as beyond the pale. Muir's pursuit of self-creation fixed on a pure version of nature, stripped of any human presence. He, like the other northern travelers, was not interested in primitivism. "Most Indians I have seen," Muir insisted, "are not a whit more natural in their lives than we civilized whites. . . . Nothing truly wild is unclean. . . ."[149] He could afford to hold his views about nature and natives. Muir lived within his own contradictions—a now wealthy man with abundant leisure—and abjured the civilized life he saw as corrupted and polluted, yet he derided those people who seemed to live closest to nature. Money brought Muir close to nature.

Chapter Six

Juneau's Industrial Sublime

Out of Fort Wrangell, steamers churned northward another hundred nautical miles to the mining center of Juneau. First west into Frederick Sound and then turning northwestward into the nearly seventy-mile stretch of the Stephens Passage, the ships carried their cargoes of tourists, miners, mail, groceries, and mining supplies to the booming village, site of the largest gold mine in the world during the late nineteenth century. Leafing through the pages of an Alaskan tour book, these tourists might have agreed with travel writer Eliza Scidmore, who marveled at the passing scenery. "There was something, too," Scidmore wrote, "in the consciousness that so few had ever gazed upon the scene before us, and there were neither guides nor guide books to tell us which way to go, and what emotions to feel."[1] Scidmore's pleasant confusion in the face of Alaskan scenes might have quickly turned to horror had she witnessed events that confronted visitors in 1883.

The regular steamer schedule that summer carried a group of tourists to an unanticipated reception at the Juneau pier. Arriving travelers could hear the rough distant clanking of the gold mine stamp mills working across the channel, smoky, wet clouds wisped in the distance behind the clapboard town hacked out between the mountains and sea. But it was a makeshift gallows—rope, noose, and lynched man—that fixed their gaze now. The body hung on the scaffolding above the oozy lawn of seaweeds left exposed by the ebbing tide. A crowd of white men all held the hanging rope.

Several Tlingit men had run afoul of a local saloonkeeper and, according to the midnight verdict of the local miner's meeting, one of the men had murdered the saloonkeeper. "It just so happened," recalled Juneau local D. A. Murphy, "that just as we hung this Indian the monthly steamer came in and tied up to the wharf and of course the people on it could see what happened." According to Murphy, "There were quite a number of tourists aboard and between sixty and seventy white men in Juneau at that time. So that we would all assume equal responsibility for hanging the Indian we all pulled on the rope." This scene must have made quite a spectacle. The tourists' experience in an unstable realm could not always be controlled and packaged.

"Later on that same afternoon the third Indian was taken. [The second presumed culprit had been shot and killed earlier by a miners' posse.] We then decided that as long as they had pleaded guilty it was useless to hold another meeting, so we hung the last Indian on the same scaffold on the beach. It so happened as we hung him the steamer left the wharf."[2] For the upscale tourists there was no escaping the sight of the dockside gallows with its mob lynching. It seemed as if the miners were hanging Indians as a matter of habit.

Lacking a guidebook that might tell them what emotions to feel as they gazed on the scene before them, the tourists slipped into the only rationale available to them. "The country is perfectly wild," noted an emigrant's guide to British Columbia's gold fields, "and a dense forest, full of warlike Indians; and, with the well-known injustice of the miner towards anything of the genus Indian or Chinaman, and their foolhardiness, they will get up a series of little amusements in the way of pistolling and scalping, quite edifying. It is the custom of miners generally to shoot an Indian . . . and it is considered a very good joke to shoot at one at long shot, to see him jump as the fatal bullet pierces his heart."[3] Indeed, the Juneau local Murphy noted that upon the return of the next steamer following the lynchings, "we had clippings from all over the world saying that we were hanging Indians just for fun." The expectation of frontier violence—its presumption as unfortunate but necessary, and so its acceptance—guided the visitors' perception of these horrors. Where hours earlier the tourists had been bargaining with natives for souvenirs, marveling at the supposed mysteries of Fort Wrangell's totem poles, and generally finding in the native presence a rich spectacle, here one day in Juneau they briefly confronted something else.

But this uncontrolled element was quickly buttonholed into the easy discourse of the frontier, a realm so free that it was believed that swift and arbitrary justice was acceptable. But the gory spectacle had not been staged for the tourists. The scaffold was built on the beach in plain view of the Indian village, "in order that it might be a lesson to them . . . when they had hung long enough, their bodies were cut down . . . it had an excellent effect on the natives afterwards. They were quite civil to the whites," as Juneau resident William Pierce observed of the lynching"[4] Edward Pierrepont, visiting southeast Alaska, had similarly arrived at the time of a hanging. In his 1885 travel account *Fifth Avenue to Alaska*, the young New Yorker noted that "while shopping for souvenirs in the Indian village, the cry 'Indians are coming!' went out." Curio shopping was not such a mundane activity after all. Pierrepont had made sure he was armed and ready on his shopping excursion. "Drawing my revolver,

I rushed out; and from every direction the miners were coming, each little log hut yielding up its owner armed with an old Hudson-Bay gun or Winchester. In a few moments all the men who possessed guns were mustered in the little open street." Pierrepont concluded that "the fight would be a bloody one . . . the flash of guns could distinctly be seen."[5] As it turned out the so-called hostile band was in fact a group of Tlingits who had captured another murderer from an earlier incident. "A great load of anxiety was lifted from all," Pierrepont wrote, "although I confess that the prospect of an Indian fight had been exhilarating." After a hasty on the spot "trial" the Sitkan man was hanged. "His hands were tied, and the noose placed around his neck. He repeated the Lord's Prayer in pretty good English. It seemed a strange coincidence that the three murderers were all Christian, converted by the faithful missionaries," Pierrepont wrote.[6]

Lamenting the rule of the lynch law, Pierrepont nonetheless placed the incidents firmly in the permissible space of "this wild territory." The visitor reflected on another incident in which the USS *Adams* shelled the Tlingit village of Killisnoo. "At first glance, the bombardment and burning of an Indian village by an American man-of-war when reported East sounds harsh; but not so to a settler in this far-off possession. . . . Murderers and desperadoes have to be hanged by lynch-law. It is impossible for one ship to be at every point along twelve hundred miles of coast at the same time." Pierrepont easily incorporated this use of violence as necessary and justifiable. "We moved away in silence, and went sadly back to the steamer" he wrote, "and, as we left this place of violence and lawless death, we felt that our government had neglected its duty in failing to organize a Christian rule over this wild territory which we had purchased. As we slowly steamed away in the dusky afternoon, we looked back from the deck; and on the gallows of new wood, standing out against the dark background, we saw the swinging body of the dead, and heard only the lapping of the wavelets on the beach, and the requiem-dirge of the moaning winds along the mountains."[7] Travelers to Alaska, such as Pierrepont and the others, knew what to do with the unexpected. These isolated incidents were not emblematic of any wider barbarisms, no darkest Africa here, no heads on pikes.[8] Instead, momentary violence, necessary to keep the natives in line, they thought, was staged to "make a deep impression on the wild and passionate nature of a savage aborigine."[9] Violence was a part of nature, part of the scenery like the waves, wind, and mountains, brief reflections of the as yet unsettled wildness of the place.

It would seem that each of the villages along the coast where Tlingit and whites crowded anxiously together had witnessed at least one lynching. In 1870 at Wrangell a similar situation led to the hanging of a local man. A Stikine Tlingit man loaded on local liquor provided illegally by white miners bit a laundress' finger. Her husband happened to be the local quartermaster sergeant with the U.S. Army. The fort dispatched an officer with twenty soldiers at midnight. Arriving at the Tlingit village, the troops lined up outside the supposed culprit's home. When the accused Tlingit emerged a rapid volley of eight shots killed him instantly. In retaliation, a relative shotgunned a white man, an ex-Confederate soldier with a long history of violence and racism directed at the Tlingit. That afternoon the Tlingit and the army post exchanged gunfire, leading to the shelling of the Tlingit village. The following day the shelling resumed at sunrise "until these helpless people begged for mercy."[10] The Tlingit man accused of the shotgun killing was surrendered. And "the man was hung in full view of the ranch [Tlingit village], and the body remained until sun-down."[11] The Tlingit had become accustomed to well-staged displays of the strangers' power, aimed less at executing the accused than at terrorizing the Tlingit who were the intended audience. On the peripheries, instead of finding more freedom, official and unofficial practices more often overasserted their authority.

Beyond the lynching, Juneau presented a stump-pocked scene of rainy desolation, erosion gutted streets, and a chaos of clapboard shacks, scattered higgledy-piggledy up the hillsides. The forests had all been cut to feed the giant boilers of the mine's hundred-odd stamp-mills.[12] Whatever went uncut succumbed to the heavy plume of smoke from the Treadwell mine's chlorination works that killed off the vegetation for a mile up and down the nearby Douglas Island's edge.[13] The scarp of the coast mountains rose up some 4,000 feet, squeezing the town between the peaks and sea. So dwarfed did the town appear that one traveler noted, "It is a toy town with toy streets."[14] Others were less impressed with the town's quaint features. "We fondly anticipated wide streets and fine buildings, and could hardly believe our eyesight when we beheld the straggling lines of tumble-down buildings, and the narrow sidewalks beside a slough of mud," noted William Wiley, traveling with his wife Sara in 1892.[15] By the time Wiley and his entourage trooped through the muddy streets, Juneau had been a mining site for more than a decade. These hills were veined with minerals.

In 1878, the U.S. government commissioned the naturalist John Muir to reconnaissance the resources in southeastern Alaska during his upcoming visit.[16] And in autumn of the following year, Muir and the Fort Wrangell Presbyterian missionary S. Hall Young embarked on a nearly thousand-mile canoe journey with four Tlingit guides. This five-week venture took them north into Glacier Bay and on their return south

Figure 24. "Juneau, Alaska," (June 1886), Winter and Pond Collection.
(Courtesy University of Washington Libraries, Special Collections)

through the Gastineau Channel, site of future Juneau. Muir's interests
and intentions were broader than simply documenting the region's supposed wilderness attributes. Despite his status as a naturalist, he traveled
officially in the name of American territorial interests, bringing back
favorable reports concerning the territory's mining potential.

Muir challenged earlier dismissals of the North's mineral potential,
and he predicted that the area southeast of present-day Juneau would
"make a second California." During his subsequent visit to Sitka in early
spring 1880, Muir met with U.S. Navy commander L. A. Beardslee and
relayed the findings of his coastal reconnaissance. He carefully detailed
a map of Glacier Bay that led to the first tourist visits to the bay several
years later, intentionally boosting another of the North's coming industries—the extensive tourism that brought thousands northward in the
years before the Klondike. But Muir had also supplied officials with
many observations about possible mineral areas where gold might be
found. All of this information, and the sketch, were published in an
official government report in 1882.

Rumors of Muir's findings spread more quickly in the small close-knit community of prospectors and military personnel then living in Sitka. Soldiers, sailors, and a number of officers had been involved in mineral exploration and development nearby since the early 1870s. Much of the region's gold was found in quartz veins, as opposed to the more easily mined placer—or free gold—ordinarily panned from the loose gravel of creeks and rivers. Quartz gold mining required substantial investment in rock-crushing stampmills and chemical-reduction facilities to extract the gold from the crushed stone. Breaking hard rock was not a job for the ragtag armies of prospectors scattered about the territory. A German mining engineer, George Pilz, had come north from California in 1879 to assist in the development of the Silver Bay mine near Sitka, a lode claim owned by several on-duty army officers and outside businessmen. The Sitka veins did not prove profitable, so Pilz encouraged new exploration. Recognizing the Tlingits' intimate knowledge of the region, he promoted their contributions to the prospecting effort. "I had made a standing offer of a bonus of 100 pairs of Hudson's Bay blankets and work for the tribe at one dollar per day, for any ore samples brought me, of rock in place" that proved valuable, Pilz recorded.[17] "Nearly every tribe brought me some—the Chilkats, the Hoonup from Chichagoff and Cross Sound and Icy Straits, the Hoochinoos from Admiralty Island, the Auks from Auke River and present Juneau, the Takoos from Takou and Windham Bay, Schucks from Sumdum and different others," Pilz wrote.[18] The Auk clan leader Cowee from the Gastineau Channel area brought Pilz a number of promising ore samples. Following up on John Muir's predictions and the information gathered from Tlingit prospectors, Pilz sponsored—grubstaked—a series of prospecting expeditions to explore the region. Richard Harris and Joseph Juneau were among more than a dozen men, including a number of Tlingit, who were paid to find and stake gold claims. And it was Harris and Juneau who eventually found prospects and staked lode claims near the Auk village on the Gastineau Channel. "It was a beautiful sight to see the large pieces of quartz, spangled over with gold," Richard Harris later said, of the autumn 1880 discovery in the Silver Bow Basin above the eventual town site, later named for his partner. The subsequent discovery of gold at Juneau, if not the direct result of Muir's report, was at least encouraged by the celebrated naturalist's promotions. By the mid-1880s the Treadwell mining complex at Juneau was the largest industrial gold mine in the world.

Russian Creole Stephen Ushin, chronicling events from his clerkship in Sitka, recalled in his journal the two most salient facts from this new development. "The quartz was discovered with the help of the Koloshes in the region of Aku-Taku. The first party of miners left Sitka for the newly-discovered gold bearing places near Taku . . . more than 20 men went with this party. A small steamboat from the man-of-war Jamestown accompanied them as a convoy," Ushin wrote.[19] The Tlingit along with the U.S. military had been active in the region's mineral exploration, which might seem more than a little incongruous. But the Auk and Taku Tlingit along the Gastineau Channel had long protected the area from the intrusions of outsiders. It would take the military presence to push development in this area.

A decade earlier, Captain John A. Henriques of the U.S. Revenue Marine had steamed the cutter *Lincoln* into the Gastineau Channel in order to investigate accusations of a hostile boarding of two American schooners by Tlingit from an Auk village. And before that the Taku Tlingit had frustrated Hudson's Bay Company efforts to establish a permanent fur trading post at Fort Durham in 1843. So that when the small band of prospectors headed out to stake new gold claims in the Silver Bow Basin, U.S. Navy Captain Henry Glass (who had succeeded Beardslee during summer 1880) sent along armed support. The small steam launch from the USS *Jamestown*, equipped with a Gatling gun, provided the right amount of intimidation.

Indeed, the Americans and British had not been reluctant to level their guns on native villages up and down the coast. The Gastineau natives knew well the devastating firepower that the visitors could muster. Captain Beardslee had similarly sent a Gatling-equipped steamer to the Chilkoot region, where white prospectors had tried in vain to negotiate safe passage over the pass into the upper Yukon River drainage area. (Beardslee had experience with opening new regions to American interests; he had, like Van Buskirk, accompanied Commodore Matthew Perry to Japan in 1853.)[20] "We exhibited to them the howitzer and gatling, firing a number of rounds from both; the action of the gatling, which was mounted on a pivot block aft, so that we could sweep two-thirds of the horizon, was particularly interesting to them, as it taught them what one man could do to a fleet of canoes coming from all directions." Several months earlier, in August 1880, more than a dozen armed sailors and officers accompanied a prospecting team to Chilkat where, not surprisingly, the organized civilian and military squad secured an opening of the pass that the Tlingit had resisted for decades. Captain Glass relied upon such tactics of intimidation, making frequent shows of his vessels' firepower to make an impression upon local Tlingit. At a neighboring village, Glass threatened that "If they harmed the whites who came among them, we would storm their village and blockade the river. He then showed them what the big guns were made of by firing quite a number of balls and bombshells . . . and the big braves didn't laugh anymore," wrote missionary Carrie Willard in December 1881.[21]

These staged bombardments by U.S. gun-ships were a common practice, as visitors noted when the navy demonstrated its guns at Juneau.[22] "The warship's commander, Captain Glass, had fired the heavy guns to prove their usefulness to the doubting Indians. This had made a great impression on the Natives," visiting German ethnographers Aurel and Arthur Krause noted in 1881.[23] But the military did not act as merely a threatening presence. At all of the early discoveries near Sitka and later at Juneau, the names of officers and enlisted men filled the claim notices. Juneau had been named briefly for Lieutenant Commander Charles Rockwell, who had overseen the work of settling mining claims and property ownership in the vicinity, though Rockwell would soon turn to Juneau as the miners' meetings asserted their control and renamed the mining outpost after one of their own. The officers "had gold fever bad," original discoverer Richard Harris wrote. "Too much praise cannot be given to the officers of the *Jamestown* as they assisted us in every manner in opening up the camp. The U.S. Navy never furnished a more honorable or obliging set of officers on our ships than the *Jamestown* had aboard at that time," Harris concluded.[24]

In April 1881 regular mail boat service had been established. By May of that year, 150 white miners and an estimated 450 Tlingit filled the haphazard town site. By 1882, "some five hundred thousand dollars had been taken out," according to an exaggerated estimate by an early Juneau stakeholder. It was estimated "some two hundred men were working, but the placer was beginning to play out."[25] In fact gold production—both placer and lode mining—reached an output of nearly $100,000 in 1881, and by 1890 nearly a million dollars in gold had been taken from the area.

This phenomenal output had been achieved through the development of the lode mines built on Douglas Island, across the Gastineau Channel from Juneau. Californian John Treadwell purchased the Paris claim from a French Canadian prospector, Pierre Joseph Erussard, in 1881. Within two years, Treadwell and a group of San Francisco investors operated a 120-stamp mill, crushing mined rock and extracting the gold through mercury amalgamation and chlorination. In 1885, the Treadwell mills processed an average of 300 tons of ore each day. By 1899 a complex of mines and mills on Douglas Island had raised ore production to several thousand tons per day, with a deafening roar of nearly one thousand stamp mills. For a generation the Treadwell complex represented the largest industrial gold-mining operation in the world, integrating the latest developments in gold extraction processes and attracting considerable capital investment.

For the crowds of travelers filling "the elegant steamers that weekly ply the inland channel from Port Townsend to Glacier Bay," these enormous mining operations fit easily into their tour agendas. "Alaska being so beautiful a country," missionary Charles Replogle wrote, "many tourists are found visiting its different places of interest through out the summer season." Their visits included the mines, as the missionary noted with the arrival of the steamer *Queen* "with about 200 tourists and the Treadwell Mines were always one of the places visited by them."[26] A critical part of the northern spectacle, aside from the glaciers and natives, included being "informed" about the "great resources of this wonderful country . . . and the extension of civilization," wrote Alexander Badlam in his popular travelogue, *The Wonders of Alaska, Illustrated.*[27] Contemporary observers would have joined mining historian T. A. Rickard in his enthusiasm for mining: "the great work of opening the dark places of the earth and of introducing civilization among the backward peoples."[28]

Alaska joined those other "dark places" in the imaginations of late nineteenth-century visitors. And as with the great Witwatersrand gold mines of South Africa, Alaska's wealth was opened up. Mining and the supposed work of civilization went hand in hand. When missionaries Charles Replogle and his wife applied for mission work, they hoped for a challenging assignment. "I might perhaps be permitted by the grace of God to see India, or it might possibly be the interior of Africa, for I had a sort consciousness that there were many workers who were willing to go to easy places, but to the hard places, the out of the way places, where men's lives were in danger, where no one else would go, would be my field! And there I was willing to go! And what could be harder than the heart of India or darkest Africa?" However, the Replogle family was sent to Juneau instead. "My wife was anxious to go," Replogle recounted. "She little dreamed that she ever would be so, but now the real time had come, and instead of darkest India, or blackest Africa, it was the snow capped peaks of Alaska that held view before our eyes."[29] The avowedly born-again Replogles set about Christianizing the several hundred Tlingit workers at the coastal gold mine. Their work of reform linked seamlessly the antipodes of the imperial mission, whether in darkest Africa or Alaska.

The mining work was not separated in the travelers' minds from the other spectacles observed on their transits northward. Mining, as one of the pinnacles of "machine civilization," represented the progressive triumph of man over nature and natives. "The greatest thing it has to show," wrote another traveler, "in proof of what treasures may yet be found in the earth, is the Treadwell Mine." "It is a veritable Vulcan's Cave, with its two hundred and forty 'stamps' resounding like so many trip-hammers that never cease their clang . . . it has stopped but once (and then only for a few minutes), running day and night, weekdays and Sundays!"[30] The mine represented a perpetual-motion machine to the tourists, running uninterrupted, harvesting money from the earth. But at the mines men's labor had been rendered invisible, as the tourists fixated on the marvels of industrial technology. "A whole mountain of free milling quartz to work on," marveled one traveler in his journal. "The rock is very low grade, however, running less than $4 to the ton average, and the rock is so soft that it can be got out and the gold extracted at the small cost of about $1.50 per ton . . . a very profitable piece of property."[31]

Machines had become the measure of progress. The Treadwell mine was all the more phenomenal because its technologies stripped value from apparently worthless rock—a true capitalist alchemy, conjuring gold from stone. The early placer finds, easily worked by individuals and small companies of men with little money and simple, even medieval equipment, had quickly been worked over. As they had said, "Alaska dust is big as wheat." Eventually harvesting new crops of gold necessitated the intervention of metropolitan capital from San Francisco, New York, and London. Individual prospectors were only the foot troops in a vanguard of industrialists with their large sums of capital and their machines, capable of working over the apparently poorer ore-bodies.[32] The myth of discovery was told and retold by the arriving strangers, celebrated as the beginning of the New North, a land opened by hardy pioneers and sustained by risk-taking capitalists. Alaska constituted "Nature's Corporation Yard," pronounced tourist Stephen Merritt during his visit to the Juneau mines.[33]

While the travelers visited Juneau's mines, they little noticed the workers who operated the machines and scraped at the quartz veins below ground. It was as if the natural wealth had been got from the ground by some magic. Instead of seeing the workers producing the gold, they saw mostly the machines. Looking at laborers, urged George Munro Grant in his 1882 *Picturesque Canada*, "in any other light than a piece of machinery, welcome him. Machinery is just what such a Province needs. It can never be developed except by the use of all kinds of labor-saving machines." "Labor is capital," Grant wrote, echoing sentiments shared widely among the capitalist classes along the American coast as well.[34] This concatenation of forces collapsed capital, labor, and nature into an ideological mix that neatly fixed the working classes within a natural stream of production.

But nonetheless the workers were there, numbering in the thousands by the time these mines stepped up their production in the 1890s.[35] Alaskan work was appealing during the last two decades of the nineteenth century. The lack of more rigorous territorial control and the close cooperation of the military with the loose government of the mining districts meant that the average worker enjoyed more freedoms than did his southern counterparts. "Living in Alaska is not so expensive as it is in Idaho or Colorado. . . . This is due to cheap transportation by steamers from southern ports," early mine worker Walter Pierce explained.[36] An Idaho editor relied upon the naturalizing metaphors of the era, seeing in the miners' wandering a trait that was "almost instinctive," for they were "the Arabs of the American wilderness, content with nothing but constant change and exploration."[37]

Where pamphlet writers advertised Alaska as "the greatest Mecca of the sight-seer on the North American continent," mine workers knew that the draw of Alaska was not due to its scenic beauty, but rather to the obvious opportunities offered by Alaskan employment. "Alaska is the Mecca for the fortune seeker," advertising brochures would soon proclaim. "This is cool work and quite easy ten hours [sic] and I will have to content myself with the wages," William Bunge reasoned.[38] Bunge and others "contented" themselves with wages for short intervals between their prospecting expeditions into the interior or further up the coast, in search of the chance of sudden wealth, far superior to the slow accumulation of wages. Others were not so enamored with the industrial labor at the mines. "Anyone in Douglas familiar with these mines at this time knows whether he earned his wages or not," J. Bernard Moore wrote in his diary.[39] "I remained there for three weeks, then made up my mind that if I wanted to kill myself there were better ways than breaking ore rock for Treadwell's rock crusher." So Moore quit and with his Tlingit wife, Klinget-sai-yet, pursued less predictable prospecting in the interior. Writing of the seemingly ever-present rumor of rich gold finds, a Juneau newspaper story highlighted the mine capitalists' predicament regarding the need for more reliable labor. "If it should reveal a big strike there," an editor lamented of a rumored discovery, "Juneau will become nearly depopulated."[40] Territorial Governor Swinefort emphasized this dilemma in his 1887 annual report, writing that "the more intelligent and ambitious men who engage with them [the Treadwell mines] are generally inclined to work no longer than may be necessary to secure a comfortable 'grub-stake' with which to go prospecting on their own account."[41]

The tourists could not help but notice the overwhelming population of Tlingit living in and around Juneau. The town "seemed to consist almost entirely of Indians," wrote one visitor.[42] A few of the more persistent travelers recognized what their cohort generally ignored, that Tlingit laborers supplied a reliable local workforce counteracting the vicissitudes of the transient white workers. "Most of the Indian men were at work in the mines," travel writer Henry Finck observed.[43] Another writer chronicled the travelers' visits to the mines. "They see natives earning $2.50 per day each in the mine," Henry Winser wrote, "and learn to their surprise that they are better workmen than the whites; they see the ore in every stage from blasting to final separation, and though they may leave with a tinge of regret that it has not been their own luck to have made so valuable a discovery, they will none the less congratulate the owners on their magnificent possession."[44] Missionary Charles Replogle reported that "the rock does not contain any great amount of gold, only averaging about a dollar and eighty-five to ninety cents a ton, which necessitates the handling of great quantities of rock, requiring much machinery and many men." Replogle counted two thousand whites and some six-hundred Indians "all for the purpose of working in the mines."[45] But few travelers actually noted the native laborers working in the mines. Of course the discovery itself was of little actual value without the massive introduction of machinery and labor to "harvest" the gold, but leisure travelers highlighted the natural wealth of precious metals stripped from the earth.

The Tlingit workers looked out for their own interests, and in contrast to their white counterparts, recognized the effectiveness of organizing themselves. "A large part of the labor employed at the various industrial establishments is drawn from the native population," according to one writer. "The natives work in the mines and in the fisheries, in the digging of ditches, and construction of trails and wagon roads, and are, as a whole, as reliable as the ordinary class of white laborers," he elaborated. But, he continued, "They understand . . . the value of their services and are not infrequently inclined to emulate the example of their white brethren and go on a strike for higher wages, or because of some real or fancied grievance."[46] Even with organized strike tactics, native workers fell within the racially marked hierarchy that determined their pay at rates lower than their white counterparts. "Wages range all the way from two to six dollars a day," according to Juneau miner Walter Pierce. "A common white laborer will get three dollars per day, a miner four, a blacksmith five, a millwright six, and an Indian two dollars per day."[47] "Wages were paid to be $8.00 per day even to the Indians," according to Bishop W. C. Bompas, ministering in the interior upper Yukon during summer 1891. Where laborers were scarce, such as in the interior gold fields, native workers could negotiate more easily their own terms of employment. Wage rates fluctuated and by the mid-1890s Tlingit workers had bargained for a bit more, as the Baedeker's guide highlighted. "Many of the best workers in the mine are natives," the guidebook noted, "who earn $2 1/2 per day."[48] Native workers gathered in the coastal work sites such as Juneau, but also the dozen or so canneries that dotted the coastal archipelago. As European American mineworker Walter Pierce noted, "The Indians come in great numbers in search of employment." The large number of native workers at these industrial facilities made higher wages more difficult to secure. "Being of different tribes," Pierce observed, "they do a great deal of quarreling among themselves, and even go so far as to kill each other. However, when it got so far as that, it became necessary for the whites to interfere, for we wanted the Indians to labor, and if they were fighting among themselves we could not get them to work."[49] Preoccupied with the principal labor of prospecting and mining, the newcomers had little time for taking care of the rudiments of everyday living. As in nearby Sitka, "The Indians supply the city with plenty of lumber, fish, and game," according to Aurel Krause.[50] For the daily chores of laundry, food provision, construction, and cooking, the European American community relied upon the Tlingit.

The Treadwell mine owners had other ways of controlling the local native workers. Bringing Chinese workers up from the south, the mine owners hoped to break the mineworkers' ability to dictate the conditions of their labor and their wages. "The miners were," according to one visitor, "most of them foreigners and Indians, which partly took the curse of never ending accidents."[51] Indeed the hazards of the open pit and deep shafts with their constant blasting put the men at considerable risk and nurtured a necessary solidarity among the workers. For several years at the Juneau mines, mine owners pitted one working population against another, with the Treadwell workers—mostly immigrant Europeans and Tlingit—losing their position to what one contemporary called derisively "the Chinese two-legged machines."[52]

Anti-Chinese sentiment swept the western United States and British Columbia during the late 1870s and 1880s. Chinese workers, predominantly men, arrived first during the California Gold Rush of 1848 and continued to fill the ranks of the region's labor force, working on the railways and mines, doing what one contemporary described as "the dirty work." Following the sharp depression in 1876, labor activists in California targeted Chinese workers, blaming them for the white workers' unemployment.[53] Anti-Chinese riots rocked West Coast cities, particularly San Francisco. This unrest led eventually to a national response when the federal government passed the Chinese Exclusion Act of 1882. A trenchant racism endured. The Chinese workers who remained in the United States, and their American-born sons and daughters, found themselves the scapegoats for the slightest economic hardships experienced by their white counterparts. Industrialists, not blind to these tensions, used Chinese workers as a wedge between labor unions and the companies. Low-paid Chinese workers, isolated by the populist racism of the white-run unions, helped ensure a steady labor supply, less likely to strike.[54]

When a Juneau visitor exclaimed, "In Alaska, too—would you believe it?—we find the soon-to-be omnipresent Chinaman," his observation registered a decades-long struggle between labor and capital.[55] The Treadwell owners recognized the pervasive anti-Chinese racism and maneuvered Chinese workers to their own advantage. The mine owners followed a pattern of bringing in Chinese workers that had started with the fish-canning industry in the late 1870s. In May 1878, for example, "The SS. California arrived with a load of building materials and laborers to build the Fish Cannery," Sitka clerk Ushin noted. "20 Chinamen were brought here. It is the first time that the Chinese have been imported here . . . this was a surprise to all Sitka; the people went to look at the Chinese and to hear them talk, as if they were some unknown species of animals," he recorded.[56] By the time Reverend Zahm visited the coast in 1885, Chinese mineworkers seemed to dominate the workforce. "In Juneau one meets them, and in the celebrated Treadwell mine, of which I have already spoken, they constitute, it would seem, a majority of the workmen employed in drilling and blasting," Zahm observed. "I have never gotten on a steamer anywhere in the territory without coming across some of them." But echoing the consistent racist stereotyping, the visitor noted, "They have fastened themselves like a cancer." During his 1885 visit, he added that "their blighting influence on the parts they inhabit" was everywhere apparent.[57] Others shared his sentiments. By the time Reverend Zahm had published this lecture a year later, the Chinese had been forced to follow another recent trend. They had been driven out of the Treadwell mines.

In 1886, "there was lots of work at the mine digging the glory hole and the local Indians wanted this work but a great many Chinese had been employed by the company and there was trouble between the natives and the Chinese over this matter," Juneau local D. A. Murphy wrote. "A citizens' committee held a meeting and decided they would ship the Chinese out of the country," he noted.[58] Murphy, like other white locals, had little sympathy for the Chinese. "It was a beautiful sight and one of the few days when the channel was smooth the day it was done," described Murphy, giving a particularly working-class perspective upon the picturesque. "There were at least fifty large Indian canoes or war boats propelled by the Indians with paddles and they were loaded with the entire Chinese population. . . . The Chinese upon being landed in Juneau were placed aboard a schooner and deported to Puget Sound."[59]

Attempts to run Chinese workers out of the towns and cities up and down the Pacific coast and in the interior had been a staple of the anti-Chinese movement. In San Francisco in the late 1870s, Dennis Kearny's Workingman's Party of California demanded that the Central Pacific Rail Company, then the largest employer of Chinese laborers, discharge these workers. Central Pacific refused and rioting white men terrorized the city's Chinese residents for days, burning, looting, and beating. When Juneau local Murphy chronicled his town's evictions, he added, "Incidentally, in connection with the removal of the Chinese there was no rioting."[60] This must have seemed a surprising fact, given the ferocity of anti-Chinese attacks during the same period. (There had been some violence, as in January, when a house in which Chinese workers were living was bombed.) The year 1885 proved brutal for Chinese communities in the West. In September 1885, a mob of 150 whites attacked the Chinese community in Rock Springs, Wyoming, killing 28 Chinese coal miners. In Idaho masked white men lynched five Chinese men. Tacoma expelled its Chinese residents. And in early 1886, riots in Seattle forced Chinese to flee the city for a short time. And these notorious events only highlighted the routine and daily oppressions suffered by these immigrant communities. This anti-Chinese sentiment had spread north by summer 1886, when the Juneau eviction took place.

But the Juneau local's account placed the Tlingit workers at the vanguard of the eviction. So, while the Juneau eviction should be counted alongside the widespread anti-Chinese actions of 1885 and 1886, the Juneau action counted Tlingit workers among the "Chinese Must Go" contingent, suggesting a much more complicated mix of racial and class antagonisms. Other contemporary accounts did not place Tlingit workers at the lead of the eviction. A Fort Wrangell newspaper noted, "The Anti-Chinese movement has reached even Alaska's far away shores. A party of men from Juneau, mostly foreigners, crossed the bay to the Treadwell Mine on Douglas Island and ordered the Chinamen employed there to leave immediately. Two small schooners were chartered by the whites, and the Chinamen hustled aboard . . . the schooners, with their unwilling passengers, numbering eighty-seven."[61] Of course this account reflected another set of biases, directed against "foreign workers" by the white missionary editors and their Tlingit converts in Fort Wrangell. Tlingit reporters blamed the white foreigners as easily as the whites had placed the Tlingit as the perpetrators. Tlingit workers did, however, organize against Chinese laborers at other worksites and no doubt played an important role in the Juneau eviction. John Muir, visiting a cannery near Sitka in 1879, noted the local Tlingit's opposition to Chinese workers taking jobs that the natives had recognized as their own. "Many Indians are also employed in the cannery," Muir wrote during his 1879 visit, "together with a few Chinamen. They receive a dollar a day. When the Chinamen came up on the steamer, the Indians at first raised a great outcry and refused to let them land, claiming that the work rightly belonged to them and it was only after being assured that no Chinamen would be employed as fishermen, and that after the Indians learned to make the cases they would all be sent back, that order prevailed. A more perfect settlement of the Chinese labor question on a small scale could not easily be found."[62] Muir found little he liked in either the canneries or the Chinese workers. "A fearful smell, a big greasy cannery and unutterably dirty, frowsy Chinamen. Men in the business are themselves canned," Muir wrote. But if Muir's observations place the Tlingit workers of the region alongside their white counterparts who were concerned with protecting what they perceived as their prerogatives, the racial relationships were more complicated.

For the Tlingit, the "Chinese question" centered on jobs, and the racial animosities that characterized the Chinese relations with Muir and most whites did not also color the Tlingit and Chinese relationships. As the traveler Edward Pierrepont noted in 1885, while visiting "a large salmon-cannery at Pyramid Harbor, we saw nineteen Chinamen and some twenty Indians working at the same long table. But for the dress and pigtail, we could not tell the Chinese from the Alaska Indians, so close was the resemblance of features. Upon inquiry we found that several Chinamen had intermarried with squaws, that they seemed to have a ready understanding of each other and could communicate through their language with greater facility than the whites. I imagine that they must have sprung from the same original stock."[63] Intermarriage between Chinese men and Tlingit women was not uncommon. "A Chinese wanted to be baptized in order to be qualified to marry a Kolosh [Tlingit] woman. The priest refused because the Chinese would not consent to cut his queue and to renounce traditions of his motherland," one writer noted in 1887.[64] Together the Tlingit and Chinese were kept at the periphery of the mining economy, close enough to serve as a labor force, but alien enough not to be allowed the prospect of laying claims of their own. Missionary Charles Replogle recognized this factor in the regional labor economy. "There was another condition which needs mention," he wrote, "the laws concerning the Indians. The Indian had no rights as a citizen, for was he not a vassal of the Government? He had been purchased from Russia with the rest of the country, and now he was but a native and not a citizen. And in that case any improvement or any mining location for him could not be maintained in court."[65] As a result of being legally excluded from seeking their own gold finds, Tlingit found themselves relegated to laboring in the white-owned industrial mines.

Tlingit mineworkers along with immigrant Europeans, evicted Chinese laborers, native marriages to Chinese men, the presence of the world's largest industrial gold-mining operation in these northern latitudes, lynchings: these facts signal a complicated history. But these facts, significant as they seem now, carried contemporary import only inasmuch as they were endowed with significance.[66] Travel writers and other interpreters of this northern territory, if they did not completely ignore Juneau's complicated social relations, then emphasized instead those aspects of the region that fit more easily into their expectations.

The travelers recognized in Juneau the same disorientation they had experienced in Fort Wrangell, remarking upon the filth and smell as they sensed it, rather than any probing consideration of the town's culture. After all, they had come to this faraway place in order to escape from social realities. In their eyes, such a place could have little culture, at least in the highbrow sense given the term by bourgeois Victorians. "Juneau is a very dirty and odoriferous hole," Eliza Clendenin proclaimed in her travel diary, "and is perfectly piggy!!!"[67] But Juneau and its adjacent mines had other significant meanings. And it was to these attractions that the travelers turned their attentions.

"It contains a vastness of resources sufficient to make it an industrial empire," Alexander Badlam wrote. "It can be made another great field for the profitable investment of American capital," he enthused.[68] Herein the landscapes of the north served to fuse the mutual destinies of the nation and nature. "Land and minerals," historian Alan Trachtenberg writes, "served economic and ideological purposes, the two merging into a single complex image of the West: a temporal site of the route from past to future, and the spatial site for revitalizing national energies."[69] This road to development relied upon a peculiarly American site: the mining camp. The mining camp sanctified the idea that individual luck and pluck marked the beginnings of expansive society in the West, and once that was exhausted, in the far North. The mining camp, peopled with rough and tumble prospectors, signaled the advance of America's frontier civilization. It carried mythic proportions, tying Alaska's gold mining to the California rush just a generation earlier. Promoters went further still, connecting Alaska's future to Alexander Humboldt's *Cosmos*. "Humboldt said, in his 'Cosmos,' that Alaska would yield more gold than all the continents put together," according to a mining company prospectus.[70] Mineral extraction formed the core experience of American frontier development. No matter that here in Juneau, whatever individualist assumptions were attached to mining, the industrial efforts were directed by metropolitan capital and the wage labor of natives and immigrants. "It has all the resemblance of a mining camp— i.e. 'everything goes what passes,'" tourist Charles Emerson remarked.[71] Emerson's comment echoed the rationalizations that others used to accept the lynchings, the evictions, and routine racisms directed upon the indigenous population. The frontier adage "everything goes what passes" served as the operating principle of northern development.

The tourist perceptions of Juneau thus ran between opposites. They fixated on the massive scale of the industrial mining operation, alongside the presence of prospectors on whom they projected a whole host of meanings. For these travelers, the landscapes of work and leisure existed side by side in an uneasy tension. On the Inside Passage, and particularly in Juneau and in the Douglas mines, the leisure class had constant interactions with workers and their work. These well-to-do visitors were not insulated from the laboring activities of the region, and observing these workers became an important part of the touring spectacle: the very sight of work brought on a swoon.[72]

"If you have never visited a mining camp and seen the miners with their picks and shovels and red shirts, you will doubtless be pleased at the opportunity which you will have at Douglas Island of looking over the Treadwell mine and seeing one of the largest quartz mills in the United States," a steamship company brochure advertised in 1887.[33] Depicting the classic image of the legions of red-shirted California forty-niners, the writer melded the prospector with his proletarian counter-

Figure 25. "Treadwell Gold Mine, Douglass [Douglas] Island," in L. Woodhull, "Photograph Album of Alaska and the Pacific Coast," c. 1889–91. (Courtesy Yale Collection of Western Americana, Beinecke Rare Book and Manuscript Library)

parts working by the clock in the massive mine and mill. Metropolitan tourists had no wish to travel so far to see workers similar to those waging sometimes open battles in the streets of gilded age America. Instead, along with visits to the mines, visitors took in sights of prospectors preparing their expeditions into the interior. Machinery ran the mines, and lone men prospected in the wilderness, pushing the boundary line of civilization ever backward. Along with the soldiers, sailors, and explorers, the prospector joined the ranks of the pioneers of empire. The proletarian mass received hardly a comment in the public and private travelogues. "It is a fitting out place for prospectors who make up their packs here and go over the mountains in search of gold," wrote one writer. "Here our miners left the boat and began looking around for Indians to carry their packs."[74] As with the industrial mine, native people did a considerable amount of the work of prospect mining. In the case of prospecting ventures into the interior, native packers carried hundred-pound loads over the difficult passes.

The visiting tourists had more interest in the white men who trooped off in search of new finds. "One of them had a most striking physique," wrote traveler Edward Parkinson, "large, powerful, and well-proportioned. In conversation with him it was ascertained that he was going to work his way over the mountains until he got to the Yukon River, then prospect along its banks until he reached the Behring Sea, where he would probably get on an American war vessel and come back to civilization. He calculated that he would be gone all summer, and would get back to the States about the middle of November."[75] Parkinson's commentary relayed the Victorian view of the wilderness as a testing ground for personal character.[76] Observing the muscular clarity of the man's motions, his work-worn clothing, the singularity of his purpose, all speaking silently of many winters of experience, the tourist's observations highlighted late nineteenth-century concerns over the physical degeneracy thought to be plaguing Anglo-Saxon Americans, as they understood themselves to be. Indoor "brain-work," the strains imposed by time discipline, the open struggle for economic survival in urban commercial society—these pressures, it was believed, drained the virile virtues from the nation's supposed best and brightest. Native-born white men's manliness was thrown into question by the social conditions that debased their physical selves. And so, elite travelers found themselves marveling over the physical stature—"large, powerful, and well-proportioned"—of the men they observed on their visits to Juneau. The contrast implied in the visitor's watching suggested the anxiety running through bourgeois men's minds. Psychologist William James compared the "tough-minded" to these rough and tumble prospectors of the mining frontier. The "tender-minded," he thought, were akin to the effete, "tenderfoot" New Englanders. "Their mutual reaction is very much like that that takes place when Bostonian tourists mingle with a population like that of Cripple Creek," James wrote. He might as well have been writing of the meetings between male tourists and the hardy men of Juneau.[77] The gold rush experience represented a paradox. It was at once a rejection of the technology of the modern, a return to a primitive economy, a nostalgic putting on of the modes and masks of the frontier past and at the same moment, contradictorily the gold seekers were the emblem of modern market culture, buying tremendous amounts of goods and services to get themselves into the northland, the land of their nostalgic dreams. In the eyes of leisure-class tourists, the prospectors became prototype adventurers, questing to escape the same culture that they most exemplified.

Prospectors themselves were not unaware of their cultural status. They recognized in themselves the projections of their traveling counterparts. "They had the conquering spirit of supermen," wrote prospector George Snow of his contemporaries, "that overcomes every obstacle; the spirit that opens the way for civilization."[78] Snow's prospecting *ubermen* enacted the conquest that Theodore Roosevelt celebrated in *The Winning of the West*. "In obedience to the instincts working half blindly within their breasts, spurred ever onward by the fierce desires of their eager hearts, they made in the wilderness homes for their children, and by so doing wrought out the destinies of a continental nation."[79] William James buffered this appeal to race destiny with a more mechanistic metaphor. "The enormous fly-wheel of society," according to William James, "it holds the miner in his darkness, and . . . it protects us from invasion by the natives of the desert and the frozen zone. It dooms us all to make the best of a pursuit that disagrees."[80] Men might not be able to choose their position within the machinery of society and economy, but they could with fortitude determine to persevere, "to make the best of a position that disagrees." James's celebration of working-class steadfastness and its unthinking physicality redounded in the minds of anxious elite men who felt increasingly effete and over-refined. In the image of the heroic prospector, some solace might be found. For James and his contemporaries, one's position within society had been fixed in positions determined by early habits. William James's colleague at Harvard University, geologist Nathaniel Shaler, shared James's idealization of the virtues of those hard-bitten characters that peopled the frontier. "This type of strong uneducated man, while he had little learning," Shaler wrote, "often had more light than those bred in academic places."[81] Tourists responded to this widespread anxiety that they were as a class compromised by their leisure and high-born upbringings. Travel to the frontier offered the possibility of contact with men of another sort. "No one could remain blind as the luxurious classes now are blind," Shaler wrote, "to man's real relations to the globe he lives on, and to the permanently sour and hard foundations of higher life." The leisure classes had made themselves victim to the new industrial order. Visits to the mining frontier placed anxious bourgeois men in contact with a working-class authenticity thought to be lacking in their everyday urban lives. Speculating on the possibility of retooling these habits at an early stage, Shaler suggested, "To coal and iron mines, to freight trains, to fishing fleets in December, to dish-washing, clothes-washing, and window washing, to road-building and tunnel-making, to foundries and stoke holes, and to the frames of skyscrapers, would our gilded youths be drafted off, according to their choice, to get the childishness knocked out of them, and to come back into society with healthier sympathies and soberer ideas." But his notion of an alternative education was just another kind of tourism, where elite youth played at being working class, but never remained in that condition because they had the resources to dabble and then return to their privileged existences. So too did the Alaskan travelers dabble, thinking that their recognitions of manliness in the passing prospectors constituted a kind of communion with these supposed brothers of the frontier. The promotional brochures advertised as much, offering Alaska "as a picturesque background, a democratic commingling of laborers, lumbermen, gold miners, sailors, loungers, Chinese and Indians."[82]

The new culture industry of the north brought tourists into close relationships with the region's productive enterprises. Working people, much like the Tlingit, became objects of tourists' interests, "a picturesque background." But this "democratic commingling" was also not an open and fluid society as represented. The tourists' narratives were laden with a stubborn class-consciousness. Their observing constituted a prurient sociological scrutiny of the working classes seen on their northern junkets, just as it was for their analyzing of native lifestyles. They rendered the prospectors as colorful rustics, but their admiring descriptions were really condescensions.

The miners held their own views of the pleasuring strangers. "Tourists in those days," remembered one old-timer, "were heartily despised by Alaskans, especially in Juneau where they took pictures of the businessmen and miners and acted as though they considered them a sort of aborigine, though some of them had come from that center of cultured New England. All sorts of jokes were played on them in spite of their self-complacent 'sophistication.' . . . The Indians also despised them."[83] While leisure gave bourgeois sightseers the opportunity to view these working environments, it did not also give these laborers passage into more comfortable lives. As one prospector noted on his return southward, the steamer on which he traveled carried the rich product of the most industrially sophisticated mining operation in the world at the time, ore blasted and processed by the labor of several hundred workers. But the hard-luck miner Ogrissek returned with nothing. Most prospectors scraped enough gold from the northern creeks to get by, but few made more than hardscrabble lives from their efforts. This fact confirmed the travelers' most deeply held beliefs in the unforgiving motion of the economy that could be "no more done away with than gravitation," as one contemporary noted. Their sightseeing both confirmed their superiority and established a vicarious infusion of the vigor of the barbarian lower classes to renew the supposedly weakened bloodlines of the elite. If they had the proper education and training, a tourist viewer could recognize the sublimity in both nature and the heroic pioneer prospectors. Far from working as a democratizing force, tourism further separated and defined the strata of class relationships in late nineteenth-century America. Tourists filled their representations with political meanings. Capitalism was natural, as much a part of the landscape as the forests and glaciers. To resist was to resist human nature.

By taking part in seeing native cultures or in observing working-class activities, the seer conferred respectability and purpose on his activity through the act of incorporating these other lives into a network of knowledge, the seat of which was the observers' own active observance. They engaged in an activity freed of the rudiments of low-brow paid entertainments in the age of Barnum. But these tourists were nevertheless entering into a vicarious relationship with the objects that they observed. Thus, even their very real experience of viewing natives and workers was mediated by the process of placing these others into an imagined and separate arena of knowledge. In observing "nature people" and laborers, tourists divined a supposedly natural connection to the world, a connection that preceded the industrial consumerist culture that the tourists sought to escape.[84] But they engaged and reproduced what they had intended to escape and reduce.[85] They were consummate "commercial persons," in Henry James's phrase. Their direct physical experience of these new situations was overcome by the imposition of their own norms and ideological filters.

Here in Juneau, natives and prospectors constituted a critical imaginative repertoire for bourgeois tourists, even to the extent that these others facilitated the travelers' own thorough self-critique. "They are patient, garrulous, plodding fellows," a traveler wrote of the native workers, "never in a nervous civilized hurry, and never at a loss to find out the means of doing whatever is required of them, their slow, cautious, complete methods always being found better than they promise, contrasting strikingly in this respect with those of the narrowly educated townsmen, educated only at the top."[86] The travelers celebrated those traits that were in fact a challenge to their own values of efficiency, discipline, and accumulation. Their observations hinged on their own self-critique, criticisms that at once positioned the sightseer in a position of self-control and self-definition. The travelers' concerns at leaving behind what she took to be her cultural center prompted a more-than-ever rigorous observance of whatever forms they thought distinguished them from the alien cultures in which they found themselves. Even as the leisure-class travelers attempted to separate themselves through their distant travels, they only reinforced their previously held ideas.[87]

"Every tourist has an opportunity of visiting, under the most advantageous and pleasurable circumstances, the greatest gold mine in the world, namely, the Treadwell Mine, on Douglas Island," the writer Henry Winser advertised.[88] The adventure of mining capital became an object of their fascination. "The property is owned by seven gentlemen," Mrs. Wood wrote, "John C. Jones of Nevada being one, and Mr. Treadwell, who stays here all to-gether, and who very politely showed us about yesterday, being another."[89] Their visits had more of the character of a personal invitation and private tour than it did a paid excursion. And indeed, it was such, as the travelers' status gained them entry into the property. "They estimate," Wood continued, "the property at 36,000,000—but you would scarcely take Mr. T for a millionaire—he looked no better than the miners. Seven years ago in San Francisco he was terribly crushed by the fall of an elevator. When he was sufficiently recovered he came up here for his health and discovered the ore which abounds on the island. He stays here altogether, is a bachelor, and I suppose has no other thought than the making of money—were it otherwise I should think he would take his share and try to find some more pleasurable existence." The tourist's comments highlighted a pervasive fixation with the mine's value, variously assessed between some $16 and $50 million, the specific amount varying through the early years. But whatever the exact amount, the valuation helped to establish the travelers' enthusiasm for the region's development, a rhetoric of progress sanctified by harvesting the wealth of nature. And the tourists resurrected that old myth of the self-made man, here in the shape of the common millionaire, "Mr. Treadwell," with "no other thought than making money."

"The finest mill of its kind in the world," remarked H. E. Morgan of the Treadwell complex.[90] Crushing 300 tons per day in 1886, the 120 stamps working around the clock in the mills helped to process $70,000 each month from the extensive quartz ledge. "No sooner is one district exhausted than another is discovered," Morgan enthused. "It is the largest gold mine in the world," repeated another travel writer in 1894, just eight years later, with now "300 stamps, dropping the year around, never stopping except on the 4th of July and Christmas. It is indeed a rare treat to walk through this mill, with two rows of stamps on each side, constantly dropping on the ore with a 'ca-chung' so rapid that a person can't 'hear himself think.'"[91] At the time about 300,000 tons of ore was consumed every month, according to this traveler. The ore went from the mine into a big funnel-shaped hopper, in the bottom of which was a crusher that let nothing through larger than a "potatoball." From here the ore went into a chute to the stamps that gradually pounded the rock fine as flour, which was then washed out of the "pit," or mill, by water

Figure 26. Far from a northern backwater, the Treadwell mines were among the largest and most sophisticated industrial gold mining operations in the world. "Battery Floor, A.T.G.M. Co's. [Alaska Treadwell Gold Mining Company] '300 Mill,'" Douglas Island, c. 1899, Treadwell, Winter and Pond Collection. (Courtesy Alaska State Library, Historical Collections)

constantly flowing under the stamps, out onto copper plates, loaded with quicksilver and charged with electricity, to which most of the native gold adhered. The refuse passed on over a rubber plate or belt that caught the sulphides, in which there was always more gold. This material was dried and put in large brick ovens; the sulphur burned out and then cooled off. The reduced ore passed through several chemical preparations and came out as gold in a liquid form. The whole works were run by water power, brought from the mountains in a big ditch that cost about a half-million dollars to construct. The energy cost savings and the close proximity to inexpensive water transportation to export the final gold product enabled the company to work ore that only averaged about $4 per ton in gold, at a profit, which was the lowest grade ore being worked by any mine in the world at the time. It was claimed that the "clean-up" was from one to one and a half million dollars in gold every year, Emerson reported.[92] So efficient was the mine operation that low-grade ore could be made to pay. This fact held visitors in a certain awe, that something so apparently worthless could be made, through the exercise of chemical, mechanical, and electrical processes, to give up its gold. "That it pays is evident from the wonderful appliances and amount of machinery. Everything seems simply perfect," a tourist marveled.[93] It appeared as a gigantic technological alchemy, this transformation of rock into gold, making something out of nothing, the ultimate expression of capitalism.

But it was the experience of venturing into the mine itself that held these tourists' attention. The mine proper was simply a huge hole in the side of a mountain that resembled a quarry. Several tunnels, however, were dug into the mountain. "Of all the horrible dins I ever heard that mill was the worst," Eliza Cleninden wrote. "It was deafening! We all then went through a darksome tunnel, where I had to walk on a rail to keep out of the mud. . . . After reaching the end of the tunnel, taking a few Kodaks and enjoying ourselves generally, [we] went out shopping again."[94] Like the curios purchased along the boardwalks of Wrangell and Juneau, the tourists' photographs helped preserve scenes as evidence of their visits. Cleninden's imagination, momentarily distracted from her shopping, fixed on the "darksome tunnel." Others commented on the adventuresome aspects of their mining visits. "About noon we crossed to Douglas Island, where is located the most remarkable mine on the coast and our experience here was most remarkable," one traveler noted. "Armed with umbrellas, waterproofs, overshoes, etc. we scrambled up the mine, a tremendous climb it was too. I supposed we were going down a shaft, consequently my surprise was great when upon reaching the spot, I found a huge quarry. They have excavated to the depth of one hundred feet or more . . . from the quarry we returned to the mill, and being provided with a guide and candles entered the tunnel, which runs back to the quarry. It was a very picturesque sight I assure you—this crowd of people marching single file, with their twinkling lights through that long dark cavern." The sight of the tourists themselves—enclosed in the darkness of the tunnel, a line of "twinkling lights"—presented a spectacle in the otherwise sightless space. In the absence of any view the travelers themselves became part of the picturesque scene. But if the experience of venturing through this unnatural tube in the rock bordered on sublimity, it was the feature of the mine operation itself that drew their wonder. The chaos and din of the mill

Figure 27. Tourists frequently toured the mines at Treadwell, Douglas Island, and some ventured up into the gold mines of the Silverbow Basin, site of the original Juneau gold discoveries (though the term "discovery" elides the Tlingit role in showing prospectors where to find the gold in the first place). "Underground at upraise of Alexander Tunnel. Alaska Perseverance Mine," Winter and Pond Collection. (Courtesy University of Washington Libraries, Special Collections)

seemed overwhelming, a sensory experience unlike any other they had known. Nature writer John Burroughs visiting the Douglas mine referred to the stamp-mill roar. "It dwarfs," he remarked, "all other rackets I ever heard. Niagara is a soft hum beside it."[95] If the size and power of natural spectacles like Niagara conjured sublimity, then the unnatural scene of the mine with its own sound and fury surpassed even the falls. In this comparison of the industrial and the natural, the one was understood as an extension of the other. Late nineteenth-century tourists moved easily between natural analogies for the industrial.

In the nineteenth century, Americans saw little contradiction between industry and nature.[96] Nor did tourists see beyond their images of machine wizardry into the laboring landscape that was all around them. The tourists' extended descriptions of the mine and its operations offer no depictions of the workers themselves. This harvest of the wealth of nature had been accomplished through technological mastery, with apparently little physical effort; no laborers complicated their scene of industrial sublime. The mine served as a marker of cultural achievement similar to the natural features, like Niagara Falls, that also held significant national value.

Traveler Stephen Merritt recognized the symbolic and actual value that was bound up in the mine and the region. "We land at the dock of these great works," he wrote, "and pass into the mills—and see the great crushers and washers, and then to the places where the washings are cooked, baked, dried, and made ready for the art of the chemistry of mining appliances. It is like Alaska, an immense plant. We believe in Alaska—its riches, honor, power." For Merritt, the mine and its operations transcended mere industry. Here was something to "believe in." Imagining the hull of the steamer *Queen* on which he was traveling ballasted with hundreds of thousands of dollars in gold, Merritt continued, "There are mines of wealth all about, and wonderful Alaska will outstrip California in the hidden metallic treasures soon to be unfolded. Wonderful country!"[97]

Far from posing a threat to the scenic grandeur that the tourists celebrated in their travel up the coast, the mines served to finish the scenery by turning up the hidden treasures of the earth. The once "green perfection" of the island forests were now, at Juneau and Douglas, smoking hills of rubble, the brown stubble of cut-off timber and mud, so much mud. But the tourists saw little compromise between the mine and its effects and the scenic landscape that they paid so much to visit. A caption describing a photograph of an eroded hydraulic mining site by F. H. Nowell (erroneously identified as placer mining) read, "a place in Alaska made even more picturesque by placer mining." "Even hydraulic mining cannot scar and disfigure this country, where a mantle of green clothes every bare patch in a second season, and mosses and lichens cover the stones and boulders," a travel writer concluded.[98] The transformation of nature fit comfortably alongside its preservation. But in terms of pure sublimity Juneau's industrial sublime ultimately registered second place in the tourists' imaginations. With "the miners thus failing us in picturesque and thrilling incidents," the tourists turned their attentions away from town and toward the supposed unpeopled spaces of the north.[99]

Chapter Seven

Orogenous Zones
Glaciers and the Geologies of Empire

Leaving the smoking, clanking mine operations at Juneau, travelers returned to the slate dark sea and coastal wilds. Steaming across the Lynn Canal, around the north end of Admiralty Island, and west through Icy Strait, the vessels carried their sightseeing cargoes to Glacier Bay. In their thoughts the travelers shifted from the technological machine culture of the massive Juneau mines to what they thought of as nature's culture at Glacier Bay. They moved easily from the noisy technological sublime to the geological sublime.[1]

Crossing the gleaming sea, "each point or peak passed brought another glacier into view, nineteen glaciers in all being visible on the way up the canal." In summer the snow streaked the low mountains' backs like zebras. The high mountains were hid in near perpetual cloud, and when visible they stood like spectral white towers above everything. "The blue expanse was streaked with a greenish gray where the turbid streams poured in from the melting glaciers," travel writer Eliza Scidmore wrote with a flourish.[2] "It is estimated that 5,000 living glaciers belong to the coast line of Alaska, hundreds of which descend to the level of the sea, many discharging small icebergs directly into the straits. The glacial record is an open book on every mountain side." A close-up look revealed that the "symmetry of its outlines and the grand slope of its broken surface are most impressive, and this mighty torrent, arresting in its sweep, shows in every pinnacle and crevice all the blues of heaven, the palest tints of beryl and glacier ice, and the sheen of snow and silver in the sunshine," Scidmore wrote. The rhetorical tropes of the nineteenth-century picturesque still found full expression in the visitors' responses to the glaciated otherness of these northern tidewaters.

Not all reactions were filled with such easy flourish. "It was a body in motion," wrote Henry Field, "as if it were a chariot on wheels, never resting, never ceasing in its march, with its cold eye fixed like the eye of death, pushing on day and night, crushing everything in its path, as if its mission on earth were simply to destroy."[3] Their sublime encounters in

Figure 28. Steamer *Queen* in ice at Glacier Bay, June 1891. (Courtesy Yale Collection of Western Americana, Beinecke Rare Book and Manuscript Library)

the face of all that grinding ice left the sightseers profoundly moved. "My first glimpse of the glacier made me feel decidedly queer—It was such a great wall of blue ice, 300 feet high and about a mile and a half long, that one can't quite take it in at first," another admitted. The sublimity of their experiences gave the travelers the sense that they were in the presence of some pure reality. Immensity staggered their imaginations. "The Muir [Glacier] is three miles long, with a perpendicular face of four hundred feet, stretching like a frozen waterfall or gigantic dam entirely across the head of the bay. Its breast is as blue as turquoise. At a distance it looks like a fillet rent from the azure sky and laid across the brow of the cliff," Charles Hallock wrote. "What a mighty power was hidden behind the dazzling drapery of its iridescent façade!" another wrote. "Standing upon its surface a short way inland, one could hear from its depths what seemed like shrieks and groans of maddened spirits torturing each other," Maturin Ballou described his visit. "Our power of appreciation is limitless, though that of description is circumscribed," he admitted.[4] Their words conformed to the peculiar nineteenth-century literary convention of claiming to be speechless. "Our bright

dream—No! All is too real, too vivid, too enduring, for any such simile."[5]
The incomparable landscape would not fit the conventions of language.
Nature existed as an ultimate grammar to which the travelers aspired
to speak. But such supposedly pure encounters with reality more often
transcended the confinement of words, or so the travelers liked to think.
They wrote copiously, nevertheless.

Strains of romanticism persisted in the landscape writing conventions
of these Victorian travelers. And these well-educated tourists would have
shared Percy Shelley's description of his experience on viewing the glaciers of Mont Blanc early in the century. The glaciated landscape
inspired "an undisciplined overflowing of the soul . . . an attempt to
imitate the untameable wildness and inaccessible solemnity from which
those feelings sprang," Shelley wrote.[6] Shelley and his romantic cohort
helped to fix glaciers as an ultimate form of the sublime.

Nature, manifest in the glaciated landscape, served as the raw material
for human cultural constructions. "To the lover of pure wildness," Muir
urged, "Alaska is one of the most wonderful countries in the world."
"Pure wildness"—only a generation or two earlier such a "love" for the
wild would have been unthinkable in the far north. Such fancy was now
possible from the comfortable safety of the steamer decks. These sightseers were disposed to visit the "wilderness" and to aestheticize its terrors because they lived safely apart from its rigors. "The careful
commercial lives we lead hold our eyes away from the operations of God
as a workman," Muir wrote.[7]

For tourists, sightseeing was a form of conspicuous consumption, or
conspicuous leisure, as Thorstein Veblen had termed it. And the attractions of these sublime mountains might be recognized by those "best
equipped by nature" to recognize the sublime in nature, and by those
who could afford the extravagance of travel. "No intelligent being can
look upon this scene without feelings of reverence and admiration for
the creator of all this wonderful grandeur," W. H. Pierce wrote, emphasizing the distinction necessary to participate in the sublime.[8] Nature,
like art, came increasingly to be understood as a part of the high culture
of wealthy elites whose financial success also denoted their additional
abilities at appreciating wider realms of value apart from the economy.

But the travelers' depictions of nature's essential meaning meant little
but comfortable sophistries to some. Would-be prospector Egan Anderson, struggling up the Valdez Glacier, wondered what he had gotten
himself into. "At times however it seems a vague and empty undertaking. Often as I have stood upon the 'bloody glacier' as my neighbor
called it and looked upon the vast extent of ice surrounded by the majestic mountains at the base of which lies a calm bay, I seem entirely lost,
and my work seems to disappear in the presence of the mighty works of

nature."[9] The landscape seemed to absorb his puny efforts. And instead of a voyage of self-discovery, Anderson, still penning his letters in his native Norwegian and far from his Minnesota farmstead, felt oddly misplaced in the mountains and glaciers of the north.

Israel Russell also found more to fear in his more direct experience of the region's glaciers during an early attempt to climb the nearby Mount St. Elias. "The white snow surface could not be distinguished from the vapor-filled air. There was no earth and no sky; we seemed to be suspended in a white translucent medium, which surrounded us like a shroud," he wrote.[10] The glacial landscape with its surface an inviting undulating sweep of pure snow deceived would-be visitors. Hidden crevasses could prove fatal quickly to the errant wanderer.

The glaciers of the bay were close and reasonably safe. Steamer captains would lay a boardwalk across short stretches of ice so that their clients could experience the glacier close up. "Why should American tourists go to Europe for scenery? The mountain scenery of Alaska is unexcelled, and its glaciers are the grandest in the world. They are so

Figure 29. "Tourists on Muir Glacier," in L. Woodhull, "Photograph Album of Alaska and the Pacific Coast," c. 1889–91. (Courtesy Yale Collection of Western Americana, Beinecke Rare Book and Manuscript Library)

pronounced by those who have visited Alaska and also Europe. For convenience of access they are unexcelled."[11] After seeing the glaciers from afar, "the next sensation in store for the tourist is the climb to the top of the glacier." Armed with alpenstock and clad in rubber galoshes, the tourists trundled out on to the glacier. "To those who are willing to undertake it, however, I suggest that when they have ascended the first mile, which will about bring them on a line with the top of the wall of the glacier, they should look back at their little tiny ship, floating like the Maid of the Mist beneath Niagara, to fully realize the immense proportions of the glacier," traveler Septima Collis recommended.[12] They felt like little people in a Brobdingnag country.

Glacier walking, if one was careless, carried significant risks. "We were cautioned to be prudent," one traveler remembered, "and not to wander too far, and were told the story of a young Methodist clergyman, who went out of sight of his companions and was never after seen or heard of."[13] "It is impossible to describe it, so I won't try . . . on the way [back down] looking down a crevasse—It was a deep blue crack in the solid ice and was beautiful. The mist was falling in a fine rain. . . . It is the most wonderful place I ever saw."[14]

It was wonderful when one could see it. Much of the time the glaciers and surrounding mountains were obscured in cloud and rain; it was a fortunate tour that enjoyed a rare sunny day at Glacier Bay. "Capt. Hunter has been coming up here for three years," one tourist remarked, "but he says he never saw anything to equal the views we have had today. It is so rarely pleasant, for if not raining, the mountains are obscured by clouds or fogs. We have all been nearly crazy today—the captain as enthusiastic as any of us, although he has been up here so many times. Every ravine contains a Glacier, but the Muir Glacier is the wonder."[15]

The rain often fell persistently, but the tourists' enthusiasm was little dampened. For tent-bound geologists, who spent weeks on end mapping the glacier and its movements, the rain brought more discomfort. "It is now about half past nine and raining pretty hard," glaciologist Harry Fielding Reid wrote during a Glacier Bay research trip in 1892. "We are lying on the blankets in the tent to keep dry and hoping for the rain to stop. We have concluded that there are many infallible signs of rain in this region. If the sun shines, if the stars appear, if there are clouds or if there are none; these are all sure indications."[16] From the comfortable safety of the steamer deck, Alaska's glaciers appeared more inviting. If the Inside Passage was a scenic bonanza for tour companies and their patrons, then Glacier Bay was paydirt. "Fully nine Alaskan tourists out of ten go for its glaciers which are seen in a magnitude and grandeur," a travel writer estimated.[17]

Figure 30. "Muir Glacier," E. J. Partridge Collection. (Courtesy University of Washington Libraries, Special Collections)

During summer 1879 John Muir made his first visit to the far north. In October he left Fort Wrangell with four Tlingit companions and an American missionary. Muir embarked upon an amazing venture, a nearly thousand-mile sea journey in an open thirty-five-foot dugout canoe. Egged on by Muir, the Tlingit crew paddled the dangerous autumn seas of the northern Inside Passage. They set forth, Muir wrote, "eager to welcome whatever wildness might offer." His Tlingit crew did not always share his eagerness, men with long experience navigating these cold and difficult waters. "They had been asking him about what possible motive I could have in climbing dangerous mountains when blinding storms were blowing," Muir noted. When he replied, "I was only seeking knowledge," one of the Tlingit responded, "'Muir must be a witch to seek knowledge in such a place as this, and in such miserable weather.'"[18]

When it came to wildness it was to the region's glaciers that John Muir turned. One of the Tlingit navigators, known to Muir as Sitka Charley, had hunted seals years earlier in Glacier Bay and regaled Muir with stories of its tremendous ice fields and mountains. At the northernmost reach of this journey, Muir entered into this glacier-rimmed bay. Their arrival was met by a shot fired over their heads, from a group of Huna seal hunters and their families occupying several huts along the beach. This warning might have suggested to Muir that he and his companions were trespassing. Instead, Muir claimed "discovery" and in council with the Huna determined to investigate the deeper recesses of the bay, hidden areas long visited by Huna hunters. Guided by a local Huna seal hunter, Muir, the missionary Young, and their four Tlingit companions navigated the iceberg-strewn waters. Entering the bay, they "discovered" the first of its great glaciers. "Its lofty blue cliffs," Muir recorded, "looming up through the draggled skirts of the clouds, gave a tremendous impression of savage power, while the roar of the new-born icebergs thickened."[19]

The missionary rested in camp the next day, a Sunday, as Muir pursued his own Sunday service, what he termed as his "glacial gospel." When the Tlingit insisted against paddling any further until the weather improved, Muir set off on foot. "Passing through rain and mud and sludgy snow, crossing many brown, boulder choked torrents, wading, jumping, and wallowing in snow up to my shoulders was mountaineering of the most trying kind," he would later recall. "After crouching cramped and benumbed in the canoe, poulticed in wet or damp clothing night and day, my limbs had been asleep. This day they were wakened and in the hour of trial proved that they had not lost the cunning learned on many a mountain peak of the High Sierra." Muir

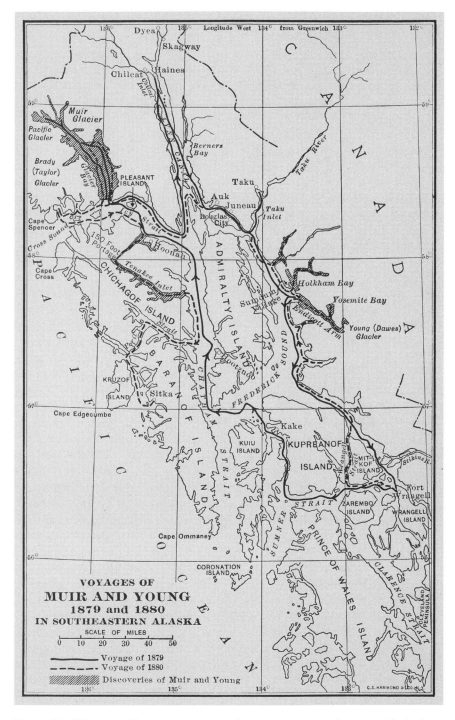

Figure 31. "Voyages of Muir and Young 1879 and 1880 in southeastern Alaska,"
in *Alaska Days with John Muir* by S. Hall Young, 1915. (Courtesy Yale Collection
of Western Americana, Beinecke Rare Book and Manuscript Library)

reached a height of fifteen hundred feet on the ridge that bordered the second of the great glaciers. When the clouds lifted, Muir saw the entire bay from this highpoint. "This was my first general view of Glacier Bay, a solitude of ice and snow and new-born rocks, dim, dreary, mysterious," he wrote.[20] "I held the ground I had so dearly won for an hour or two," Muir wrote of his strenuous conquest, his moral equivalent of war. "Sheltering myself from the blast as best I could," Muir recalled, "while with benumbed fingers I sketched what I could see of the landscape, and wrote a few lines in my notebook." Hunkered down, recording his experiences, Muir mirrored in part what writer Paul Fussell termed "the athletic, paramilitary activity of exploration."[21] He turned discomfort on its head and relished adapting himself to difficult conditions, making an otherwise hostile nature into an ally. "Storms are never counted among the resources of a country," Muir noted, "yet how far they go towards making brave people."[22]

Muir's ascetic exploits, often fasting, always chaste, mirrored a widening Christian commitment to health and manliness in late nineteenth-century culture.[23] But his efforts to find experience at the limits of endurance also sought to overturn a well-entrenched aestheticism. Taking religion out of the church into the great outdoors marked a turn in Christian practice that slipped the ecclesiastical style of a feminized laity. And according to Henry James, it was not only the church-going ladies who had gotten hold of the nation's cultural direction. "The whole generation is womanized," Basil Ransome proclaimed in James's *The Bostonians,* "the masculine tone is passing out of the world; it's a feminine, nervous, hysterical, chattering, canting age, an age of hollow phrases and false delicacy and exaggerated solicitudes and coddled sensibilities, which if we don't soon look out, will usher in the reign of mediocrity, of the feeblest and flattest and most pretentious that has ever been."[24] While Muir did not address specifically the fate of masculine character, he might have uttered Ransome's definition of manliness: "the ability to endure, to know and yet not fear reality, to look the world in the face and take it for what it is." Like his Sierra colleague Clarence King, author of *Mountaineering in the Sierra,* Muir made nature appreciation a strenuous activity.[25] Glacier science was an adventure. These excursions were not the aimless ramblings of a mere tourist. They carried a purpose. Nature appreciation and rigorous science need not be mutually exclusive. Recalling Clarence King's complaint that his society had turned to an effete aestheticism—"It's all Bierstadt and Bierstadt and Bierstadt nowadays!, What has he done but twist and skew and distort and discolor and belittle and bepretty this whole doggonned country? Why, his mountains are too high and too slim; they'd blow over in one of our fall winds"—Bierstadt, King concluded, "hasn't what old Ruskin calls for."[26] Muir was no more accepting of the tourist imagination suggested by the painter Bierstadt's inauthentic presentations. "What a show they made with their ribbons and kodaks!" Muir noted of the tourists all agape at the glacier scenery of Alaska. "All seemed happy and enthusiastic, though it was curious to see how promptly all of them ceased gazing when the dinner bell rang."[27] No "mere nature-lovers," King and Muir through their wanderings and writings opened a new space for nature writing and nature viewing. Muir's sang-froid, his downplayed accommodation to nature's extremes was its own form of bravado. "How cordial the blast, the beating of the rain, the rush of the dark clouds about the brows of the mountains!" Muir wrote.[28] In its way, Muir's work constituted a challenge to the domestic sentimental fictions of late Victorian America.

In league with his intellectual forebear Henry David Thoreau, Muir believed in "the tonic of wilderness."[29] Body and soul might be rejuvenated in outdoor communion, according to Muir. "Air yourself on the ice-prairies," he advised.[30] Suffering from a bronchial infection and urged by his doctor to avoid strenuous outdoor activity, Muir headed to Alaska instead. "Feeling sure that I would learn something and at the same time get rid of a severe bronchial cough" that had plagued him for several months, Muir spent several days alone exploring the glaciers. "My throat grew better every day until it was well, for no lowland microbe could stand such a trip," he wrote enthusiastically of his rough remedy.[31] Even bouts of snowblindness could be turned into redemptive penitence. "Now on this shattered ice I need my eyes, but the snow, gyrating, whirling, and sifting, the very incarnation of spasmodic hysterical mirth, fills them, and I am blinded by kisses, delicious in the eye, and sweet."[32] Too much of a good thing, however, affected even the usually imperturbable Muir. "Nearly blind. The light is intolerable . . . I have had too much sunshine," he was forced to admit finally.[33] Seeing double and plunging into water-filled crevasses, hypothermic and exhausted, he straggled back to camp at the base of the glacier. But his faith in the curative powers of the ice mountains went undiminished. "In God's wildness lies the hope of the world—the great fresh unblighted wilderness. The galling harness of civilization drops off, and the wounds heal ere we are aware."[34]

While Muir claimed to have "discovered" Glacier Bay during his 1879 trip, he was by no means the first nonnative to have visited there. The U.S. Revenue steamer *Wayanda* had navigated the bay in 1868 with the assistance of a Russian pilot. And in all likelihood, the Russians had been there before. In 1877, Lieutenant Charles Erskine Scott Wood hiked into the Glacier Bay basin. Wood would depart the north prematurely in order to serve as an aide-de-camp to General Howard during the Nez

Perce campaign. He had originally headed north with the intention of climbing Mount Saint Elias, then suspected to be the highest peak in North America. His Tlingit guides refused to go further up the storm-beaten coast, suggesting instead that Wood and his partner climb another mountain. "One mountain is as good as another. There is a very big one. Go climb that if you want to," Tah-ah-nah-kléh, his Tlingit guide, advised. The expedition ended before it had begun. After the departure of his climbing partner, Wood persevered, returning to explore the mountainous coast and the hidden glacier-filled bay. Following his "discovery," Wood hired local seal hunters to take him by canoe back to his ship at Sitka. Wood's account, "Among the Thlinkits in Alaska," published in *Century Magazine* in 1882, came several years after Muir's own celebrated and well-advertised promotion of the glacier bay. But where Wood's account detailed the customs of the native people he met during his travels, Muir fixated on the region's glacial geology. Unlike Muir, Wood mentioned his trip through Glacier Bay only in passing. He expressed far more interest in the region's people, where Muir obsessed on the glacial topography. Wood, a published poet, a painter, and a lawyer, showed no interest in being known as the bay's discoverer. And Wood in his article noted that a Tlingit familiar with the bay recalled that "within his own lifetime this place had been solid ice."[35] "Glacier Bay is undoubtedly young as yet," Muir wrote later. "Vancouver's chart, made only a century ago [1794], shows no trace of it, though found admirably faithful in general. It seems probable, therefore, that even then the entire bay was occupied by a glacier of which all those described above, great though they are, were only tributaries."[36] The bay that Muir "discovered" and made famous had not existed even a century earlier.

Muir's discovery and Glacier Bay's subsequent status as the pinnacle of the Inside Passage tour would not have been made known save for the promotional skills of a steamboat captain and one of his passengers. In 1883, guided by a rough sketch drawn by Muir in 1879, a sketch passed on to Captain Carroll by Lieutenant Beardslee, the steamer master eased the side-wheel steamer *Idaho* into the Muir Glacier fiord. Swinging to and fro up the narrow channel, taking soundings with a lead line and dodging the floating icebergs calved from the face of the glacier, Carroll positioned his vessel below the immense glacier. "Now that was quite as good as a real voyage of exploration," wrote Eliza Scidmore, standing alongside the venturesome captain that July morning.[37] The captain's investigation was not idle curiosity. Carroll recognized the scenic value of the glacier to future tours. (Carroll's entrepreneurial spirit carried over into other activities as well. In 1885 officials seized his ship in Port Townsend with 659 pounds of opium. Another 3,000 pounds was later discovered in his Kasaan, Alaska, warehouse along Alaska's Inside Passage.)[38] For more than two decades Captain Carroll continued his visits every couple of weeks through the summers on the tourist route to the north. Eliza Scidmore, a one-time society reporter, recorded this first steamer visit and thereby wrote herself into a new career. She published her initial accounts in the *St. Louis Globe-Democrat* and the next summer in the *New York Times*. In 1885 Scidmore published the first guidebook to the region, titled *Alaska, Its Southern Coast, and the Sitkan Archipelago*. Returning north during five summers over the succeeding decade, Scidmore became a recognized expert on Alaska, assisting in the 1890 federal census. She would later author the Appleton's guidebooks to Alaska, as well as a series of articles on the region that appeared in national magazines. It was Scidmore who fixed Muir with the title of discoverer. Writing in her popular guidebook that Muir, "as far as known, was the first white man to visit and explore the glaciers of the bay. . . . Professor Muir, strapping a blanket on his back, and filling his pockets with hard tack, started off unarmed, and spent days of glacial delight in the region."[39]

For Muir, the "discovery" of what came to be called Glacier Bay bordered on rapture. His wilderness ecstasies were reactions against the growing commercial and industrial culture of North America, what he called "the descent, deathlike apathy of weary civilized people, in whom natural curiosity has been quenched in toil and care and poor, shallow comfort."[40] His forays were escapes from industrial society's supposed ravages upon the human soul. The glacial expanse was for Muir "a picture of icy wildness unspeakably pure and sublime."[41] Here in the north Muir celebrated what he believed to be a "pure" encounter with nature. Reality was not some social construction, nor the artifice posed by civilization. For Muir, his experiences in nature were sublime encounters with this reality. And these encounters were so profoundly moving that Muir felt himself to be in touch with his god and eternity. In touch with Alaska's glacial wilderness Muir felt himself lifted out of history into a timeless realm where the distinction between the human and nature evaporated. "Most people are *on* the world, not in it—have no conscious sympathy or relationship to anything about them—undiffused, separate, and rigidly alone like marbles of polished stone, touching but separate," Muir wrote in his journal while traipsing across the Muir Glacier. The sublime encounter, as historian David Nye writes, left observers like Muir so moved that they were incapable of reflecting on the historical context of their own experiences.[42] Visitors such as Muir failed to see time—specifically geological time—as a social relation, a naturalized idea that removed indigenes from the view.

This romantic sublimity retained a sacred quality. In these glaciated mountains, Muir believed, "In very foundational truth we had been to church and had seen God."[43] Though Darwinian sociology infused much of what these educated tourists thought about the north, secular views coexisted with the sacred. "If a man had never thought of his maker he certainly would here, purely from instinct," prospector Fred Forster wrote in his diary while crossing an Alaskan glacier.[44] Forster's "instinct," a contemporary notion, fixed itself to traditional pieties. "There were many of us, however, who felt as if we were standing in the audience chamber of the Creator, and looking upon a new creation, very far away from the every day world we had always known," Matilda Barns Lukens wrote. It was far easier to recognize their god in this remote place, far removed from the every day. "Tears stood in many eyes, and an anthem of praise would better have expressed the pent-up emotion," she continued.[45] The correspondence between material nature and the transcendent spirit found in the travelers' impressions registered the ongoing influence of American transcendentalism and the romantic conventions of the sublime and picturesque. And these now traditional attitudes mixed with more recent scientific theories. Muir, in particular, sought to integrate the new science into a holistic vision of the natural world and his god. "One learns that the world," Muir wrote, "though made, is yet being made, that mountains long conceived are now being born, channels traced for coming rivers, basins hollowed for lakes; that moraine is being ground and outspread for coming plants—coarse boulders and gravel for forests, finer soil for grasses and flowers—while the finest part of the grist, seen hastening out to sea in the draining streams, is being stored away in darkness and builded particle on particle, cementing and crystallizing, to make the mountains and valleys and plains of other predestined landscapes, to be followed by still others in endless rhythm and beauty."

Muir's naturalism incorporated the sacred and the emerging science of ecology. His fascination with glaciation proposed a comprehensive and integrative approach to the physical world that complemented Ernst Haeckel's idea of ecology, first articulated in 1866. Humankind existed "on level with and part and parcel" of all life, "a small part of the one great unit of creation," Muir wrote.[46] "Every traveler," wrote travel writer Charles Taylor, "is affected to a certain extent by the scenes through which he passes [and they] have an influence upon his whole being."[47] This glacial metaphysic rested upon the premise that experiences in nonhuman nature were purer and more real than other activities.

John Muir's first impressions of Glacier Bay held for many later visitors as well. The iceberg-strewn bay was, Muir wrote, "a solitude of ice and snow and newborn rocks, dim, dreary, mysterious."[48] For others the scene at Glacier Bay conjured the sounds of battle. "Loud reports as of rifle guns would fill the ear, coming from the cracking behind the solid moving mass . . . a rattle of musketry," Charles Harrison observed.[49] The calving of ice from the vertical sides of the three-hundred-plus-foot face of Muir Glacier "is not unlike artillery firing," another wrote. It might seem strange at first that in the presence of a scene so purportedly "natural" these visitors would constantly compare the sounds with that of battle. But given their living in the aftermath of the Civil War and its constant memorialization, cannon and rifle fire were a common sound. "Reflections from the land appear in darksome shades across the water, and from the looming icebergs in tremulous semblances, ghost-like and pallid. . . . You gaze into them as into the arcane of the empyrean, with some vague awe of their mysterious source, and the intangible causes which give them birth," travel writer Ernest Ingersoll described.[50] In the face of nature's violence, indeed the very visage of death to some, the visitors found experiences that they believed to be authentic. Sensations associated with violence and death were deemed authentic experiences, not trivial leisures.

Intent on removing from their excursions any taint of pure ease, the tourists characterized their ventures in productive terms. Muir's visits and those of the many tourists who followed his path north were not merely nostalgic anti-modern retreats into a wild nature that contrasted with the alienating aspects of industrial culture. Like their curio purchasing, their sightseeing was filled with the ardor of work. These were educating excursions. "We finally got our eyes open and saw all the icebergs in the bay, we having come to the Muir Glacier, we were well repaid for getting up," remarked Eliza Cleninden.[51] Leisure, like labor, was increasingly organized and rationalized.[52] Cleninden's "leisure" was judged in terms of its worth. And worth here was characterized in wage-like terms. The latent metaphor of labor and time—so crucial to industrial capitalist society—had embedded itself within the unthinking vocabulary of its members.

It has been argued that in the latter decades of the nineteenth century Americans had outgrown the usefulness of the landscape conventions of the picturesque and the sublime, borrowed as they were from European traditions. Intent upon distancing themselves from Europe and its cultural definitions a number of authors have observed that Americans invented a new language that turned increasingly toward a nationalistic identification that fused nature and the nation. "Awed by the wonder of the scene, we ceased to speak, and over the frozen waste there seemed to rest a almost oppressive stillness, which was at length broken by strains of music. A gentleman of another party was mounted on a pinnacle so far away that he appeared a mere black dot to us, but, on account of the extreme clearness of the air, his sweet voice, and even the words of 'America' came to us over the fields of ice."[53] Natural history and national futures were entwined in the travelers' minds.

Approaching the Muir Glacier at the head of Glacier Bay, visitors placed the sight in context with other natural spectacles. "I take Niagara for comparison, because there is at the first glance a certain resemblance between the glacier and the cataract—a likeness in shape and form and color, as in the elements of which they are composed," wrote one traveler.[54] "Composing" a scene from the raw material of nature before him, the writer relied on the descriptive conventions of the picturesque. Another wrote, "In Alaska a glacier is a wonderful torrent that seems to have been suddenly frozen when about to plunge into the sea. . . . Imagine a glacier three miles wide and 300 feet thick at its mouth. Think of Niagara Falls frozen stiff, add thirty-six feet to its height, and you have a slight idea of the terminus of Muir Glacier."[55] As noted previously, historian Elizabeth McKinsey in her study of Niagara Falls argues that changes in the image of the falls after about 1860 indicated "a profound shift in attitude toward nature. Both the actual scenes of the Falls [marred by excessive tourism] and the aesthetic assumptions of artists who journeyed there reveal the eclipse of the sublime as a motive force in American culture."[56] But the sublime had not so much been eclipsed as it had turned up elsewhere. The landscape convention's real force emerged from its role as a marker of status. Wealthy tourists in late nineteenth-century America rejected the overdetermined venues of mass commercial tourism and sought out new and as yet unwritten landscapes to fulfill their ideal relationships between themselves and nature. Their relationships, though, were as much about reinforcing their privileged positions within society as they were about any pure link with the natural world itself. Where one chose to venture helped to determine one's class identity. The sublime had not been eclipsed; it had gone north.

"And the grand iceberg!—so cold yet so majestic, so solid yet so unsubstantial, so massive yet so ethereal," mused popular naturalist and travel writer Ernest Ingersoll.[57] His words signal the core of the sublime imagination. The glaciers, according to Ingersoll, conformed to Immanuel Kant's definitions of the sublime as shifting between the mathematical sublime—incomparable size—and the dynamic sublime—confrontation with a powerful and terrifying force.[58] The normative function of nature representations continued to hold sway through the now-conservative convention of the sublime. Their descriptions were hegemonic constructions invoking a supposedly common aesthetic.[59] The spectacle at Glacier Bay was not simply an immediate appreciation of this strange ice world, but a social relation between people mediated by the simulation of a pure aesthetic experience.[60]

While older conventions of aesthetic definition endured, so, too, did new tendencies expose themselves in the travelers' writings. If the Kantian sublime rested upon "boundlessness," then the tourists shifted between a sense of infinite possibilities, and the fixed probabilities of numbers. They gave a number to whatever they could—the glacier's height, "36 feet" higher than Niagara, the glacier's width, its length. After taking soundings near the toe of his namesake glacier, Muir concluded that "were the water and rocky detritus cleared away, a sheer precipice of ice would be presented nearly two miles long and more than a thousand feet high."[61] "It is said that all the glaciers in Europe combined could not make one the size of this," A. E. Browne wrote in his diary.[62] "So massive, yet so ethereal"—as Ingersoll's juxtapositions indicate, a tension existed between nature as a source of rational order versus nature as a source of spiritual and emotional experience.

The travelers' descriptions moved easily within this shifting paradox of nature as order and nature as disorder, between the rational and the irrational, the glacier as a machine and the glacier as a living body. The glacier was a "savage old mill of God," according to Muir.[63] The glacier was "a body in motion . . . a chariot on wheels." The glacier was a living body, but also a mechanism, ceaseless and repetitive in its actions. Machine life and organic life were not incompatible. Indeed the body had come increasingly to be seen as a machine itself. The life process was a machine process. William James talked of contemporary society as "the giant fly-wheel of civilization," and Henry Adams likened industrial civilization to a "dynamo" and to humans as "thermodynamic mechanisms." Physician George Beard diagnosed contemporary maladies as disturbances in the body's electric circuitry. And geologist Clarence King spoke of "the mechanism of civilization" and "the complex machinery of life."[64] Even Muir likened the world of natural forces to those of human artifice. "To think that all this mighty glacial geological engine shaping the world," he wrote, "is made up of tiny and frail frost-flowers, like children on a frolic."[65]

New master metaphors had taken hold. Included among these comprehensive metaphors was, of course, the assumption that nature's economy, a theatre of competition and survival of the fittest, matched the human economy. This understanding helped to fix nature's order as a mirror of the supposed free markets of the industrialized world. "Nature's Corporation Yard. O glory to God for the privilege of being in this wonderfully gloriously grand place! The Glacier! The Glacier! Stands out before us," wrote Stephen Merritt. Mixing human and natural economies, as historian Donald Worster has argued, travelers transformed "nature into a reflection of the modern corporate, industrial system."[66] But never content to rest with one metaphorical mode, these writers freely mixed their interpretative approaches. "You take your glass and behold it is plainly a living glacier," Merritt continued, "taking up your attention now, as a plain but cultured woman takes your whole heart and soul more and longer than a flashy, foolish, dressy woman."[67] The diarist's allusion to the glacier as woman echoed the art critic John Ruskin's view of the earth as body. "Mountains are the bones of the earth," he wrote. "Vegetation, water, even clouds provide adornments, like the folds of the dress and fall of the hair." In order to recognize the sublimity of the mountain landscape, the artist-observer must study the "bare ground," "divested of vegetation," undisguised by "the clothing of the landscape."[68] Ruskin insisted on seeing the earth "in its naked purity." "Mountains," Ruskin proclaimed, "are the beginning and the end of natural landscape." Mountains were seen as touchstones of the aesthetic sensibility, a long usage that gave this geologic space what seemed to be a fixed and canonic meaning. These ideas' availability indicated the tourists' own privileged status. The northern tourists would have agreed with Ruskin. Their interpretations of the glaciated region were voiced in sensuous terms as they comprehended the strange view within the then-available range of ideas and attitudes. Muir filled his writing with allusions to nature gendered as female: "The mighty and majestic curves drawn into noble firmness," "wide-bosomed hollows," "All Alaska fresh and sweet," "the shady recesses of the mountains where the young glaciers are nursed."

Tourists had been trained through a long literary tradition to see nature as female. Their highly gendered and class-specific ways of seeing implicated the human in nature. The sexual, aesthetic, scientific, and economic commingled; no one element could be easily separated from the rest. Gazing upon the mountain landscape was itself a kind of appreciation consistent with late Victorian mores that identified women as guardians of purity. But it was equally a kind of possession, suggesting, in the words of historian Annette Kolodny, "the female principle of gratification itself, comprising all the qualities that Mother, Mistress, and Virgin traditionally represent for men."[69]

In Alaska, space was biography. "Alaska is an epoch in our lives," one tourist proclaimed. The scenes through which a traveler passed had "an influence upon his whole being." "Our bright dream," one writer concluded, "No! All is too real, too vivid, too enduring, for any such simile. Familiar scenes and prosaic duties may once more engross us, but our trip to Wonderland will remain to the end of our lives a bright chapter in our experience, to whose glowing pictures we shall continually recur with ever-increasing delight."[70] Managing their perceptions like snap-shots visitors might return again and again to sights signifying their past experiences of the real. "No camera, no pencil, no vocabulary can do more," wrote traveler Septima Collis, "than produce a desire to see for one's self. I can only say that it has been my fortune to behold much that is grand in nature and in art at home and abroad, but the hours spent at Muir Glacier made the great event of my life."[71] Another travel writer agreed: "To see the Muir Glacier is an event in one's life. . . . It is a sight which does not fade in the distance."[72] What was most real to them was nature itself. But this nature was not self-evident; it was in no way simply transparent. The glacier that these well-heeled tourists viewed was not the same glacier that the Tlingit seal hunters saw, nor the same as that of the prospectors' experience. Instead, the glacier, like the other sightseeing objects captured along their Inside Passage tours, was both a part of the forces of production that had made the new north accessible to their viewing and a part of the products of those forces.

The new technologies of transportation—the railroads and the steam-ships—facilitated the incorporation of the north's resources into the national and international economy. These new technologies included the transformation of the north as an object of touristic consumption. This discovery gave the north new use values. Old spatial boundaries had been bridged. And, upon this new empire of nature, once presented and consumed, these travelers exerted their own power of persuasive incorporation. Their writings, their guidebooks, travelogues, their pho-tographs and lantern slides, their conversations and souvenirs, all broad-cast a view of the North to a wider national audience. Alaska was secured safely within the fixed social hierarchies of their bourgeois vision of the territory's worth. Deterritorialized, the image of northern nature, like the region's other resources—its furs, fish, timber, and gold—was made an object of universal exchange.[73] Stripped of the peculiarities of its local meanings, the new territory was re-territorialized as a new addition to the American empire, though the Americanized version of this impe-rial encounter substituted conquest with pioneering. "Among the gla-ciers of Alaska is an epoch in our lives never to be forgotten, the quiet grand beauty of the Arctic Circle," Stephen Merritt proclaimed. Claimed as a uniquely individual experience, each traveler located her-self in relation to fixed ideas of nature. Each glorification of nature also reduced nature to a memento. Identities were fixed in relation to that which the nineteenth-century sightseers recognized as the ultimate real-ity, "too real, too vivid." The consumptive political economy of tourism stripped the "aura" of things—glaciers, mountains, the air and the water—from their specific spatial relations, reproducing them "in a lev-eling, automatic, statistically rationalized form." "That which withers in the age of mechanical reproduction," as Walter Benjamin understood this phenomenon, "is the aura of the work of art [we might substitute nature itself]. . . . To pry an object from its shell, to destroy its aura, is the mark of a perception whose 'sense of the universal equality of things' has increased to such a degree that it extracts it even from a unique object by means of reproduction."[74]

The aesthetic and scientific became kinds of discipline. But not in the usual sense, as in a field of study, though they were these as well. Rather aesthetic and scientific practices disciplined their practitioners, organizing and dictating how knowledge would be shaped, determining what might be said. How else can we explain the repetitive similarities of their written words?

Nature was a book, with a discernable language, a transferable language. The world outside was a series of intelligible objects.[75] "Glaciers, avalanches and torrents," Muir insisted, "are the pens with which Nature produces written characters most like our own." Bourgeois observers inherited a normative grammar through which they described and wrote, viewed and interpreted the landscapes along their tour north and its zenith, their visits to Glacier Bay.

The world to the sightseers was made up of superimposed surfaces, sediments, strata, great uplifted orogenies and ground-down, polished granites, rouche moutons, nunitaks, morrainal debris, and erratics. The world was knowledge. The scientific consciousness, wedded to the landscape aesthetic, imagined drawing the whole world into what Foucault stresses as a single "science of order." The travelers performed as amateur geologists and glaciologists, absorbing a smattering of terminology that added heft to their collective aesthetic voice. They ably employed this geological terminology, claiming their observations as something broader than simple sightseeing. Their pretense as natural historians, as active observers of the geological frontier of knowledge, in this activity gave sanction to practices that might otherwise have drawn their contempt as empty leisure. The tourists' movements were utilitarian. Their tourism was in fact the very duty of citizenship, investigating the nation's most recent territorial acquisitions. "A stretch of territory that is not only the pride of every native of the United States, but the subject of never ceasing wonders of educated foreigners who come to our shores with the special purpose of journeying over the same ground," as one traveler recited.[76] Or as another pronounced, "I never saw anything that approaches this scene. How proud I feel that it belongs to us, that I have an individual share in it."[77] Seeing constituted possession. And possession portended a bright future for the region. "May not a similar change be wrought in the part of the world of which I have been speaking?" wrote one traveler. "Who knows? In our age of steam and electricity, it is almost rash to predict anything as impossible to the genius of progress and civilization."[78] Dreams of possession proceeded. Progress had been predetermined, according to their capitalist logic of ownership. Their natural histories legitimated the process of domination. Their collective bourgeois belief in assured progress was guided by what Thorstein Veblen called "a sense of fortuitous necessity in the sequence of phenomena."[79] For all their insistence upon an ordered and rational nature, at its core their belief in their science and their nature aesthetic rested upon its own metaphysic. Fin-de-siècle culture rested upon a belief system—science—that, in the words of geographer Bruce Braun, was "assumed to exist independent from culture, religion or politics, and thus could be explained by reference to Nature alone."[80] Veblen, critiquing this leisure culture at the end of the century, recognized as much when he analyzed what he called "The Belief in Luck." This faith was, in Veblen's words, an "animistic sense of relations and things that imputes a quasi-personal character to facts." Alongside Victorian claims to rational superiority and enlightened objectivism lay a profound animism. Simultaneous with industrial organization, which "assumes more and more of the character of a mechanism," the animistic "habit of mind" survives in the "modern reminiscence of the belief . . . in the guidance of the unseen hand."[81] The beginnings of ecological naturalism inherent in Muir's writing and in the tourists' experience of Alaska lent support to the imperial assumption that historical causality—that unseen hand—predestined these European Americans to northern domination.[82] The recognition of a natural order legitimated the other hierarchies that arose on this northern frontier.

After Alaska's purchase from the Russians in 1867, predictions regarding Alaska's future worth did not hold out much hope for what some referred to derisively as "Icebergia," and "Seward's Folly." "It is a paradise for the naturalist," wrote one early Alaskan, "a happy hunting ground for the ethnologist, a new and boundless field for the geologist, . . . It is, and will be for years to come, a perfect treasure trove for these gentlemen; but alas! It bids fair from what we now know, never to be a treasure trove for the miner."[83] Such predictions proved fabulously inaccurate. In fact it would be the observations of these gentlemen naturalists that would eventually reveal the resource potential of the north to the United States and Canada.

These men—for they were mostly so—collected information and catalogued the region's landforms, flora and fauna, and native peoples, subjugating landscapes and whole cultures to bits of knowledge, and returned home to write up their discoveries. The representations of the north and their concentration of knowledge about the subarctic helped to fix outlying regions into a global system of capital development. The activities of traveling gentleman scholars were instrumental to the administration of territorial expansion. One such mobile agent of empire was John Muir.

As one of his biographers notes, "Muir believed with evangelical passion that nature's glaciers could form men as well as mountains." Muir, touting what he called his "glacier gospel," saw his Alaskan ventures as pilgrimages as much as they were scientific ventures. Indeed Muir saw in this glaciated region a source for profound moral guidance, where he touched his God's greatest productions. The science of glaciology was still young. And Muir, blending the roles of natural historian and scientist, recognized the rewards for careful observation and on-the-ground knowledge. The self-taught naturalist had already established his scientific reputation with his theory that glaciers had formed California's Yosemite Valley. He overturned the reigning theory that Yosemite's deep U-shaped valleys were not formed by glaciation, but rather by a sudden subsidence. If that was so, Muir wondered, then where did the landmass go? His theory of Yosemite glaciation earned him a national audience.

Earlier in the century, Louis Agassiz had proposed that much of the earth had been recently covered by a single ice age, and that the record of this phenomenon could be found nearly everywhere. The Austrian-born Harvard geologist went so far as to travel to Brazil in search of evidence of previous glaciation in the tropics. On his return, his lectures titled "Traces of Glaciers under the Tropics" confirmed, at least in his own mind, the former existence of an icecap across the entire Americas, indeed the entire world. Charles Darwin concluded that Agassiz was "glacier-mad." "Since I saw the glaciers," Agassiz wrote, "I am quite of a snowy humor, and will have the whole surface of the earth covered with ice, and the whole prior creation dead by cold." But Agassiz's theory that great ice sheets had once spread across entire continents, including the tropical regions, was more fancy than fact. Nonetheless Muir's documenting of glacial signs in Yosemite helped to extend the theory of a previous ice age. And while he may not have been "glacier-mad" like Agassiz, Muir was more than a bit obsessed with glaciers. He intended to establish the fact of a widespread past ice age by exploring evidence of past and present glaciation in the far north. "Many detailed proof-facts will be required to compel the assent to this in the mind of most geologists on account of the defectiveness of glacial education in general and in special," Muir wrote. "But the glacial millennium will come."

Muir made a series of trips north to Alaska in 1879, 1880, 1881, 1890, and 1899, to document the extent of the region's glaciation. Despite his expressions of disgust at advertisers of wilderness, he increasingly advertised the northland's features. His prolific writing and lecturing contradicted his earlier stance that, in his words, "The best things and thoughts we get from Nature we dare not tell," he said to a friend. "To lay out all his delicate treasures for the coldly critical eye of an unimaginative world seemed a kind of betrayal."

According to a traveling companion, Muir's mission was to find and study the forests, mountains, and glaciers. " 'We are going to write some history, my boy,' Muir would say to me, 'think of the honor! We have been chosen to put some interesting people and some of nature's grandest scenes on the page of the human record and on the map.' " Muir's extended lecture tours, his newspaper articles and magazine stories, and his later books advertised Alaska to the curious metropolitan masses. And his promotion of northern scenery took root in the national imagination. The tidewater ice field at the head of Glacier Bay was named the Muir Glacier after its supposed discoverer. The prophet of wilderness helped to spawn the cultural incorporation of the north, naturalizing the nation's claim to the region's scenic resources. Muir recognized as much when he wrote, "Since I made my first excursions and called attention to the wild scenery of Alaska through the newspapers, a bright and lively stream of tourist travel has been developed."[84] The monumental beauty and grandeur of Alaska's mountains served as a scenic anchor to the era's competitive nationalism. "The area drained by this one grand glacier," wrote Muir of his namesake glacier, "can hardly be less than seven or eight hundred miles, and probably contains as much ice as all the eleven hundred Swiss glaciers combined."[85] America may have lacked the sublime ruins of antiquity, but its vast landforms surpassed Europe's Alps. The troops of scientists attracted to the region by Muir's promotions soon recognized Alaska's significance to the wider study of ice ages. "This whole region forms a magnificent field for the study of glacial phenomena," wrote an English geologist during an 1884 visit.

Muir's writings and public lectures were never mere scientific lectures, nor were they simply philosophical sermons of his glacial gospel. He was best known for his aesthetic fixation with Alaska's natural beauty. But Muir poses a more interesting, complicated, and—indeed given his popular representation—conflicted persona. In 1878, the U.S. government commissioned Muir to explore southeastern Alaska. Thus his interests and intentions were broader than simply documenting the region's supposed wilderness attributes. Accordingly the explorer naturalist cooperated with military officials in Alaska, providing them with extensive information on his reconnaissance, and he brought back favorable reports concerning the territory's mining potential. Thus, Muir challenged earlier dismissals of the North's potential.

Muir predicted that the area southeast of present-day Juneau would "make a second California." He delivered this report to U.S. military officials in Sitka during early spring 1880. He carefully detailed a map of Glacier Bay that led to the first tourist visits to the bay several years later, intentionally boosting one of the North's earliest industries—the extensive tourism that brought thousands northward in the years before the Klondike. Interested Sitka prospectors, as detailed in the previous chapter, paid careful attention to Muir's suggestions and decided to explore several of the gold-bearing areas described by the celebrated naturalist. The subsequent discovery of gold at Juneau, if not the direct result of Muir's report, was at least encouraged by Muir's promotions. By the mid-1880s the Treadwell mining complex at Juneau was the largest industrial gold mine in the world.

But Muir's promotions did not end in Sitka. On his return from his initial Alaska venture in January 1880, Muir gave a series of illustrated lectures in the Northwest and California. In Portland, Oregon, he gave three lectures, titled "The Glaciers of Alaska and California," "Earth Sculpture, the Formation of Scenery, the Influence of Glaciers in the Development of Mines, and the Gold Mines of Alaska," and "Resources and Gold Fields of Alaska."[86] Alongside his later denunciations of miners as greedy despoilers of Alaska's wilderness, Muir's advocacy of mining ventures appears contradictory.

Muir's geology mixed aesthetic representations with more pragmatic concerns for value. He wove through his discussions of glaciers an enthrallment with nature's monumental wonders and what he believed were the practical relationships between glacial action and gold prospects. His geology had room for aesthetic emotions alongside more mundane economic considerations. And his articulate boosterism had the effect of incorporating the north as both a scenic resource and a mineral one. He believed that the glacial record was, in his words, "an open book on every mountain side." By reading the rocks, Muir hoped that Americans might approach their God, but also their gold. The glaciers did the work of a multitude of miners, exposing auriferous deposits, so that men might more easily find the valuable mineral. Glaciers made scenery and made gold seeking easier.

In his lectures he pronounced that "Alaska will be found at least moderately rich in the precious metals," he predicted. Gold and scenery would come to be regarded as "the most important and reliable of her resources." Glacier study served as a subset of the work of geology. And during the nineteenth century this work was the work of mineral discovery, differentiating minerals based on their inherent worth. "Glaciers," Muir instructed, "make the deepest mark of any eroding agent, and write their histories in un-erasable lines. And so we can . . . read the history of glaciers. Glaciers are the pens with which Nature produces written characters most like our own."

Glaciers past and present, thus, made the northern landscape legible, where the trained eye could decipher the mineral meanings otherwise hidden from view. Although Muir acted only as a peripheral agent of the state, his aesthetic and scientific incorporation of Alaska's visual and material resources had the effect of a cultural appropriation of these indigenous spaces.

In a series of San Francisco newspaper stories, Muir explained that the lack of gold production in the north was due to the fact that even the coastal mountains had not been extensively explored. "While the interior region is still a virgin wilderness—all mineral wealth about as darkly hidden as when it was covered by ice-mantel of the glacier period," he concluded. By learning how to read the rocks, Muir encouraged a new fluency in the language of glaciology. A new generalized literacy might allow newcomers to see into the otherwise hidden value of the land. He urged miners from Nevada and California to push their way over the whole territory to "make it tell its wealth."

Muir's writing brought new and valuable information about Alaska to important metropolitan audiences. His travel writing and his lecture tours played a critical role in providing a written landscape for metropolitan audiences interested in northern development. He helped to lay the imaginative foundation upon which the gold seekers' dreams were to be built. Northern territory was made *legible* through these geological ways of seeing. Geology was so entwined with the pragmatic pursuit of mineral wealth that even Muir found it impossible to restrain himself from indulging in speculative activity.

Muir helped to promote the idea of a "gold belt theory." According to this theory, Muir wrote in 1880, "the gold rocks of British Columbia and Alaska . . . seem to be the equivalents of those in California," suggesting the extension of an auriferous belt northward. And Ivan Petroff echoed this theory of a sweep of gold-bearing rocks that ran continuously from the placer gravels of California through to the Arctic. He authored the 1880 Alaska census and described this gold-bearing belt that "crosses into our Alaskan boundary away back, and concealed from the sea by the towering summits of the Coast Range . . . our miners [there] . . . they shall find the free gold and rich quartz in unwonted abundance." With these predictions Alaskan promoters such as Petroff and Muir hoped to inspire the energies of numerous individual prospectors, who would open the country through their wandering efforts to discover precious metals in the frozen gravels of northern creeks.

Muir's ideas regarding northern development extended beyond gold mining. *The Alaskan* in August 1889 ran a story complimenting the "bold project of Professor John Muir to build a railroad to Europe through the Yukon and Bering straits. Senator Stanford, agreeing entirely with Muir, advises building of a permanent bridge across the Bering Strait as the width of it, according to his opinion, is only 25 miles; three islands in that Strait can be easily connected by a bridge. Redwood, as the best material for marine buildings, may be brought from California."[87] Muir's northern boosterism foresaw a more comprehensive integration of the north into a global transportation scheme, one that might unite the new world with the old via a Siberian connection.

Muir's random promotions of the northern mineral potential were assisted by a far more powerful motor for shaping individual decisions to seek gold. The General Mining Law of 1872 established mineral prospecting and mining as the highest use of new territory. Indeed, the law effectively zoned nearly all public lands for mining, including Alaska after 1884. The language of the law could not have been clearer. The law stated that "The mineral lands of the public domain, both surveyed and unsurveyed, are hereby declared free and open to exploration and occupation by all citizens." This simplified and uniform property regime had in a few words swept the furthest reaches of the nation's territorial acquisitions into a legible and coherent system, easily manipulable from the center. The law encouraged, even compelled, individuals to advance into new territories. And so, the mining law had arranged the self-interest of individuals so as to lead to the strengthening of the state's forces from within. Its aim to encourage specific types of behavior succeeded in forming a legion of gold-seeking expeditions that would probe the corners of the new U.S. acquisition. Prospecting became the very duty of citizenship in the north. Even the tourists demonstrated a fascination with the technical language of geology and its ability to uncover the hidden values of the earth. "Fragments and rounded pebbles of red and gray granite, limestone, marble, schistose slate, porphyry, and quartz were picked up," wrote one northern traveler to Glacier Bay in the 1880s. "Many bits of quartz and marble were deeply stained with iron," according to Eliza Scidmore, who demonstrated her grasp of the new geologic lexicon, an understanding that connected her and her touring companions to the supposed mineral future of the region. "The Polish mining engineer with the party assured us," she wrote, "that all Glacier Bay was rich in the indications of a great silver-belt, and held up carbonates, sulphates, and sulpherets to prove his assertion."[88] Late nineteenth-century education promoted nature study. A consensus emerged by 1900 regarding the value of nature study. Such study under the dictum, "nature, not books," emphasized experiential engagement with the natural world.[89] The tourists followed suit. The natural science of geology became an arena for the amateur and expert. As a science, it established an easily communicated lexicon that allowed the newcomers—tourists and prospectors alike—to probe the region's potential worth.

This new language of earth and mineral fixed the North with new qualities, ones that could be quickly incorporated into national political and economic rationalities through the instrument of the mining law and their earth science. Drawing the region into global circuits of capital accomplished the task of what several historians have termed "incorporation"—the assertion of national authority, the penetration of a national market, and finally the establishment of the national culture and settlement of citizens from the national core.

Making sense of their surroundings, Muir and his cohort had in effect *made* their surroundings.[90] Their geologic facts were made within *historical* rather than *natural* systems of meaning. Or perhaps more specifically, nineteenth-century men such as Muir naturalized all systems of meaning, making gold a universal product of nature holding a timeless value. The new geologic discourse assumed that its rationale existed separate from culture, that mineralogic study could be explained by reference to nature alone, rather than a dynamic culture. The transformation of nature's material resources rested on the increasingly elaborate representations of those resources through the science of geology. Geological "facts," it was believed, existed out there to be discovered. But geologic facts did not exist to be discovered. Instead geological science served as an instrument of political and economic extensions, helping to order territories that existed at the margins of late nineteenth-century capital. Colonial discourses naturalized the processes of domination. Geology was one such discourse.

Fearful of the United States' thirst for territory, Canada in the 1880s set about marking the boundaries of its own northern interests. In 1887 George Mercer Dawson, the assistant director of the Geological Survey of Canada, embarked on a year-long survey of the Yukon District. That Canada chose to fix its northern borders and assert its authority over the Yukon through the instrument of a geological and natural history survey suggested the important role that science had claimed within the modernizing nation-state. Far from serving as a disinterested pursuit of general scientific knowledge, Dawson's geologic work helped extend Canadian political and economic interests, and importantly, his survey challenged American expansionist impulses in the far north. The Canadian survey fixed the dominancy of the geological survey's mapping of the earth's surface as the scientific corollary to the nation's imperial and commercial expansion.[91] And like his American counterparts, Dawson identified a gold zone in British Columbia and the Yukon District of the

Northwest Territory. "Project the axis of this zone northwesterly and," he insisted, "we have a zone of upward of 500 miles in length, some of it in Alaska, more of it in the Northwest Territory, and much of it in British Columbia, which will yet be the scene of numerous mining enterprises, both on the quartz and the placer, the former practically inexhaustible."[92] Using their earth science, Dawson and his cohort speculated about the possibilities embedded in those unseen lands, thus opening space for new political and economic goals. Maps with special symbols and colors revealed the otherwise unseen substrata of the continent. As one geographer writes, "the emphasis on mapping gave geology a uniquely territorial dimension which accorded well with the interests of both landed property and imperialism." To further these nation-building agendas, Canada, following the United States, sought to institute more uniform legal definitions of mining lands. And like the United States, the Canadians prized the mineral character of the north above all else. The division of territory into "mining districts" administered by a hierarchy of mining recorders and overseen by a Gold Commissioner emphasized the Canadian government's recognition of mining as the highest and best use of the land. After his 1887 survey, Dawson dubbed the Yukon region "Canada's Great Reserve."[93] His geological survey served as a means to attract development capital. And it provided the administrative apparatus that encouraged individual prospecting activity in the subarctic north. Individual and corporate risk-taking behavior was made more likely through the rationalizing strategies of the state.

Understanding the glacial past of the interior proved critical to Dawson and the Canadian's predictions of the north's mineral potential, as it had for Muir and the Americans. The study of the glacial phenomenon had, Dawson insisted, "a direct value in its connection with the distribution of the placer gold deposits and on the existence and position of the buried channels of rivers and streams, in which some of the richest of those deposits are often found to occur." Reading the glacial past might lead gold seekers to hidden treasure, according to Dawson. "The greater part of the 'fine' gold found along the river-bars and banks of the larger streams in the Yukon district is doubtless proximately derived from the gravels and other superficial deposits in which these streams have re-excavated their beds since the period of glaciation," Dawson speculated.[94] Ironically, the glacial knowledges assumed by men such as Dawson and Muir presumed too much. Muir imagined sweeps of archaic ice caps wherever he traveled in the north. He found evidence of glaciation where no glaciers had in fact existed.[95] And Dawson predicted the movements of vanished glaciers over much of the northland, suggesting that those glaciers' traces held important clues to the placement of gold in the Yukon gravels. Geologist George Frederick Wright followed this conventional wisdom regarding the increasingly rich prospects found in the interior Yukon. When prospectors discovered the rich Klondike fields, some of the densest concentrations of placer gold ever found, speculation as to the "mother lode"—that is, the source of the gold— centered upon glacial analysis. In "The Geology of the Yukon Region, the Mother Lode and the Glacial Deposits," Wright noted, "The discovery of gold in large quantities on the Yukon River is by no means unexpected. . . . Little is known about the geology of the Yukon River, where the Klondyke mines have been found. Being placer mines, the gold may have been transported many miles. The means of transportation are both glaciers and rivers . . . Dawson and Professor Russell both report well defined terminal moraines across the upper Yukon Valley. The source of the Klondyke gold therefore is from the south."[96] Dawson had noted that vanished ice sheets had once flowed north, supposedly carrying their auriferous deposits across the Yukon interior. But this was not the case. Cold as the interior Yukon valleys of Canada and Alaska were, much of the region had not been glaciated. The Klondike gold and the deposits throughout the gold-rich region were untouched by glacial action.

In George Dawson's mind, Canada's physical structure helped to determine the very existence of the nation itself. "The same or very similar types of geological structure," he argued, "with their accompanying and dependent features of surface form, are very widely extended. Great distances may be traversed without notably changing the conditions and no examination of a single province suffices to give an idea of the whole."[97] Canada's uniformity reinforced the national character, even made possible a national character. The nation was united by its geologic similarity. Not only was geology a natural science, but the nation was naturalized as an inevitable product of the ground itself, the inner strata of bedrock. Canada was imagined, in the words of one of Dawson's contemporaries, as a "Mineral Nation."

The prospect of mineral wealth below the ground helped assure settlement above ground, or at least so the boosters hoped. "We may be prepared at any time," Dawson predicted, "to hear of the discovery of important mineral deposits, which will afford the necessary impetus, and may result, in the course of a few years, in the introduction of a considerable population into even its most distant fastnesses."[98]

In the far north national history and natural history commingled as the United States and Canada traced their northern borders and claimed the future mineral wealth that lay within their new acquisitions. As these nations naturalized their vast new territories, so too did they endow their possessions with primordial claims. But these were not vacant lands. The newcomers' occupation required another step. Their task was, to paraphrase Mary Louise Pratt, to reinvent Alaska and the Yukon as backward and neglected, to encode its noncapitalist landscapes and societies as manifestly in need of the rationalized exploitation the Americans and Canadians could bring.

When John Muir recorded his first visit to Glacier Bay, he described it as "a stern solitude of ice and snow and raw, newborn rocks, dim, dreary, mysterious." He had in effect erased the native presence from the bay, a presence long established by local Tlingit seal hunters, one of whom had guided Muir to the very bay that he claimed to have "discovered." Muir was not unusual in the ease with which he ignored the native presence. "Alaska has no history," insisted one observer, "except a geological history." Nineteenth-century travelers typically viewed native peoples as a fleeting presence in the wilderness landscapes of the north—"the beaver and otter far back on many a rushing stream, Indians floating and basking along the shores, the leaves of the forest drinking the light and the glaciers on the mountains tracing valleys for rivers." The Tlingit and other coastal people appeared as a part of the picturesque or not at all, as was the case for one travel writer who wrote, "Still appalling was the absence of human beings. I looked for Indians, but . . . all was silence and solitude. It was a fresh new world, waiting for the footsteps of future generations." "No natives are to be seen; not a sound falls upon the ear save the hoarse cannonading of the glacier," travel writer Maturin Ballou observed.[99] The rhetorical practice of native erasure contradicted the actual and important working presence of native people. Native workers piloted the steamers, caught and canned the salmon, labored in the region's mines, served as sex workers in the scrappy mining and fishing outposts along the coast, helped map the interior, and importantly, they were often the discoverers of gold.

"The primeval forces that mould the face of the earth," noted one traveler, "were at work, and it was all so far away and out of the everyday that we might have been walking a new planet, fresh fallen from the Creator's hand."[100] Such description should not be dismissed simply as evidence of nineteenth-century literary extravagance. The above-mentioned quote was a repetition of the reigning geologic theory, first articulated by James Hutton at the beginning of the nineteenth century. In short, the observable causes of geologic change in the present— glaciation, erosion, sedimentation, uplift, subsidence, and volcanics— were at work in the past. The face of the earth changed in response to these forces, but the forces themselves did not change. Enthralled with the prospect of geologic time, scientists imagined the prospect of a

Figure 32. Edward Curtis would establish his reputation after 1907 with the publication of *The North American Indian*. Completed in 1930, this monumental work eventually encompassed twenty volumes in a series including more than 2,000 photographs. Curtis, who staged many of his photographs, has been credited with helping to create a nostalgic and inaccurate popular image of Native Americans. His work during the 1899 Harriman expedition to Alaska is refreshingly free of the stagecraft that would make his later work so controversial. "Sealers' Camp in Glacier Bay." Photograph by Edward Curtis. (Courtesy Yale Collection of Western Americana, Beinecke Rare Book and Manuscript Library)

much longer earth history, so deep as to be beyond one's imagining. The span of human history shrank to a mere fraction of earth history.

But intense disagreements arose over the character of geologic change. Visitors to the north, lay people and scientists alike, were attuned to this controversy. In their travels to Glacier Bay they entered into one of the era's most contested scientific disputes. Again tourists covered their leisurely travels with an exterior rhetoric of rigorous intellectual debate. "The landscape is a unique study in geology," wrote traveler A. L. Lindsley in his *Sketches of an Excursion to Southern Alaska the Voyage*.[101] He went on to detail the poles of the ongoing debate over the character of past earth history—whether change occurred catastrophically with sudden and massive geologic events, or whether change occurred slowly and progressively over great expanses of time. "The uniformitarian," Lindsley wrote, "will be sadly perplexed to account for these precipitous heights and abysmal depth on the theory of the slow and imperceptible action of natural forces. On the other hand, the theory of catastrophism will find abundant illustration through these channels." He argued that the "slow disintegrating processes required by the theory of uniformity to break down the sides of these lofty cliffs, and to carve out and excavate these unfathomable cliffs, would consume eras of duration, the magnitude of which would surpass the wildest geologic calculations." The passage north and the evidence of Glacier Bay suggested in Lindsley's reasoning that "in an instant, a vast geologic convulsion, which shot through the Earth, as chain lighting through the sky, and split off a portion of the continental mass, which, falling into the sea, was dislocated and dissolved by the in-rushing waters, into the thousand islands that are now scattered along the coast. . . . Perchance the anthropoids, reeling on these dizzying heights, rocked in the throes of these convulsions, gazed down into fathomless abysses. But for a moment only, for then came the irresistible forces of the sea, pouring through innumerable cataracts the overwhelming flood." Diluvian theories of a Noachian flood were never far from the imaginations of late nineteenth-century Americans, who continued to search for some bridge between their new science and their old religion. This traveler had no explanation for the geologic catastrophe that he imagined as the formative influence upon the southeastern coast of Alaska. Nonetheless, the dramatic landscapes of the Inside Passage conjured visions of dramatic whirlwinds of past change. "Castastrophes," as geologist Clarence King explained, "are far more surely proved by the observed mechanical rupture, displacement, engulfment, crumpling, and crushing of the rocky surface of the globe."[102] All of this was on display along the Inside Passage, and especially at Glacier Bay ringed by tremendous oceanside mountains.

Other earth observers such as Muir held to the established tenets of uniformitarianism. "Nature never leaps," argued Muir, repeating the core of uniformitarian theory, "which means that God never shouts or spouts or speaks incoherently. The rocks and sublime canyons, the waters and winds, and all life structures . . . are words of God."[103] Catastrophism implicated diety in a world of random, even chaotic destruction. And Muir disputed the evidence of an unpredictable and violent god. "God is living and working, working like a human being by human methods and though essentially always unsearchable and infinite yet writing passages that we can understand and coming within the range of our sympathies . . . God is connected by such means as glaciers to us and to all his creation," Muir wrote.

The region's glaciated landscape provided visible evidence of ages of slow, incremental change. "The proofs of glacial action are also abundant," Lindsley observed, "and appear in the most interesting forms. The slowly sculptured rocks, the glaciers still in operation and beds of extinct glaciers are everywhere in view, suggesting long ages of time to account for the changes which this imperceptible force has wrought upon the landscape." He predicted a resolution of the long-running geologic debate. "The advocates of the contending theories may shake hands over these chasms . . . for it shall come about at the last, doubtless, that both theories shall be accepted and the antagonism cease," Lindsley concluded.

In the glacier zone, time became *seen*, visible in the calving bergs, heard in the booming, fracturing ice. "They are what are scientifically designated as 'living glaciers,'" wrote one visitor, "that is huge bodies of frozen snow that are in continual motion, wearing down and grinding into shape the surface of the earth. In them one sees the primordial forces that made the earth what it is; that ground the rock into the soil which gives us food and flowers; that made this earth useful to man and beautiful. To watch this action is one of the keenest delights in a trip to Alaska."[104]

The history of glacial action, according to travel writer Alexander Badlam, helped to explain the "topographic history of the continental United States and Alaska." Tourists visiting the active glaciers of the bay were afforded "a living laboratory" in which to understand the forces of past change.[105] The first tourist visits to the bay in 1883 and the promotions of the glaciers as a monumental scenic destiny attracted the interests of the scientific community. English geologist G. W. Lamplugh visited Glacier Bay the following year. He complained about the inaccuracy of newspaper accounts that had been widely quoted, accounts that had also attracted his attentions to this otherwise remote location, hitherto unknown outside of Alaska. "In a recent number of *Nature* an abstract is made of a San Francisco newspaper account of the 'Great Glacier' of Alaska. This account is not very accurate," he noted. But he remained enthusiastic about the region's possibilities. "I spent a few hours on this glacier during a flying visit to Alaska in the summer of 1884. . . . This whole region forms a magnificent field for the study of glacial phenomena," Lamplugh wrote.[106] "And to any geologist who may follow," he continued, "I would especially say— . . . wherever there

is stained ice on the top of the glacier, trace out the source of the discol-
ourations." Lamplugh believed he had discovered the remnants of
meteorites on the glacier's surface. Though the geologist could not have
known it at the time, the evidence of interstellar debris was a clue to the
kinds of catastrophe that might have accounted for the "vast geologic
convulsion, which shot through the Earth, as chain lighting through the
sky" that Lindsley and the Castastrophists understood as the random
and chaotic history of the planet's past.[107]

A succession of scientific expeditions followed on these initial visits to
Glacier Bay. In 1886 geologist and Reverend George Frederick Wright
spent a month trying to calculate the rate of the Muir Glacier's movements. Wright's subsequent articles and book drew explicit links
between earth history and human history.[108] His glacier studies in Alaska
and elsewhere in the United States necessitated "a considerable extension of man's antiquity as usually estimated." "I see no reason," Wright
concluded, "why these views should seriously disturb the religious faith
of any believer in the inspiration of the Bible."[109] Staking and triangulat-
ing, Wright established estimates of the glacier's movement at an
extraordinary forty feet per day, sometimes as much as seventy feet.
While this speed seemed impossible to many, it did account for the
incredibly active terminus of the Muir Glacier that constantly calved ice
into the bay. In 1890 Muir returned for a fourth time to his namesake
glacier and stayed through the summer with a team of scientists, including Israel Russell of the United States Geological Survey and geologist
Harry Fielding Reid. Encamped on the moraine adjacent to the glacier's
toe, the group built a rough cabin and became something of an attraction to the thousands of tourists visiting that summer. Reid would return
two years later to continue his survey of the bay and its glaciers. Muir
made a final trip to "his" glacier with railroad magnate Edward H. Harriman during summer 1898.

For these scientists, time had been made visible. The past was writ
large in the movements of ice, conjuring up the visage of past and future
ice ages. Space here was not isolated from geologic time. Space was geologic time, surging and shaping the entire sweep of the landscape. The
visible present was linked to the abysses of deep time. An Alaskan writer
suggested as much when he noted in the late 1880s "a large portion
of Alaska still passes through the glacial period." Alaska represented a
remnant of the past. Physical travel to Alaska was like traveling back into
time, to the glacial period. One might witness the deep geological past
in the present while traveling in Alaska. And according to those with
active imaginations, "it was not unreasonable to suppose that in the
unknown and unexplored regions there are large food resources available for the support of such animals as natural history puts under the
generic name of 'Mammoths.'" Mammoth flesh and tusk preserved in

ice, a raw remnant of the Pleistocene, dredged from some frozen hillside permafrost, turned up occasionally at interior trading posts. According to one report, "At one of the posts an agent had questioned the aborigines and learned from the man who led the hunt in which the ivory was taken that the party had encountered a bull and cow of the mastodon species."[110] Alaskan travelers, whether they believed "Mammoth" stories (and most did not), did believe that they were wanderers on a prehistoric planet.

Hubert Bancroft in his sweeping history of Alaska echoed this sense of territorial prehistory. "The limit of the history of western North America is reached . . . what a land is this of which to write a history? Bleak, swampy, fog-begirt, and almost untenanted except by savages—can a country without a people furnish material for a history?"[111] Geology served as a text through which an educated observer might literally read the landscape, giving it an imagined past, a deep past before human time, a text that voided the human presence as only a recent incursion. This textual reading graphically removed native people from the land, stripping them of "ownership" by giving the terrain a past so old, so ancient, so as to preclude any legitimate claims to possession or right of place, except to those skilled in the new geologic readings of the land. " 'Nature alone is antique,' says Carlyle. The past history of Alaska, except for a comparatively short period, is a blank to the people of the nineteenth century," observed travel writer Maturin Ballou.[112] The geologic perspective lent scientific validity to the idea that these primeval landscapes naturally harbored particularly primitive human inhabitants.

Given the easy equation of geological and evolutionary theories, ancient landscapes were associated with underdeveloped human societies, doomed to extinction in the minds of many nineteenth-century Americans and Canadians. According to Herbert Spencer, a proponent of social Darwinist ideologies, northern native people were "feeble unorganized societies . . . at the mercy of their surroundings." They were, according to popular survival-of-the-fittest theories, "incapable of surviving in the struggle for life." Of the northern coastal people, one writer noted that readers "may feel a scientific curiosity in inspecting this division of the race. It is a new variety of the human species, which may at least serve as a study in anthropology," he wrote. Indeed, nineteenth-century anthropology had produced a taxonomy of different cultures placed on a temporal scale of development. This evolutionary hierarchy determined that as stratigraphic geology presented a vertical comparison of the past and present, so too did anthropology fix particular human populations to particular spatial locations, and, in the case of the north, fixed native peoples in an evolutionary gradation far below the supposed superior development of the European newcomers. "One can imagine," a guidebook writer wrote, "only the revels of chaos and the scroll rolled back to the genesis of creation."[113] Nature, above all, was a map of eternal hierarchies. Questions about geologic time tied the science of geology to large epistemological questions concerning human origins and the tensions inherent between evolutionary biology and theology.[114]

Anthropology's temporal perspective enabled imperial states, in the words of historian Prasenit Duara, "to make claims on alien peoples and territories by producing the latter as primordial objects of caretaking."[115] The Tlingit and other northern people were, in the eyes of the newcomers, a primitive race whose "history was lost in the shadows of antiquity." As one writer observed, "their oral traditions were as vague as the sea mists." The native people were seen as just another physical feature of the landscape, like the rocks and mists. The interwoven discourses of anthropology and geology gave a rationale to the power relations between natives and newcomers—the savage natives needed civilized guidance. And since their science determined naturalized orders of human and geologic time, European Americans' and Canadians' power over natives was also determined to be part of the natural order of things.

This penchant for order led to calls for protecting native people from the onslaught of time and their supposedly inevitable demise. An Alaskan missionary encouraged such protective benevolence. He urged, "Let us preserve as relics of a prehistoric past our predecessors on this continent," he wrote.

The Indian is to this day but little understood. By some he is looked on as an animal, by others as almost a hero of romance. The ideal Red-skin, the painted and much adorned native with lofty sentiments, is certainly, as far as my experience goes, a very rare being at the present day, if indeed his existence at any time is not to be considered mythical. A creature, half child-half animal, a mixture of simplicity and ferocity, certainly exists; but though a partial civilization may have varnished his exterior, beneath the thin crust the savage nature lurks, ever ready to break forth, like those volcanic mountains whose pure snows only hide the molten lava within.[116]

Geologic metaphors worked to characterize the hidden stratigraphies embedded within the human. The truth always lay somewhere just beneath the surface, ready to erupt. The landscape became a reflection of social relations. By visiting alien cultures late nineteenth-century observers might travel back in human evolutionary time, just as they traveled back in geologic time. The far North might then serve as a grand museum with its living relics of the past—glaciers and Natives.

What these northern newcomers took as natural was for the Tlingit and other northern people an alien way of living in the world. The Tlingit endowed all nature with spirit life, according to a late nineteenth-century ethnographer. "Natural phenomena and inanimate objects all possessed something which made itself felt or became visible under certain conditions," ethnographer George Emmons wrote.[117] A limitless number of spirits were believed to be in the world, inhabiting virtually all space. There were spirits in the sun, moon, sea, salmon, streams, and glaciers. Spirits controlled glaciers.[118] The winter wind, called "hoon," was the breath that poured from the interior down over the glaciers to the coast.[119] The spirit of the glacier itself, sit' tu yégi, was manifest in the cold wind. The Tlingit called Glacier Bay, Gathéeni—"the bay where the glacier lived."[120] Living in close proximity to such active glaciers meant that locals had a relationship with the occasional massive and rapid ice movements called surges. "The Tlingit believe that the corpse of a human or of a dog is so offensive to the glacier that it will retreat," according to anthropologist Frederica de Laguna.[121] And according to western observers, the Tlingit would offer sacrifices in order to stop these occasional glacier advances. "In the early days, when the glaciers of Glacier Bay were advancing, the [Tlingits] threw a slave into a crevasse and so propitiated the Ice Spirit, and the glacier retreated," so reported a late Victorian ethnographer. Given such opposed ways of engaging with the external world, it was no wonder that white and native societies had difficulty communicating. The coastal native people suffered from a superstitious relation to nature in the eyes of European Americans. Given the Tlingit's hold on what they believed to be a primitive emotionalism, whites believed that their possession could go ahead logically with little consideration of the Alaskan natives.

Between 1200 and 1700 the glaciers were smaller than they were in the mid-nineteenth century. The Little Ice Age marked a significant advance of coastal tidewater glaciers between 1700 and the mid-nineteenth century when conditions warmed again and the glaciers retreated.[122] The Glacier Bay Huna's oral traditions record the destruction of villages by the sudden advance of the tidewater glaciers. Tlingit oral traditions record glacier surges, earthquakes, and tsunamis that occurred in the eighteenth century, and perhaps earlier.[123] In some cases Tlingit clan myths narrated their peoples' birth from the glacier itself. Such geo-myths likely document Tlingit migrations in the eighteenth century from the interior during periods of extensive glaciation that extended to the open coast.[124]

"They said the way it was moving, the way it was growing, was faster than a running dog," a Huna story described a glacier advance.[125] "It was like after a war," recorded another story. "There was nothing. This is how it was," as a Tlingit story recorded the history of a village's destruction during a glacial advance.[126] While the Huna at Glacier Bay did not use the scientific tools of cause and effect as understood by the newcomers, they did possess through long practice an intimate and detailed understanding of the region's geology.[127] The Tlingit would have understood geologist Clarence King's characterization of the geologic theory of catastrophism, even if they understood it in different terms. "Catastrophism," King argued, "is therefore the survival of a terrible impression burned upon the very substance of human memory."[128]

Indigenous appreciation for these northern spaces was dismissed as primitive and unreasoned by European Americans. The newcomers' science displaced the mythological discourses of Tlingit. In the place of these pre-scientific relationships between nature and culture, the newcomers understood their world through a "perspectivalist fiction of being outside the object of inquiry."[129] Their scientific logic relied upon the "useful fiction of a distancing vision." That is, the viewer trained his analyses upon the world of fixed natural forces, rather than a world constituted through the revolving constructions of a dynamic and contemporary culture. Since the Tlingit and other northern people left the region's resources underutilized, since they were supposedly ruled by their environment, the north was left fiscally barren. Geological ways of seeing nature assumed that what was viewed was outside of the economy. Nature preexisted the human economy. The newcomers' natural history created new fields of knowledge production and established hierarchies of information that allowed for the progressive incorporation of nature, in the new terminology—natural resources—into capital. "Alaska has no history, except a geological history, which is of interest to men of science," concluded writer Henry Field, thereby stripping all indigenous claims to time and space.[130] The European American separation of natural history from social history belied the degree to which the social created the natural, and hence this separation disguised the degree to which discourses like geology were a diffused exercise of power. Muir's focus on geology allowed him, and those who followed his lead—the tourists and scientists—to avoid deterministic questions arising from human evolution and biology.[131] With the elision of the productive enterprise constituted by tourism and natural history, whole landscapes gained an exchange value.

The act of seeing in its essence rejected this level of profit imperatives, insisting that what was viewed was outside of the economy, preexisting it, and having a separate source of value, one that was inherent in its very naturalness. Geologic and ethnographic information gathering were conscious efforts to objectively categorize and observe new regions of the globe. As such scientists and tourists elided their critical role as part of the productive enterprise of expanding late nineteenth-century capitalism whereby whole landscapes gained a monetary exchange value. And having established mineral value as a fixed thing, where value was inherent in its very nature, gold then became naturally selected as a money form. Natural history's separation from social history was in no way problematic for these bourgeois travelers.[132] Marx's reminder that value was not a fixed thing, but rather a social relationship signified by material nature played no part in the conventional wisdom of the mind-set of late Victorian imperialists. Gold seeking served to bring this natural money form from nature into the economy. Traipsing across the subarctic in search of the soft yellow metal, one hardly needed to provide an explanation. It was the thing to do, the new cultural commonsense.

If geology and anthropology had been naturalized, then so too was economic production made a feature of natural law. The late nineteenth-century writer Charlotte Perkins Gilman confirmed as much when she announced, "Economic production is the natural production, is the natural expression of human energy,—not sex-energy at all, but race energy . . . socially organized human beings tend to produce as a gland to secrete: it is the essential nature of the relation."[133] And so, with gold and gold seeking in the nineteenth century we can observe the most elemental form of the relationship between nature and capital. Gold, the thing itself which signified pure capital, wedded the human economy to nature's geology. In a world of imagined social Darwinian struggle seizing mineral lands ensured racial survival. Nineteenth-century expansionists need not dwell over the ethics of conquest, since natural law deemed it so: "human beings tend to produce as a gland to secrete." Capitalism—here through the signifier of gold—was an inevitable, universal product of nature. Even biological nature was viewed as a subset of an inevitable productive impulse. Human nature was viewed as fixed to capitalism. Capitalism became natural. To resist it was unnatural. "So easily we glide," wrote the late Victorian theorist of imperialism J. A. Hobson, "from natural history to ethics, and find in utility a moral sanction for the race struggle. Now, Imperialism is nothing but this natural history doctrine regarded from the standpoint of one's own nation."[134]

Scientific discourse had naturalized the processes of dispossession. "Race energy," the industrious vigor supposedly represented by Anglo-Saxons, determined by natural law that this group above all others was destined to dominate. The structures of their rationalist geologic dogma were but one part of a larger structure of meaning that supplanted the prescientific discourses of the north's indigenous populace. These northern visitors' initial cognitive acts, their interpretations of the north's deep and un-peopled geologic past and renderings of the region's mineral potential, set the stage upon which subsequent transformations unfolded. These disciplinary transformations were a bourgeois attempt to find a language that might bring all things into relation. Their travels and studies were in part an effort to effect an understanding, but one that also resulted in control. "Here all belonging the mineral kingdom awaits the coming of man," one travel writer proclaimed.[135] "Equality is not the rule," he continued, "yet every intelligent effort will be rewarded . . . Alaska! The last West, the great domain of the North . . . the secret of its riches has been well kept; and now an invitation, limited by nature, is extended the present generation—a reserve held for countless ages, denied to all others. The wisdom of Providence is most clearly established. In a land of sunshine, a vast country could be pillaged in a few seasons; with sunshine, the sustenance and need of unborn generations might be destroyed; with seasons moderating, ice disappearing, His will may be surmised."[136]

In the late nineteenth century no one would have seriously questioned the nature of gold, the practice of geology, or the discourse of anthropology. There were, of course, strident debates about all of these subjects—gold versus silver, uniformity versus catastrophe, degeneration versus polygenesis—but their essential practices were assumed. This being said, there were also inconsistencies, contradictions, and profound anxieties generated by the thrall of naturalism. To be sure, the claims made upon northern resources and native land by European Americans and Canadians were guaranteed by arguments that naturalized and legitimated dispossession. But, these same discourses raised profound concerns. Alongside confident assertions of a progressive resource development and conquest of native space and nature lay darker questions.

The late nineteenth-century world presented a competitive arena where, it was believed, vast hostile and uncontrollable forces intersected. American sociologist William Graham Sumner warned his contemporaries that the utmost one could do was "to note and record their course as they are carried along in the great stream of time." Darwinian sociology had called progressive history into question. "Such attitudes exemplified the naturalistic determinism that originated with Darwin and Spencer," historian John Higham observes, "and became increasingly oppressive as the century waned. Until the 1890s American intellectuals had tempered the naturalistic creed with a supreme confidence in their own destiny. But evolutionary thought gradually slipped into a darkened vision of a blind and purposeless universe."[137] The same progressive scientific theories that enabled the spread of European societies also carried the seeds of a profound anxiety. Max Nordau ended his book *Degen-*

eration with the conclusion that the age was suffering from "a compound of feverish restlessness and blunted discouragement . . . vague qualms." He joined others in a fin de siècle warning of the "Dusk of Nations."

"Over the entire landscape nature seemed dead," wrote Glacier Bay visitor Charles Hallock. "Not a living thing appeared. . . . Desolation reigned throughout, for there was nothing to sustain life. The creation was all new, and the glacier was still at work gradually preparing it for the abode of organic life. Darkness only was needed to relegate us to the primorgium of chaos." These remnants of past ice ages upset comfortable notions of providential history. Natural forces might portend an uncontrollable, ungoverned, and ultimately hostile universe. Given the contemporary theories of climate change, a less secure vision of the future lurked. Yes, the glaciers appeared to be in retreat at Glacier Bay and along the southeastern Alaska coast, but for how long?[138]

Cyclical views of history challenged those of progressive development.[139] Systems of information like geology, posited upon a positivist development of knowledge, suddenly suggested a reversal of optimistic evolution. Late Victorians shuddered at the prospects of the threat of global cooling and their own racial degeneration. In the fin de siècle the only thing that seemed certain was that change was certain. The perennial critic John Ruskin in an 1884 essay broke from his earlier aesthetic optimisms. In "The Storm Cloud of the Nineteenth Century," he brooded gloomily over future prospects of flood and storm. Drawing on then-recent conclusions regarding the physics of entropy—that is, the random dissolution of the universe, the tendency of all matter toward disorder—Ruskin concluded that the late nineteenth-century weather patterns portended chaos on a global scale, suggesting a world ungoverned. A poison wind blew over the civilized world, according to Ruskin's apocalyptic prognostications.[140] Ruskin saw no possibility for order in such a universe. The certainty of positive knowledge was no longer so certain. No unseen hand, no visible hand, no hand at all.

While his 1884 lectures focused primarily upon atmospheric elements, Ruskin's thought drew from his long-term interests in glaciology. A running argument with the glaciologist John Tyndall—"Tyndall['s intention was] to keep the scientific world in darkness as to the real nature of glacier motion"—filled these lectures and much of Ruskin's work.[141] The metaphor of a glacier's inscrutable movements was never far from Ruskin's assessments of social change. The glacier's cold and restless mass moving onward day by day portended vast destructive global forces at work, geologically and socially. In 1854, Ruskin, then visiting the glaciated valley of Chamonix, France, wrote, "Every day here I seem to see farther into nature, and into myself, and into futurity."[142] By the century's end another vision intruded into the romantic sublime of his world's progressive mentality: "A wind of darkness" now blew. "I believe that the powers of Nature are depressed or perverted, together with the Spirit of Man."[143] "Harmony is now broken, and broken the world round . . . month by month darkness gains upon the day," Ruskin concluded.[144] "What old Ruskin called for" was no longer the comfortable security of the romantic sublime, but rather disorder and chaos.

"The destructive invasion of northern lands by the slow-marching ice of the glacial period" portended a radically contingent history.[145] What if history's *longue durée* only endured briefly between episodes of unpredictable catastrophic punctuations and mass extinctions? C. A. M. Taber agreed. In his 1896 book *The Coming Ice Age,* he argued that new cycles of glaciation were a certainty. And with these inevitable episodes of global cooling came the threat of civilization's demise. Clarence King warned, "Here in America our own species has seen the vast massive eruptions of Pliocene basalt, the destructive invasion of northern lands by the slow-marching ice of the Glacial period."[146] "Climatic catastrophes," he prophesied, "could not fail to have a disastrous effect on much of the organic world . . . catastrophic in their effect upon the life of America." "The glacier," King continued, "is at once the remnant and the reminder of the Ice Age of prehistoric times, when great seas were frozen into solid ice, that swept over great continents, carrying away whole mountain tops." "Here we are face to face with the grim destroyer," he wrote, "Have we any way to stop him in his course? Has he not given us proof already of his power to bear down all resistance?" "Suddenness, world-wide destructiveness," reasoned King, "are the characteristics of geological changes."[147] Thorstein Veblen's caustic depiction of the leisure class' fortuitous animism no longer appeared so fortunate.

The belief in luck had been shaken. What the expansionists understood as their providential destiny no longer looked to be so provident. A revealing continuity existed between the discourse of geology, especially glaciology, and questions of racial destiny.[148] Catastrophism tied geologic futures to human ones. Human evolution, once viewed as a gradual process in Darwinian theory, suddenly held out a much darker probability. "Successive faunas and floras were created only to be extinguished by general cataclysms," King predicted.[149] Even Louis Agassiz's theologic scientism believed that god used ice ages in order to wipe out existing life forms. "A vast mantle of ice and snow covered the plains," he wrote, "the valleys and the seas. All the springs were dried up, the rivers ceased to flow. To the movements of a numerous and animated creation, succeeded the silence of death."[150] These extinctions prepared the way for a new creation. And in Agassiz's racialist view of multiple human species, certain races emerged stronger and destined to dominance. Agassiz clung conveniently to his view of white racial superiority amidst these geological contingencies. But the Victorian foundations of geology teetered at the end of the century.[151] Others saw only chaos as a secular world supplanted the sacred.

The imperial journey to the north brought travelers face to face with the ice age remnant. History was a visual spectacle in the form of a glacier. Their travels into glaciated nature suggested visits back in time. But their travels also suggested visits to a possible future, one darker and less hopeful. In the subarctic north, the geographical periphery became a site of central cultural significance where turn-of-the-century social, economic, and political questions arose in seemingly marginal discussions over the order and disorder of nature.

These questions of nature's teleology were, however, obscured by other conundrums that the tourists faced at the glacier's edge. Rumors circulated about a phantasm hovering in the play of light above the ice fields. Sir Edward Belcher, visiting a tidewater glacier near to Glacier Bay in the early 1840s, was one of the first to question the visual mirage of a great city across the surface of the glacier. "What could produce these special forms? If one could fancy himself perched on an eminence about 500 feet above a city of snow-white pyramidal houses with smoke-coloured flat roofs covering many square miles of surface and rising ridge above ridge in steps, might form some faint idea of this beautiful freak of nature," Belcher wrote.[152] "The reflection of a great and strange city upon its glassy surface . . . suspended in the air" might be seen, according the Pacific Coast Steamship Company's advertising.[153] "The streets of this strange city are very wide . . . in the streets many people are seen moving about, dressed in loose flowing garments, with something after the fashion of Turkish caps upon their heads . . . large dogs with lion-like heads and manes . . . the picture resembles a Japanese city," the brochure described the seeming city. Others thought the metropolis resembled Bristol, England. The Baedeker's guide expressed a more skeptical view. "Mirages are of common occurrence at the Muir Glacier, and have given rise to the so-called 'Phantom City' of which fanciful illustrations are given in some books describing this region," the guidebook noted.[154] One travel writer suggested that though a number of others vouched for having seen the so-called Silent City themselves, civilized and educated people should not be given over to such preposterous claims.[155] In other versions of the story, some Glacier Bay miners holding a gold pan skimmed with quicksilver were said to have seen a city as well—these observers noted that what they were seeing was in fact a sunken city reflected onto the clouds overhead and then immediately back into the quicksilvered pan of the imaginative gold prospectors. Another glacier-visiting prospector claimed to have actually visited the mysterious city itself and "found that the place was laid out in streets with blocks of strange-looking building, what appeared to be mosques, towers, ports, etc., and every evidence of having been built by art. The whole was not of solid ice, though it seemed to be, but blows from a hatchet on one of the walls disclosed the fact that beneath this barrier of ice was some sort of building material."[156] The illusions witnessed by the tourists were the result of a complex mirage common in the Arctic and over glaciated landscapes where warm and cold air masses mixed. Such mirages, known as Fata Morgana, often gave the appearance of built structures—castles or cities—superimposed over the surface of the ice. The travelers incorporated these illusions into their own imperial repertoire. The alien landscapes were imbued with as much importance as were the "alien" cultures that inhabited the non-European imperial spaces of the globe. Like the Orientalist representations of the conjured cities hovering in the ice mirage, the landscapes of the north were imbued with political and cultural significance.

Was there a hidden significance in this late nineteenth-century chicanery? Or were these doctored pictures and first-hand accounts more straightforward than that—simply a hoax, easily recognized and all the

Figure 33. "Prof. Willoughby's 'Silent City,' Muir Glacier," 1889. (Courtesy Yale Collection of Western Americana, Beinecke Rare Book and Manuscript Library)

Figure 34. "Taber's Silent City, Glacier Bay," 1889. (Courtesy Yale Collection of Western Americana, Beinecke Rare Book and Manuscript Library)

less important for its failure to steal the confidences of its viewers? Perhaps the confabulation was little more than a Barnumesque trick.[157] "The public," as Barnum recognized, "appears disposed to be amused even when they are conscious of being deceived."[158] Barnum biographer Neil Harris identifies the role of these Barnum-like hoaxes in training Americans to absorb knowledge. "This was an aesthetic of the operational," Harris writes, "a delight in observing process and examining for literal truth. In place of intensive spiritual absorption, Barnum's exhibitions concentrated on information and the problem of deception." Through this "operational aesthetic," onlookers were relieved from the burden of coping with more abstract problems. "Beauty, significance, spiritual values, could be bypassed in favor of seeing what was odd, or what worked, or was genuine," he argues.[159] The so-called Phantom City of Glacier Bay deflected tourists' fears of the unknown, their sense of their having no significance in the face of all that grinding ice.

These visual tests provoked sightseers to consider the veracity of the glacier representations. When given a choice between fact and fake, tourists welcomed this exercise in recognition. Recognizing the trickery in the doctored photographs reversed the false effect. Uncovering the truth affirmed the underlying reality of the glaciated landscape itself. If large epistemological questions had been raised by photographic hoax—that is, the question of what was real?—then the resolution of these indeterminate depictions in effect determined what was real and what was fake. The illusion produced and advertised an experience for tourists that rendered the glacier as that which was most real, most natural, and most uncorrupted.

The photographic trick produced the essential opposition that might have characterized the Inside Passage itself. The trip north, but especially its finale, the visit to Glacier Bay, divided the real from the fake, nature from culture, the purity of the natural from the corruptions of the unnatural city, the best citizens from the worst. "Civilized and educated people" would "not be given over to such preposterous claims," one writer reflected on the story of the Phantom City. The hopeless mass of Americans, the elite believed, appeared happy to pay to be fooled, if they were fooled well. These others would likely have been taken in by such chicanery. The wealthy happily recognized their superiority to those class and ethnic others who enjoyed low forms of amusement and spectacle, and who were supposedly taken in by low deceptions. Their bourgeois venture north reinforced their sense of their class status. The trip was, according to the advertisers, "the object of a lifetime. There is nothing like it. Without doubt it is 'the biggest show on earth.' "[160] Their Inside Passages were circuses of the real. These sorts of distractions deflected the travelers' attentions away from the potentially ominous implications of the ice age north.

Nature originated in its opposite. It was no coincidence that the glacier and the city were imagined together in one simultaneous visual spectacle. Though the photographic and descriptive hoax was false, the hovering presence of the "city wilderness" was ever present in their metropolitan minds. At Glacier Bay nature, grandly represented by the inscrutable force of the glacier, contrasted with the city. Nature and culture could not be understood apart until they were placed together.[161] The northern ice cap did not immediately pose the specter of doom that the visiting scientists had portended. Instead nature came to represent an immutable reality opposed to the changling city. The city's uncertainties were counterposed to nature's eternal certitudes. The wilderness of empire countered the metropolis that bourgeois contemporaries characterized as the "storm center" of civilization, scene of the coming apocalypse. "The city," the evangelical Protestant Josiah Strong wrote in 1886, "is the nerve center of our civilization. . . . It is also the storm center."[162] Cities were "pestilential human rookeries . . . reeking with poisonous and malodorous gases," Strong announced.[163] Overfilling with alien races, "the city has become a serious menace to our civilization," wrote Strong, who echoed widespread anxiety over the growing immigrant population from eastern and southern Europe.[164] Some said the world would end in ice. But the metropolitan travelers feared not ice, but fire, an urban conflagration. Their passages into nature were not always returns to some past pristine arrangement when humans lived in harmony with nature. More often nature was cast as a vacant space, timeless and immemorial, and freed of the troubling presence of other humans. Bourgeois nature was a realm of stability and natural hierarchies in opposition to an urban, industrial world of flux and disorder.

Conclusion
Inside Passage

We are all tourists now, and there is no escape.
—*Claude Lévi-Strauss*, Tristes Tropiques

Alaska steamer excursions made a final stopover at Sitka. The regular mail ships remained for a full twenty-four hours, but the tour ships made shorter visits. "Sitka faces full upon the sea, overlooking a harbor that is dotted as full of small islands as a pepper box is with holes," wrote one visitor of the island's position.[1] The Sitka stop usually came at the end of the nearly two-week trip and boat-bound travelers felt pent up and ready to return south. But this final stop gave the tourists one last chance to take final snapshots and make curio purchases. In addition to offering the now familiar visits to the Tlingit villages, Sitka presented the novelty of vestiges of a former Russian colony. Located on the west side of Baranof Island, Sitka served as the headquarters for the Russian-American Company beginning in 1804 until the American purchase in 1867. The company's chief manager Alexander Baranov had established Novo Arkhangelsk, as it was then called, after a series of battles with the Sitka Tlingit, notably the capture of the Russians' original base at nearby Redoubt St. Michael in 1802.

Russian settlement in Sitka left its nostalgic traces—conspicuously a "castle" and the Russian Orthodox Church. After American occupation, the U.S. Navy reorganized the Tlingit village, making it "safe" for travelers, and the missionary Sheldon Jackson established an Indian school and a museum. In the tourists' eyes, the remnants of the colonial past gave Sitka a deeper history, that is, a longer European presence. And the contrast between the failed Russian mercantilist experiment and the American entrepreneurial spirit presaged the eventual success of so-called "Yankee" enterprise. Like the Tlingit villages elsewhere along the coast that were stamped with a particular character—that is, savage—the former Russian colony bore the mark of degradation. Russian mercantilist culture, held under the thrall of tsarist control, represented an economic relic according to the American visitors. To the bourgeois onlookers capitalism was moving Alaska progressively forward. Russia represented the past and the demise of an archaic form of governance and economy.

Travel writers did not hesitate to compare Alaskan's historical structures favorably in contrast to Europe's monuments. And Russian Alaska offered reminders of old Europe. "Baranoff Castle is not a grim, ivy covered, and decaying stronghold, with turrets, battlements and keep, but a plain, square substantial, yellow frame building, surmounted by a little look-out tower," travel Henry Winser wrote.[2] The Russian fur trade manager had built the so-called castle as a residence and defense against the Tlingit. Fire all but destroyed the building in 1894, leaving only its ruins as an object of tourist interest. What these writers did not consider was that Sitka was as much a part of Asian history as it was a part of European, or in its Eurocentric spatialization "Western" history.[3] But when these travelers thought of home, it was to the east that they turned, perhaps to California, but their golden state only represented a further development of a great westward movement that had begun centuries earlier in Europe. Through these human-made monuments, visiting Americans celebrated their possession not only of the territory, its scenery, and its inhabitants, but also of the region's past, a curious colonial past that signaled their national greatness. The American takeover also signaled the removal of a colony. The newcomers' free-market attitudes elided the fact that one colonial regime had been replaced with another, and that monopoly rule and domination of native Alaska had only accelerated with the American takeover.

Soon after the American purchase travel guides suggested that Alaska was "not likely ever to be much frequented by travelers, yet one now and then finds his way there."[4] An 1872 description hardly encouraged visitors. "Sitka, the seat of government, is really the only point in Alaska where the United States is able to exercise more than a nominal authority. It has a population of about 1,500, of whom 1,000 are Indians, and is, beyond doubt, the dirtiest and most squalid collection of log-houses on the Pacific slope."[5] The anonymous travel writer painted a picture of Sitka living under the threat of Indian attack. "The Indians are never allowed inside the stockade after nightfall, while a guard is kept constantly on the alert with rifles loaded, and a field-battery of Parrott guns kept constantly trained on the Indian village, adjoining the town, and a man-of-war lies anchored in the harbor, with her guns pointed at the Sitka village." During the summer season in 1877, when the mail boat *California* arrived a Sitka local noted the arrival of "one unknown tourist." The sleepy former colony was scarcely the Mecca for the traveler that it would soon become.[6]

American occupation hardly brought the boon to Sitka that eager boosters had projected. Sitka declined in population, while Juneau's settlement steadily increased. Travel writers almost uniformly lamented the fact that the American government had done so little to develop Sitka. Matilda Lukens, touring the north in 1889, noted the commercial decline following the American takeover of Sitka; "The town to-day though is without commerce," she wrote in her travel diary.[7] Lukens did not consider her own presence, and that, like Fort Wrangell, the commercial value in Sitka "at this time consists almost entirely in the curio trade during the tourist season."[8] Tourism had been made into a central feature of the region's commerce; even though it did not appear so to the tourists themselves.

Excursionists traipsed through the town, past the Russian blockhouse and Russian cemetery, to the Russian Orthodox Church and along the harbor's tide line to the Tlingit village, "a long row of cheaply built houses fronting on the beach." "Each house is numbered, and the village is under the strict surveillance of an officer of the Navy," wrote traveler William Webb.[9] A quick visit to the Sitkan Mission and Sitka Industrial and Training School convinced the visitors that the forces of progress were at work in the new territory, despite the slow development of the town. Under the direction of Sheldon Jackson, the Presbyterian mission trained Tlingit children in supposedly useful skills. Tlingit youth were incorporated into the region's wage labor economy. The industrial school instructed children in skills related to the tourist economy—curio production, weaving, and carving. Jackson and the other missionaries in Sitka and the other coastal missions advocated an enlarged role for Alaskan tourism in the region's economy. Jackson used his Sitka museum, which opened in 1889, to showcase coastal crafts.[10] What the visiting tourists could not purchase in the museum they could find replicas of for sale on the boardwalks of Sitka's main avenue.

"Inhabited by whites, Indians and Russian peasants," Sitka was, according to one travel writer, "the typical little Alaska town." Former Russian fur traders and company agents had intermarried into the coastal native populations. Far from peasants, the Russians represented a thorough integration of European and indigene such that a large population of creoles served as the intermediaries between Sitka natives and the American newcomers. But for the sightseers the Russian creole and native past served as an epic backdrop to the newcomers' own history of successful expansion.[11] Incorporating this rich cultural legacy—the Russian and Tlingit pasts—enhanced the Americans' own history, especially in contrast to Europe's relics of antiquity.[12] "See Alaska before you see

Europe!" writer Ella Higginson trumpeted, "Then you will be able to gaze unmoved upon the glories and the wonders of the old world; and when your indifference is commented upon you may put on a blasé air and say carelessly: 'Oh, I have been to Alaska.'"[13] The Russian colonial past served as a pretext for nostalgia and quaintness. Such pretext was an act of distancing that elevated the American present.

The new inroads made by American culture came with a cost, at least in the eyes of the travelers. The precious quaintness the tourists valued appeared to have been sullied by the Americans' arrival. Sitka was ruined, according to several observers. "There are no totem poles . . . to lend outward interest to the villages, and the Indians themselves are too much given to ready-made clothes and civilized ways to be really picturesque," Eliza Scidmore insisted.[14] The tourists themselves seemed to have been the cause of this lost authenticity. Lamenting changes in the much vaunted woven Tlingit baskets available in Sitka, another writer observed, "Since the tourist has invaded Sitka and these baskets have become regular merchandise, the Indians are copying designs from dress goods, carpets and curtains, and have adopted the aniline dyes. Thus their basketry is fast losing its charm." Along with the loss of authentic bric-a-brac, tourists bemoaned what they perceived as the vanishing Tlingit culture. "Year by year too, it becomes more and more difficult to obtain even this fleeting glimpse of these interesting people." The Tlingit were another object for their viewing and this was being lost, or so they believed. "The old, old story of the gradual disappearance of the aboriginal in face of the advancing tide of civilization is being repeated in Alaska. Dissipation and disease have joined hand in wreaking the extermination of the Thlinket, while by the rapidly dwindling remnant, old customs, old myths, and old beliefs are being forgotten or allowed to fall into desuetude."[15] But, if the "manners and customs of the squat sturdy slant-eyed villagers" seemed to be slipping away, the scenery as yet remained. "The almost sensational scenery of Alaska, it is true, can be appreciated and enjoyed to the full as the steamer takes its rapid way through the inland waters and along the rugged coast line," even if the soul of Alaska appeared to be extinguished.[16] Following the now requisite curio shopping, the tourists embarked their steamers for the trip home. Safe in their alienated form of nostalgia, the tourists trucked their collected loot and idealized memories home.

After a final stopover in Sitka the tourists steamed south, back outside, back to their cities with their accustomed comforts. "Southward, until fair faces greet us instead of the scowling visages of the Si-wash; until summer-tide takes us by the hand and leads our thoughts away from ice-rivers and gloomy snow-fields; until the past fades and the present comes

Figure 35. "Native Women Weaving Baskets, Sitka, Alaska," 1897, Winter and Pond Collection. (Photograph courtesy Alaska State Library, Historical Collections)

to cheer and bless us," mused travel writer James Dennis, "and Alaska—golden, sunny, fair, muddy, gloomy, stormy, contradictory Alaska—seems more a fairy dream—a realization of the mythic Hesperides—the lost Atlantis—the fabled eden—than a reality; and not only a part and parcel of this little planet; but also—our country!"[17] The travelers' attitudes were a concatenation of feelings and ideas. Their travels were an extension of American nationalism into the new territory, "our country!" The nation's center had shifted and the travel writing of the period helped to fix this new geography.

In 1872 a guidebook stated, "No territory of equal extent on the globe, except Central Africa, is so little known."[18] But by 1890, another travel writer announced, "The interior of the country is not as little explored as people generally suppose. There is very little that has not been seen by prospectors, travelers, adventurers, and explorers. Its character is pretty well understood by such people."[19] Travelers linked unthinkingly this Alaskan lebensraum to imperial expansion in the tropics. "Men have been found willing to dare the insalubrious exhalations of the Isthmus of Panama, to live in the jungles of India, to endure the

Figure 36. The economic independence that many Tlingit women found through their management of the curio trade slipped away as European-American entrepreneurs sought greater control over the profitable trade. White-run businesses concentrated production into easily managed workshops, often employing Tlingit men. Tlingit women did continue to dominate the gender-specific basket production. P. E. Kern's Curio Workshop, Skagway, c. 1900. (Courtesy Rauner Special Collections Library, Dartmouth College)

blazing suns of Africa, to tempt death upon the gold coast," an Alaskan writer argued.[20] But the north was deemed superior to the febrile tropics and its climate was assumed to be particularly suitable to the immigration of northern Europeans. Tourist promotions and travelers themselves presented Alaska as huge in scale. An earlier generation of promoters had compared American landscapes of the West to the Alps, looking for the American Switzerland. However, Alaska proportions dwarfed its European counterparts. Tourists in their way helped to incorporate Alaska, as they had already done for the West more generally, into a national culture.

But these ventures were more than celebrations of the new national space. Their northern sojourns afforded a certain class of privileged Americans and Europeans a respite from the anxieties of their everyday lives, the space for both a physical and spiritual regeneration, an escape from the city summer and the tumult of the fin de siècle. "Here I revel in visions," a traveler wrote, "no thought of life's sorrows or pain." Alaska presented, according to this diarist, the "key to my dreamland and fancy, my refuge from gloom and despair."[21]

The Alaska excursion gave the bourgeois tourists more than solo experiences in a dreamy natural world; it provided this class with an exclusive traveling holiday with a community of generally like-minded men and women. "Agreeable companionship and other social pleasures will," Dennis recalled, "render the homeward voyage possibly even more truly enjoyable than were those first few days before the barriers of reserve were broken down, and when the rapid succession of one sublime and unlooked-for spectacle after another kept the mind in a state of perpetual tension."[22] The Alaska vacation rejuvenated the wealthy tourists, preparing them to reenter the hurly-burly of their urban lives. The north Pacific coast with its briny air and mountain breezes offered a cure. Its salubrious airs restored and refreshed. "Having arrived Home: You will find your eyes clear and sparkling, your appetite keen, your step more elastic, your general health immensely improved, and in case you were not up to a proper and healthy standard when you started out, your avoirdupois increased anywhere from five to thirty pounds," the Pacific Coast Steamship Company brochure advertised.[23] But these trips were not only aimed at individual rejuvenation and the immediacy of experience. The tours also rewarded travelers with a new cultural capital. Back home in the domestic spaces, exclusive clubs, and managers' offices the tourists' experiences became complete. "You will have lots of stories to tell of your experiences, which will make you the lion of your social gathering and the envy of those who stayed home or went to the springs," an advertising brochure concluded.[24] Tourists did not perceive themselves to be the victims of unscrupulous advertisements. "One venturesome traveler after another, to the surprise, and not unfrequently against the advice and remonstrance of his friends, ventures forth to put the claims and pretensions of the railroad and steamship companies to the test," a traveler noted, "and return to be the hero of the social circle in which he moves."[25] Status was lifestyle and increasingly lengthy summer vacations became another requirement to maintaining one's image and identity. Two weeks spent aboard the coastal steamship tour, coupled with the requisite foray to Yosemite Valley and Yellowstone, or Glacier and Grand Canyon National Parks, cross-country rail trips, nights in comfortable hotels and resorts—all this filled the summertime.

Travelers were often gone for a couple of months, but they carried their culture of privilege and status with them, recreating among their self-selected traveling companions the kind of society they had left behind. Here culture in the form of experience appeared separate from the political and economic entitlements that made their leisured touring possible. Their published travel narratives performed a social function, as these texts helped to underpin the power of their class position, though never directly. That was, after all, the point: the travelers' appreciation of wild nature and the curiosities of native Alaska was a direct experience, the kind of passage that unraveled the truth about the places they visited. But these extravagances emphasized and exhibited cultural distinctions and differences and formed a crucial feature of American social stratification. "Travel," according to a Great Northern Railway promotional pamphlet, "for business or pleasure, is now almost a fine art . . . the patriotic American is just awakening to the fact that the United States and its possessions contain a greater diversity of climate than any other nation on the face of the globe."[26] The "right kind" of citizens recognized this fact. Their visits helped place Alaska within the imagined national domain. Citizenship in a democracy might be broadly construed, but the "best" citizens were those who could afford the leisure to consider questions of national scope and "fine arts."

The well-heeled travelers were not only producers of the "New Alaska"; their ideas about the place were also produced for them. "People look at what they are told to look at or at what has been named," John Muir wrote of the tourist throng. "Nameless things, however fine, go unnoticed," he lamented.[27] The new travel industry marketed experience as a commodity. Advertising nature and natives in undifferentiated forms, travel marketing synthesized new desires. The tourists in their way were like the prostitutes they derided on their visits to the coast's frontier villages. The travelers were both buyer and bought. Increasingly the tourists became a mass article, moved about like coastal cargoes, purchasers of the immaterial, transient experiences sold by the largest corporations of the period, the rail companies and their allied steamer companies. "Value transforms," Karl Marx wrote, "every product of labor into a social hieroglyph. People then try to decode the meaning of the hieroglyph in order to get behind the secret of their own social product." Like Marx's oft-cited example of the whore, the image of the tourist reveals this secret "like a rebus."[28] "Whereas every trace of the laborer who produced the commodity is extinguished when it is torn out of context by its exhibition on display," to paraphrase Marx, in the tourist, who existed at the opposite end of the exchange from the whore, the commodity and the content remain visible. Unlike the prostitute, the tourist synthesized the form of the commodity and the productive capital behind the enterprise. Here the tourists placed their leisure-class status on display. Still hidden was the trace of the labor that had made all the fortunes, large and small, which made possible the tourists' journeys. The high-brow travelers were perverse dialectical images, flaunting their privilege. Indeed some of the travelers, like the Northern Pacific Railroad executive Henry Villard, directed the major corporations of the era. Their seemingly passive touring de-centered their roles as sightseers, avoiding the appearances of an active and powerful subject. Here the tourists escaped their own social realities, all the while exercising broad powers to define what could be said.

Value, as Marx reminds us, was not a fixed thing, but rather a social relationship signified by material nature. But nature was never simply *there* to be seen and interpreted. It too became a social product and relationship, continuously repackaged in aesthetic terms as a "fine art," a sublime realm, the site of immense and valuable resources, a region capable of acting as a mirror to its visitors' inner identities, a place to confirm one's manliness or a stage for the New Woman of the fin de siècle. In late nineteenth-century tourism one might glimpse the nature of metropolitan social realities at the margin of American empire. The travelers' "technologies of the self," their journal keeping and their vacationing with its mix of leisure and health maintenance, was the product of a particular history. Their psychological version of human identity was a product of this late nineteenth-century moment. The modern natural sciences tied bodies to nature, and so men's and women's relations to the "wild" and the "savage" carried layers of meaning. The travelers' dominance lay in their power to narrate, both to themselves in their private words and to a wider national audience in their published travelogues.[29]

But these early tourists straddled a paradoxical position between dictating the new regime of travel and having it ordered for them. Guidebooks and travel books provided written imagined spaces that helped to form future tourist's behavior, informing them of what to see, how to act, what to buy. Much of the experience was invested in being able to say at the end of it all that one had "done Alaska," to having "Kodak'd" images of natives and nature. Places became "identified as scheduled moments of departure and arrival," as Alan Trachtenberg observes; these experiences were like the industrial commodities produced by the time-efficient factory, also a timed element of production.[30] The experience had value because it could be stored and related at a later time where the trip communicated one's cultured identity. Identity could be derived from travel and an increasing world of goods came to include increasingly a world of experience as goods. Modern selves were actively creating themselves through their arrangements of commodities that in this case appeared to have no material traces.[31] Thus identities formed through the careful consumption of even more carefully advertised and fashioned experiences.

These situations seemed all the more real because they were so immaterial, because they disguised their existence as commodities. How could this touring be consuming since in the end, aside from the requisite curios, nothing was bought? But these experiences were in fact the reverse. They were perversely more commercial in their very obscuring of the act of purchase. Here there were no visible traces, save the stories and curios of one's travels. The trace of the wage laborer on whose appropriated efforts in the form of capital the touring leisure class spent their summers was nowhere in sight. The onlookers saw little of the rearrangement of native lives brought on by their visits. The view of nature and natives from the deck of the steamer appeared as natural. Instead, the appearance of nature and natives was the social product of the tourists' and the natives' relative positions within a national and international economy.[32] As traveler William Seward Webb wrote, "it was something more than a trip of pleasure, as indeed, it could not but be to any business man." In their nearly four-month tour, Webb and his family intended "to be entirely independent of time-tables . . . under such a scheme the party would be relieved of any anxiety they might otherwise have had in regard to making connections."[33] Like Webb, the Inside Passage vacationers believed that they lived briefly beyond the scale of their industrial society. But these tourists did not somehow slip the bounds of civilization into the liminal wilderness spaces of empire. The tourists were incorporating arms of that empire, both consuming and producing the new reach of national power into the new northern territory, "something more than a trip of pleasure." The leisure-class triumph was its ability to inscribe its ideology into a then-reforming national culture. The achievement of the bourgeoisie, the anthropologists Jean and John Camaroff write, was its stress on "utilitarian individualism and the virtues of the disciplined, self-made person; on private property and status as measures of success, poverty as appropriate sanction for failure; on enlightened self-interest and the free market as an instrument of the common good; on reason, and method, science, and technology, as the key to the progress of mankind."[34] In their Alaska reflections, the leisure-class travelers assumed all of these ideas to be given facts. American progress could proceed in the north with these supposedly natural virtues in full view. Alaskan travelers mixed nature and culture, rendering their own perspectives as that of the nation's itself. As replications of ruling ideas about the natural evolution of species and specie, the tourists' views showed little evidence of departing from the mental consensus of their capitalist society. "The number of people in our country who are willing and able to enter into the modes of thought of other nations is altogether too small," wrote the well-traveled student of the northwest Franz Boas. "The American," he concluded, "who is cognizant only of his own standpoint sets himself up as arbiter of the world."[35] And it was their view that came to dominate. Boas's own work, largely generated from time spent along the Inside Passage, suggests that paradigms of understanding might change. But this would take some time.

"While the eye of almost the entire world is directed to the wonders of the comparatively unexplored regions of the far northwest," Alexander Badlam wrote, "and while the elegant steamers that weekly ply the inland channel, from Port Townsend to Glacier Bay are crowded to their utmost capacity, it would seem an opportune time to publish an illustrated work on the wonders of Alaska."[36] Collectively this spate of travel writing met a demand for work chronicling the nation's newest territories in their increasingly geographically conceived world. Eager readers, whether they intended to travel north or not, bought these books and magazines. "Books on California and Alaska," travel writer Henry Finck noted, "exist in abundance, if not superabundance."[37] The words read became their own reality, helping to build a new vision of the North. "Thirty years ago what would have been the mental picture of Alaska that a pupil interested in the study of geography could have been able to fashion for himself from the information within his reach?" one writer queried. "A meager paragraph in print and a narrow space on the atlas represented nearly all his sources of information," he answered. "A stray book of travels might have come within the reach of a reading youth, and have afforded some new starting-points for flights of the imaginations to those far-away regions."[38] By the 1890s, accounts from all corners of the globe filled the shelves and stands, and the imaginations of the reading public. But, it would not do to overstate the significance of the Alaskan tourist trade. Alaska visits increased, but tourism in the

North accounted for only a small percentage of the overall national tourist traffic.[39] However, Alaskan travel contributed in its small way to a wider global view that helped to make possible the claims by the metropolitan centers of power over those as yet unincorporated regions.

In order to understand the ideology behind the travelers' texts, we must understand the role of these writings both within their individual circumstances and role of the writing freed of these authors' own relationships.[40] Many of these writers were women taking advantage of the opportunities that travel writing provided to escape the confines of Victorian domesticity. Some, such as Eliza Scidmore, relied upon her writing and travel to launch a professional career. Her missionary parents' extensive journey to Japan and China excited Scidmore's own interest in travel. She began her career as a society reporter in Washington, D.C., writing for the *New York Times* and the *St. Louis Globe-Democrat*. But while the capital remained her base, Scidmore shifted from the confining strictures of high-society reporting to far-flung ventures in the West, Alaska, and eventually throughout Asia. She spent a considerable amount of time traveling in Alaska and wrote her first book, *Alaska: Its Southern Coast and the Sitkan Archipelago*, in 1885. For Scidmore, travel writing offered access to the public sphere and an arena for establishing herself as an authority on topics usually reserved as a male enterprise.[41] Scidmore's guidebook and her later authoring of the popular Appleton's guides, as well as dozens of articles in major newspapers and magazines, fixed her status as a "New Woman." Through travel writing she exercised a new-found freedom, pushing against entrenched gender norms, especially in such a male-dominated region of the country. Her expertise earned her an appointment to help conduct the 1890 census in Alaska.

While these traveling women used their writing to open new fields of possibility, they nevertheless were positioned by their society as custodians of bourgeois respectability, a distinction that often rested upon class and racial ideals.[42] As such, women like Scidmore found access to new-found power within a role acceptable to the wider patriarchal culture. Her new autonomy was still cast within the prevailing culture of imperialism, what women's rights activist Susan B. Anthony famously called this "exclusively masculine form of government." While Scidmore's work challenged societal expectations regarding women's roles, her travel reporting was not entirely a departure from her society's prevailing ideologies. And so Scidmore and other women's travel writing replicated the ruling ideas bound up in the era's enchantment with its new possession and its aesthetic passions. These women often found themselves in contradictory positions where they occupied a dominant position due to imperialism, but a subordinate place in a patriarchal society.[43] Most often these women's written observations did not contest the dominant imperial representations. They reiterated these representations first before initiating a challenge to the patriarchal presumptions of their own society.

Women and men did not experience travel in precisely the same ways, though their written words suggest a similarity. Women found both an actual space in which they might literally expand their horizons and a discursive space where women writers found new voices and audiences, and the recognition as authoritative speakers about subjects outside the private domestic sphere. In this way these women writers and the other women travelers contested the patriarchal strictures of the late nineteenth century. But they also brought some of the essences of American domesticity out of the home and into this wider world—ideas of scientific racism and Social Darwinism. Not that these ideas were not already at work, because they were, but the moral authority of bourgeois women gave these domestic ideas new force.[44] The frequent attention to curio buying fit within these gendered norms where consuming habits fell into expected female roles. "Things 'accumulate' in Alaska," travel writer Ella Higginson wrote, "When our top berth was so full of curios that the very eagles quarreled with the bear on our totem poles and we could not get our trunks closed unless some nice man sat upon them—as he always did—we began to hate the sight of our clothes because of the valuable space they occupied."[45] But if the subjects of these writers' attentions did not break out of gendered norms, the very fact of their writing and of their traveling, often with other women companions, did open new realms of freedom and possibility for bourgeois women at the turn of the century. "Don't be afraid to travel alone in Alaska," Higginson urged, "even if you are cross-eyed; you will be taken care of. Chivalry has its birthplace in that sublime land."[46]

Regardless of the gendered aspects of Alaskan travel writing, Americans read the flood of writing that poured from the far north. The focus on travel in this work seemed to have stripped these descriptions of their political meanings. But the attention to leisure in these texts elided their incorporating actions. In the late nineteenth century, the bourgeois ideal of a homogenous American was struggling to take shape. There were many Americans and many Americas. But the forces of mass consumption, print capitalism, and certainly a growing travel industry helped to create a broad national identity. Travel literature proffered a normalized view of nature. "The mystery of its silent spaces," a prospector rhapsodized at the turn of the century, "seemed to hold them with an irresistible attraction—they were fascinated by its broad rugged

Figure 37. "Scene Across Bay from Muir Glacier, July 19, 1899." Photograph by Fred W. Carlyon. (Courtesy University of Washington Libraries, Special Collections)

splendor."[47] Leisure-class images of a romantic and wild nature came to dominate. They made of Alaska a new economy of appearances, and their normative views of nature spread. The domestication of the out-doors spilled over into efforts to control of the so-called "out-of-doors" people—the lower class, working-class people, those who were feared as the mob, and the indigenous people distrusted as savages supposedly living outside of the economy.[48] Natural scenery had been converted into a commodity. The social transformation of nature on the Alaska coast made way for other conquests. The West and then the North emerged as a form of consciousness that resisted the social fragmenta-tion of the late nineteenth century. And attitudes toward the North in particular suggested a racial nostalgia for an idealized era of conquest and settlement without the assumed hazards of race mixing as understood at the end of the century. Bourgeois travelers situated their individuality in nature. They had made nature a form of bourgeois consciousness. There were, of course, competing versions of nature's meaning, but the high-brow vacationers and their class largely claimed the power to determine which meanings would prevail. The leisure class claimed to appreciate the "fine art" of the mountain landscapes. In fact the tourists' view of nature mirrored their own history writ large on a world they had come to call natural. Nature's monuments encountered on their passage north were really monuments to their own significance. One might turn Frederick Jackson Turner's oft-cited thesis—"the wilderness masters the colonist"—on its head. The tourist mastered the wilderness. "The fact was, that here was a new product that was American," inverting Turner's meaning.[49] The American "product" was the idea of the wilderness itself.[50] The more natural the scenery appeared, to repeat Don Mitchell's observation, the more effectively it naturalized power.

Tourists performed as parts of the machinery of the state, but not in any ordinary sense. They were all the more effective because they were not an official institution of the state apparatus. The type of power they exercised moved invisibly without the imprimatur of state activity, even as they effected the critical functions of imperial expansion.[51] Tourism was as much a part of the conquest and incorporation of the north as other state institutions, like the military and the territorial government. The leisure class acted without being seen to act. They acted without even recognizing their own actions. Tourism was a coercive institution without the edifice of institutional visibility. It was no institution at all, and thus, all the more powerful.[52] Their experiences, commodified and sold like a product, left material traces. The tourists' presence helped to transform the north. It still does.

"So it is a long farewell to the land of ice and snow," Alaskan traveler Charles Taylor wrote, "May your charming recesses, your hoary giants, and your veiled princesses remain forever undisturbed by the spirit of progress, and man's insatiable desire for your subterranean treasures."[53] Taylor's desire for undisturbed wilderness had already met with the forces of progress. In August 1896 on a remote creek deep in the Yukon, a Tagish man, his nephew, and Anglo-American brother-in-law discovered gold. The history of the North shifted suddenly with the Klondike Rush. Over the next several years thousands of eager Argonauts rushed to the Klondike in an often-vain search for the soft yellow metal. Gold rushers, like their tourist predecessors, lived contradictory lives. Gold rushing was at once a rejection of modern technology, a return to a primitive economy, a nostalgic putting on of the modes and masks of the frontier past, and at the same moment the gold seekers were the emblem of modern market culture, buying tremendous amounts of goods and services to get themselves into the northland, the land of their dreams.

They were prototypes for all adventurers then and now. Like the tourists, they yearned to escape the very culture that they most exemplified. Gold seekers thought they had returned in a loose fashion to collective relations, rigorous and masculine enforced codes of conduct, and the law of the trail. They believed that they had returned to an older set of collective productive relations, but this return to the premises of an older moral economy was mostly superficial. The groups of men who traipsed north were organized phenomenally under privately held cor-

Figure 38. "Packers ascending summit of Chilkoot Pass, May 1898." Photograph by Eric A. Hegg. (Courtesy Yale Collection of Western Americana, Beinecke Rare Book and Manuscript Library)

porations, with stock owned by investors and the rules of the game determined by profit returns to those often home-bound investors, speculators experiencing the rush vicariously through the risk of their investments. The same apparatus that had so efficiently guided tourists to the north for nearly two decades prior to the rush now provided the information, the transportation, and the imagination for the gold Argonauts. In addition to the desire for wealth, or simply economic independence, gold seekers, like their leisure-class contemporaries, also found some respite in their otherwise difficult passages into the interior. "I tell you I love the freedom of this wild land," wrote one prospector. "Why a man is as free as air. No whistles or bells, no time or dates, even the days of the week are forgotten," he continued.[54] The gold seeker's words mirrored the discursive practices evidenced in the travelers' diaries and published writing. Nature, capital, and culture were all bound in the turn-of-the-century symbolic order. The aesthetics of the bourgeois leisure culture spread itself widely.

"For years Alaska has been looked upon as merely a land for the tourist and the pleasure seekers," a gold rush–era travel brochure noted. "Its glaciers and its mountains, its wealth of scenery that cannot be equaled elsewhere in the world, rendered it a wonderland," according to the advertisement, "that filled the beholder with admiration of its beauty and grandeur. To-day Alaska is the Mecca for the fortune seeker."[55] The tourists, as the brochure acknowledged, had preceded the gold seekers, setting the stage for these later prospecting travelers. Scidmore, Ingersoll, Muir, and others wrote guides marketed to the legions of gold seekers eager for information about the passage north. As a result the tourist's passage mixed easily with the prospector's venture, such that the would-be miners' journals mirrored the vacationing interests of their touring predecessors. The travel writers' representations of nature helped to fix the north as a scene of vast resources, both scenic and mineralogic. Their words were central to the material transformation of nature into capital in the north.

Discursive practices in the decades before the gold rush formed the imaginative foundation, indeed even the directions upon which the gold seekers would plan their northern ventures. The actions of tourists and travel writers helped to produce the conditions upon which the gold seekers would rely as they followed the watery trail northward. The realities of travel and life in the interior North certainly challenged the placid summer coastal perspectives conjured by steamship luxury. The view from the promenade deck could have hardly seen into the interior's rigors, much less the challenges presented by winter's lock on the region. Nevertheless, the flood of travel writing guided the Argonauts on their excursions.

The gold rush has usually marked a deep divide in northern history, a divide between the relatively unchanging pre-rush era and the rapid transformation following the gold finds. Taking seriously the discursive practices that helped guide the rush north and that preceded the gold discovery requires that we see into the social and economic facts long obscured by the celebratory rush narratives.[56] Instead of seeing the gold rush as the beginning of an era, we might understand the rush years as the culmination of a series of events that began with the first movements of tourists northward. If gold, as Marx said, was the "Lord of Commodities," then the north's scenic resources proved to be a more robust good. In the end, the gold ran out, leaving Alaska with its most durable and culturally complicated resource, the scenery itself. "There is one other asset of the territory not yet enumerated—imponderable and difficult to appraise, yet one of the chief assets of Alaska, if not the greatest," Chief Geographer of the United States Geologic Survey Henry Gannett wrote, "This is the scenery."[57] As the rush subsided after 1900, the tour promoters recognized as much. "The Alaska coast is to become the show-place of the earth, and pilgrims, not only from the United States, but from far beyond the seas, will throng in endless procession to see it," a brochure predicted. "Its grandeur is more valuable than the gold or the fish or the timber, for it will never be exhausted," the advertisement concluded, perhaps too optimistically.[58] "I suppose that most persons imagine that the City of San Francisco marks the western boundary of the great Republic. So far from this being the case, it is practically the geographical center. Reckoning from the meridian of New York, San Francisco is between 46 and 47 deg. west, while the western boundary of Alaska extends beyond 90 deg. thus the United States of North America stretch in an unbroken line—save for the incursion of the State of British Columbia—on quarter round the globe."[59] Each retelling of Alaska's spatial enormity reconstituted again and again the power of the nation with its continental imperial ambitions.[60] Its center was not Washington or London, but the diffuse experiences of thousands of well-to-do travelers, jotting their feelings and observations.

Unease loomed, in the minds of a few, over the world that they bought. "In vain have we annex'd Texas, California, Alaska, and reach north for Canada and south for Cuba. It is as if we were somehow being endow'd with a vast and more and more thoroughly appointed body and then left with little or no soul," Walt Whitman had warned.[61] Indeed, even as a legion of American travelers incorporated Alaska into the body of the nation, these northering pilgrims appeared guided by the "materialistic experiences" and "a certain highly deceptive superficial popular intellectuality" that Whitman had feared. It is easy to cynically

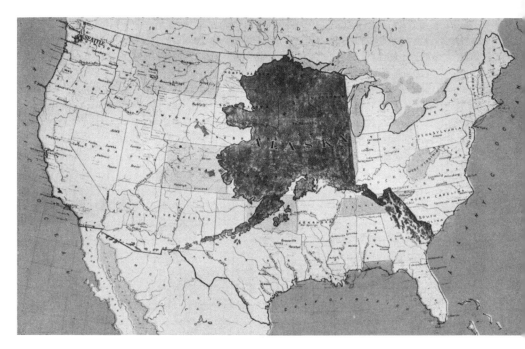

Figure 39. Postcard highlighting Alaska's size with respect to the contiguous United States. "A comparison of Alaska and the United States as to Area," c. 1900. "That the area of Alaska is vast is a well-known fact; but few persons realize that it is nearly one-sixth as large as the entire United States, and more than one-seventh as large as the whole of Europe . . . It is as far from the northern to the southern point of Alaska as from Maine to Florida, and as far from its eastern boundary to its westernmost as from Washington to California." Raymond & Whitecomb's Tours advertisement (Boston: 1898), 27. Photograph by F. H. Nowell. (Courtesy University of Washington Libraries, Special Collections)

disdain the tourists' experiences, in part because these experiences are so clearly part of our present.[62]

The late nineteenth-century tourist imagination has endured, continuing unbroken into the present. The notion that nature offered and offers some timeless and essential secret behind the superficial features of the modern world was itself a construction of these fin-de-siècle travelers. The nature of empire had been fabricated within the ideological forms of late nineteenth-century imperialism.[63] Alaskan vacationers replaced Tlingit landscapes with their own visions of nature as empty wilderness, and their vistas made way for further conquests. Northern development would not have been possible save for the aesthetic dispossessions that created new ways of seeing the north as a land of untapped resources. The vestiges of this colonial mind lie active, but hidden beneath the surface of the present. The idea of untrammeled wilderness obscures its imperial beginnings. Insulated from the politics of its creation, wilderness endures as an unnatural history. For every tourist site, there has always existed another just over the horizon, places to be made into the next new destination where the visitor might claim discovery. We are all tourists now.

Epilogue
Out of Alaska

In August 1897 John White tossed up a half-crown to decide whether to book passage to Canada or Africa. Another restless Brit like Edward Glave, White worked as a clerk for a Fleet Street firm in London. He first found escape with the Greek foreign legion, fighting in the Greco-Turkish War of 1897. Returning to England, his "fate had been decided by the flip of a coin."[1] White headed to Canada.

"Adventure," he wrote in a letter to his father, "is like any other stimulant; the habit acquired is hard to abandon and satisfaction is found only in successive and possibly larger doses. Pity not the hobo who . . . sees a constant change in the panorama of nature . . . Pity the wage-slave condemned to a monotonous round of toil and tarnished pleasure in the city."[2] Not unlike Glave, young John White sought some imagined freedom at the empire's peripheries. An "English son of the colonies" with a bible and revolver in his kit, he enlisted in the British navy, cruising the British Columbia coast. Quickly jumping ship, White rushed north to seek gold in the Klondike. He never reached the interior and instead worked as a "mucker" in the coastal construction trades. "I hope '98 will see me settled with a comfortable mine outside my cabin door. If I discover a creek, I will name it "Pharsala" after a battle in Greco-Turkish war in which legion forces were outnumbered by Turkish cavalry." Like most northern Argonauts, White found no gold. Instead, he and thousands of others ended up toiling in the very wage regime that they sought to escape. Frustrated with the low pay, White "led a gang of 300 strikers against the authorities and got worsted with a horrible crack on the head which laid me senseless for several days."[3] Sentenced to six months in the Sitka jail, he secured an early release and a commission in the United States Army.

Abandoning Alaska for the Philippines, White found in the Spanish-American War that "larger dose" of adventure he had been seeking. "We were within 50 yards of the enemy several times but they always vamoosed before we could apply cold steel," he wrote home. Later he added that "We had some nice fighting here," noting his unit having killed some 200 Philippinos. His exploits seem apocryphal, but, save for some narrative enhancement, White's life was no fiction. "Did you ever read that poem "The White Man's Burden" by Kipling?," White inquired in a letter to his father in England.[4] Self-exiled to colonial service, the twenty-year old celebrated his deliberate strenuous life, an Englishman fighting for American empire. How transparent nationality seemed to be, so long as Anglo-Saxonism held constant in the racial logic of the era. White fashioned himself as a stock character in a Boys Own Adventure Story. Was he, like Edward Glave before him, a product of his childhood reading, of imperial adventure stories? "We are the creatures of our light literature much more than is generally suspected in a world which prides itself on being scientific and practical and in possession of incontrovertible theories," the novelist Joseph Conrad reflected.[5]

Not yet ready to give up his tropical conquests, White joined the Philippine constabulary in 1901, rising to the rank of colonel, and serving as superintendent of the Iwahig Penal Colony, eventually retiring in 1914. "The pacification and building-up of the Philippines have been but the rolling on of that restless wave which surmounted the Rockies to eddy and swirl for a while on the Pacific Coast; but only to regain its momentum, and then sweep majestically on across the Pacific until its combers sprayed the breed of Boone and Crockett and Kit Carson over those Eden Isles of the Far East, that are our Far West," he wrote in his memoir.[6] White's Americanization was complete.

His peripatetic life led him inexorably into the First World War when he joined the American Expeditionary Force as a pilot. By 1920 he had returned to the United States, enlisting in the recently established National Park Service. Trading one uniform for another, White rose through the ranks from ranger and chief ranger to park superintendent and regional director, leapfrogging across the west at Death Valley, Grand Canyon and Sequoia. "Our national parks are often but islands of rescued scenery . . . in the midst of an exploited region," he wrote, echoing a consistent theme of rescue that punctuated his entire life. Elected in 1935 to the Sierra Club Board of Directors as an honorary life member, White joined John Muir's society as enthusiastically as he had overseen the protection of the wilderness advocate's "Giant Forest" in the heart of Sequoia. "California," White reflected, "held forth two promises to adventurous men in the mid-nineteenth century: one was the sparkle of gold and man-made treasure; the other was beauty, wilderness beauty that had outlasted both gold and man in time."[7] John White's imperial roving led him to nature, as had Muir's wanderings before him. And the nature these men beheld concealed the violence of its construction, the colonial conquests that had remade nature into un-peopled spaces.

Why this vignette at the end? The drama of a whole life contained in White's letters suggests not abstraction, but the symbolic weight of real events. Foreign wars in Greece, the Philippines, and the skies over France, the cruel illusion of gold rushing, labor struggles, and wilderness administration—varieties of experience welded into one man's life. The idea of wilderness effused by John White towards the end of his life found root in his imperial jaunts. The experience of one prepared him for the experience of the other. Dominion over natives and nature—territorial gains—sprang from his own occupations as soldier, gold seeker, and ranger. The wilderness idea safely insulated his culture's nature myth from the political contexts of its creation. Stitching together his temporary world, White's life marked the disappearance of boundaries as his experiences connected the once disparate spaces of his colonial travels.

And what of the others? John Muir had stood on the promenade deck of the railroad magnate E. H. Harriman's steamer the *George W. Elder* in June 1899 gazing at the Klondike gold seekers crowding Skagway's shoreline. John White worked amongst that rabble. The Harriman expedition members like Muir had no need, nor interest, in seeking the soft yellow metal. Two years earlier surveying the same hurried scene, "Muir was vastly amused by the motley crowd of excited men, their various outfits, their queer equipment, their ridiculous notions of camping and life in the wilderness," his friend S. Hall Young had remembered. "A nest of ants," he called them, "taken to a strange country and stirred up with a stick."[8] Money had brought Muir closer to a particular idea about nature. His elite connections and his own personal wealth—he had married into a California agricultural fortune—allowed him to assume his own perspective as absolute, universalizing his own bourgeois values through the commercial experience of the tourist. Asked if he might join the gold rushers, Muir replied, "Do they think I'm daft . . . when I go into that wild it will not be in a crowd like this or on such a sordid mission. Ah! My old friend, they'll be spoiling our grand Alaska." Muir saw nature as a recreational wilderness. "The regular tourist, ever on the flow, is one of the most characteristic productions of the present century; and however frivolous and inappreciative the poorer specimens may appear, viewed comprehensively they are a most hopeful and significant sign of the times, indicating at least the beginning of our return to nature,—for going to the mountains is going home," he had once enthused.[9]

A decade later at the age of seventy-three Muir boarded a steamer for

South America and eventually Africa. On reaching the South African coast line, he noted that it was "charmingly sculptured like those of Alaska bays."[10] From the "shop-like windowed spaces" of his comfortable state room, Muir's view unified all space, capably bringing together qualities and categories that seem at odds with one another. Across southern Africa by rail and north to East Africa to Uganda and the coast at Zanzibar and Mombasa, Muir detailed his wandering across this "hot wild" continent. But Muir's writing betrayed an almost premeditated blindness. He obsessed on the landscape—its trees and rocks—and left hardly a mention of the Africans in his letters and journal notes. Tourists like Muir could escape their own social realities, ignoring the empire that made possible their travels. "This society," the critic Guy Debord writes, "eliminates geographical distance only to reap distance internally in the form of spectacular separation."[11] And, so stood Muir. Celebrating the commercial experiences of the tourist from the train window or aboard his comfortable steamer, he neatly separated out the baobob tree and the zebra from all that humanity. Nature and culture existed as separate realms for Muir, the latter always threatening to subsume the former. Muir returned home to California and fought in vain to keep a dam from stopping up the Hetch Hetchy River in his beloved Yosemite. He died on Christmas Eve 1914.

Travel writer Eliza Scidmore joined the National Geographic Society in 1890, just five years after the success of her first guide book on Alaska. For the next thirteen years she would serve as correspondence secretary, associate editor, foreign secretary, and finally, as the first female member of the society's board of managers. The society and its publications celebrated the distinctiveness of the globe's separate spaces, but also effected the opposite, advertising and assimilating the world into something at once understandable and connected in the imagination of Americans. Scidmore, who honed her writing skills in Alaska, enjoyed a prolific career and published books on Japan, China, Indonesia, and India. Alaska had served for Scidmore as a "draw-bridge to Asia," as Secretary of State William Seward who had arranged the Alaska purchase once predicted. Always narrated through the sightseeing eyes of the tourist, her books and articles helped to describe and define this Asian world for concerned Americans. More interested in Asian culture and politics than in its natural spaces, she nonetheless betrayed the imperial imagination's race logic, describing Asia's essential otherness: the Chinese—the "yellow people"—as "the most incomprehensible, unfathomable, inscrutable, contradictory, logical, and illogical people on earth," or the "marvel" of "British energy" in its colonizing work.[12] A long-time supporter of Japan, Scidmore died in 1928, and her ashes were interred in Yokohama at the request of the Japanese government, another empire.

The neurasthenic minister Stephen Merritt returned to his Manhattan home after his Alaska tour, apparently cured. For more than fifty years Rev. Merritt had occupied various Methodist-Episcopal pulpits, but he was best known as the undertaker of the rich and famous, having arranged General and President Ulysses S. Grant's funeral in particular. He died in 1917 at the age of eighty-three. The veteran undertaker's will divided less than ten thousand dollars between his widow and daughter.

In 1896 Phillip Van Buskirk returned from his Alaska trip without having found a wife. He returned to his Snohomish homestead that he had dubbed the Lone Hill Ranch. Discontent and admittedly lonely, he never really settled down there, drifting instead up and down the West Coast and Puget Sound. In June 1903 Van Buskirk visited an old friend in Bremerton, Washington. He had known Timothy Sheean for more than twenty-seven years. Sheean invited his old bachelor friend to move in with him. Van Buskirk eagerly accepted. He prepared to return to Snohomish, sell the Lone Hill Ranch, and join Sheean. On his way to the boat in June 1903 he died suddenly of a massive stroke. The old sailor was buried in the Bremerton Navy Yard cemetery with full naval honors.[13]

Jack Dalton, Edward Glave's Alaska exploring partner, stayed on in the north. The trail he and Glave had "pioneered" over the long-established aboriginal Chilkat Trail would become an important link to the interior gold fields with the start of the Klondike gold rush. For a brief moment, Dalton found pay dirt charging tolls for the stampeders who chose to follow the Dalton Trail to the Klondike interior. The imaginative Dalton eventually drove thousands of head of cattle and horses to supply the mining boomtown of Dawson, a city reputed in 1898 to be the largest city west of Chicago and north of San Francisco. His bonanza was short-lived, as the gold fields of the Klondike played out. Had he lived long enough, Edward Glave would have been gratified to know that his well-publicized attempt to open interior Alaska to commerce had succeeded.

Glave returned to Africa in 1893. For nearly two years he transited the continent from the Indian Ocean west to the Congo. Glave reported on the rapidly deteriorating conditions in the interior, on "rubber and murder, slavery in its worst form." He confronted the unfolding horrors of Belgian King Leopold's so-called Congo Free State. "War has been waged all through the district of Equator, and thousands of people have been killed and homes destroyed," he recorded in one of a series of dramatic articles published in *Century* magazine.[14] In fact, the scale of violence was almost unprecedented as millions of Congolese perished.

"This forced commerce is depopulating the country," Glave announced. His writing from the interior caught the world's attention and his words would help to spur calls for reform in the Belgian colony. "Twenty-one heads," Glave described ominously, "were brought to the falls, and have been used by Captain Rom as a decoration round a flower-bed in front of his house!" Joseph Conrad would draw on Glave's accounts as he fashioned his own narrative of the atrocities perpetrated by colonialism in *Heart of Darkness*, borrowing the brutal details of these heads staked on posts ornamenting the broken fence around Mistah Kurtz's Inner Station.

But Glave would not survive his final African venture. Succumbing to fever at Matadi on the lower Congo River in May 1895, he died at thirty-two. He believed that through the simple exercise of his will, he might conquer and subdue the human darkness—slavery and slaughter—plaguing central Africa. Glave's faith in the power of his own creative will was itself a fiction, grounded in his self-fashioning as an intrepid explorer, a soldier of civilization fighting against the supposed darkness. Glave had zigzagged between the antipodes of his imperial world from wilderness Alaska to Africa, from the Inside Passage to Kurtz's Inner Station. He never imagined the irrational and relativistic world that his contemporary Joseph Conrad understood. He did not succumb to his pessimism, his sense of the futility of action, a world seemingly doomed to repeat itself forever. But while Glave did not adopt Conrad's self-conscious critique of the modern world that the Europeans and their settler societies had wrought, he was caught unconsciously in a paradox as both antagonist and advocate for the imperial world he helped to create. "We must not condemn the young Congo Free State too hastily or too harshly," he wrote, qualifying his critique. "They have opened up the country, established a certain administration. . . . Their commercial transactions need remedying, it is true," he had concluded. While the methods of empire may have proved at times unsound, the imperial project remained intact. And so, Darkest Alaska joined its tropical counterpart Darkest Africa.[15] If not quite a colder Congo, Alaska, nevertheless, served the American imperium—first as a territorial claim, then as anchor to one of America's most pervasive myths, its national origin story cast in the theatre of a supposedly vacant wilderness frontier. The latter would mask the explicitness of the former.

What then should we make of this strange epic of conquest peopled by Gilded Age misfits, wilderness visionaries, Park Avenue scions, soldiers of fortune, and muckraking internationalists? Blurring boundaries with their travels, diverse historical actors linked their world, connecting Alaska—America's first overseas colony—with other imperial spaces. The ex-sailor returned wifeless to his homestead. The society reporter turned travel writer served as the National Geographic Society's first executive secretary and went on to write a series of books covering Asia. The wilderness visionary wandered abroad to Africa comparing his notions of wilderness Alaska to Africa, omitting the people all the while. And the tourists came and went with an indelible routine. They still do.

Notes

Prologue

Note to epigraph: Octavio Paz, "Envoi," quoted in Henri Lefebvre, *The Production of Space,* trans. Donald Nicholson-Smith (Cambridge: Blackwell, 1991), n.p.

1. Johann Baptist Homann, *Generalis Totius Imperii Russorum,* 1723.

2. Carey McWilliams, *California: The Great Exception* (New York: Current Books, 1949).

3. Jonathan Swift, *Gulliver's Travels,* (reprint, 1726; New York: Penguin Books, 1985), 150.

4. Jonathan Swift, *"Poetry a Rhapsody",* (1733). *The Selected Poems, Jonathan Swift,* ed. A. Norman Jeffares, (London-K. Cathie, 1992).

5. Susan Stewart, *On Longing: Narratives of the Miniature, the Gigantic, the Souvenir, the Collection* (Durham: Duke University Press, 1993).

6. Swift, *Gulliver's Travels,* 343–44.

7. Stewart, *On Longing,* 80.

8. McWilliams, *California: The Great Exception,* 4.

9. Septima Collis, *A Woman's Trip to Alaska* (New York: Cassell, 1890), 72.

10. Bernard Bendel, "The Alexander Archipelago," *Proceedings of the Agassiz Institute* (Sacramento, 1873), 26.

11. Charles Hallock, *Our New Alaska* (New York: Forest and Stream Publishing Co., 1886), 36.

12. The 1890 United States Census announced the formal closure of what it called "the frontier," defined by population per square mile.

13. 11th United States Census, Alaska, 250.

14. For the term "bourgeois," as used here and throughout this study, I accept Karl Marx's definition: "By bourgeoisie is meant the class of modern capitalists, owners of the means of social production and employers of wage labor." See Karl Marx and Frederick Engels, *Manifesto of the Communist Party,* ed. Eric Hobsbawm (1848; New York: Verso, 1998), 34. Some readers will no doubt be troubled by the term. However, the most typical American term for such a class—that is, *middle class*—does not convey the same meanings as *bourgeoisie.* Raymond Williams noted, "A *ruling* class, which is the socialist sense of bourgeois in the context of historical description of a developed capitalist society, is not easily or clearly represented by the essentially different *middle* class. For this

reason, especially in this context and in spite of the difficulties, bourgeois will continue to have to be used." Williams, *Keywords: A Vocabulary of Culture and Society* (New York: Oxford University Press, 1983), 48.

15. Robert Service, "The Law of the Yukon," *Collected Poems of Robert Service* (New York: Dodd, Mead and Co., 1940), 10–12.

16. Theodore Roosevelt, *The Winning of the West*, vol. 1 (New York: G. P. Putnam's Sons, 1906), 17.

Introduction

1. Elaine Scarry, *Resisting Representation* (New York: Oxford University Press, 1994), 53.

2. William Christie Macleod, *The American Indian Frontier* (New York: Alfred A. Knopf, 1928), vii–viii.

3. *The Soul of Alaska: A Comment and a Description* (New York: Gorham, 1905), 7.

4. Mary Hallock Foote, *A Victorian Gentlewoman in the Far West* (San Marino, Calif.: Huntington Library Press, 1972), 265.

5. Associated Press, "In Darkest Alaska," *Daily Northwestern*, Oshkosh, Wis., October 18, 1901, 1.

6. William Appleman Williams, *The Tragedy of American Diplomacy* (New York: Dell, 1962), 18.

7. Amy Kaplan, "Left Alone with America," in *Cultures of United States Imperialism*, ed. Amy Kaplan and Donald E. Pease (Durham: Duke University Press, 1993), 13.

8. W. A. Williams, quoted in Kaplan and Pease, *Culture of United States Imperialism*, 11.

9. William Robbins, *Colony and Empire: The Capitalist Transformation of the American West* (Lawrence: University Press of Kansas, 1994).

10. Karl Marx and Frederick Engels, *Manifesto of the Communist Party* (1848; reprint, New York: Verso, 1998), 39.

11. James Ferguson, *The Anti-politics Machine: "Development," Depoliticization, and Bureaucratic Power in Lesotho* (Minneapolis: University of Minnesota Press, 1994), 21.

12. *Alaska and the Yukon Valley: How to Get There* (Nashville: Brandon Printing Company, 1897), 6.

13. My intention here is neither to duplicate these travelers' fictive distortions, nor to ignore material conditions along the passage itself and beyond in the wider metropolitan world, fueling the dramatic changes in the north.

14. John Sears, *Sacred Places: American Tourist Attractions in the Nineteenth Century* (Amherst: University of Massachusetts Press, 1989), 4.

15. Ibid., 52.

16. Daniel Defert, "The Collection of the World: Accounts of Voyages from the Sixteenth to the Eighteenth Centuries," *Dialectical Anthropology*, 7 (1982): 11–20.

17. Raymond Williams, *Marxism and Literature* (New York: Oxford University Press, 1977), 132.

18. Ibid., 132–33.

19. Ibid.

20. Don Mitchell, *The Lie of the Land: Migrant Workers and the California Land-*

scape (Minneapolis: University of Minnesota Press, 1996) 2. See also W.J.T. Mitchell, ed., *Landscape and Power* (Chicago: University of Chicago Press), 1–34.

21. "Alaska" (Raymond and Whitcomb Tours, promotional brochure, 1898), Yukon Archives, Whitehorse, Yukon Territory.

22. Lefebvre, The *Production of Space*, 329.

23. Walter Benjamin, *The Arcades Project,* trans. Howard Eiland and Kevin McLaughlin (Cambridge: Harvard University Press, 1999), 19.

24. The chapter title plays on the geological term *orogeny,* or mountain-building processes.

25. Neil Smith, *Uneven Development: Nature, Capital, and the Production of Space* (New York: Basil Blackwell, 1984), 20.

26. McWilliams, *California, The Great Exception.*

Chapter 1. Continental Drift

1. C. E. S. Wood, "Among the Thlinkits in Alaska," *Century Magazine* 24, no. 3 (July 1882), 323.

2. James Alton James, *The First Scientific Exploration of Russian America and the Purchase of Alaska* (Evanston, Ill.: Northwestern University Press, 1942), 45.

3. Paul Carter, *The Road to Botany Bay* (New York: Knopf, 1988), 81.

4. William Henry Dall, *Alaska and Its Resources* (Boston: Lee and Shepard, 1870); Frederick Whymper, *Travel and Adventure in the Territory of Alaska* (London: John Murray, 1868).

5. Debra Lindsay, *Science in the Subarctic: Trappers, Traders, and the Smithsonian Institution* (Washington, D.C.: Smithsonian Institution Press, 1993), 110.

6. Martin Green, *The Great American Adventure* (Boston: Beacon Press, 1984), 4.

7. Whymper, *Travel and Adventure,* 87.

8. Ibid., viii.

9. Ibid., viii; 87–88.

10. Walter Lafeber, *The New Empire: An Interpretation of American Expansion, 1860–1898* (1963; reprint, Ithaca: Cornell University Press, 1998), 33.

11. Some Canadian Liberal Party supporters encouraged U.S. annexation in the Canadian West. See David Wroebel, *The End of American Exceptionalism* (Lawrence: University Press of Kansas, 1993); Jean Barman, *The West Beyond the West: A History of British Columbia* (Toronto: University of Toronto Press, 1991).

12. Abby Woodman Johnson, *Picturesque Alaska: A Journal of a Tour Among the Mountains, Seas, and Islands of the Northwest, from San Francisco to Sitka* (Boston: Houghton, Mifflin, 1889), 69.

13. The supposed "blood-tie" of Anglo-Saxonism was not without substantial tension, as evidenced in the Venezuela dispute of 1895 and ongoing disputes over sealing rights in the Arctic and boundary lines between Alaska and British North America.

14. Charles Darwin, *The Descent of Man* (London: John Murray, 1888), 142.

15. Josiah Strong, *Our Country: Its Possible Future and Its Present Crisis* (New York: American Home Missionary Society, 1885), 218.

16. Norris, quoted in Larzer Ziff, *The American 1890s: Life and Times of a Lost Generation* (New York: Viking Press, 1966), 265.

17. Strong, *Our Country,* 29; quoted in Lafeber, *The New Empire,* 74.

18. In 1879 nearly a million tourists visited Switzerland; more than 200,000

were Americans. See Eric Hobsbawm, *The Age of Empire* (London: Abacus, 1987), 14.

19. Edward Whymper, *Scrambles Amongst the Alps* (1871; reprint, London: John Murray, 1936), 332.

20. Fergus Fleming, *Killing the Dragon: The Conquest of the Alps* (New York: Atlantic Monthly Press, 2002).

21. Oliver Wendell Holmes, Jr., "The Soldier's Faith," 1895; Theodore Roosevelt, *The Strenuous Life: Essays and Addresses* (New York: Century Company, 1900), 8.

22. Dall, *Alaska and Its Resources,* 293.

23. Ralph Waldo Emerson, *Journal,* quoted in Stephen Fender, *Plotting the Golden West: American Literature and the Rhetoric of the California Trail* (New York: Cambridge University Press, 1981), 11. Travel writing as a popular genre was by no means new, though the genre did enjoy a wider appeal as print capitalism made these works more available. See Patrick Brydone, "The Eighteenth Century Traveller as Representative Man," in Warner G. Rice, ed., *Literature as a Mode of Travel: Five Essays and a Postscript* (New York: New York Public Library, 1963), 53–67.

24. William Francis Butler, *The Great Lone Land: A Narrative of Travel and Adventure in the North-west of America* (London: S. Low, Marston, Low and Searle, 1872); Butler, *The Wild North Land: Being a Story of a Winter Journey, with Dogs, across Northern North America* (London: S. Low, Marston, Low and Searle, 1873).

25. William Francis Butler, *The Campaign of the Cataracts; Being a Narrative of the Great Nile Expedition of 1884–5* (London: Sampson, Low, Marston, Searle and Rivington, 1887).

26. Frederick Schwatka, *Along Alaska's Great River: A Popular Account of the Travels of the Alaska Exploring Expedition of 1883, Along the Great Yukon River* (New York: Cassell, 1885).

27. *New York Times,* September 21, 1886, quoted in Beau Riffenburgh, *The Myth of the Explorer: The Press, Sensationalism, and Geographical Discovery* (New York: Oxford University Press, 1994), 110.

28. Schwatka, *Along Alaska's Great River,* 179.

29. Details of E. J. Glave's biography drawn from *Biographie Coloniale Belge,* vol. II (Brussels: Institut Royal Colonial Belge, 1951), 415–17; *A nos Héros Coloniaux morts pour la Civilisation (1876–1908)* (Brussels: Ligue du Souvenir congolais, c. 1931), 84, 88, 91.

30. E. J. Glave, *Six Years of Adventure in Congo-Land* (London: Sampson, Low, Marston, 1893), 16.

31. Rudyard Kipling, "The Song of the English," *The Seven Seas* (London: Methuen, 1896).

32. Joseph Conrad, *Heart of Darkness* (1899; reprint, New York: Norton, 1988), 7.

33. See Paul Zweig, *The Adventurer: The Fate of Adventure in the Western World* (Princeton: Princeton University Press, 1974), 6–7.

34. Glave, *Six Years of Adventure in Congo-Land,* 15.

35. Ibid.

36. Ibid. Conrad would later write of his own hankerings for distant travel inspired by "map-gazing." Pointing as a youth to the map of Africa, Conrad recollected that he announced, "When I grow up I shall *go there*" (13). See Conrad, *A Personal Record* (London: J. M. Dent & Sons, 1912).

37. Robert Louis Stevenson, *Memoirs and Portraits* (New York: C. Scribner's Sons, 1887), 159.

38. George R. Sims, *How the Poor Live* (London: Chatto & Windus, 1883), 5.

39. David Reed, *The Popular Magazine in Britain and the United States, 1880–1960* (London: British Library, 1997), 85.

40. This understanding of what Benedict Anderson calls "print-capitalism" has become a commonplace in historical studies. Anderson treats this print culture in his *Imagined Communities: Reflections on the Origins and Spread of Nationalism* (New York: Verso, 1983), especially chapter 2.

41. Frederic Jameson, *Postmodernism, Or the Cultural Logic of Late Capitalism* (Durham: Duke University Press, 1992), 286.

42. Roger Pocock, *The Frontiersman*, 185. See discussion in Robert H. MacDonald, *The Language of Empire: Myths and Metaphors of Popular Imperialism, 1880–1918* (New York: Manchester University Press, 1994).

43. Margaret Atwood, "In Search of Alias Grace: On Writing Canadian Historical Fiction," *American Historical Review*, 103 (December 1998), 1504.

44. With Glave my story begins arbitrarily. I could have begun anywhere. Why here? Why not? By entering the narrative here, we upend the expected, casting the reader into the midst of a life. Our historical narratives are always formed in retrospect, even this one. But by casting a random beginning, I hope to, at least in part, reclaim some sense of contingency.

45. Charles Booth, *Life and Labour of the People of London*, rpt., 3rd edition (New York: Macmillan, 1902–3), 1:66–68; quoted in Judith Walkowitz, *City of Dreadful Delight* (Chicago: University of Chicago Press, 1992), 34.

46. The similarities here are unmistakable. Conrad's Marlow narrated: "'Now when I was a little chap I had a passion for maps. I would look for hours . . . and lose myself in the glories of exploration. At that time there were many blank spaces on the earth and when I saw one that looked particularly inviting on a map, (but they all look that) I would put my finger on it and say: When I grow up I will go there.'" See Conrad, *Heart of Darkness*, 11.

47. Glave, *Six Years of Adventure in Congo-Land*, 16.

48. Ibid., 11.

49. Conrad, *Heart of Darkness*, 10.

50. Conrad, *Heart of Darkness*, 35.

51. Glave, *Six Years of Adventure in Congo-Land*, 27.

52. See Frantz Fanon, *Wretched of the Earth* (New York: Grove Press, 1963), for the clearest evocation of the oppositional perspectives of the colonized and colonizer, especially his description of the "settler's town" and the "native town" on pages 38–40.

53. Conrad in *Heart of Darkness* never identifies the river that Marlow journeys up. The point is that the river could be *any* river—imperial ubiquity, if that isn't redundant. But the reader becomes quite uncomfortable with not knowing exactly where he or she is. Readers feel betrayed. Are these things a writer must tell? Did I forget to add the detail? Why does it matter? In effect the whole apparatus of knowing where precisely one is at any one time within a global imaginative reach—the reader's present—is not separable from the origins of this imaginative field in these late nineteenth-century explorations that set out to fill in the blank spaces on the map, "geography militant," as Conrad described it. The reader's distress confirms just how intricately we are tied to the very activity that the history is narrating. The power to narrate and to know precisely where on the globe we are, these are the inheritances of past imperialisms. We are those militancies' inheritance, and our desires, indeed the expectation to know precisely where the action is, comes from this past. In this way this chapter seeks

to extort interpretative significance from the reader's experience of reading. The reader enacts the expectation that Alaska is in play while in fact they are reading about Africa. The reader transposes Alaska with Africa, the experience of global reach is accomplished, and the reader has already compared Africa and Alaska unwittingly.

54. J. Conrad, "Geography and Some Explorers," quoted in Ian Watt, *Conrad in the Nineteenth Century* (Berkeley: University of California Press, 1979), 146.

55. Henry Morton Stanley, *The Congo and the Founding of the Free State* (London: Sampson, Marston, Searle, Rivington, 1885), 237.

56. George Grenfell, *George Grenfell and the Congo*, 2 vols., (New York: D. Appleton, 1910), 1:445. Grenfell had established a mission at Bolobo in 1886, downstream of Glave's trading station.

57. Adam Hochschild, *King Leopold's Ghost* (New York: Houghton Mifflin, 1998), 50.

58. Glave, *Six Years of Adventure in Congo-Land*, 44.

59. Eric R. Wolf, *Europe and the People Without History* (Berkeley: University of California Press, 1982). Wolf delves into this theme of European expansion whereby non-Europeans were denied history. All history began with the arrival of the European, at least according to the colonizers.

60. Hugh Trevor-Roper, *The Rise of Christian Europe,* (New York: Harcourt, Brace & World, 1905), 9.

61. Herman Melville, *Moby Dick; or, The Whale* (1851; reprint, New York: Penguin Books, 1972), 261.

62. Claude Lévi-Strauss, *Tristes Tropiques* (1955; reprint, New York: Penguin Books, 1973), 48.

63. Not all those who fled the civilized confines returned; some slipped out beyond the pale. The French poet Arthur Rimbaud sought refuge in Africa as well, escaping into the anonymity of the desert wilderness of North Africa in order to flee the sexualized lines of force in Europe. Rimbaud quit writing at nineteen and found some solace as a trader and gun-runner.

64. Conrad, *Heart of Darkness.* Conrad wrote in his author's note that "'*Heart of Darkness,*' is experience, too; but it is experience pushed a little (and only very little) beyond the actual facts of the case for the perfectly legitimate, I believe, purpose of bringing it home to the minds and bosoms of the readers" (5).

65. Kurtz was a composite of probably several historical and imagined figures. But Ian Watt highlights Stanley's importance. Watt wrote, "Stanley is probably of central importance, though not so much as a basis for the character of Kurtz as for the moral atmosphere in which he was created." See Watt, *Conrad and the Nineteenth Century*, 145.

66. Engels, quoted in Raymond Williams, *The Country and the City* (New York: Oxford University Press, 1973), 231.

67. William Booth, *In Darkest England and the Way Out* (London: International Headquarters of the Salvation Army, 1890).

68. *Frank Leslie's Illustrated Newspaper,* vol. 70, April 5, 1890, 190.

69. Ibid.

70. I have inverted David Spurr's formulation: "global systems of representation." To be sure, the intent of these discursive strategies was to effect "global systems." However, these systems did not achieve their goal of true global embrace. Instead, the representations extended the appearance of globalism, even as the colonized resisted the supposed "global systems." Colonial discourse was never complete in its dispossessions. See David Spurr, *Rhetoric of Empire* (Dur-

ham: Duke University Press, 1993), 10. The critical analysis of colonialism should not recapitulate the totalizing vision and discourse of colonialism itself.

71. *Frank Leslie's Illustrated Newspaper,* June 20, 1891.

72. Frank Luther Mott, *A History of American Magazines, 1885–1905,* vol. 4 (Cambridge: Harvard University Press, 1957), 96.

73. J. K. Noyes, *Colonial Space: Spatiality in the Discourse of German South West Africa, 1884–1915* (Philadelphia: Harwood Academic Publishers, 1992), 17.

74. *Frank Leslie's Illustrated Newspaper,* November 15, 22, 29, 1890; December 6, 13, 20, 27, 1890; and January 3, 10, 1891.

75. It was no accident that in Joseph Conrad's short story, "The Secret Agent," the narrative circled around a plot to blow up the observatory at Greenwich.

76. *Frank Leslie's Illustrated Newspaper,* vol. 70, April 5, 1890, 190.

77. E. J. Glave, "Pioneer Packhorses in Alaska," *Century Magazine,* vol. 44 (September 1892), 671.

78. Glave, "Pioneer Packhorses in Alaska," *Century Magazine,* vol. 44 (October 1892), 869.

79. Ibid., 870.

80. E. J. Glave collection, folder 1, journal entry, August 9, 1890, Special Collections, University of Alaska at Fairbanks.

81. E. J. Glave collection, folder 1, journal entry, May 18, 1891, Special Collections, University of Alaska at Fairbanks.

82. E. H. Wells, *Frank Leslie's Illustrated Newspaper,* June 21, 1890, 419.

83. E. J. Glave, *Frank Leslie's Illustrated Newspaper,* 70, no. 1815, (June 28, 1890), 419.

84. Glave, "Pioneer Packhorses in Alaska," 671.

85. Glave canoed down the Tatshenshini River, though he thought he was navigating the Alsek River. A trip down the Alsek would likely have proved fatal to Glave and his cottonwood dugout companions, Dalton, Shank, and a "shaman." Turnback canyon on the Alsek has Class V and VI rapids.

86. Carter, *The Road to Botany Bay,* 340.

87. George Davidson, "Explanation of an Indian Map of the Rivers, Lakes, Trails, and Mountains from the Chilkaht to the Yukon, Drawn by the Chilkaht Chief Kohklux in 1869," *Mazama,* 2, no. 2(1901), 75–82.

88. Eliza R. Scidmore, "The Northwest Passes to the Yukon," *National Geographic,* 9, no. 4 (April 1898).

89. George Davidson, U.S. Coast Survey, Pacific Coast, Coast Pilot of Alaska, from southern boundary to Cook's Inlet, (Washington, D.C.: (U.S. Government Printing Office, 1869), 113–14.

90. Carter, *The Road to Botany Bay,* 337.

91. Julie Cruikshank, *Reading Voices, Dan Dha Ts'Edenintth'E: Oral and Written Interpretations of the Yukon's Past* (Seattle: University of Washington Press, 1997).

92. *Frank Leslie's Illustrated Newspaper,* "Our Alaska Expediton," vol. 70, April 12, 1890, 222.

93. Glave, "Pioneer Packhorses," 671.

94. Mary Louise Pratt, *Imperial Eyes: Travel Writing and Transculturation* (New York: Routledge, 1992), 153.

95. E. J. Glave collection, folder 1, journal entry, March 22, 1891, Special Collections, University of Alaska at Fairbanks.

96. Glave, "Pioneer Packhorses in Alaska," 679.

97. Ibid., 672.

98. Ibid., 682.

99. *New York Times*, September 21, 1886, quoted in Riffenbaugh, *Myth of the Explorer*, 110.

100. Matthew F. Jacobson, *Barbarian Virtues: The United States Encounters Foreign Peoples at Home and Abroad, 1876–1917* (New York: Hill and Wang, 2000), 21.

101. E. J. Glave collection, folder 1, journal entry, March 22, 1891, Special Collections, University of Alaska at Fairbanks.

102. Ibid.

103. E. J. Glave collection, folder 1, journal entry, August 15, 1891, Special Collections, University of Alaska at Fairbanks.

104. E. J. Glave collection, folder 1, journal entry, September 20, 1891, Special Collections, University of Alaska at Fairbanks.

105. Williams, *The Country and the City*, 302.

106. Glave, *Six Years of Adventure in Congo-Land*, 12–13.

107. Anthropologist Nicholas Thomas writes, "An understanding of a pluralized field of colonial narratives, which are seen less as signs than as practices, or as signifying practices rather than elements of a code. In this emphasis I am inspired by, if not rigorously following, the work of Pierre Bourdieu; his interest in located subjectivities informs an analytic strategy which situates colonial representations and narratives in terms of agents, locations and periods; these terms are conducive to a far more differentiated vision—of colonialisms rather than colonialism." *Colonialism's Culture: Anthropology, Travel, and Government* (Princeton: Princeton University Press, 1994), 8.

108. Conrad, *Heart of Darkness*, 31.

Chapter 2. Alaska with Appleton's, *Canada by* Baedeker's

1. Harry Ricketts, *The Unforgiving Minute: A Life of Rudyard Kipling* (London: Chatto and Windus, 1999), 158. Andrew Lycett, *Rudyard Kipling* (London: Weidenfeld and Nicolson, 1999).

2. Rudyard Kipling, *American Notes, Rudyard Kipling's West* (1891; reprint, Norman: University of Oklahoma Press, 1981), xv.

3. Rudyard Kipling, *From Sea to Sea, Letters of Travel, Vol. 2* (New York: Doubleday and McClure, 1899), 53.

4. Kipling, *American Notes*, 84.

5. Ibid., 85.

6. J. Valerie Fifer, *American Progress: The Growth of the Transport, Tourist, and Information Industries in the Nineteenth-Century West* (Chester, Conn.: Globe Pequot Press, 1988), 311.

7. Timothy Mitchell, *Colonising Egypt* (Cambridge: Cambridge University Press, 1988). Edmund Swinglehurst, *The Romantic Journey: The Story of Thomas Cook and Victorian Travel* (London: Pica Editions, 1974).

8. Kipling, *American Notes*, 87.

9. Henry Morton Stanley, *My Early Travels, Vol. 1* (New York: Charles Scribner's Sons, 1895), 146.

10. Kipling, *American Notes*, 85.

11. Ibid., 90.

12. Henry James, *Italian Hours*, ed. John Auchard (University Park: Pennsylvania State University Press, 1992), 89.

13. Edward Hungerford, "Our Summer Migration: A Social Study," *Century Magazine*, 42 (August 1891), 569.

14. Anne F. Hyde, *An American Vision: Far Western Landscape and National Culture, 1880–1920* (New York: New York University Press, 1990), 109.

15. Henry Finck, *The Pacific Coast Scenic Tour* (New York: Charles Scribner's Sons, 1890), 235.

16. 11th United States Census, Alaska, 1890, 250.

17. Stephen Merritt, "From Ocean to Ocean," 1892, 40, Huntington Library, Pasadena, Calif.

18. See Edward Wakefield, "Nervousness, The National Disease of America," *McClure's* 2 (February 1894), and S. Weir Mitchell, *Wear and Tear: Hints for the Overworked* (Philadelphia: Lippincott, 1891).

19. George Beard, *American Nervousness: Its Philosophy and Treatment* (Richmond: J. W. Fergusson and Sons, 1879), 1.

20. Ibid.

21. George Beard, *American Nervousness: Its Causes and Consequences* (New York: G. P. Putnam's Sons, 1881), vi.

22. Ralph Waldo Emerson, quoted in Leo Marx, *The Machine in the Garden: Technology and the Pastoral Ideal in America* (New York: Oxford University Press, 1964), 17.

23. George Beard, *American Nervousness: Its Causes and Consequences,* quoted in F. G. Gosling, *Before Freud: Neuresthenia and the American Medical Community, 1870–1910* (Urbana: University of Illinois Press, 1987), 11.

24. Mitchell, *Wear and Tear,* 7–8.

25. Beard, *American Nervousness: Its Causes and Consequences,* 133.

26. Mitchell, *Wear and Tear,* 74.

27. Beard, *American Nervousness: Its Causes and Consequences,* 133.

28. Marc Cook, *The Wilderness Cure* (New York: William Wood, 1881), 13.

29. Ibid.

30. Ibid., 20.

31. Ibid., 31.

32. Ibid., 49.

33. Ibid., 105.

34. Charles Loring Brace, *The Dangerous Classes of New York* (New York: Wynkoop and Hallenbeck, 1872), 29.

35. Cook, *The Wilderness Cure,* 108.

36. Merritt, "From Ocean to Ocean," 40.

37. Finck, *The Pacific Coast Scenic Tour,* 234.

38. Merritt, "From Ocean to Ocean."

39. William Seward Webb, *California and Alaska over the Canadian Pacific Railway* (New York: G. P. Putnam's Sons, 1890), vi.

40. I. Winslow Ayer, *Life in the Wilds of America* (Grand Rapids: Central Publishing Company, 1880), 15, 527; quoted in Earl Pomeroy, *In Search of the Golden West: The Tourist in Western America* (New York: Knopf, 1957), 93.

41. Dona Brown, *Inventing New England: Regional Tourism in the Nineteenth Century* (Washington, D.C.: Smithsonian Institution Press, 1995), 5.

42. Beard, *American Nervousness: Its Causes and Consequences,* 103.

43. Ibid., 112.

44. Webb, *California and Alaska and Over the Canadian Pacific Railway,* v–vi.

45. Carter H. Harrison, *A Summer's Outing and the Old Man's Story* (Chicago: Dibble Publishing, 1891), 9–10.

46. Frederick Schwatka, *Wonderland; or, Alaska and the Inland Passage, With a Description of the Country Traversed by the Northern Pacific Railroad,* with John Hyde (St. Paul, Minn.: Northern Pacific Railroad, c. 1886), 84.

47. Beard, *American Nervousness: Its Causes and Consequences*, 298.

48. Webb, *California and Alaska and Over the Canadian Pacific Railway*, v.

49. Kipling, *American Notes*, 104.

50. Harrison, *A Summer's Outing*, 12.

51. R. W. Meade, "Alaska," *Appleton's Journal*, 6 (1871), 126.

52. Kipling, *From Sea to Sea*, 55–56.

53. John Muir, *Picturesque California and the Region West of the Rocky Mountains from Alaska to Mexico* (San Francisco: J. Dening, 1888), 193.

54. John Muir, "Notes of a Naturalist," "John Muir in Alaska—Wrangel Island and its Picturesque Attractions," *Daily Evening Bulletin*, September 6, 1879, p. 1, col. 1, reprinted in Robert Engberg and Bruce Merrell, eds., *John Muir: Letters from Alaska* (Madison: University of Wisconsin Press, 1993), 11.

55. Linnie Marsh Wolfe, ed., *John of the Mountains: The Unpublished Journals of John Muir* (Boston: Houghton Mifflin, 1938), 246, 248–49.

56. Ibid., 261.

57. E. L. Doctorow, *Ragtime* (New York: Random House, 1975), 182.

58. Marsh Wolfe, ed., *John of the Mountains*, 204–5.

59. Ibid., 206.

60. Steven J. Holmes, *The Young John Muir: An Environmental Biography* (Madison: University of Wisconsin Press, 1999).

61. William James, *Varieties of Religious Experience*, quoted in Kim Townsend, *Manhood at Harvard: William James and Others* (New York: W. W. Norton, 1996), 170.

62. William W. Stowe, *Going Abroad: European Travel in Nineteenth-Century American Culture* (Princeton: Princeton University Press, 1994), xii.

63. Thorstein Veblen, *The Theory of the Leisure Class* (1899; reprint, New York: Signet, 1953), 30.

64. John F. Sears, *Sacred Places: American Tourist Attractions in the Nineteenth Century* (Amherst: University of Massachusetts Press, 1989), 52.

65. Marsh Wolfe, ed., *John of the Mountains*, 302.

66. Stowe, *European Travel*, 19.

67. John Muir, "Alaska's Glaciers," *San Francisco Daily Evening Bulletin*, 1879, reprinted in Engberg and Merrell, eds., *Letters from Alaska*, 32.

68. S. Hall Young, *Alaska Days with John Muir* (New York: Fleming H. Revell, 1915).

69. Thomas Richards, *The Imperial Archive: Knowledge and the Fantasy of Empire* (New York: Verso, 1993), 1.

70. Alan Trachtenberg, *The Incorporation of America: Culture and Society in the Gilded Age* (New York: Hill and Wang, 1982), 59.

71. Karl Baedeker, *The Dominion of Canada, with Newfoundland and an Excursion to Alaska, Handbook for Travellers* (Leipzig: Karl Baedeker Publisher, 1894), 228.

72. Septima Collis, *A Woman's Trip to Alaska*, preface, n.p.

73. M. Wood, travel diary August 6, 1887, entry, Beinecke Rare Book and Manuscript Library, Yale University.

74. Eliza Clendenin, travel diary, July 1894, Yale Collection of Western Americana, Beinecke Rare Book and Manuscript Library.

75. *Appleton's Hand-Book of American Travel* (New York: D. Appleton, 1872), 309.

76. Brown, *Inventing New England*, 28.

77. Lester A. Beardslee, "Chilcat and Chilcoot," To the "Sportsman Tourist," *Forest and Stream*, 15 (November 25, 1880), 325.

78. George H. Hotchkiss, "The Midnight Sun," September 19, 1889, Beinecke Rare Book and Manuscript Library, Yale University.

79. Cook, *The Wilderness Cure,* 60.

80. L. Marsh Wolfe, ed., *John of the Mountains,* 261.

81. Eric J. Leed, *The Mind of the Traveler: From Gilgamesh to Global Tourism* (New York: Basic Books, 1991), 189.

82. Charles H. Gates, *Yellowstone National Park and Alaska* (Toledo, Ohio, 1900), 2.

83. Finck, *The Pacific Coast Scenic Tour,* 231.

84. E. Ruhamah Scidmore, *Alaska: Its Southern Coast and the Sitkan Archipelago* (Boston: D. Lothrop, 1885), 289.

85. Marsh Wolfe, ed., *John of the Mountains,* 261.

86. *Appleton's Hand-Book of American Travel,* 308.

87. Scidmore, *Alaska,* 289.

88. See Paul Carter, *The Road to Botany Bay* (New York: Knopf, 1988).

89. Quoted in Walter Benjamin, *The Arcades Project,* trans. Howard Eiland and Kenin McLaughlin (Cambridge: Harvard University Press, 1999), 77.

90. Quoted in Susan G. Davis, *Spectacular Nature: Corporate Culture and the Sea World Experience* (Berkeley: University of California Press, 1997), 31–32.

91. Finck, *The Pacific Coast Scenic Tour,* 231.

92. "Alaska, Land of Gold and Glacier" (Chicago: Poole Brothers, 1896), 4, promotional pamphlet, Great Northern Railway, Beinecke Rare Book and Manuscript Library, Yale University.

93. Conevery Bolton Valencius, *The Health of the Country: How American Settlers Understood Themselves and Their Land* (New York: Basic Books, 2002).

94. Marsh Wolfe, ed., *John of the Mountains,* 317.

95. Ella Higginson, "The Voyage of All Voyages," *Washington Magazine* 1, no. 4 (June 1906), 339.

96. "To Alaska by Canadian Pacific Route," Canadian Pacific Railway Company, advertising pamphlet, 1892, British Columbia Archives, Victoria, B.C.

Chapter 3. Scenic Bonanza

1. Stephen Merritt, "From Ocean to Ocean," July 8, 1892, entry, Huntington Library, Pasadena, Calif.

2. John Muir, *Picturesque California and the Region West of the Rocky Mountains from Alaska to Mexico* (San Francisco: J. Dening, 1888), 194.

3. Henry Finck, *The Pacific Coast Scenic Tour* (New York: Charles Scribner's Sons, 1890), 237.

4. Edward Pierrepont, *Fifth Avenue to Alaska* (New York: G. P. Putnam's Sons, 1885), 154.

5. Karl Marx, *The Grundrisse,* trans. Martin Nicholaus (New York: Vintage, 1973), 524.

6. Wolfgang Schivelbusch, *The Railway Journey: Trains and Travel in the 19th Century* (New York: Urizen Books, 1979), 43.

7. Jean Baudrillard, *America* (New York: Verso, 1988), 6.

8. Eliza R. Scidmore, *Alaska, Its Southern Coast and the Sitkan Archipelago* (Boston: D. Lothrop, 1885), 3.

9. W. H. Pierce, *Thirteen Years of Travel and Exploration in Alaska, 1877–1889* (1890; reprint, Anchorage: Alaska Northwest Publishing, 1977), 43.

10. George A. Ogrissek, Alaskan Gold Rush diary and sketchbook, folder 1,

Memoranda of the Second Trip To Alaska, from Feb'y 24 1899 to Sep. 6, 1899; July 17, 1899, entry, Beinecke Rare Book and Manuscript Library, Yale University.

11. John Muir, *Alaska via Northern Pacific* (Northern Pacific Promotional Pamphlet, 1891), 7, Beinecke Rare Book and Manuscript Library, Yale University.

12. Paul Carter, *The Road to Botany Bay* (New York: Knopf, 1988), 240.

13. Linnie Marsh Wolfe, ed., *John of the Mountains: The Unpublished Journals of John Muir* (Boston: Houghton Mifflin, 1938), 261.

14. Ibid., *John of the Mountains*, 261–62.

15. George Monro Grant, *Picturesque Canada; The Country As It Was and Is. with Over Five Hundred Engravings on Wood* (Toronto: Belden Bros., 1882), 867.

16. Percy Bysshe Shelley, *History of a Six Week's Tour through Part of France, Switzerland, Germany, and Holland, with letters descriptive of a sail round the Lake Geneva, and of the Glaciers of Chamouni* (London: T. Hookham, 1817), vi.

17. John Ruskin, *Modern Painters, Vol. IV, Of Mountain Beauty* (1856; reprint, London: George Allen, 1906), esp. chapters 1–4.

18. Scidmore, *Alaska*, 16.

19. Finck, *Pacific Coast Scenic Tour*, 237.

20. John Ruskin, *Modern Painting*, vol. 4 (New York: Wiley & Halsted, 1859), 365.

21. Mrs. M. Wood, travel diary, August 6, 1887, entry, Beinecke Rare Book and Manuscript Library, Yale University.

22. Merritt, "From Ocean to Ocean," July 1892, 103.

23. S. Hall Young, *Alaska Days with John Muir* (New York: Fleming H. Revell, 1915).

24. H. W. Seton-Karr, *Shores and Alps of Alaska* (London: Sampson Low, Marston, Searle & Rivington, 1887), n.p.

25. Septima Collis, *A Woman's Trip to Alaska: Being an Account of a Voyage through the Inland Seas of the Sitkan Archipelago in 1890* (New York: Castleton, 1890), 86.

26. Ralph Admari, "Ballou, the Father of the Dime Novel," *American Book Collector*, 4, 128 (September–October 1933), and Henry Nash Smith, *Virgin Land: The American West as Symbol and Myth* (1950; reprint, Cambridge: Harvard University Press, 1978), 87–88.

27. Maturin M. Ballou, *The New Eldorado, A Summer Journey to Alaska* (Boston: Houghton and Mifflin, 1890), iii.

28. Carter, *Road to Botany Bay*, 246.

29. Ernest Ingersoll, "To Alaska, by the Canadian Pacific Railway" (Montreal: Passenger Department, Canadian Pacific Railway, 1888), 3.

30. Quoted in Anne Hyde, *An American Vision: Far Western Landscape and National Culture, 1880–1920* (New York: New York University Press, 1990), 102.

31. Elliott F. Shepard, "The Riva, New York and Alaska," privately published pamphlet, 1887, Beinecke Rare Book and Manuscript Library, Yale University.

32. T. W. Ingersoll, *Picturesque Alaska, In Photogravure, From Recent Negatives* (New York: Albertype, 1890), n.p.

33. S. Hall Young, *Hall Young of Alaska, "The Mushing Parson"* (New York: Fleming H. Revell, 1927), 268.

34. Collis, *A Woman's Trip to Alaska*, 149.

35. Jonathan Crary, *Techniques of the Observer: On Vision and Modernity in the Nineteenth Century* (Cambridge: MIT Press, 1992), 17.

36. E. P. Thompson, "Time, Work-Discipline and Industrial Capitalism," *Past and Present*, 38 (1967), 56–97.

37. "All About Alaska," Pacific Coast Steamship Co. (San Francisco: Goodall, Perkins, 1888), 3.

38. Christopher Herbert calls this a "congruent metaphorical construction." See Herbert, *Culture and Anomie: Ethnographic Imagination in the Nineteenth Century* (Chicago: University of Chicago Press, 1991), 72.

39. Ernest Gruening, *The State of Alaska: A Definitive History of America's Northernmost Frontier* (New York: Random House, 1954), 76.

40. "All About Alaska."

41. The Canadian Pacific Navigation Company was acquired by Canadian Pacific in 1900 and became the foundation for the CPR's Princess fleet of steamers cruising from Seattle and Vancouver north to Alaska. See John Murray Gibbon, *Steel of Empire: The Romantic History of the Canadian Pacific* (New York: Tudor Publishing, 1937), 354.

42. Will Lawson, *Pacific Steamers* (Glasgow: Brown, Son & Ferguson, 1927), 203.

43. Ingersoll, "To Alaska"; "All About Alaska."

44. Ingersoll, "To Alaska," 3.

45. Eliza Clendenin, travel diary, June 6, 1894, entry, Beinecke Rare Book and Manuscript Library, Yale University.

46. Charles H. Gates, *Yellowstone National Park and Alaska. White Pass, 1900: Going via Steamer on the Great Lakes and Canadian Pacific R.R. Returning via Northern Pacific RR. and Steamer on the Great Lakes* (Toledo, Ohio, 1900), 6.

47. Scidmore, *Alaska*, 132.

48. Ibid., 108.

49. Collis, *A Woman's Trip to Alaska*, preface.

50. Lewis and Dryden, *Maritime History of the Pacific Northwest*, ed. E. W. Wright (Portland, Ore., 1895), 150.

51. E. Katherine Bates, *Kaleidoscope: Shifting Scenes from East to West* (London: Ward and Downey, 1889), 226.

52. Ibid., 262.

53. Ibid., 227.

54. Oscar Bike manuscript, letter, Bike to Mr. Bennett, June 5, 1898, Beinecke Rare Book and Manuscript Library, Yale University.

55. "All About Alaska."

56. The associated railroads were Union Pacific, Oregon Railway and Navigation Co., Northern Pacific, and Canadian Pacific.

57. C. E. S. Wood, "Among the Thlinkits in Alaska," *Century Magazine*, 24, no. 3 (July 1882), 339.

58. Alexander Badlam, *The Wonders of Alaska, Illustrated* (San Francisco: Bancroft, 1890), 11.

59. Ingersoll, "To Alaska," 5.

60. Catherine Cocks, *Doing the Town: The Rise of Urban Tourism in the United States, 1850–1915* (Berkeley: University of California Press, 2001).

61. Newton H. Chittenden, *Settlers, Prospectors, and Tourists Guide or Travels Through British Columbia* (Victoria, B.C.: no publisher, 1882), n.p.

62. Crary, *Techniques of the Observer*, 6.

63. Catharine E. Beecher, *The American Woman's Home, or, Principles of Domestic Science* (1869; reprint, Hartford, Conn.: Stowe-Day Foundation, 1975), 91, 94.

64. Bryan J. Wolf, "How the West Was Hung, or When I Heard the Word 'Culture' I Take Out My Checkbook," *American Quarterly*, 1992.

65. Quoted in Lawrence W. Levine, *Highbrow, Lowbrow: The Emergence of Cul-*

tural Hierarchy in America (Cambridge: Harvard University Press, 1988), 161; see also E. L. Godkin, "Chromo-Civilization," *The Nation*, September 24, 1874.

66. Oliver Wendell Holmes, "The Stereoscope and the Stereograph," *Atlantic Monthly* 3, no. 20 (June 1859), 738–48.

67. Albert E. Osborne, *The Stereograph and the Stereoscope, with special maps and books forming a travel system. What they mean for individual development. What they promise for the spread of civilization* (New York: Underwood & Underwood, 1909), 72.

68. Carter H. Harrison, *A Summer's Outing and the Old Man's Story* (Chicago: Dibble Publishing, 1891), 12.

69. Kenneth Burke, "Literature as Equipment for Living," *The Philosophy of Literary Form: Studies in Symbolic Action* (1941; reprint, Berkeley: University of California Press, 1974), 229.

70. Charles Hallock, *Our New Alaska* (New York: Forest and Stream Publishing, 1886), 1.

71. Ibid.

72. Collis, *A Woman's Trip to Alaska*, preface, n.p.

73. "Alaska, Land of Gold and Glacier," Great Northern advertising pamphlet (Chicago: Poole Bros., 1896), 3.

74. John Hyde, *Northern Pacific Railway Tour: The Pacific Northwest and Alaska; with a Description of the Country Traversed by the Northern Pacific Railroad* (St. Paul: W. C. Riley, 1889), 6.

75. Ibid., 7.

76. Henry M. Field, *Our Western Archipelago* (New York: Charles Scribner's Sons, 1895), 94.

77. Ibid., 90.

78. Aylett Cotton Rains Papers, Memoir, Summer 1894, n.d., Bancroft Library, University of California, Berkeley.

79. Field, *Our Western Archipelago*, 189.

80. Ibid., 90.

81. J. A. Zahm, *Alaska, the Country and its Inhabitants, a Lecture* (South Bend, Ind.: Notre Dame University Press, 1886), 14.

82. Pierrepont, *Fifth Avenue to Alaska*, 149; John Douglas Belshaw, "Mining Technique and Social Division on Vancouver Island, 1848–1900," *British Journal of Canadian Studies*, 1986 (1), 45–65.

83. Rebecca Solnit, *River of Shadows: Eadweard Muybridge and the Tehcnological Wild West* (New York: Viking, 2003), 52–53, 276.

84. R. W. Meade, "Alaska," *Appleton's Journal*, 6 (1871), 126.

85. J. H. Gray, "Alaska, Stikine River," *New Dominion Monthly*, 21 (1878).

86. Henry Villard, *Journey to Alaska*, reprinted from *New York Evening Post* (New York, 1899), 36.

87. Robert Wooster, *Nelson A. Miles and the Twilight of the Frontier Army* (Lincoln: University of Nebraska Press, 1993), 135.

88. Ibid., 136–37.

89. Nelson A. Miles, *Personal Recollections* (New York: Werner, 1896), 419.

90. "All About Alaska," 19.

91. Frederick Schwatka, *Along Alaska's Great River* (Chicago: Henry Publishing, 1898), 16.

92. Ingersoll, "To Alaska," 22.

93. Ronald P. Rohner, ed., *The Ethnography of Franz Boas, Letters and Diaries of Franz Boas, Written on the Northwest Coast from 1886 to 1931* (Chicago: University of Chicago Press, 1969), letter dated June 1, 1889, 13.

94. Ibid., 5–6.

95. George Vancouver, *A Voyage of Discovery*, quoted in Joe Upton, *Journeys Through the Inside Passage: Seafaring Adventures Along the Coast of British Columbia and Alaska* (Anchorage: Alaska Northwest Books, 1992).

96. Canadian Hydrographic Service, *Sailing Directions, British Columbia Coast*, 2 vols. (Sidney, B.C.: Department of Fisheries and Oceans).

97. Martha Ferguson Mckeown, *The Trail Led North: Mont Hawthorne's Story* (New York: Macmillan, 1948), 96.

98. Ibid., 97.

99. Aurel Krause, *To the Chukchi Peninsula and to the Tlingit Indians, 1881/1882: Journals and Letters by Aurel and Arthur Krause*, trans. Margot Krause McCaffrey (Fairbanks: University of Alaska Press, 1993), 26.

100. Ibid., 240.

101. Bernard Bendel, "The Alexander Archipelago," *Proceedings of the Agassiz Institute* (Sacramento, Calif., 1873), 27.

102. Fred Rogers, *Shipwrecks of British Columbia* (Vancouver: J. J. Douglas, 1976), 63; E. W. Wright, ed., *Lewis & Dryden's Marine History of the Pacific Northwest* (Portland, Or.: Lewis & Dryden Printing Co., 1895); Gordon R. Newell, ed., *The H. W. McCurdy Marine History of the Pacific Northwest* (Seattle: Superior, 1966).

103. Scidmore, *Alaska*, 18.

104. Finck, *Pacific Coast Scenic Tour*, 240.

105. Edmund Burke, *Philosophical Inquiry into the Origin of Our Ideas of the Sublime and Beautiful* (Glasgow: University Press, 1818), 36.

106. Elizabeth McKinsey, *Niagara Falls: Icon of the American Sublime* (New York: Cambridge University Press, 1985), 8.

107. Henry Jacob Winser, *The Great Northwest* (St. Paul: W. C. Riley, 1889), 404.

108. Hyde, *Northern Pacific Tour*, 6.

109. Max Weber, *The Protestant Ethic and the Spirit of Capitalism* (1904–5; reprint, New York: Charles Scribner's Sons, 1976), 167.

110. Angela Miller, *The Empire of the Eye: Landscape Representation and American Cultural Politics, 1825–1875* (Ithaca: Cornell University Press, 1993), 11.

111. Sylvia Plath, "Ocean 1212-W," *The Listener*, no. 70, August 29, 1963.

112. Gates, *Yellowstone National Park and Alaska*, 10.

113. Ibid.

114. Matilda Barns Lukens, "The Inland Passage: A Journal of a Trip to Alaska," 1889, 35–36, Beinecke Rare Book and Manuscript Library, Yale University.

115. Oscar Bike Papers, letter dated June 5, 1898, Juneau, Bike to Mr. Bennett, Beinecke Rare Book and Manuscript Library, Yale University.

116. Ingersoll, "To Alaska," 31.

117. Schwatka, *Along Alaska's Great River*, 22.

118. Eleanor W. MacDonald, "Here and There in Alaska," *The Pacific Monthly*, 683.

119. Scidmore, *Alaska*, 16.

120. Bert Webber, *Wrecked Japanese Junks Adrift in the North Pacific Ocean* (Fairfield, Wash.: Ye Galleon Press, 1984).

121. Kipling, *American Notes*, 6.

122. Quote from Riffenbaugh, *Math of the Explorer*, 76.

123. Ingersoll, "To Alaska," 26.

124. Muir, *Travels in Alaska*, 176. Muir noted this phosphorescence, writing, "Every stroke of the oar made a vivid surge of white light, and the canoes left shining tracks."

125. William Carlos Williams, *In the American Grain* (New York: New Directions, 1956), v.

126. M. Wood, travel diary, Alaska, August 17, 1887, entry.

127. Oscar F. Bike Papers, letter dated June 5, 1898.

128. Scidmore, *Alaska*, 152.

129. Ibid., 296.

130. C. C. Hine, *A Trip to Alaska: Being A Report of a Lecture, Given with Stereopticon Illustrations* (Milwaukee: King, Fowle, and Co., 1889), 9.

131. Wood, travel diary, Alaska, August 17, 1887, entry.

132. Ibid.

133. Newton Chittenden, *Hyda Land and People* (Victoria, B.C.: Printed by Authority of the Government, 1884), 38.

134. Finck, *Pacific Coast Scenic Tour*, 244.

135. *San Francisco Bulletin*, quoted in "All About Alaska," Pacific Coast Steamship Company (San Francisco: Goodall, Perkins, 1887), 17.

136. Winser, *The Great Northwest*, 88–89.

137. See Gordon Hendricks, *Albert Bierstadt: Painter of the American West* (New York: H. N. Abrams, 1974); Nancy K. Anderson and Linda S. Ferber, *Albert Bierstadt: Art and Enterprise* (New York: Hudson Hills Press, 1990).

138. Will Lawson, *Pacific Steamers* (Glasgow: Brown, Son & Ferguson, 1927), 203.

139. Albert Bierstadt Collection, Bierstadt to Rose Bierstadt, letter dated September 18, 1889, Boston Museum of Fine Arts, Boston, Mass.

140. Scidmore, *Alaska*, 28.

141. John Muir, quoted in Nancy Lord, *Green Alaska*, 77.

142. Patricia Roppel, "Loring," *Alaska Journal*, 5, no. 3 (summer 1975), 171.

143. Schwatka, *Along Alaska's Great River*, 36.

144. William H. Goetzmann and William N. Goetzmann, *The West of the Imagination* (New York: Norton, 1986).

145. Wolfe, "How the West Was Hung," 418–438.

146. Merritt, diary, 15.

Chapter 4. Frontier Commerce

1. Philip Clayton Van Buskirk Papers, Journals, August 8, 1896, entry Manuscript and Archives, University of Washington, Seattle.

2. B. R. Burg, *An American Seafarer in the Age of Sail: The Erotic Diaries of Philip C. Van Buskirk, 1851–1870* (New Haven: Yale University Press, 1994), 148.

3. George Chauncey, *Gay New York: Gender, Urban Culture, and the Making of the Gay Male World, 1890–1940* (New York: Basic Books, 1994), 79.

4. William Douglas Johns, "The Early Yukon, Alaska and the Klondike discovery as they were before the Great Klondike Stampede . . . By one who was there" (manuscript, 1942), 2–3, Manuscript and Archives, University of Washington, Seattle.

5. Van Buskirk diary, Burg, *An American Seafarer*, 44.

6. Ibid., 82.

7. See Robert K. Martin, *Hero, Captain, and Stranger: Male Friendship, Social Critique, and Literary Form in the Sea Novels of Herman Melville* (Chapel Hill: University of North Carolina Press, 1986).

8. Van Buskirk diary, Burg, *An American Seafarer*, 82.

9. Ibid., xi.

10. See David Montgomery, *Workers' Control in America* (New York: Cambridge University Press, 1979), 13–14.

11. Chauncey, *Gay New York*, 78. The nineteenth-century sailor Chauncey observes, "seen as young and manly, unattached, and unconstrained by conventional morality, epitomized the bachelor subculture in the gay cultural imagination."

12. Van Buskirk diary, quoted in Burg, *An American Seafarer*, 161.

13. See E. Anthony Rotundo, *American Manhood: Transformations in Masculinity from the Revolution to the Modern Era* (New York: Basic Books, 1993), 277–78; and Ronald Hyam, *Empire and Sexuality: The British Experience* (Manchester: Manchester University Press, 1992), 7.

14. Michel Foucault, *The History of Sexuality: An Introduction, Volume I* (1979; reprint, New York: Vintage Books, 1990), 42, 103. "The nineteenth-century homosexual, became a personage, a past, a case history, and a childhood, in addition to being a type of life, a life form, and a morphology . . . nothing that went into his total composition was unaffected by his sexuality," Foucault observed of the new persecution of what came to be seen as peripheral sexualities. If, to paraphrase Foucault, Van Buskirk "the sodomite had been a temporary aberration," then Van Buskirk the homosexual "was now a species."

15. Quoted in John D'Emilio and Estelle B. Freedman, *Intimate Matters: A History of Sexuality in America* (New York: Harper & Row, 1988), 227, 225–26.

16. Rotundo, *American Manhood*, 276.

17. Daniel J. Kevles, *In the Name of Eugenics: Genetics and the Uses of Human Heredity* (Cambridge: Harvard University Press, 1995), 85.

18. Gail Bederman, *Manliness and Civilization: A Cultural History or Gender and Race in the United States* (Chicago: University of Chicago Press, 1995), 201.

19. Karl Pearson, "Reproductive Selection," in *The Chances of Death and Other Studies in Evolution* (London: Edward Arnold, 1897), 102, quoted in Robert A. Nye, "Sociology: The Irony of Progress," in J. Edward Chamberlin and Sander L. Gilman, eds., *Degeneration: The Dark Side of Progress* (New York: Columbia University Press, 1985), 65.

20. Ann Stoler, *Race and the Education of Desire: Foucault's History of Sexuality and the Colonial Order of Things* (Durham: Duke University Press, 1995), 40.

21. Max Nordau, *Degeneration* (London: William Heinemann, 1895), 16.

22. J. Edward Chamberlin and Sander L. Gilman, eds., *Degeneration: The Dark Side of Progress* (New York: Columbia University Press, 1985), 112.

23. See Felicity A. Nussbaum, *The Autobiographical Subject: Gender and Ideology in Eighteenth-Century England* (Baltimore: Johns Hopkins University Press, 1989).

24. C. E. S. Wood to Lute Pease, February 22, 1928, quoted in Sherry L. Smith, *Reimagining Indians: Native Americans through Anglo Eyes, 1880–1940* (New York: Oxford University Press, 2000), 23.

25. Edward Said, *Orientalism* (New York: Vintage, 1978), 189–91.

26. Rudyard Kipling, *The Seven Seas* (London: Methuen, 1896).

27. Stoler, *Race and the Education of Desire*, 167.

28. Anne M. Butler, *Daughters of Joy, Sisters of Misery, Prostitutes in the American West, 1865–1890* (Urbana: University of Illinois Press, 1985); Marion S. Goldman, *Gold Diggers and Silver Miners: Prostitution and Social Life on the Comstock Lode* (Ann Arbor: University of Michigan Press, 1981); Jeff Rettmann, "Business, Government, and Prostitution in Spokane, Washington, 1889–1910," *Pacific Northwest Quarterly*, 89, no. 2 (spring 1998).

29. Hyam, *Empire and Sexuality*, 144–45.

30. George W. Bailey, *Alaska and Its People: Giving Statistics as to the Numbers, Location, Pursuits, and Social Condition of the Inhabitants; The Climate, Productions, and General Resources of the Country and of The Commerce, Ocean Currents, Etc.* (Washington, D.C.: U.S. Government Printing Office, 1880), 44.

31. Johan Adrian Jacobsen, *Alaskan Voyage, 1881–1883*, trans. Erna Gunther (Chicago: University of Chicago Press, 1977), 7.

32. Robin Fisher, *Contact and Conflict: Indian-European Relations in British Columbia, 1774–1890* (Vancouver: University of British Columbia Press, 1992), 113.

33. Ibid., 19.

34. Sylvia Van Kirk, *Many Tender Ties: Women in Fur-Trade Society, 1670–1870* (Norman: University of Oklahoma Press, 1980), 26.

35. Jennifer S. H. Brown, *Strangers in the Blood: Fur Trade Company Families in Indian Country* (Vancouver: University of British Columbia Press, 1980), 60. Brown writes that "many northern Indian groups customarily established friendship bonds with strangers not by means of impersonal diplomatic contracts and trappings such as the early London committee had proposed to use, but by lending or exchanging wives or daughters." And Hudson Bay Governor George Simpson noted that "the offer of their Wives and Daughters is the first token of their Friendship and hospitality."

36. La Pérouse, quoted in Philip Fradkin, *Wildest Alaska* (Berkeley: University of California Press, 2001), 56.

37. Leland Donald, *Aboriginal Slavery on the Northwest Coast of North America* (Berkeley: University of California Press, 1997), 250.

38. Gilbert Malcolm Sproat, *The Nootka: Scenes and Studies of Savage Life*, ed. Charles Lilliard (1868; reprint, Victoria, B.C.: Sono Nis Press, 1987), 89–92.

39. Gilbert Sproat, cited in Leland Donald, *Aboriginal Slavery on the Northwest Coast of North America* (Berkeley: University of California Press, 1997), 234–35.

40. Stephen M. Ushin, diary, 1874–1881, 1883–1889, Box 2, June 13, 1874, entry, Charles S. Hubbell Collection, Box 2, Manuscript and Archives, University of Washington, Seattle.

41. Ushin, diary, June 17, 1874, entry. Seattle.

42. Ernest Gruening, *An Alaskan Reader: 1867–1967* (New York: Meredith Press, 1967).

43. K. T. Khlebnikov, *Colonial Russian America: Kyrill T. Khlebnikov's Reports, 1817–1832*, trans. Basil Dmytryshyn (1861; reprint, Portland: Oregon Historical Society, 1976), 71.

44. P. N. Golovin, *The End of Russian America: Captain P. N. Golovin's Last Report*, trans. Basil Dmytryshyn (1862; reprint, Portland: Oregon Historical Society, 1979), 64.

45. It was later named Fort Wrangell by the British for the Russian governor Ferdinand Petrovich von Wrangell.

46. Pavel N. Golovin, Russian Navy, *The End of Russian America: Captain P.N. Golovin's Last Report*, trans. Basil Dmytryshyn and E. A. P. Crownhart-Vaughn (1862; reprint, Portland: Oregon Historical Society, 1979), 63–64.

47. Van Kirk, *Many Tender Ties*, 27.

48. Ibid., 28–29.

49. Constantine, vol. 3, miscellaneous documents, 1870–1908, letter from Bompas, followed May 1893 letter with another to the Dept. of Interior dated December 9, 1893, Charles Constantine Papers, National Archives of Canada, Ottawa, Ontario.

50. Van Kirk, *Many Tender Ties,* 240.

51. Attributed to George Pilz, quoted in R. N. DeArmond, *The Founding of Juneau* (Juneau: Gastineau Channel Centennial Association, 1966), 45.

52. John C. Callbreath, diary, February 12, 1882, entry, Charles S. Hubbell Collection, Box 3, Manuscript and Archives, University of Washington, Seattle.

53. Ushin, diary, May 1874.

54. William Henry Collison, *In the Wake of the War Canoe* (1915; reprint, Victoria, B.C.: Sono Nis Press, 1981), 99.

55. William Dall, quoted in Julia McNair Wright, *Among the Alaskans* (Philadelphia: Presbyterian Board of Publication, 1883), 110.

56. Emil Teichmann, *A Journey to Alaska in the Year 1868: Being a Diary of the Late Emil Teichmann* (Kensington: Cayme Press, 1925).

57. Ibid., 187–91.

58. William Gouverneur Morris, *Report upon the Customs District, Public Service, and Resources of Alaska Territory* (Washington, D.C.: U.S. Government Printing Office, 1879), 62.

59. Bailey, *Alaska and Its People,* 40.

60. The 1884 Organic Act applied the Oregon code of laws to Alaska. Not until 1906 would the district be granted the right to send a delegate to Congress. In 1912 the Second Organic Act provided for territorial status.

61. William Healey Dall, *Alaska as It Was and Is, 1865–1895* (Washington, D.C.: Philosophical Society of Washington, 1895).

62. Morris, *Report upon the Customs District, Public Service, and Resources,* 62.

63. William G. Morris, Report on the Resources of Alaska, 62, quoted in William R. Hunt, *Distant Justice: Policing the Alaska Frontier,* (Norman: University of Oklahoma Press, 1987), 10.

64. Callbreath, diary, May 1887.

65. Ibid., December 1887.

66. Several Stikine Tlingit clan chiefs requested the establishment of schools soon after the American occupation; see Polly Miller, *Lost Heritage of Alaska: The Adventure and Art of the Alaskan Coastal Indians* (Cleveland: World, 1967), 180–85.

67. Ted C. Hinckley, "The Presbyterian Leadership in Pioneer Alaska," *The Journal of American History,* 52, no. 4 (March 1966), 742–56. Note well that a visiting Tsimshian had begun introducing Christianity to the Stikine Tlingit a year earlier.

68. Jackson and the Presbyterians modeled their missions, in part, upon the quite successful efforts of Anglican missionary William Duncan, who had established a school mission at Metlakatla in northern British Columbia in 1862. Duncan, never ordained, was forced out of his position in 1887 and he and eight hundred of his Tsimshian followers emigrated to Annette Island in Alaska, where they established a new town site. See Brian C. Hosmer, *American Indians in the Marketplace: Persistence and Innovation Among the Menominees and the Metlakatlans, 1870–1920* (Lawrence: Kansas University Press, 1999).

69. Collison, *In the Wake of the War Canoe,* 100.

70. Carrie Willard, *Life in Alaska: Letters of Mrs. Eugene S. Willard,* ed. Eva McClintock (Philadelphia: Presbyterian Board of Publication, 1884), 21.

71. Judith R. Walkowitz, *Prostitution and Victorian Society: Women, Class, and the State* (New York: Cambridge University Press, 1980).

72. Wright, *Among the Alaskans,* 14.

73. Marsh Wolfe, eds., *John of the Mountains,* 275.

74. Sheldon Jackson, *Alaska, and Missions on the North Pacific Coast* (New York: Dodd, Mead, 1880), 118.

75. Ibid., 116.

76. Ibid.

77. Homi Bhabha, *The Location of Culture* (New York: Routledge, 1994), 70.

78. W. H. Pierce, *Thirteen Years of Travel and Exploration in Alaska, 1877–1889* (1890; reprint, Anchorage: Alaska Northwest Publishing, 1977), 115.

79. *San Francisco Chronicle,* November 23, 1884, quoted in Ted C. Hinckley, *Alaskan John G. Brady, Missionary, Businessman, Judge, and Governor, 1878–1918* (Columbus: Ohio State University Press, 1982), 67.

80. John C. Callbreath, diary, January 19, 1897, entry Charles S. Hubbell Collection, Box 4, Manuscript and Archives, University of Washington, Seattle. The Oregon legislature had prohibited intermarriage "between Whites and Indians or half-Indians" in 1866. The ban on intermarriage remained Oregon law until May 1951. After the Alaska Organic Act of 1884, Oregon law was adopted in Alaska.

81. A. P. Swineford, *Alaska: Its History, Climate, and Natural Resources* (Chicago: Rand, McNally, 1898), 132.

82. William Johns, Memoir, 51, Manuscript and Archives, University of Washington, Seattle.

83. Ibid.

84. The historical record does not allow for an adequate recounting the perspectives of Tlingit sex workers. "One must recognize the inherent empirical limits for studies," historian Timothy Gilfoyle writes. "Prostitutes represent one of the ultimate subaltern subjects, outcasts from not only the dominant culture but often those subcultures labeled 'subordinate'—women, working classes, social minorities, radicals, religious dissidents. Source materials that articulate the voices of prostitutes simply do not exist in many cases." "Prostitutes in History: From Parables of Pornography to Metaphors of Modernity," *American Historical Review* (February 1999), 137–38.

85. Livingston F. Jones, *A Study of the Thlingets of Alaska* (New York: Fleming H. Revell, 1914), 214–15.

86. Bailey, *Alaska and Its People,* 42.

87. William Dall, "Late News from Alaska," *Science,* 6 (July 31, 1885), 96.

88. Franz Boas, *The Social Organization and the Secret Societies of the Kwakiutl Indians* (Washington, D.C.: U.S. Government Printing Office, 1897), 358–59; quoted in Douglas Cole and Ira Chaikin, *An Iron Hand Upon the People: The Law Against the Potlatch on the Northwest Coast* (Seattle: University of Washington Press, 1990), 76.

89. Ibid., 77.

90. Philip Drucker, *Cultures of the North Pacific Coast* (San Francisco: Chandler, 1965), 53.

91. Ibid., 185.

92. George Emmons noted, "The Chilkats and Chilkoots, as well as the Takus and Stikines, marry quite frequently with the women of interior tribes . . . these intertribal marriages gave the husband the privileges of the wife's people and country, in trading, fishing, and hunting." *The Tlingit Indians,* ed. Frederica de Laguna (Seattle: University of Washington Press, 1991), 31.

93. Bernard Bendel, "The Alexander Archipelago," *Proceedings of the Agassiz Institute* (Sacramento, Calif., 1873), 31.

94. Anne McClintock, *Imperial Leather: Race, Gender, and Sexuality in the Colonial Contest* (New York: Routledge, 1995), 286.

95. Ibid., 56.

96. E. Ruhamah Scidmore, *Alaska: Its Southern Coast and the Sitkan Archipelago* (Boston: D. Lothrop, 1885).

97. The naturalization of the bourgeois home as the site of a rational and modern sexuality arose during the nineteenth century. "Sexuality was carefully confined," Foucault wrote, "it moved into the home. The conjugal family took custody of it and absorbed it into the serious function of reproduction. On the subject of sex, silence became the rule. . . . A single locus of sexuality was acknowledged in social space as well as at the heart of every household, but it was a utilitarian and fertile one: the parent's bedroom. The rest had only to remain vague; proper demeanor avoided contact with other bodies, and verbal decency sanitized one's speech." Though, of course, Foucault's characterization of "the repressive hypothesis" was intended to contradict it, insisting instead that Victorian bourgeois culture represented an exceptional increase in discourses of sexuality. See generally Foucault, *History of Sexuality, Vol. I,* esp. pp. 3–4.

98. See Stoler, *Race and the Education of Desire,* 40–41; Foucault, *History of Sexuality,* 108.

99. James G. Brady, quoted in Ted C. Hinckley, *Alaska's Tlingit and the Euramerican Frontier, 1800–1912* (New York: University Press of America, 1996), 67.

100. George W. Stocking, Jr., *Victorian Anthropology* (New York: The Free Press, 1987), 228–37.

101. Septima Collis, *A Woman's Trip to Alaska: Being an Account of a Voyage through the Inland Seas of the Sitkan Archipelago in 1890* (New York: Castleton, 1890), 100.

102. Regenia Gagnier, *The Insatiability of Human Wants: Economics and Aesthetics in Market Society* (Chicago: University of Chicago Press, 2000), 4.

103. Dipesh Chakrabarty writes, "The assumption that cultures were not properly understood until the 'domestic' had been opened up to scholarly (or governmental) scrutiny, itself belonged to an intellectual tradition that objectified the idea of culture." "The Difference—Deferral of a Colonial Modernity: Public Debates on Domesticity in British Bengal," in Frederick Cooper and Ann Laura Stoler, eds., *Tensions of Empire: Colonial Cultures in a Bourgeois World* (Berkeley: University of California Press, 1997), 375.

104. Oscar Wilde, *"The Ballad of Reading Gaol and Other Poems"* (Mount Vernon, N.Y.: Peter Pauper Press, 1947).

105. Burg, *An American Seafarer,* 129.

106. Ibid., 143–44.

107. Same-sex relations among the Tlingit have received little attention in the ethnographic literature, aside from the report from Etienne Marchand in his *A Voyage Round the World . . . During the Years 1790, 1791, and 1792,* trans. and ed. Charles P. C. Fleurieu (London: Longman and Rees, 1801) 1: 370. Marchand reported that "there were a few male homosexuals among the Tlingit," though Frederica de Laguna notes that they "remained, apparently, outside of all marriage alliances." See de Laguna, ed., *The Tlingit Indians* by George Thornton Emmons (Seattle: University of Washington Press, 1991), 270.

108. "Notes of a Naturalist: John Muir in Alaska—Wrangel Island and its Picturesque Attractions," *Daily Evening Bulletin,* September 6, 1879, 1, in Robert Engberg and Bruce Merrell, eds., *Letters from Alaska, John Muir* (Madison: University of Wisconsin Press, 1993), 12.

109. Van Buskirk, diary, Wrangell, August 13, 1896, entry, Manuscript and Archives, University of Washington, Seattle.

110. Roger Casement called the Irish "The White Indians of Ireland." See Michael Taussig, *Shamanism, Colonialism, and the Wild Man: A Study in Terror and Healing* (Chicago: University of Chicago Press, 1987).

111. See Philip Deloria, *Playing Indian* (New Haven: Yale University Press, 1998).

112. McClintock, *Imperial Leather*, 52.

113. Eugene Talbot, *Degeneracy: Its Causes, Signs and Results*, quoted in Nancy Stepan, "Biology: Races and Proper Places," in J. Edward Chamberlin and Sander Gilman, eds., in *Degeneration: The Dark Side of Progress* (New York: Columbia University Press, 1985).

114. Willard and McClintock, eds., *Life in Alaska*, 10.

115. Vincent Colyer, quoted in Wright, *Among the Alaskans*, 1883.

116. Michael Paul Rogin, *Fathers and Children: Andrew Jackson and the Subjugation of the American Indian* (New Brunswick, N.J.: Transaction Publishers, 1991), xv.

117. Richard Dellamora, *Masculine Desire: The Sexual Politics of Victorian Aestheticism* (Chapel Hill: University of North Carolina Press, 1990), 3.

118. Stoler, *Race and the Education of Desire*, 188.

119. Foucault, *History of Sexuality*, 121.

120. Roland Barthes, *Mythologies*, trans. Annette Lavers (New York: Hill and Wang, 2000), 33.

121. E. Katherine Bates, *Kaleidoscope, Shifting Scenes from East to West* (London: Ward and Downey, 1889), 226.

122. Foucault, *History of Sexuality*, 105.

Chapter 5. Totem and Taboo

1. C. E. S. Wood, "Among the Thlinkits in Alaska," *Century Magazine*, 24, no. 3 (July 1882), 323.

2. Stephen Merritt, "From Ocean to Ocean," travel diary, June 1894, Huntington Library, Pasadena, Calif.

3. Michel Foucault, *The History of Sexuality: An Introduction, vol. 1*, (New York: Vintage Books, 1990), 3.

4. J. A. Zahm, *Alaska, the Country and its Inhabitants, a Lecture* (South Bend, Ind.: Notre Dame University Press, 1886), 5.

5. George Wardman, *A Trip to Alaska A Narrative of What Was Seen and Heard during a Summer Cruise in Alaskan Waters* (San Francisco: Samuel Carson, 1884), 48–49.

6. Mrs. M. Wood, diary, August 12, 1887, entry, Beinecke Rare Book and Manuscript Library, Yale University.

7. S. Hall Young, *Hall Young of Alaska* (New York: Fleming H. Revell, 1927), 81.

8. *Alaska Appeal*, July 15, 1879, quoted in Donald Craig Mitchell, *Sold American: The Story of Alaska Natives and Their Land, 1867–1959* (Hanover: Dartmouth College, 1997), 100–101.

9. William Ridley, *Warriors of the North Pacific: Missionary Accounts of the Northwest Coast, the Skeena and Stikine Rivers and the Klondike*, ed. Charles Lillard (Victoria, B.C.: Sono Nis Press, 1984), 188.

10. John Muir, *My First Summer in the Sierra* (1911; reprint, New York: Penguin Books, 1987), 226. While Muir described Sierra natives, his disgust with native lifestyles extended to southeastern Alaska.

11. Wardman, *A Trip to Alaska*, 50.

12. George H. Hotchkiss, "The Midnight Sun," Sept. 19, 1889, manuscript, Beinecke Rare Book and Manuscript Library, Yale University.

13. Charles J. Gillis, *The Yellowstone Park and Alaska* (New York: J. J. Little, 1893), 47.

14. Claude Lévi-Strauss, *The Way of the Masks*, trans. Sylvia Modelski (Seattle: University of Washington Press, 1979), 101, 35–38.

15. Henri Lefebvre, *The Production of Space*, trans. Donald Nicholson-Smith (Cambridge: Blackwell, 1991), 68.

16. Sigmund Freud, quoted in David Harvey, *Justice, Nature, and the Geography of Difference* (Oxford: Blackwell, 1996), 155.

17. Foucault, *History of Sexuality*, 151.

18. Carter H. Harrison, *A Summer's Outing and the Old Man's Story* (Chicago: Dibble Publishing, 1891), 6.

19. Maturin M. Ballou, *The New Eldorado: A Summer Journey to Alaska* (Boston: Houghton Mifflin, 1890), 195.

20. Collis, *A Woman's Trip to Alaska: Being an Account of a Voyage Through the Inland Seas of the Sitkan Archipelago in 1890* (New York: Castleton, 1890), 185.

21. Henry M. Field, *Our Western Archipelago* (New York: Charles Scribner's Sons, 1895), 119.

22. Frederick Schwatka, *Along Alaska's Great River* (Chicago: Henry Publishing, 1898), 51.

23. John A. Henriques, *Alaska, Facts About the New Northwest* (Ohio, 1872), 6.

24. John Muir, *Travels in Alaska* (Boston: Houghton Mifflin, 1915), 65.

25. Robert J. C. Young, *Colonial Desire: Hybridity in Theory, Culture and Race* (New York: Routledge, 1995), 180.

26. Charles E. Hamilton, "Legends and Customs of the Tisimshean Indians," *The Curio, An Illustrated Monthly Magazine*, 1 (September 1887–February 1888), 220.

27. Young, *Colonial Desire*, 180.

28. See Joyce Chaplin, *Subject Matter: Technology, the Body, and Science on the Anglo-American Frontier, 1500–1676* (Cambridge: Harvard University Press, 2002).

29. Guy Debord, *The Society of the Spectacle* (1967; reprint, New York: Zone Books, 1995), 120.

30. Collis, *A Woman's Trip to Alaska*, 100.

31. Ann Laura Stoler, *Race and the Education of Desire* (Durham: Duke University Press, 1995), 176.

32. A. E. Browne, diary, "A Trip to California, Alaska, and the Yellowstone Park, April 20th to July 10th 1891," vol. 2 (Philadelphia), 165, Beinecke Rare Book and Manuscript Library, Yale University.

33. Wardman, *A Trip to Alaska*, 12.

34. "All About Alaska," Pacific Coast Steamship Company (San Francisco: Goodall, Perkins, 1887), 11–12.

35. Matilda Barns Lukens, "The Inland Passage," journal, 1889, Beinecke Rare Book and Manuscript Library, Yale University.

36. Sigmund Freud, *Totem and Taboo: Some Points of Agreement Between the Mental Lives of Savages and Neurotics*, trans. James Strachey (New York: W. W. Norton, 1950), 2.

37. Frederick Cooper and Ann Laura Stoler, eds., *Tensions of Empire: Colonial Cultures in a Bourgeois World* (Berkeley: University of California Press, 1997), 25–26.

38. Foucault, *History of Sexuality*, 103.

39. Gilles Deleuze and Félix Guattari, quoted in Young, *Colonial Desire*, 168.

40. "City of Palaces: Picturesque World's Fair Chicago" (W. B. Conkey, 1894), 71.

41. Robert W. Rydell, *All the World's a Fair: Visions of Empire at American International Expositions, 1876–1916* (Chicago: University of Chicago Press, 1984); Tony Bennett, *The Birth of the Museum* (New York: Routledge, 1995), 77.

42. William Johns Manuscript, 12–13, Manuscripts and Archives, University of Washington, Seattle.

43. Franz Boas, *The Ethnography of Franz Boas: Letters and Diaries of Franz Boas, Written on the Northwest Coast from 1886–1931*, ed. Ronald P. Rohner (Chicago: University of Chicago Press, 1969), 98.

44. Boas, *The Ethnography of Franz Boas*, 6. By the late 1890s it was generally believed that all the indigenous coastal people of Alaska came from Asia. However, at least one writer suggested another possibility, that the Haida of the Queen Charlotte Islands were descended from Central American peoples. F. E. Frobese came to this conclusion through a comparative examination of Hydah stonework and carving design. He also linked Hydah material culture to Polynesian origins. See *The Origin and Meaning of the Totem Poles in South Eastern Alaska* (Sitka: Alaska Printing Office, 1897), 7–8. The Beringia hypothesis may not be the only explanation for North American settlement, as these maritime transits indicate.

45. John Muir, *Picturesque California and the Region West of the Rocky Mountains from Alaska to Mexico* (San Francisco: J. Dening, 1888), 209.

46. Warburton Pike, *Through the Subarctic Forest: A Record of a Canoe Journey from Fort Wrangel to the Pelly Lakes and Down the Yukon River to the Bering Sea* (London: Edward Arnold, 1896), 62.

47. Scidmore, *Alaska*, 89.

48. Ibid.

49. A. L. Lindsley, *Sketches of an Excursion to Southern Alaska* (1881), 50.

50. Johannes Fabian, *Time and the Other: How Anthropology Makes Its Object* (New York: Columbia University Press, 1983).

51. Field, *Our Western Archipelago*, 138.

52. Wardman, *A Trip to Alaska*, 60.

53. Edward Pierrepont, *Fifth Avenue to Alaska* (New York: G. P. Putnam's Sons, 1885), 156.

54. Ivan Petroff, *Population and Resources of Alaska*, 1880, 10 Census, published 1881, 85.

55. Alfred P. Swineford, "Report of the Governor of Alaska to the Secretary of Interior, 1888" (Washington, D.C.: U.S. Government Printing Office, 1888), 33.

56. Swineford, quoted in Pacific Coast Steamship Company, *All About Alaska* (San Francisco: Goodall, Perkins, 1888), 57. "Report of the Governor of Alaska to the Secretary of Interior, 1887" (Washington, D.C.: U.S. Government Printing Office, 1887).

57. R. T. Williams, *The British Columbia Directory*, 1882–1883 (Victoria, 1883), 14.

58. Ernest Ingersoll, "To Alaska by the Canadian Pacific Railway" (Montreal: Passenger Department, Canadian Pacific Railroad, 1888), 40.

59. John Edward Boyer Papers, "The Log of our Trip to Alaska Panhandle," August 11–18, 1912, Manuscripts and Archives, University of Washington, Seattle.

60. Herbert Spencer, *The Principles of Sociology*, vol. 1 (New York: D. Appleton, 1897), 60.

61. Timothy Mitchell, *Colonising Egypt* (Berkeley: University of California Press, 1991).

62. Frances Knapp, *The Thlinkets of Southeastern Alaska* (Chicago: Stone and Kimball, 1896), 11.

63. Mitchell, *Colonising Egypt*, xiv.

64. Alexander Whyte to his wife, letter dated February 23, 1898, Fort Wrangell, Alexander Whyte and Family Papers, Minnesota Historical Society, St. Paul, Minn.

65. Wardman, *A Trip to Alaska*, 33.

66. Muir, *Travels in Alaska*, 38.

67. John Muir, *The Cruise of the Corwin* (New York: Houghton Mifflin, 1917), 110–11.

68. Walter Benjamin, *Illuminations* (New York: Schocken Books, 1969), 256.

69. E. Macdonald, "Here and There in Alaska," The *Pacific Monthly*, V-15, 1902 685.

70. William H. Dall, quoted in Philip L. Fradkin, *Wildest Alaska: Journeys of Great Peril in Lituya Bay* (Berkeley: University of California Press, 2001), 81.

71. Charles Emerson, "A Trip to Alaska," self-published diary, 1895, 4.

72. Lloyd Winter and Percy Pond, *The Totems of Alaska* (New York: Albertype Company, 1905).

73. James Clifford, *The Predicament of Culture: Twentieth-Century Ethnography, Literature, and Art* (Cambridge: Harvard University Press, 1988), 228.

74. James Teackle Dennis, *On the Shores of an Inland Sea* (Philadelphia: J. B. Lippincott, 1894), 33.

75. "All the Year Round Tours, to Tropical Climes and the Frigid Zone" (San Francisco: Pacific Steamship Company, 1903).

76. Frederic Schwatka, *Summer in Alaska* (St. Louis: J. W. Henry, 1893), 27.

77. Sophia Cracroft, *Lady Franklin Visits Sitka, Alaska, 1870: The Journal of Sophia Cracroft, Sir John Franklin's Niece*, ed. R. N. DeArmond (Anchorage: Alaska Historical Society, 1981), 68.

78. Scidmore described this attack on the authority of the Tlingit shaman, noting that the U.S. Navy "broke the power of shamanism in the archipelago by repeated rescues of those charged with witchcraft, by fine and punishment of tribe and shamans, and finally by taking the shamans on board his ship, shaving off and burning their long sacred hair." "The First District from Prince Frederick Sound to Yakutat Bay," in *Report on Population and Resources of Alaska at the Eleventh Census: 1890* (Washington, D.C.: U.S. Bureau of the Census), 42–53.

79. R. N. De Armond, *Lady Franklin Visits Sitka, Alaska, 1870, The Journal of Sophia Cracroft, Sir John Franklin's Niece* (Anchorage: Alaska Historical Society, 1981), 3.

80. Douglas Cole, *Captured Heritage: The Scramble for Northwest Coast Artifacts* (Seattle: University of Washington Press, 1985), 45.

81. Muir, *Travels in Alaska*, 276.

82. Macdonald, "Here and There in Alaska," 685.

83. James Swan, quoted in Cole, *Captured Heritage*, 100.

84. Ella Higginson, "The Voyage of All Voyages," *Washington Magazine*, June 1906, 338.

85. A. E. Browne, diary, "A Trip to California, Alaska, and the Yellowstone Park," 177.

86. Karl Baedeker, *The Dominion of Canada with Newfoundland and an Excursion to Alaska: Handbook for Travelers* (Leipzig: Karl Baedeker Publisher, 1894), 156.

87. Scidmore, *Alaska*, 38.

88. Molly Lee, "Appropriating the Primitive: Turn-of-the-Century Collection and Display of Native Alaskan Art," *Arctic Anthropology*, 28, no. 1 (1991), 6–15.

89. Eliza Scidmore, "Alaska Mining Regions," *Harpers Magazine*, 1892, 471.

90. Scidmore, *Alaska*, 105.

91. Carrie Willard, *Life in Alaska: Letters of Mrs. Eugene S. Willard*, ed. Eva McClintock (Philadelphia: Presbyterian Board of Publication, 1884), 39.

92. Eliza Scidmore, *Appleton's Guide-Book to Alaska* (New York: D. Appleton, 1898), 115.

93. William Douglas Johns, "The Early Yukon, Alaska and the Klondike discovery as they were before the Great Klondike Stampede . . . By one who was there" (Manuscript, 1942), 49, Manuscript and Archives, University of Washington, Seattle.

94. Frances Knapp and Rheta Louise Childe, *The Thlinkets of Southeastern Alaska* (Chicago: Stone and Kimball, 1896), 103; Scidmore, *Alaska*, 176; Collis, *A Woman's Trip to Alaska*, 104–8; Lukens, "The Inland Passage," 54.

95. Lukens, "The Inland Passage," 54.

96. "All About Alaska," 12.

97. The word *kitsch* comes from the German *kitschen*, "to put together sloppily."

98. Browne, diary, "A Trip to California, Alaska, and the Yellowstone Park, April 20 to July 10.

99. Dennis, *On the Shores of an Inland Sea*, 32.

100. Scidmore, *Alaska*, 91.

101. Henry T. Finck, *The Pacific Coast Scenic Tour* (New York: Charles Scribner's Sons, 1890), 241.

102. Ingersoll, "To Alaska," 39.

103. Scidmore, *Alaska*, 91.

104. Philip J. Deloria, *Playing Indian* (New Haven: Yale University Press, 1998), 92–94.

105. Caroline Frear Burk, "The Collecting Instinct," *The Pedagogical Seminary*, 7(2), July 1900.

106. Stephen Greenblatt, "Resonance and Wonder," in *Exhibiting Cultures: The Poetics and Politics of Museum Display*, ed. Ivan Karp and Steven D. Lavine (Washington D.C.: Smithsonian Institution Press, 1991), 49–50.

107. Hotchkiss, "The Midnight Sun."

108. Ballou, *The New Eldorado*, 226–27.

109. Jean-Joseph Goux, *Symbolic Economies, After Marx and Freud*, 1973, trans. Jennifer Curtiss Gage (Ithaca: Cornell University Press, 1990), 62.

110. Karl Marx wrote, "Objects that in themselves are no commodities, such as conscience, honour, etc. are capable of being offered for sale by their holders, and of thus acquiring, through their price, the form of commodities. Hence an object may have a price without having value." Karl Marx, *Capital, An Abridged Edition*, ed. David McLellan (New York: Oxford University Press, 1995), 63.

111. Michel Foucault, *Madness and Civilization* (New York: Vintage Books, 1988), 11.

112. Walter Benjamin, *The Arcades Project*, trans. Howard Eiland and Kevin McLaughlin (Cambridge: Harvard University Press, 1999), 7.

113. Lloyd Macdowell, "Alaska Indian Basketry" (Seattle: Alaska Steamship Company, 1906), n.p.

114. Prasenjit Duara, *Rescuing History from the Nation: Questioning Narratives of Modern China* (Chicago: University of Chicago Press, 1995), 14.

115. Charles Horton Cooley, *Human Nature and the Social Order* (1902; reprint, New Brunswick, N.J.: Transaction Publishers, 1992), 3.

116. Duara, *Rescuing History from the Nation*, 13–14.

117. Marx, *Capital*, 42.

118. Michael Taussig, *Shamanism, Colonialism, and the Wild Man: A Study in Terror and Healing* (Chicago: University of Chicago Press, 1987), 5.

119. Ella Higginson, *Alaska: The Great Country* (New York: Macmillan, 1908), 72.

120. Knapp and Childe, *The Thlinkets of Southeastern Alaska*, 156.

121. Frazer understood totemism as a system of cooperative magic, which Freud summarized as "a magical producers' and consumers' union." James G. Frazer, *The Golden Bough: A Study in Magic and Religion* (1890; reprint, New York: Papermac, 1994).

122. Ibid., 234.

123. James G. Frazer, *Totemism* (Edinburgh: A & C. Black, 1887).

124. Marx, *Capital*, 45.

125. Francis Galton, ed., *Vacation Tourists and Notes of Travel*, vol. 1 (London, 1860), preface.

126. Charles Darwin, *The Descent of Man* (London: J. Murray, 1871), 542.

127. Sigmund Freud, *Group Psychology and the Analysis of the Ego*, S.E., XVIII, 69, quoted in Peter Gay, *Freud for Historians* (New York: Oxford University Press, 1985), 146.

128. Benjamin, *The Arcades Project*, 212.

129. Aurel Krause, *The Tlingit Indians: Results of a Trip to the Northwest Coast America and the Bering Strait* (1885), Trans. Erna Gunther (Seattle: University of Washington Press, 1956) 104.

130. Nicholas Thomas, *Colonialism's Culture: Anthropology, Travel and Government* (Princeton: Princeton University Press, 1994), 81.

131. Paul Carter, *The Road to Botany Bay* (New York: Knopf, 1988), 119.

132. Charles Hallock, *Our New Alaska* (New York: Forest and Stream Publishing, 1886), 26.

133. James G. Frazer, *The Golden Bough*, quoted in Christopher Herbert, *Culture and Anomie: Ethnographic Imagination in the Nineteenth Century* (Chicago: University of Chicago Press, 1991), 254.

134. Frederick Whymper, *Travel and Adventure in the Territory of Alaska* (London: John Murray, 1869), 36.

135. Garret Wolseley, *Fortnightly Review* (1888), 692.

136. Higginson, *Alaska, The Great Country*, 11.

137. Foucault, *History of Sexuality*, 124.

138. Duara, *Rescuing History from the Nation*, 48–49.

139. Eliza Ruhamah Scidmore, "The First District of Alaska from Prince Frederick Sound to Yakutat Bay," in Robert P. Porter, *Report on Population and Resources of Alaska at the Eleventh Census: 1890*, (Washington, D.C.: U.S. Government Printing Office, 1893), 44.

140. Benjamin, *The Arcades Project*, 19.

141. Susan Stewart, *On Longing: Narratives of the Miniature, the Gigantic, the Souvenir, the Collection* (Durham: Duke University Press, 1993), 163.

142. Ella Higginson, "The Voyage of All Voyages," *Washington Magazine*, June 1906, 336.

143. *The Curio, An Illustrated Monthly Magazine,* 1 (September 1887), 1.

144. Homi Bhabha, *The Location of Culture* (New York: Routledge, 1994), 85–92.

145. Benjamin, *The Arcades Project,* 210. Marx also helps to make the connection between the both actual and metaphorical uses of the "body" in order to understand the intimacies between the market and the parlor, between the public and the private, between the society and the individual. "In bourgeois society *the commodity-form* of the product of labor—or the value-form of the commodity—is the *economic cell-form.* Certainly the body, as an organic whole, is more easy of study than are the cells of that body, but only this 'microscopic anatomy,' this atomic science of value can radically dispel the enigma of the established value form." See Robert Tucker, ed., *Marx-Engels Reader,* (New York: Norton, 1978), 295, preface to the 1st German edition of *Capital.*

146. Terry Eagleton, *Marxism and Literary Criticism* (Berkeley: University of California Press, 1976).

147. S. Hall Young, *Alaska Days with John Muir* (New York: Fleming H. Revell, 1915), 75–76.

148. Henry David Thoreau, "Ktaadn" (1848) in "The Maine Woods" (1864) in *The Writings of Henry David Thoreau,* vol. 3 (New York: Houghton Mifflin, 1906), 86.

149. John Muir, *My First Summer in the Sierra* (New York: Penguin Books, 1987), 226.

Chapter 6. Juneau's Industrial Sublime

1. Eliza R. Scidmore, *Alaska, Its Southern Coast and the Sitkan Archipelago* (Boston: D. Lothrop, 1885), 139.

2. Juneau's law enforcement was under miner's law from February 1881 until July 1884, when the first governor, district judge, and U.S. marshall were appointed under the first Alaska's Organic Act.

3. M. Claudet, *The Handbook of British Columbia and Emigrant's Guide to the Gold Fields with Map and Two Illustrations,* (London: W. Oliver, 1862).

4. W. H. Pierce, *Thirteen Years of Travel and Exploration in Alaska, 1877–1889* (1890; reprint, Anchorage: Alaska Northwest Publishing, 1977), 37.

5. Edward Pierrepont, *Fifth Avenue to Alaska* (New York: G. P. Putnam's Sons, 1885), 210–11.

6. Ibid., 214.

7. Ibid., 193, 215.

8. Clarence L. Andrews, "Biographical Sketch of Captain William Moore," *Washington Historical Quarterly,* 22, no. 2 (April 1931), 110. Historian Andrews noted only four "lynchings" in territorial Alaska.

9. Stephen M. Ushin, diary, 1874–1881, 1883–1889, Box 2, March 1, 1880, entry. Charles S. Hubbell Collection, Box 2, Manuscript and Archives, University of Washington, Seattle.

10. Vincent Colyer, Secretary to Board of Indian Commission, "Bombardment of Wrangel, Alaska," *Report of the Secretary of War, Secretary of Interior, and Letter to the President* (Washington, D.C.: General Printing Office, 1870), 508.

11. First Lieutenant William Borrowe, letter dated February 8, 1870, published in *Report of the Secretary of War, et al.* (Washington, D.C.: Government Printing Office, 1870), 4.

12. Robert Williams, diary, Juneau, March 22, 1898, Williams Family Papers,

Minnesota Historical Society. Williams noted, "There is considerable timber about, or was rather, till cut down leaving stumps everywhere."

13. Eliza Scidmore, *Appleton's Guide-Book to Alaska* (New York: D. Appleton, 1898), 86.

14. Juliette C. Reinicker, letter to Clara, April 1, 1898, "Fourth of July Creek: The Story of Alfred G. McMichael's Trip to Alaska, 1898," Yukon Archives, Manuscript collection.

15. William H. Wiley and Sara King Wiley, *The Yosemite, Alaska, and the Yellowstone* (London: Offices of Engineering, 1893), 153.

16. T. A. Rickard, *Through the Yukon and Alaska* (San Francisco: Mining and Scientific Press, 1909), 37. Rickard wrote that "in 1878 John Muir was deputed by the United States government to explore southeastern Alaska." According to Rickard, Muir reported that an area between Windham Bay on Stephens Passage sixty-five miles southeast of the present site of Juneau, and Sullivan Island sixty-miles northwest, in Lynn Canal, "would make a second California" (18).

17. George Pilz, communication to Judge James Wickersham, quoted in R. DeArmond, *The Founding of Juneau* (Juneau: Gastineau Channel Centennial Association, 1966), 20.

18. Communication to Alfred H. Brooks, U.S. Geological Survey, quoted in DeArmond, *The Founding of Juneau*, 20.

19. Ushin, diary, November 17, 1880, November 25, 1880, March 1, 1880, and April 10, 1881, entries.

20. DeArmond, *The Founding of Juneau*, 38.

21. Carrie Willard, letter to friends, Haines, December 13, 1881, *Life in Alaska, Letters of Mrs. Eugene S. Willard*, ed. Eva McClintock (Philadelphia: Presbyterian Board of Publication, 1884), 127.

22. Barry Gough dubbed the British naval activity along the coast, "the gunboat frontier." See Gough, *Gunboat Frontier: British Maritime Authority and Northwest Coast Indians, 1846–1890* (Vancouver: University of British Columbia Press, 1984).

23. Aurel and Arthur Krause, *To the Chukchi Peninsula and to the Tlingit Indians, 1881/1882: Journals and Letters by Aurel and Arthur Krause*, trans. Margot Krause McCaffrey (Fairbanks: University of Alaska Press, 1993), 116.

24. Richard Harris letter, quoted in DeArmond, *The Founding of Juneau*, 66.

25. William Douglas Johns, "The Early Yukon, Alaska and the Klondike discovery as they were before the Great Klondike Stampede . . . By one who was there" (manuscript, 1942), 35, Manuscript and Archives, University of Washington, Seattle.

26. Charles Replogle, *Among the Indians of Alaska* (London: Headley Brothers, 1904), 16–17.

27. Alexander Badlam, *The Wonders of Alaska, Illustrated* (San Francisco: Bancroft, 1890), iii, iv.

28. T. A. Rickard, quoted in Gray Brechin, *Imperial San Francisco: Urban Power, Earthly Ruin* (Berkeley: University of California Press, 1999), 57.

29. Replogle, *Among the Indians of Alaska*, 5, 7.

30. Henry M. Field, *Our Western Archipelago* (New York: Charles Scribner's Sons, 1895), 105.

31. Thomas W. Moore, "Account of Travels," c. March 1898, 27, Manuscript collection, British Columbia Archives.

32. Donald Denoon, *Settler Capitalism: The Dynamics of Dependent Development in the Southern Hemisphere* (Oxford: Clarendon Press, 1983), 127.

33. Stephen Merritt, "From Ocean to Ocean," July 8, 1892, entry, 103, Huntington Library, Pasadena, Calif.

34. George Munro Grant, *Picturesque Canada; The Country As It Was and Is, with over Five Hundred Engravings on Wood* (Toronto: Belden Brothers, 1882), 880.

35. George A. Ogrissek, Alaskan Gold Rush diary and sketchbook, folder 1, Memoranda of the Second Trip To Alaska, from Feb'y 24 1899 to Sep. 6, 1899, August 1, 1899, entry, Beinecke Rare Book and Manuscript Library, Yale University.

36. Walter Pierce, quoted in DeArmond, *The Founding of Juneau.*

37. Mark Wyman, *Hard Rock Epic: Western Miners and the Industrial Revolution, 1860–1910* (Berkeley: University of California Press, 1979), 58.

38. William H. Bunge Papers, letter to his father, dated Juneau, June 15, 1899, Minnesota Historical Society.

39. J. Bernard Moore, *Skagway in Days Primeval: The Writings of J. Bernard Moore, 1886–1904* (Alaska: Lynn Canal Publishing, 1997).

40. *Juneau Free Press,* quoted in *West Shore,* no. 13 (April 1887), 344.

41. Governor Swinefort's annual report, 1887, quoted in "All About Alaska," Pacific Coast Steamship Co. (San Francisco: Goodall, Perkins, 1888), 57.

42. Wiley and Wiley, *The Yosemite, Alaska, and the Yellowstone,* 155.

43. Henry T. Finck, *The Pacific Coast Scenic Tour: From Southern California to Alaska, the Canadian Pacific, Yellowstone Park, and the Grand Canyon* (New York: Charles Scribner's Sons, 1890), 241.

44. Henry Jacob Winser, *The Great Northwest; A Guide-Book and Itinerary for the Use of Tourists and Travelers over the Lines of the Northern Pacific Railroad, Its Branches and Allied Lines* (St. Paul: W. C. Riley, 1889), 426–27.

45. Replogle, *Among the Indians of Alaska,* 13.

46. "All About Alaska," 57.

47. Pierce, *Thirteen Years of Travel and Exploration in Alaska,* 34.

48. Karl Baedeker, *The Dominion of Canada with Newfoundland* (Leipzig: Karl Baedeker Publisher, 1894), 234. Elsewhere native workers negotiated even higher wage rates, often competitive with their white counterparts. According to Bishop W. C. Bompas, ministering in the upper Yukon during summer 1891, "Wages were paid to be $8.00 per day even to the Indians." Bishop Bompas to Lieutenant Governor, Canada, letter dated December 3, 1891, William Ogilvie files, MG 30 B22, vol. 1, National Archives of Canada, Ottawa, Ontario.

49. Pierce, *Thirteen Years in Alaska,* 35.

50. Krause, *To the Chukchi Peninsula and to the Tlingit Indians,* 112.

51. Johns, "The Early Yukon," 6.

52. Van Horne letterbooks, microfilm reel M-2288, letter to a Mr. Cotton, who had written a number of anti-Chinese editorials to which Van Horne responded, October 6, 1896, Corporation Records, Canadian Pacific Railway, MG III, 20, National Archives of Canada, Ottawa, Ontario.

53. There had been earlier violent episodes, such as in Los Angeles in 1871, when a white mob murdered eighteen or nineteen Chinese immigrants.

54. See Gunther Barth, *Bitter Strength: A History of the Chinese in the United States, 1850–1870* (Cambridge: Harvard University Press, 1964); Alexander Saxton, *The Indispensable Enemy* (Berkeley: University of California Press, 1971).

55. J. A. Zahm, *Alaska, the Country and its Inhabitants, a Lecture* (South Bend, Ind.: Notre Dame University Press, 1886), 16.

56. Ushin, diary, May 14, 1878 entry.

57. Zahm, *Alaska, the Country and its Inhabitants.*

58. D. A. Murphy, "Frontier Incidents at Juneau," in Herbert L. Heller, ed., *Sourdough Sagas: The Journals, Memoirs, Tales and Recollections of the Earliest Alaskan Gold Miners, 1883–1923* (New York: The World Publishing Company, 1967), 25–26.

59. Ibid., 26.

60. Ibid.

61. *The Glacier* 1, no. 10 (September 1886).

62. Linnie Marsh Wolfe, ed., *John of the Mountains: The Unpublished Journals of John Muir* (Boston: Houghton Mifflin, 1938), 259–60.

63. Pierrepont, *Fifth Avenue to Alaska*, 177.

64. Ushin, diary, July 1878 entry.

65. Replogle, *Among the Indians of Alaska*, 29.

66. Roland Barthes, *Mythologies*, trans. Annette Lavers (1957; reprint, New York: Hill and Wang, 2000), 111.

67. Eliza Clendenin, diary, Juneau, July 15, 1894, entry Beinecke Rare Book and Manuscript Library, Yale University.

68. Badlam, *The Wonders of Alaska*, 126.

69. Alan Trachtenberg, *The Incorporation of America: Culture and Society in the Gilded Age* (New York: Hill and Wang, 1982), 17.

70. California-Klondyke Mining and Exploration, 1897, Beinecke Rare Book and Manuscript Library, Yale University.

71. Charles Emerson, "A Trip to Alaska," self-published diary, 1895, 2.

72. Neil Smith, *Uneven Development: Nature, Capital, and the Production of Space* (Oxford: Basil Blackwell, 1984), 16.

73. "All About Alaska," 11.

74. Edward S. Parkinson, *Wonderland; or, Twelve Weeks in and out of the United States* (Trenton, N.J.: MacCrellish and Quigley, 1894), 186.

75. Ibid.

76. See Michael Smith, *Pacific Visions: California Scientists and the Environment, 1850–1915* (New Haven: Yale University Press, 1987), 62.

77. William James, *Pragmatism and Four Essays from the Meaning of Truth* (Cleveland: Meridian, 1961), 22–23; quoted in Christopher Lasch, *The True and Only Heaven: Progress and Its Critics* (New York: W. W. Norton, 1991), 349.

78. George Snow Papers, manuscript memoir, c. 1896, 2, Baker Library Manuscript Collections, Dartmouth College, Hanover, N.H.

79. Theodore Roosevelt, *The Winning of the West*, 1889, quoted in Trachtenberg, *The Incorporation of America*, 13.

80. William James, quoted in Kim Townsend, *Manhood at Harvard: William James and Others* (New York: W. W. Norton, 1996), 174.

81. Nathaniel Shaler, *The Autobiography of Nathaniel Southgate Shaler, with a Supplementary Memoir by His Wife* (Boston: Houghton Mifflin, 1909), 98–99. 336–37; quoted in Townsend, *Manhood at Harvard*, 112.

82. Ernest Ingersoll, "To Alaska," (Montreal: Passenger Dept., Canadian Pacific Railway, 1888), 23.

83. Johns, "The Early Yukon," 44.

84. Christopher Gair quotes what William Graham Sumner calls a general "rule . . . that nature peoples call themselves 'Men,' and regard others as 'something else—perhaps not defined—but not real men.'" Sumner, *Folkways: A Study of the Sociological Importance of Usages, Manners, Customs, Mores, and Morals* (1906), quoted in Christopher Gair, *Complicity and Resistance in Jack London's Novels: From Naturalism to Nature* (Lewiston, N.Y.: Edwin Mellen Press, 1997), 13.

85. Jean-Christophe Agnew, "The Consuming Vision of Henry James," in Richard Wightman Fox and T. J. Jackson Lears, ed., *The Culture of Consumption: Critical Essays in American History, 1880–1980* (New York: Pantheon Books, 1983), 74.

86. Frederick Whymper, *Travel and Adventure in the Territory of Alaska* (London: John Murray, 1869), 264.

87. Stephen Fender, *Plotting the Golden West: American Literature and the Rhetoric of the California Trail* (New York: Cambridge University Press, 1981), 8.

88. Winser, *The Great Northwest*, 420.

89. Mrs. M. Wood, diary, August 11, 1887, entry, Beinecke Rare Book and Manuscript Library, Yale University.

90. Letter H.E. Morgan to Lumpliegh, May 10, 1886, George W. Lumpliegh Manuscript Collection, British Columbia Provincial Archives, Victoria, British Columbia.

91. Emerson, "A Trip to Alaska," 4.

92. Ibid., 4–5.

93. Wood, diary, August 11, 1887, entry.

94. Cleninden, Diary, July 15, 1894, entry.

95. John Burroughs, "Narrative of the Expedition," Harriman-Alaska Expedition, 1:29, Bancroft Library, Berkeley, Calif.

96. Leo Marx, *The Machine in the Garden: Technology and the Pastoral Ideal in America* (New York: Oxford University Press, 1964); John Sears, *Sacred Places: American Tourist Attractions in the Nineteenth Century* (Amherst: University of Massachusetts Press, 1989).

97. Merritt, "From Ocean to Ocean," 109.

98. Scidmore, *Alaska*, 91–92.

99. Ibid., 87.

Chapter 7. *Orogenous Zones*

1. Michael L. Smith, *Pacific Visions: California Scientists and the Environment, 1850–1915* (New Haven: Yale University Press, 1987), 71.

2. Eliza Scidmore, *Alaska: Its Southern Coast and the Sitkan Archipelago* (Boston: D. Lothrop, 1885), 101.

3. Henry M. Field, *Our Western Archipelago* (New York: Charles Scribner's Sons, 1896), 114.

4. Maturin M. Ballou, *The New Eldorado: A Summer Journey to Alaska* (New York: Houghton Mifflin, 1890), 277.

5. John Hyde, "Northern Pacific Tour" (St. Paul: W. C. Riley, 1889), 68.

6. Percy B. Shelley, *History of a Six Week's Tour Through Part of France, Switzerland, Germany, and Holland, with Letters Descriptive of Sail around Lake Geneva, and of the Glaciers of Chamouni* (London: T. Hookham, 1817), vi.

7. John Muir, "Alaska-Land. A Perfect Day," *Daily Evening Bulletin*, November 13, 1880, 4, col. 1, reprinted in *Letters from Alaska, John Muir*. See also John Muir, *Travels in Alaska* (Boston: Houghton Mifflin Co. 1915), 234–42.

8. W. H. Pierce, *Thirteen Years of Travel and Exploration in Alaska, 1877–1889* (1890; reprint, Anchorage: Alaska Northwest Publishing, 1977), 46.

9. Letter from Valdez to Han Anderson, March 9, 1898, Anderson Family Collection, Egan Anderson, Yukon Archives, Whitehorse, Yukon Territory.

10. Israel Russell, "Mount Saint Elias Revisited," *Century Magazine* (June 1892), 196.

11. Pierce, *Thirteen Years of Travel*, 47.

12. Septima Collis, *A Woman's Trip to Alaska: Being an Account of a Voyage Through the Inland Seas of the Sitkan Archipelago in 1890* (New York: Castleton, 1890), 155.

13. Charles J. Gillis, *The Yellowstone Park and Alaska* (New York: J. J. Little, 1893), 43.

14. Eliza Cleninden, diary, July 16, 1894, entry, Beinecke Rare Book and Manuscript Library, Yale University.

15. Mrs. M. Wood, diary, August 12, 1887, entry, Beinecke Rare Book and Manuscript Library, Yale University.

16. Dave Bohn, *The Wondrous Scene: Early Engravings, Drawings, Paintings, and Photographs of the Landscape Now Known as Glacier Bay National Monument* (Berkeley: Goose Cove Press, 1973), n.p.

17. Carter H. Harrison, *A Summer's Outing and the Old Man's Story*, (Chicago, Dibble Publishing, 1891), 145.

18. John Muir, "The Discovery of Glacier Bay," *Century Magazine*, 50, no. 2 (1895), 234, 237.

19. Ibid., 236.

20. Ibid., 237.

21. Paul Fussell, *Abroad: British Literary Traveling Between the Wars* (New York: Oxford University Press, 1980), 39.

22. Linnie Marsh Wolfe, ed., *John of the Mountains: The Unpublished Journals of John Muir* (Madison: University of Wisconsin Press, 1979), 312; Lawrence Buell, *The Environmental Imagination: Thoreau, Nature Writing, and the Formation of American Culture* (Cambridge: Harvard University Press, 1995), 192–96.

23. Clifford Putney, *Muscular Christianity: Manhood and Sports in Protestant America, 1880–1920* (Cambridge: Harvard University Press, 2002); Ann Douglas, *The Feminization of American Culture* (1977; reprint, New York: Farrar, Straus and Giroux, 1998); Michael Rosenthal, *The Character Factory: Baden-Powell's Boy Scouts and the Imperatives of Empire* (New York: Pantheon Books, 1986).

24. Henry James, *The Bostonians* (1885; reprint, New York: Modern Library, 1984), 293.

25. This linking of masculine adventure and "geologizing" was not entirely new. Horace-Bénédict de Saussure celebrated the mutual benefits of mountain climbing and geology during his eighteenth-century travels in the European Alps. See Eric J. Leed, *The Mind of the Traveler: From Gilgamesh to Global Tourism* (New York: Basic Books, 1991), 198–204. See also Archibald Geikie, *The Founders of Geology* (London: Macmillan, 1905).

26. Clarence King, *Mountaineering in the Sierra Nevada* (1871; reprint, New York: W. W. Norton, 1935), 210.

27. Muir, *Travels in Alaska*, 245.

28. Marsh Wolfe, ed., *John of the Mountains*, 312.

29. Henry David Thoreau, "Walking," in *Henry David Thoreau: Collected Essays and Poems* (New York: Houghton Mifflin, 2001).

30. Marsh Wolfe, ed., *John of the Mountains*, 317.

31. Muir, *Travels in Alaska*, 247.

32. Marsh Wolfe, ed., *John of the Mountains*, 321.

33. Muir, *Travels in Alaska*, 257.

34. Marsh Wolfe, ed., *John of the Mountains*, 317.

35. C. E. S. Wood, "Among the Thlinkits in Alaska," *Century Magazine*, 24, no. 3 (July 1882), 335.

36. Muir, "The Discovery of Glacier Bay," 242.

37. Scidmore, *Alaska*, 134.

38. William R. Hunt, *Alaska* (New York: W. W. Norton, 1976), 44.

39. Scidmore, *Alaska*, 134.

40. Muir, "The Discovery of Glacier Bay," 240.

41. Ibid., 238.

42. David Nye, *American Technological Sublime* (Cambridge: MIT Press, 1994), xiv.

43. John Muir, "Alaska Glaciers: Graphic Description of the Yosemite of the Far Northwest," San Francisco *Daily Evening Bulletin,* September 27, 1879, p. 1, col. 1; reprinted in Robert Engberg and Bruce Merrell, eds., *Letters From Alaska* (Madison: University of Wisconsin Press, 1993), 32.

44. Fred J. Forster Manuscript, letters to George L. Estes, Rochester, New York, April 22, 1898, Beinecke Rare Book and Manuscript Library, Yale University.

45. Matilda Barns Lukens, "The Inland Passage: A Journal of a Trip to Alaska" (no publisher, 1889), 35–36.

46. John Muir, *Thousand Mile Walk to the Gulf,* quoted in Donald Worster, *Nature's Economy: A History of Ecological Ideas* (New York: Cambridge University Press, 1994), 185.

47. Charles M. Taylor, Jr., *Touring Alaska and the Yellowstone* (Philadelphia: George W. Jacobs, 1901), 7.

48. John Muir, journal entry, 1879, quoted in Engberg and Merrell, eds., *Letters from Alaska*, 45.

49. Harrison, *A Summer's Outing*, 146.

50. Letter from Valdez to Han Anderson, March 9, 1898, Anderson Family Collection, Egan Anderson, Yukon Archives.

51. Cleninden, diary, July 16, 1894, entry.

52. John Urry, *Consuming Places* (New York: Routledge, 1995), 6.

53. William H. Wiley and Sara King Wiley, *The Yosemite, Alaska, and the Yellowstone* (London: 1893), 164.

54. Field, *Our Western Archipelago*, 113.

55. "To Alaska by Canadian Pacific Route" (Canadian Pacific Railway Company, 1892), n.p., British Columbia Provincial Archives, Victoria, B.C.

56. Elizabeth McKinsey, *Niagara Falls: Icon of the American Sublime* (New York: Cambridge University Press, 1985), 8.

57. Ernest Ingersoll, "To Alaska," (Montreal: Passenger Department, Canadian Pacific Railway, 1887), 45.

58. Nye, *American Technological Sublime*, 7–8.

59. Kate Soper, *What Is Nature? Culture, Politics, and the Non-Human* (Cambridge: Blackwell, 1995), 215.

60. Guy Debord, *The Society of the Spectacle*, trans. Donald Nicholson-Smith (1967; reprint, New York: Zone Books, 1995).

61. Muir, "The Discovery of Glacier Bay," 245.

62. A. E. Browne, diary, "A Trip to California, Alaska, and the Yellowstone Park, April 20th to July 10th 1891," vol. 2 (Philadelphia), 186, Beinecke Rare Book and Manuscript Library, Yale University.

63. Engberg and Merrell, eds., *Letters from Alaska*, 32, excerpted from "Alaska Glaciers: Graphic Descriptions of the Yosemite of the Far Northwest," *San Francisco Daily Evening Bulletin*, September 27, 1879, p. 1, col. 1.

64. Clarence King, "Catastrophism and the Evolution of Environment, An Address," delivered at the Sheffield Scientific School of Yale College, June 26, 1877, 4, 8.

65. Marsh Smith, ed., *John of the Mountains*, 318.

66. Worster, *Nature's Economy*, 292.

67. Stephen Merritt, "From Ocean to Ocean," travel diary, 1894, 106, Huntington Library, Pasadena, Calif.

68. John Ruskin, quoted in Michael Smith, *Pacific Visions*, 83.

69. Annette Kolodny, *The Lay of the Land: Metaphor as Experience and History in American Life and Letters* (Chapel Hill: University of North Carolina Press, 1975), 4, 150.

70. Hyde, "Northern Pacific Tour," 94.

71. Collis, *A Woman's Trip to Alaska*, 149.

72. Field, *Our Western Archipelago*, 116.

73. Gilles Deleuze and Félix Guattari, *Anti-Oedipus: Capitalism and Schizophrenia*, trans. Robert Hurley (1977; reprint, Minneapolis: University of Minnesota Press, 2000), 200–261.

74. Walter Benjamin, "The Work of Art in the Age of Mechanical Reproduction," in *Illuminations*, trans. Harry Zohn (New York: Schocken Books, 1968), 221.

75. Eduard J. Dijksterhuis, *The Mechanization of the World Picture*, trans. by C. Dikshoorn (Oxford: Oxford University Press, 1969).

76. William Seward Webb, *California and Alaska Over the Canadian Pacific Railway* (New York: G. P. Putnam's and Son, 1890), v.

77. Matilda Barns Lukens, "The Inland Passage," 37.

78. J. A. Zahm, *Alaska, the Country and its Inhabitants, a Lecture* (South Bend, Ind.: Notre Dame University Press, 1886), 27.

79. Thorstein Veblen, *The Theory of the Leisure Class* (1899; reprint, New York: New American Library, 1953), 184.

80. Bruce Braun, *The Intemperate Rainforest: Nature, Culture, and Power on Canada's West Coast* (Minneapolis: University of Minnesota Press, 2002), 44–50.

81. Veblen, *Theory of the Leisure Class*, 183–84. See also Mark Seltzer, *Bodies and Machines* (New York: Routledge, 1992), 61–62.

82. Soper, *What Is Nature?* 149–52.

83. Henry Elliott, "Ten Years Acquaintance with Alaska, 1867–1877," *Harper's Monthly*, 55 (Nov. 1877), 802.

84. Marsh Wolfe, ed., *John of the Mountains*, 308.

85. Muir, *Travels in Alaska*, 220.

86. Frank Buske, "John Muir's Alaska Experience," in Sally Miller, ed., *John Muir: Life and Legacy* (Stockton, Calif.: Holt-Atherton Center, 1985), 117–18.

87. *The Alaskan*, no. 189, August 17, 1889, Hubbell File, Journal of Stephen Ushin, Manuscripts and Archives, University of Washington. See also Richard J. Orsi, " 'Wilderness Saint' and 'Robber Barron': The Anomalous Partnership of John Muir and the Southern Pacific Company for Preservation of Yosemite National Park," in Sally Miller, ed., *John Muir: Life and Legacy* (Stockton, Calif.: Holt-Atherton Center, 1985), 138.

88. Scidmore, *Alaska*, 143.

89. Sally Gregory Kohlstedt, "Nature, Not Books: Scientists and the Origins of the Nature-Study Movement in the 1890s," *Isis*, 96 (2005), 324.

90. Jean-Christophe Agnew, "History and Anthropology: Scenes from a Marriage," *Yale Journal of Criticism*, 3, no. 2 (1990), 32.

91. Robert A. Stafford, "Annexing the Landscapes of the Past: British Imperial Geology in the Nineteenth Century," in John M. MacKenzie, ed., *Imperialism and the Natural World* (Manchester: Manchester University Press, 1990), 67–89.

92. George M. Dawson, *Report on an Expedition in the Yukon District, N.W.T. and Adjacent Northern Portion of British Columbia* (1887; reprint, Whitehorse, Y.T.: Yukon Historical and Museum Association, 1987), 27.

93. Ibid., 30.

94. Ibid., 43.

95. John Muir, *The Cruise of the Corwin; Journal of the Arctic Expedition of 1881 in Search of De Long and the Jeannette* (New York: Houghton Mifflin, 1917), appendix: "The Glaciation of the Arctic and Subarctic Regions Visited During the Cruise."

96. "All About the Klondike Gold Mines" (New York: Miners' News Publishing Co., 1898), 10–11, Minnesota Historical Society.

97. Dawson, quoted in Karl Baedeker, *The Dominion of Canada, with Newfoundland and an Excursion to Alaska, Handbook for Travellers* (Leipzig: Karl Baedeker Publisher, 1894), xxxiv.

98. Dawson, *Report on an Expedition in the Yukon District*, 30.

99. Ballou, *The New Eldorado*, 277.

100. Scidmore, *Alaska*, 79.

101. A. L. Lindsley, *Sketches of an Excursion to Southern Alaska, the Voyage* (Portland, Ore., 1881), 4.

102. King, "Catastrophism and the Evolution of Environment," 26.

103. Marsh Wolfe, ed., *John of the Mountains*, 153–54.

104. Trevor Corry, "The White Pass and Yukon Route—The Scenic Railway of the World" (White Pass and Yukon Railway, 1900), 5, Yukon Archives.

105. Alexander Badlam, *The Wonders of Alaska, Illustrated* (San Francisco: Bancroft, 1890).

106. G. W. Lamplugh, "Notes on the Muir Glacier of Alaska," *Nature* 33, January 28, 1886; quoted in Bohn, *The Wondrous Scene*, 63.

107. Stephen Jay Gould, *Time's Arrow, Time's Cycle: Myth and Metaphor in the Discovery of Geological Time* (Cambridge: Harvard University Press, 1987); Duncan Steel, *Rogue Asteroids and Doomsday Comets* (New York: Wiley, 1995); Mike Davis, *Dead Cities and Other Tales* (New York: The New Press, 2002), 306–59.

108. G. F. Wright, "The Muir Glacier," *American Journal of Science*, 33, series 3, January 1887; *The Ice Age in North America, and Its Bearings upon the Antiquity of Man* (New York: D. Appleton, 1891).

109. Wright, *The Ice Age in North America*, viii.

110. Mammoths and mastodons had initially been classed in the same zoological order, Proboscidea. More recently taxonomists have relegated them to two separate families—mastodons to the family Mammutidae, and mammoths to the family Elephantidae. The frozen carcasses of either the mastodon or the wooly mammoth might be found in the northern interiors of Alaska and the Yukon. See E. C. Pielou, *After the Ice Age* (Chicago: University of Chicago Press, 1991), 108–10. Both species went extinct around 10,000 years ago at the end of the Pleistocene epoch.

111. Hubert H. Bancroft, *History of Alaska* (San Francisco: A. L. Bancroft & Co., 1886), 3. Canadian historian W. L. Morton, writing more recently, echoed the theme of native erasure: "The ultimate and the comprehensive meaning of Canadian history is to be found where there has been no Canadian history, in the North" (Morton, 1970). W. L. Norton, "The North in Canadian Historiography," *Transactions of the Royal Society of Canada*, 1970 8: 40.

112. Ballou, *The New Eldorado*, 187.

113. Ingersoll, "To Alaska," 48.

114. Stephen J. Pyne, *How the Canyon Became Grand: A Short History* (New York, Viking, 1998), 102.

115. Prasenjit Duara, *Rescuing History from the Nation: Questioning Narratives of Modern China* (Chicago: University of Chicago Press, 1995), 14.

116. Frederick Whymper, *Travel and Adventure in the Territory of Alaska* (London: John Murray, 1868), 38.

117. George Emmons, *The Tlingit Indians*, ed. Frederica de Laguna (Seattle: University of Washington Press, 1991), 368.

118. John Swanton, *Social Conditions, Beliefs, and Linguistic Relationship of the Tlingit Indians*, Bureau of American Ethnology, 26th Annual Report (Washington, D.C.: Smithsonian Institution Press, 1908), 453.

119. Emmons, *The Tlingit*, 102.

120. Susie James, "Glacier Bay History," in Nora Marks Dauenhauer and Richard Dauenhauer, eds., *Haa Shuká, Our Ancestors: Tlingit Oral Narratives* (Seattle: University of Washington Press, 1987), 245.

121. Frederica de Laguna, *Under Mount Saint Elias*, Smithsonian Contributions to Anthropology, vol. 7 (Washington, D.C.: Smithsonian Institution Press, 1972), 239.

122. Brian Fagan, *The Little Ice Age, How Climate Made History, 1300–1850* (New York: Basic Books, 2000); John Imbrie and Katherine Palmer Imbrie, *Ice Ages: Solving the Mystery* (Cambridge: Harvard University Press, 1986); Pielou, *After the Ice Age*.

123. Philip L. Fradkin, *Wildest Alaska: Journeys of Great Peril in Lituya Bay* (Berkeley: University of California Press, 2001).

124. De Laguna, *Under Mount Saint Elias*, 25–28, 286–87.

125. James, "Glacier Bay History," 251; Wayne Suttles, ed., *Handbook of North American Indians, Northwest Coast*, vol. 7 (Washington, D.C.: Smithsonian Institution Press, 1990), 206.

126. A. Marvin, "Glacier Bay History," in Nora Marks Dauenhauer and Richard Dauenhauer, eds., *Haa Shuká, Our Ancestors: Tlingit Oral Narratives* (Seattle: University of Washington Press, 1987), 291.

127. Keith H. Basso, *Wisdom Sits in Places: Landscape and Language Among the Western Apache* (Albuquerque: University of New Mexico Press, 1996); Julie Cruikshank, *The Social Life of Stories: Narrative and Knowledge in the Yukon Territory* (Lincoln: University of Nebraska Press, 1998); Hugh Brody, *Maps and Dreams* (New York: Pantheon Books, 1982).

128. King, "Catastrophism and the Evolution of Environment," 5.

129. Martin Jay, "Scopic Regimes of Modernity," in Hal Foster, ed., *Vision and Visuality* (Seattle: Bay Press, 1988), 24–25.

130. Field, *Our Western Archipelago*, 95.

131. Claude Lévi-Strauss, *Tristes Tropiques* (1955; reprint, New York: Penguin Books, 1973), 70–71. Lévi-Strauss writes, "At a different level of reality, Marxism seemed to me to proceed in the same manner as geology and psychoanalysis (taking the latter in the sense given it by its founder). All three demonstrate that understanding consists in reducing one type of reality to another; that the true reality is never the most obvious; and that the nature of truth is already indicated by the care it takes to remain elusive."

132. Raymond Williams, *Problems in Materialism and Culture* (London: Verso, 1980), 76.

133. Charlotte Perkins Gilman, "The Yellow Wallpaper," in Ann J. Lane, ed., *The Charlotte Perkins Gilman Reader* (New York: Pantheon Books, 1980), 116; see also the discussion in Walter Benn Michaels, *The Gold Standard and the Logic of Naturalism* (Berkeley: University of California Press, 1987), 3–14.

134. J. A. Hobson, *Imperialism: A Study* (1901; reprint, Ann Arbor: University of Michigan Press, 2000), 156.

135. *Alaska and the Yukon Valley: How to Get There,* (Nashville: Brandon Printing Company, 1897), 5.

136. Ibid., 6.

137. John Higham, "The Reorientation of American Culture in the 1890s," in John Weiss, ed., *The Origins of Modern Consciousness* (Detroit: Wayne State University Press, 1965).

138. Pierce, *Thirteen Years of Travel and Exploration in Alaska,* 47; George Davidson, (U.S. Coast Survey, Pacific Coast, Coast Pilot of Alaska (Washington, D.C.: GPO, 1869), 196, Noting the decrease in the glacier's sizes along the coast, Davidson theorized that "the climate is becoming dryer and warmer." "The glaciers along the coast are numbered in the hundreds. The large majority of them belong to a class called dead glaciers. They do not move nor flow. They are rapidly melting away. Every summer reduces their size. This must be due to a change in climate, and indicates that the climate is much warmer now than when those huge masses of ice were formed."

139. John Ruskin drew connections between a 1783 volcanic eruption with its global cooling and the 1883 eruption of Krakatoa and the cold summers that followed.

140. Thomas Richards, *The Imperial Archive: Knowledge and the Fantasy of Empire* (New York: Verso, 1993), 85–88; Raymond E. Fitch, *The Poison Sky: Myth and Apocalypse in Ruskin* (Athens: Ohio University Press, 1982), 2–46; Michael Wheeler, ed., *Ruskin and Environment: Storm Cloud of the Nineteenth Century* (New York: Manchester University Press, 1995).

141. John Ruskin, "The Storm-Cloud of the Nineteenth Century," in E. T. Cook and Alexander Wedderburn, eds., *The Works of John Ruskin*, vol. 34 (London: George Allen, 1908), Lecture II, February 11, 1884, 62.

142. Fitch, *The Poison Sky*, 288.

143. John Ruskin, *Fors Clavigera, Letter 66,* quoted in Fitch, *The Poison Sky*, 6.

144. Ruskin, "The Storm-Cloud of the Nineteenth Century," 78.

145. King, "Catastrophism and the Evolution of Environment," 4.

146. Ibid., 19. Clifford Geertz, *The Interpretation of Cultures* (New York: Basic Books, 1973), 47–48. "The final phases (final to date, at any rate) of the phylogenetic history of man took place in the same grand geological era—the so-called Ice Age—as the initial phases of his cultural history. Men have birthdays, but man does not. What this means is that culture, rather than being added on, so to speak, to a finished or virtually finished animal, was ingredient, and centrally ingredient, in the production of that animal itself. The slow, steady, almost glacial growth of culture through the Ice Age altered the balance of selection pressures for the evolving *Homo* in such a way as to play a major directive role in his evolution."

147. King, "Catastrophism and the Evolution of Environment," 8.

148. Eric Lott, *Love and Theft: Blackface Minstrelsy and the American Working Class* (New York: Oxford University Press, 1993).

149. King, "Catastrophism and the Evolution of Environment," 8.

150. Louis Agassiz, quoted in Lorenzo Burge, *Pre-Glacial Man and the Aryan Race* (Boston: Lee and Shepard, 1887), 52.

151. American historian Ellsworth Huntington in the early twentieth century would begin to tie these climatological changes to civilizational decline. Climate shifts were identified as "one of the controlling causes of the rise and fall of the

great nations of the world." Huntington, quoted in David Arnold, *The Problem of Nature: Environment, Culture and European Expansion* (Cambridge: Blackwell, 1996), 31–34.

152. Sir Edward Belcher, *Voyage of the Sulphur During the Years 1836–42* (London, 1843), 78–80.

153. "All About Alaska," 61–2.

154. Karl Baedeker, *The Dominion of Canada with Newfoundland* (Leipzig: Karl Baedeker Publisher, 1894), 236.

155. Badlam, *The Wonders of Alaska*.

156. Ibid.

157. See Neil Harris, *Humbug: The Art of P. T. Barnum* (Chicago: University of Chicago Press, 1973).

158. P. T. Barnum, *Humbugs of the World*, 1865.

159. Harris, *Humbug*, 78–79.

160. "All About Alaska," 3.

161. Kenneth Burke, "Literature as Equipment for Living," in *The Philosophy of Literary Form: Studies in Symbolic Action* (1941; reprint, Berkeley: University of California Press, 1974), 302.

162. Josiah Strong, *Our Country: Its Possible Future and Its Present Crisis* (1886; reprint, Cambridge: Harvard University Press, 1963), 171.

163. Strong, *Our Country*, quoting from *The Bitter Cry of Outcast London*, 174.

164. Ibid., 172.

Conclusion

Note to epigraph: Claude Lévi-Strauss, *Tristes Tropiques* (New York: Atheneum, 1974), 50–51.

1. Eleanor W. Macdonald, "Here and There in Alaska," *The Pacific Monthly*, 15 (1902), 684.

2. Henry Jacob Winser, *The Great Northwest* (St. Paul: W. C. Riley, 1889), 434.

3. James Clifford, *The Predicament of Culture: Twentieth-Century Ethnography, Literature, and Art* (Cambridge: Harvard University Press, 1988), 303.

4. *Appleton's Hand-Book of American Travel* (New York: D. Appleton, 1872), 309.

5. Ibid., 310.

6. Stephen Ushin, journal, Hubbell Collection, Manuscript and Archives, University of Washington.

7. Matilda Barns Lukens, travel account, 46, Beinecke Rare Book and Manuscript Library, Yale University.

8. "Alaska, Sights and Scenes for the Tourist" (Omaha: Knight, Leonard, 1891), 26.

9. William Seward Webb, *California and Alaska and Over the Canadian Pacific Railroad* (New York: G. P. Putnam's Sons), 224–25.

10. Macdonald, "Here and There in Alaska," 683.

11. Paul Carter, *The Road to Botany Bay* (New York: Knopf, 1988), xviii.

12. Historian John Sears has highlighted this contrast between the United States and Europe. "But because of America's relationship to Europe and to its own past, because its cultural identity was not given by tradition but had to be created, tourist attractions have played an especially important role in America," Sears writes. John Sears, *Sacred Places: American Tourist Attractions in the Nineteenth Century* (Amherst: University of Massachusetts Press, 1989), 4.

13. Ella Higginson, "The Voyage of All Voyages," *Washington Magazine*, June 1906, 336–39.

14. Eliza R. Scidmore, *Appleton's Alaska Guide-book* (New York: Appleton, 1898), 175.

15. *The Soul of Alaska: A Comment and a Description* (New York: Gorham, 1905), 12.

16. *The Soul of Alaska*, 12.

17. James T. Dennis, *On the Shores of an Inland Sea* (Philadelphia: J. B. Lippincott, 1894), 78.

18. *Appleton's Hand-Book of American Travel*, 308.

19. Alexander Badlam, *The Wonders of Alaska, Illustrated* (San Francisco: Bancroft, 1890), 126.

20. G. F. Wright, *The Ice Age in North America, and Its Bearings Upon the Antiquity of Man* (New York: D. Appleton and Co., 1891), 79.

21. George H. Hotchkiss, "The Midnight Sun," September 19, 1889, manuscript, Beinecke Rare Book and Manuscript Library, Yale University.

22. Dennis, *On the Shores of an Inland Sea*, 439.

23. "All About Alaska," Pacific Coast Steamship Company (San Francisco: Goodall, Perkins, 1887), 13.

24. "All About Alaska," 14.

25. Winser, *The Great Northwest*, 404.

26. "Alaska, Land of Gold and Glacier" (Chicago: Poole Brothers, 1896).

27. Marsh Wolfe, eds., *John of the Mountains*, 379.

28. Karl Marx, *Capital*, abridged (New York: Oxford University Press, 1995), 45.

29. Edward Said, *Culture and Imperialism* (New York: Vintage Books, 1993), xiii.

30. Alan Trachtenberg, *The Incorporation of America: Culture and Society in the Gilded Age* (New York: Hill and Wang, 1982) 59.

31. Dean MacCannell, *The Tourists: A New Theory of the Leisure Class* (Berkeley: University of California Press, 1999), 21. MacCannell writes, "Increasingly, pure experience, which leaves no material trace, is manufactured and sold like a commodity." The Alaskan tourists' presence left plenty of material traces, however.

32. Marx, *Capital*, 45.

33. Webb, *California and Alaska*, v–vi.

34. Jean and John Camaroff, *Ethnography and the Historical Imagination* (Boulder: Westview Press, 1992), 187.

35. Franz Boas, *The Shaping of American Anthropology, 1885–1911: A Franz Boas Reader*, ed. George W. Stocking, Jr. (New York: Basic Books, 1974), 332.

36. Badlam, *The Wonders of Alaska*, n.p.

37. Henry T. Finck, *The Pacific Coast Scenic Tour; From Southern California to Alaska, the Canadian Pacific Railway, Yellowstone Park, and the Grand Canyon* (New York: Charles Scribner's Sons, 1890), preface.

38. Willey, *The Yosemite, Alaska, and the Yellowstone*, 9.

39. J. Valerie Fifer, *American Progress: The Growth of Transport, Tourist, and Information Industries in the Nineteenth-Century West* (Chester, Conn.: Pequot Publishing, 1988).

40. Terry Eagleton, *Marxism and Literary Criticism* (Berkeley: University of California Press, 1976), see esp. chapter 4.

41. This is not to suggest that Scidmore's position was entirely unique. She followed a well-established genre of female travel literature, though its devotees were not large in number.

42. Frederick Cooper and Ann Laura Stoler, eds., *Tensions of Empire: Colonial Cultures in a Bourgeois World* (Berkeley: University of California Press, 1997), 25–26.

43. Sara Mills, *Discourses of Difference: An Analysis of Women's Travel Writing and Colonialism* (New York: Routledge, 1992), 63.

44. See Laura Wexler, *Tender Violence: Domestic Visions in an Age of U.S. Imperialism* (Chapel Hill: University of North Carolina Press, 2000), 22.

45. Higginson, "Voyage of All Voyages," 338.

46. Ibid.

47. George Snow Papers, "Snow Papers of the Yukon," 2, Dartmouth College Library, Hanover, N.H.

48. T. J. Jackson Lears, "Mass Culture and Its Critics," in Mary Kupiec Cayton, Elliott Gorn, and Peter W. Williams, eds., *Encyclopedia of American Social History*, vol. 3 (New York: Charles Scribner's Sons, 1993), 1591.

49. Frederick Jackson Turner, "The Significance of the Frontier in American History," in John Mack Faragher, ed., *Rereading Frederick Jackson Turner* (1893; reprint, New York: Henry Holt, 1994), 33–34.

50. There was a peculiar circularity at work here. As Michael Taussig writes, we should have no naïve acceptance of the "reified world that capitalism creates, a world in which economic goods known as commodities and, indeed, objects themselves [in the present study, nature] appear not merely as things in themselves but as determinants of the reciprocating human relations that form them." See Michael T. Taussig, *The Devil and Commodity Fetishism in South America* (Chapel Hill: University of North Carolina Press, 1980), 229.

51. Gilles Deleuze, *Foucault*, trans. Sean Hand (Minneapolis: University of Minnesota Press, 1988), 26.

52. This argument relies upon Foucault's analysis of what he termed "governmentality." See Graham Burchell, et al., *The Foucault Effect: Studies in Governmentality, with Two Lectures by and an Interview with Michel Foucault* (Chicago: University of Chicago Press, 1991), esp. 87–105.

53. Charles M. Taylor, *Touring Alaska and the Yellowstone* (Philadelphia: George W. Jacobs, 1901), 282.

54. Fred J. Forster to George Estes, April 22, 1898, Estes Papers, Beinecke Rare Book and Manuscript Library, Yale University.

55. "To the Klondike and Alaska Gold Fields via the ACC," 1898, Yukon Archives (PAM 1898–33), Whitehorse, Yukon Territory.

56. Art historian Jonathan Crary writes, "How one periodizes and where one locates ruptures or denies them are all political choices that determine the construction of the present. Whether one excludes or foregrounds certain events and processes at the expense of others affects the intelligibility of the contemporary functioning of power in which we ourselves are enmeshed." One might speculate as to the peculiar resilience of the gold rush narrative. See Jonathan Crary, *Techniques of the Observer* (Cambridge: MIT Press, 1990), 7.

57. Henry Gannett, "The General Geography of Alaska," *National Geographic*, May 1901.

58. "All the Year Round Tours, to Tropical Climes and the Frigid Zone," Pacific Steamship Company, San Francisco, 1903, Yukon Archives, Whitehorse, Yukon Territory.

59. William H. Wiley and Sara King Wiley, *The Yosemite, Alaska, and the Yellowstone* (London: Offices of Engineering, 1893), ix.

60. For a related analysis, see Edward M. Bruner and P. Gorfain, "Dialogic Narration and the Paradoxes of Masada," in Stuart Plattner and Edward Bruner, eds., *Text, Play, and Story: The Construction and Reconstruction of Self and Society, 1983 Proceedings of the American Ethnological Society* (Washington, D.C.: American Ethnocological Society, 1983), 59.

61. Walt Whitman, "Democratic Vistas," in James E. Miller, Jr., ed., *Complete Poetry and Selected Prose by Walt Whitman* (1871; reprint, Boston: Houghton Mifflin, 1959), 461–62.

62. For an example of such disdain see the work of travel writer Paul Theroux, or historian Hal K. Rothman, *Devil's Bargains: Tourism in the Twentieth-Century American West* (Lawrence: University Press of Kansas, 1998), esp. 1–9.

63. Michel Foucault, "Nietzsche, Genealogy, History," in D. Bouchard, ed., *Language, Counter-Memory, Practice: Selected Essays and Interviews* (Ithaca: Cornell University Press, 1977), 142. See also Patricia Nelson Limerick, *Legacy or Conquest: The Unbroken Past of the American West* (New York: Norton, 1987).

Epilogue

1. John Roberts White Collection, Letter dated September 1, 1897, Special Collections, University of Oregon.

2. Ibid.

3. White Collection, Letter dated May 1, 1899, Special Collections, University of Oregon.

4. White Collection, Letters dated June 9, 1899 and Nov. 4, 1899, Special Collections, University of Oregon.

5. Joseph Conrad, *Chance; A Tale in Two Parts* (New York: W. W. Norton, 1968), 288.

6. John R. White, *Bullets and Bolos: Fifteen Years in the Philippine Islands* (New York: Century Company, 1928), xiv.

7. John R. White, *Sequoia and Kings Canyon National Parks* (Stanford, Calif.: Stanford University Press, 1948), ix.

8. S. Hall Young, *Alaska Days with John Muir* (New York: Fleming H. Revell, 1915), 210.

9. John Muir, "Summering in the Sierra," *San Francisco Daily Evening Bulletin*, August 24, 1876. Quoted in Bruce Merrell, "'A Wild, Discouraging Mess': John Muir Reports on the Klondike Rush," *Alaska History* (Fall 1992), 33.

10. Michael P. Branch, ed., *John Muir's Last Journey: South to the Amazon and East to Africa, Unpublished Journals and Selected Correspondence* (Washington, D. C.: Island Press, 2001), 143.

11. Guy Debord, *Society of the Spectacle* (New York: Zone Books, 1994), 120.

12. Susie Lan Cassel, "Scidmore, Eliza Ruhamah," in *American National Biography*, John A. Garraty and Mark C. Carnes, eds. (New York: Oxford University Press, 1999), 479.

13. Robert D. Monroe, "Sailor on the Snohomish," *Journal of Everett and Snohomish County History* (Summer 1982).

14. Edward James Glave, "Cruelty in the Congo Free State: Concluding Extracts from the Journals of the Late E. J. Glave," *Century Magazine*, 54, no. 5 (1896), 709.

15. If these vignettes seem forced, then consider one final coincidence. "These papers, along with three or four books, are all I have been able to realize of a determination conceived three decades ago at Matadi on the banks of the

Congo. I came there seeking 'adventure,' jealous of older contemporaries to whom that boon had been offered by the First World War. . . . The adventures that Africa afforded were tawdry enough, but it became the setting for a sudden epiphany (if the word be not too strong) of the pressing necessity for expounding my America to the twentieth century. . . . It was given to me, equally disconsolate on the edge of a jungle of central Africa, to have thrust upon me the mission of expounding what I took to be the innermost propulsion of the United States, while supervising, in that barbaric tropic, the unloading of drums of case oil flowing out of the inexhaustible wilderness of America." The historian Perry Miller prefaced his Puritan history *Errand into the Wilderness* with these reflections from Matadi where Glave had died. See Perry Miller, *Errand into the Wilderness* (Cambridge, Mass.: Harvard University Press, 1956), xvii. There on the banks of the Congo, Miller recognized the "fundamental theme" of American history, the supposed uniqueness of the American past, having escaped the experience of imperialism. "The field of American studies was conceived on the banks of the Congo," historian Amy Kaplan has written, critically recognizing Miller's influence. See Amy Kaplan, " 'Left Alone with America': The Absence of Empire in the Study of American Culture," in *Cultures of United States Imperialism*, Amy Kaplan and Donald E. Pease, eds. (Durham, N.C.: Duke University Press, 1993), 3.

Index

curio trade and, 168–70; deterritorialization of Alaska and, 229; glaciers and, 212–16, 226–27; on gold mining, 191–93; identity and, 13, 181–82; idleness and, 57; images of travel and, 86–87; impact on Alaska, 9–10; journal-keeping, 74–75; in Juneau, 200, 201; Kipling on, 46, 47, 48, 57; labor unrest and, 89–91; landscape and, 70–74, 75, 77, 108–9, 230–31; leisure and, 56; masculinity and the frontier, 202–4; native Alaskans and, 135, 143–55; nature and, 266–67; nineteenth century notions of tourism and, 13; notions of pioneers, 107–8; numbers in Alaska, 6, 49; power of the worldview of, 13–14; the preimagining of experience and, 86; the "primitive" and, 172–73; prospectors and, 201–6; racialism and, 148–49; scientific and aesthetic consciousness in, 230; self-critique, 205–6; sex and, 142; sublime experience, 100–102, 226–27; time and, 55; touring as work, 225; touring of Tlingit homes, 135; Treadwell mine complex and, 192, 206–10; wilderness cures, 51–53; women travelers, 82, *83*; writing by, 57. *See also* Touring elites

Trachtenberg, Alan, 200, 267

Travel and Adventure in the Territory of Alaska (F. Whymper), 19–20

Travel guides, 62, 64, 67, 267

Travel technology: deterritorialization of landscape, 70

Travel writers, 78–79; influence on gold seekers, 274–75; Eliza Scidmore's career, 224; women, 269–70; world-as-exhibition viewpoint, 157

Travel writing: British, 24–26; commodification of nature, 66, 79; demand for and growth in, 268–69; early descriptions of Alaska, 5; the economy of desire and, 79; incorporating actions of, 270–71; intellectuals and, 174–75; significance of, 12, 42–43; George Sims on London, 24–25; subjectivities projected outward, 65; tourists as consumers of, 79, 267; women writers, 269–70

Treadwell, John, 191

Treadwell mine complex, *168, 201*; Chinese labor and, 196, 197; deforestation caused by, 187; growth of, 191; tourist

descriptions of, 192, 206–10; value of, 206; world's largest industrial gold mine, 189, 191, 234

Trevor-Roper, Hugh, 28

Tsimshian, 303n68

Turner, Frederick Jackson, 138, 272

Turner, J. M. W., 73

"Turnerian Picturesque," 73

Tyndall, John, 251

Uniformitarianism, 242–43

Union Pacific railway, 81

United States: compared to Europe, 323n12; expansionism and, 94–95

U.S. Army, 128, 129

U.S. Coast and Geodetic Survey, 35

U.S. Department of War, 93–94

U.S. Navy, 129, 190–91, 309n78

U.S. Revenue Marine, 190

Urine, 145

Ushin, Stephen, 124, 189–90, 197

Utilitarian individualism, 268

Valdez Glacier, 214

Value: Marx on, 266

Van Buskirk, Philip, *115*, 133, 144, 147; Kadishan and, 160; later life of, 282; military career, 114; notions of identity and, 137–39; observations of an Alaskan town, 139; relationship to children, 138; sexuality and, 116–18, 119, 120, 137–38, 141, 301n14; travel to Alaska, 113–14

Vancouver, George, 35, 97, 122–23

Vancouver (Canada), 47, 85

Van Kirk, Sylvia, 126

Veblen, Thorstein, 252; on belief in progress, 231; "conspicuous consumption," 68, 214; "conspicuous leisure," 214; notions of the primitive and, 175; on tourism, 56, 60

Venereal disease, 124

Victoria, Queen of England, 21

Victoria (Canada), 85, 95–96, 122

Victorian parlors, 179, 181–82

Villard, Henry, 94, 266

Wachusett (ship), 99

Wages: of natives, 314n48

Wardman, George, 154

Watkins, Carelton E., 91

Watt, Ian, 290n65

Acknowledgments

Books take the shape of one's experiences and reflect the places where one has lived. This one is no exception. I first went to Alaska the day after graduating from high school. On that first venture, I climbed Mt. McKinley—Denali—during a forty-day traverse from the mining camp of Petersburg on the mountain's south side to the park road at Wonder Lake on the north. That climb led to others and to a succession of summers spent working and climbing in Alaska. A year's worth of days spent crossing glaciers with names like Tazlina, Nelchina, Tokositna, and Kahiltna left a deep imprint upon me and tied me intimately to the ways in which Americans see wilderness. Several years living and working in East Africa taught me the inadequacy of North American ideas about nature and wilderness, including my own. Experiences in Kenya, Tanzania, and Uganda impressed upon me the continuing power of the colonial past and the ongoing rule of global capital in the present.

The mark of a number of my teachers may be discerned readily in the following pages. Others, less directly involved in this project have set a high standard of scholarship and spurred me on through their teaching and mentoring over the years. More than anyone, my adviser and mentor Johnny Faragher role-modeled the practice of history. He gave of his own time unstintingly. His workingman's mastery of the craft helped turn this historian's apprentice into a journeyman historian. Jean-Christophe Agnew has always inspired me with his critical attentions and direction. Robin Winks set a high bar for the standards of historical scholarship in his students. Jim Scott and the Agrarian Studies Program at Yale University nurtured my intellectual curiosities during my graduate years, leading me down new theoretical paths. Jim, too, teaches by his own generous example. John Demos, Robert Harms, Howard Lamar, David Montgomery, and Alan Trachtenberg offered counsel and invaluable intellectual direction to me at various points during my years at

Yale. At the University of Colorado–Boulder Yvette Huginnie, Patty Limerick, Ralph Mann, and Charles Wilkinson helped bring me in from the cold. I had been working as a mountain guide for nearly a decade. I remember telling Charles that I could not become a lawyer because it would require too much time spent indoors—whoops. I owe a debt to all the writers whose work helped to inform my own thoughts. Early on in my studies, I was fortunate to have met historian Morgan Sherwood who suggested further work on Alaskan tourism. I followed his sage advice.

This study relied upon a number of archive and library collections. I owe a great deal to the efforts of numbers of unknown staff, as well as the archivists and librarians with whom I worked directly, at the following institutions: University of Alaska, Fairbanks; Yukon Territorial Archives; Klondike Historical Park in Skagway, Alaska; Glenbow Museum Archives; Provincial Archives of British Columbia; Manuscripts and Archives, and Special Collections at the University of Washington; the Oregon Historical Society; the University of Oregon Special Collections; Bancroft Library; Huntington Library; Minnesota Historical Society; Wisconsin Historical Society; National Archives of Canada; Dartmouth College Library; and Sterling and Mudd Libraries and the Beinecke Rare Book and Manuscript Library at Yale. At the Beinecke, Western Americana curator George Miles deserves special mention for his unflagging and generous support.

I received financial assistance from the Andrew W. Mellon Foundation, the Fulbright Fellowship program, the Canadian Embassy, the Huntington Library, the Beinecke Rare Book and Manuscript Library, Yale University, and most recently, Montana State University. As my archival schedule and funding support indicates, this project started with a different goal in mind. I had anticipated writing a history of the Klondike gold rush. My research kept leading further into the past and by the time I had completed the research for a Klondike history, I also had another project in hand. That this present study is in part the product of my work in Canadian archives will not be apparent to many readers. But I am grateful for the many courtesies shown to me during my year studying in Canada. In particular, the staff, faculty, and students at Yukon College in Whitehorse proved particularly welcoming. My Canadian experience and the research conducted there will no doubt influence my future writing. A Woodrow Wilson Fellowship through the Townsend Humanities Center at the University of California, Berkeley provided an ideal environment for completing this work. At Berkeley, Nancy Peluso, Candace Slater, Richard Walker, Michael Watts, and many others suggested new theoretical directions.

My peripatetic research trail has left me indebted to a rather far-flung group of family, friends, and colleagues. In Seattle, my sister Marcie and John McHale opened their home to me, as did Dr. Sarah Dick (incidentally the great-grand-daughter of the founder of Petersburg, Alaska). In Portland, my brothers, Russell and Douglas, and their families hosted my too-brief stopovers. In Berkeley, Julie Greenberg, Jake Kosek, and Geoff Mann offered inspired distractions. Jeff and Shelley Brinck in Salt Lake City reminded me that western rivers and good friends can restore even the most archive-wearied soul (the deconstructive conclusions of this study not withstanding). Bob Allison in Denver always welcomed me during my cross-country jaunts and for trips into the mountains. Longtime friends Jim Phillips and Lesley Reid in Canmore, Alberta, hosted me between long driving stints across Canada. Andrew McCabe and his family, and Julie Morton made their homes my home in the Adirondacks and Vermont during much of my time in the East.

New Haven, Connecticut, and Yale University were amazing places to spend my graduate student years—New Haven because it proved to be a diverse and surprisingly beautiful city, and Yale because it exceeded its reputation as a dynamic and rigorous community of scholars. My colleagues Michelle Anderson, Matthew Babcock, Kat Charron, Jon Coleman, Ray Craib, Cathy Gudis, Karl Jacoby, Ben Johnson, James Kessenides, Dan Lanpher, Ted Liazos, Rick Lopez, Christian McMillen, Marina Moskowitz, J. C. Mutchler, Michelle Nickerson, Aaron Sachs, and others made the intellectual life complete in addition to their friendship. The community away from the university afforded a welcome balance. Louise de Carrone and the regular Lulu's Cafe crowd upheld the deep traditions of coffeehouse politics and camaraderie. Jeff Hardwick read nearly every word, often in far rougher forms. I can't hold him accountable for the end result, but he did help make the end possible. Illisa Kelman heard more about this book than she probably ever wanted. She always listened and encouraged. Colleagues and friends Allegra and Andrew Hogan made their home my true second home. I learned more from Andrew, a photographer, about the ways of seeing than he might realize. I don't know if he anticipated that the dinners I swapped for installing their woodstove chimney would end up being nearly nightly events over several years. I could talk to Allegra about history forever.

At Penn Press, my editor Bob Lockhart and series editor Peggy Shaffer helped smooth the process of completing the manuscript. My colleagues and students at Montana State University also helped ease the task. Thanks to Kirk Branch, Diane Cattrell, David Cherry, Susan Cohen, Dan Flory, Kristen Intemann, Susan Kollin, David Large, Tim LeCain, Deidre Manry, Dale Martin, Michelle Maskiell, Mary Murphy, Michael Reidy, Bob Rydell, Sara Pritchard, Lynda Sexson, Billy Smith, Brett Walker,

Yanna Yannakakis, and recent postdocs Arn Keeling and Bob Wilson. In Bozeman, friends Barb Cestero, Randa Chehab, Tim Conlan, Patricia Cosgrove, Sarah Davies, Aiden Downey, Chuck Steen, Erich Pessl, and Juliette Vail have helped make Bozeman my home. Jennifer Chrisman has shared that home with me. Her companionship and inspiration helped make possible the completion of this book. My parents, Judy and Bill Campbell, have supported me over the years with their enthusiasm and interest in my work. My father died suddenly before he could see the book in print. He taught me how to live and I dedicate this book to his memory.